More of the Best of Bon Appétit

More of the Best of Bon Appétit

THE KNAPP PRESS
PUBLISHERS
LOS ANGELES

Bon Appétit is a registered trademark of Bon Appétit Publishing Corp. Used with permission.

Copyright © 1984 by Knapp Communications Corporation

Published by The Knapp Press
5900 Wilshire Boulevard, Los Angeles, California 90036

Library of Congress Cataloging in Publication Data
Main entry under title:

More of the best of Bon appétit.

    Includes index
    1. Cookery, International.   I. Bon appétit.
TX725.A1M67 1984   641.5   84-14368
ISBN 0-89535-136-6

On the cover: *Roasted Pepper Salad with Feta and Shrimp, Almond Charlotte*

Printed and bound in the United States of America

10 9 8 7 6 5 4 3 2 1

Contents

Foreword

❖　❖　❖　❖　❖　❖　❖　❖　❖　❖　❖　❖　❖　❖

In 1979 we created the first collection of *Bon Appétit* magazine's very best recipes. We called it, naturally enough, *The Best of Bon Appétit*. You, our readers, responded with overwhelming enthusiasm; to date, over 600,000 copies are in print, and time after time we keep getting requests for *more* of *Bon Appétit*'s best recipes.

Here it is: *More of the Best of Bon Appétit*, an *all-new* collection of the most outstanding recipes that have appeared in the magazine since 1980.

For those of you who know and love the first collection, you'll feel comfortably at home. We've kept the same convenient chapter organization that helps you pinpoint exactly the right recipe for the right course or occasion. There are over 400 recipes in all, from *Autumn Soup* to *Zucchini Lasagne*, *Apricot-Stuffed Lamb Chops* to *Fresh Oranges with Orange Zabaglione*. And there's page after page of helpful tips and hints on breadmaking, pastas and

pizzas, perfect sauces and foolproof cakes. . . .

But whether or not you own a copy of *The Best of Bon Appétit*, you'll find this second collection fresh, involving, exciting—filled with recipes and ideas that reflect our ever-growing awareness of what it means to cook and eat well, with style, flair, and quality. Want new tastes? Try *Three Melon Soup of Summertime* . . . *Veal with Cucumbers and Morels* . . . *Breast of Duck with Lingonberry Sauce and Onion Marmalade* . . . *Mesquite-Grilled Fresh Tuna with Tomato-Basil Sauce* . . . *Sautéed Spinach with Pear* . . . *Warm Scallop and Avocado Salad* . . . *White Chocolate Ice Cream*. . . .

Something ethnic or international? How about Indonesian *Zesty Barbecued Fish* . . . *Navaho Fry Bread* . . . *Thai Stuffed Mussels* . . . *Cajun Martinis* . . . *Boiled Beef German Style* . . . Greek *Spinach-Stuffed Leg of Lamb* . . . French *Sausages Wrapped in Buckwheat Crepes* . . . Indian *Chicken in Silky Almond Sauce* . . . Chinese *Fireworks Shrimp* . . . Italian *Hazelnut Cookies*. . . .

And for all that's new and exotic, you'll also find dozens of recipes comfortingly down-home, outstanding versions of familiar old favorites. *Southern Fried Chicken* . . . *Roast Turkey with Cornmeal* . . . *Brown Buttermilk Bran Muffins* . . . *Hot Mulled Cider* . . . *Fresh Tomato Soup* . . . *Standing Rib Roast of Beef* . . . *Minted Peas in Boston Lettuce Cups* . . . *Native American Cranberry Sauce* . . . *Strawberry-Glazed Cream Cheese Cake*. . . .

The best recipes deserve the best pictures, and we give you 48 pages of them. To delight you. Make your mouth water. Inspire you with scores of serving ideas.

It's even more of the very best—appetizers, beverages, fabulous soups, entrées of every description, vegetables, side dishes, salads and dressings, tempting sauces and condiments, breads, cakes, pies, cookies, irresistible desserts—all for you!

BON APPETIT!

1 ❖ Appetizers

Pâtés and Spreads

❖ ❖ ❖ ❖ ❖ ❖ ❖ ❖ ❖ ❖ ❖ ❖ ❖ ❖

ALSATIAN CHARCUTERIE PLATE

(Assiette Charcutière Alsacienne)

The centerpiece of this dish is an exceptional pâté dotted with whole chicken livers and pistachios.

6 servings

- 4 cups 1-inch cubes skinned chicken (about one 5-pound roaster)
- 3¾ cups 1-inch cubes fresh pork fatback (about 1 pound)
- 1 cup 1-inch cubes loin *or* rib veal chop (about 8 ounces)
- 1 cup 1-inch cubes loin *or* rib pork chop (about 8 ounces)
- 1 cup Sercial Madeira *or* Rainwater Madeira
- 2 large onions, thinly sliced (about 2 cups)
- 3 medium shallots, thinly sliced (about ½ cup)
- 2 medium garlic cloves, finely chopped
- 1 teaspoon dried thyme, crumbled
- 1 bay leaf
- 8 chicken livers (preferably pale colored), trimmed (5 to 6 ounces)
- 2 to 3 tablespoons Cognac *or* Armagnac *or* other brandy
- 2 center slices stale French bread, crusts trimmed, crumbled (1 cup crumbs)
- 6 eggs, beaten
- 24 pistachio nuts, blanched and peeled

- 1 teaspoon Quatre-Epices (see following recipe)
  Salt and freshly ground pepper
  Dash of Cognac *or* Armagnac *or* other brandy (optional)

- 1 tablespoon all purpose flour
- 1¼ teaspoons salt
- ½ teaspoon freshly ground pepper

- 1 tablespoon salt
- 2 medium cucumbers, peeled and thinly sliced
- 2 tablespoons white wine vinegar
  Very small pinch of sugar
  Salt and freshly ground pepper
- 6 tablespoons corn oil
- 1 pound young spinach leaves, stemmed
- 2 tablespoons chopped fresh dill *or* 2 teaspoons dried, crumbled
- 2 green onions, very thinly sliced diagonally
- 12 paper-thin slices Westphalian ham *or* other smoked and cured ham

Combine chicken, fatback, veal and pork cubes in large glass baking dish. Sprinkle with Madeira. Add onions, shallots, garlic, thyme and bay leaf. Place livers in small dish. Top with 2 to 3 tablespoons Cognac. Refrigerate both dishes 2 days, turning ingredients occasionally to marinate.

Stir breadcrumbs into eggs and let stand several minutes until crumbs

absorb egg. Meanwhile, transfer chicken mixture to processor or blender using slotted spoon. Add 2 marinated chicken livers and process until smooth using on/off turns. Transfer mixture to bowl of electric mixer (fitted with paddle attachment, if available). Remove remaining 6 livers from marinade using slotted spoon; set aside. Stir marinades into breadcrumb mixture. With machine running, gradually beat breadcrumb mixture into meat mixture. Stir in nuts and Quatre-Epices. Season with salt and pepper. (To check seasoning, pinch off small piece of forcemeat and fry until cooked through. Cool completely. Taste cooked forcemeat and season uncooked forcemeat with salt and pepper if necessary.) Add dash of Cognac. Discard bay leaf.

Preheat oven to 350°F. Butter two 8½ × 4½ × 3-inch loaf pans. Pack ¼ of forcemeat into bottom of each pan. Mix flour with 1¼ teaspoons salt and ½ teaspoon pepper in small bowl. Lightly dredge remaining 6 livers in flour, patting off excess. Press 3 livers down center of forcemeat, spacing evenly. Spread remaining forcemeat evenly over. Tap pans sharply on work surface to remove any air bubbles. Cover with foil. Set pans in large baking dish. Add enough boiling water to come halfway up sides of pans. Bake until fat is liquefied, about 30 minutes. Remove foil and continue baking until fat runs clear and skewer inserted in centers of terrines comes out hot and dry, about 45 minutes.

Set terrines aside. Pour hot water out of baking dish. Rinse dish with cold water. Return terrines to dish. Fill dish with cold water. Cover tops of terrines with plastic wrap or foil. Weight each with heavy object (such as large can or brick) and let cool. Refrigerate. (*Can be prepared up to 1 week ahead.*)

To serve, sprinkle 1 teaspoon salt over cucumbers in colander. Set aside 30 minutes to drain. Combine vinegar and sugar with salt and pepper to taste in large bowl. Whisk in oil 1 drop at a time. Rinse cucumbers well; pat dry. Add cucumbers and spinach to vinaigrette and toss gently. Line half of each plate with layer of spinach leaves. Top with cucumbers. Sprinkle dill and green onion generously over top. Arrange 1 slice of terrine on other side of plate. Roll pieces of ham into cornucopias and place 1 roll on each side of terrine. Serve well chilled.

Quatre-Epices

  2 teaspoons ground allspice
  2 teaspoons ground coriander
  2 teaspoons dried tarragon
  1 teaspoon ground cinnamon
  1 teaspoon freshly grated nutmeg
  ½ teaspoon ground cardamom
  ½ teaspooon dried marjoram
  ⅛ teaspoon ground cloves

Mix all ingredients in blender at high speed until finely powdered.

SHRIMP MOUSSE WITH PEAS

A lovely terrine of spring colors. The secret of the mousse's creamy lightness is to make sure that all ingredients are very cold when blended. Must be prepared one day in advance. Shrimp mousse can also be prepared in batches in a blender.

6 servings

  ⅔ cup frozen tiny peas, thawed *or* cooked sugar snap peas
  2½ tablespoons minced fresh chives *or* garlic chives* Generous pinch of sugar Salt

  2 12-ounce fillets of sole *or* flounder about same length as terrine mold
  1 tablespoon dry white wine
  ¾ pound medium shrimp, shelled and deveined
  1 large shallot, coarsely chopped
  1 egg white
  ½ teaspoon salt
  1 cup whipping cream
  1 tablespoon fresh lemon juice
  Green Herb Sauce (see following recipe)

Pat peas dry. Transfer to processor. Add 1 tablespoon chives with sugar and mix using on/off turns until coarsely chopped, or chop by hand. Add salt. Chill.

Sprinkle fillets with wine. Cover and refrigerate until ready to use.

Freeze processor work bowl, Steel Knife and top at least 1 hour. Refrigerate all remaining ingredients.

Position rack in center of oven and preheat to 350°F. Generously butter 3-cup nonmetal rectangular terrine. Cut 4 shrimp into quarters and set aside. Place remainder in chilled processor work bowl. Add shallot and blend well using on/off turns. Mix in egg white and salt. With machine running, add cream in steady stream, mixing only until cream is blended, about 1 minute; *do not overmix or cream will form butter.* Remove Steel Knife from work bowl and scrape off all mousse. Stir in lemon juice, reserved shrimp and remaining chives.

Spread slightly less than half of mousse in prepared mold. Pat chilled fish dry. Lay 1 fillet down length of mousse and press down along center, forming trough. Mound peas down length of fillet and, using hands, mold almost to enclose. Set remaining fillet over peas with wide end of top fillet joining narrow end of bottom fillet. Add remaining mousse to cover fillets completely. Smooth top and tap mold sharply on work surface several times to eliminate air pockets. Cover with piece of buttered foil, buttered side down; seal edges tightly.

Set mold in large pan. Add hot water to halfway up sides of mold. Bake until knife inserted in center comes out with only several flecks of mousse, about 30 minutes; *do not overcook.* Remove from hot water. Let cool to room temperature. Refrigerate overnight.

To serve, dip mold in hot water. Loosen edges with knife and invert onto platter. Let stand at room temperature 45 minutes. Cut terrine into ½- to ¾-inch-thick slices, bracing end with wide spatula. Arrange on individual plates. Pour sauce in 2 arcs around each slice and serve immediately.

*Available in oriental markets.

Green Herb Sauce

Makes about 2 cups

  2 small green onions
  2 egg yolks, room temperature
  2 generous teaspoons Dijon mustard
  1 tablespoon fresh lemon juice
  ⅔ to 1 cup vegetable oil
  1 tablespoon minced fresh parsley
  3 tablespoons chopped fresh chervil *or* 3 tablespoons minced fresh parsley
  2 large fresh basil leaves *or* generous pinch of dried, crumbled
  ½ to ⅔ cup half and half Salt and freshly ground pepper
  2 tablespoons minced fresh chives

Chop onions in processor or blender using on/off turns. Add yolks, mustard and lemon juice and mix until smooth and creamy, about 1 minute. With machine running, add ⅔ cup oil in slow steady stream, stopping occasionally to scrape down sides of container. Add remaining oil as necessary until sauce is consistency of mayonnaise. Blend in parsley, chervil and basil. With machine running, gradually add enough half and half to attain consistency of whipping cream. Season with salt and pepper. Add chives to sauce just before serving.

LABNA

This tangy fresh yogurt "cheese" spread is easy to make. Whether eaten alone or on bread with a sprinkling of green onion, Labna is delightful. It can be prepared 2 days ahead, covered and refrigerated.

16 to 18 servings

- **8 cups (2 quarts) plain yogurt made from whole milk**
- **1 teaspoon salt**

Blend yogurt and salt. Line strainer with several layers of dampened cheesecloth. Set over large bowl. Pour yogurt into lined strainer. Cover loosely with plastic wrap and refrigerate overnight for whey to drain. Discard drained liquid. Turn contents of strainer into chilled bowl to serve.

SMOKED TROUT MOUSSE WITH RYE HEART TOAST

Makes 2 to 2½ cups

- **1 pound smoked trout, skinned and boned**
- **½ cup sliced green onion**
- **¼ to ⅓ cup loosely packed fresh dill *or* 1 teaspoon dried**
- **2 tablespoons plus 2 teaspoons fresh lemon juice**
- **¼ teaspoon freshly ground pepper**
- **1 cup whipping cream**
  Salt (optional) and freshly ground pepper
  Additional fresh lemon juice
- **1 fresh dill sprig (garnish)**
  Rye Heart Toast (see following recipe) *or* crisp crackers

Combine trout, green onion, dill, lemon juice and ¼ teaspoon pepper in processor and chop finely using 5 to 6 on/off turns, or mince finely by hand and turn into blender. With processor or blender running, slowly add cream and blend well. Taste and adjust seasoning with salt, pepper and lemon juice. Transfer to crock or serving bowl. Cover with plastic wrap. Chill several hours or over-

night. Garnish with dill. Serve with Rye Heart Toast or crackers.

Rye Heart Toast

- **1 1-pound loaf very thinly sliced rye bread**

Preheat oven to 375°F. Using 2-inch heart-shaped cookie cutter, cut out as many hearts as desired from bread (reserve trimmings to make crumbs for another use). Arrange hearts in single layer on ungreased baking sheets. Bake, turning once, until crisp and lightly colored, 4 to 6 minutes per side. Transfer to rack to cool.

CROCKED SHRIMP AND CHEESE WITH CUCUMBER ROUNDS

This zesty spread also goes well with toast points and crackers.

10 servings

- **2 cups water**
- **1 cup dry white wine**
- **1 lemon, sliced**
- **2 garlic cloves, peeled**
- **1 teaspoon black peppercorns**
- **1 teaspoon yellow mustard seed**
- **1 pound uncooked medium shrimp**

- **9 ounces cream cheese**
- **3 anchovy fillets, rinsed**
- **3 tablespoons butter, room temperature**
- **1 tablespoon fresh lemon juice**
- **1 to 2 teaspoons Dijon mustard**
- **2 small green onions, minced**
- **1 tablespoon capers, rinsed and drained**
  Salt and freshly ground pepper
- **2 cucumbers, cut into thin rounds**

Combine water, wine, lemon, garlic, peppercorns and mustard seed in medium saucepan and bring to boil over high heat. Cover partially and let boil 10 minutes. Reduce heat to medium-low, add shrimp

and simmer 2 minutes. Set aside to cool. Chill shrimp in cooking liquid overnight.

Drain shrimp well; remove shells and devein. Combine cream cheese, anchovies, butter, lemon juice and mustard in processor or blender and mix until smooth. Add shrimp and chop finely using on/off turns. Transfer to medium bowl. Blend in green onions, capers and salt and pepper. Pack mixture into crock or bowl. Cover and refrigerate overnight. To serve, center crock on platter and surround with cucumber slices.

CRUSHED CHICK PEAS WITH CILANTRO

Can be prepared 2 days ahead, covered and refrigerated.

Makes 3½ cups

- **6 tablespoons finely chopped sweet yellow Bermuda onion***
- **6 tablespoons olive oil (preferably extra virgin)**
- **2 15-ounce cans chickpeas, rinsed and drained**
- **½ cup tahini (sesame seed paste)****
- **¼ cup tightly packed fresh cilantro (coriander) leaves**
- **¼ cup minced fresh chives *or* green onion**
- **⅓ to ½ cup fresh lemon juice**
  Salt and freshly ground pepper
  Cilantro leaves (garnish)

Puree onion with oil in processor or blender. Add chickpeas, tahini, cilantro and chives and mix using on/off turns until chickpeas are finely chopped but still retain some texture. Turn into serving bowl. Stir in lemon juice and salt and pepper to taste. Serve at room temperature. Garnish with fresh cilantro leaves.

*If unavailable, use pungent onion and soak in fresh lemon juice 40 minutes to mellow. Drain well before using.

**Available at Middle Eastern markets and natural foods stores.

Hors d'Oeuvres

MUSHROOMS STUFFED WITH PESTO AND CHEESE
(Funghi Ripieni con Pesto)

Serve these as a first course or with grilled fish, poultry or veal chops.

6 servings

    Olive oil
12 large firm white
    mushrooms, stems removed
    and caps wiped clean
1   small lemon, halved
½   cup (about) Fresh Basil
    Pesto (see following recipe)
⅓   cup freshly grated Parmesan
    or Romano cheese

Preheat oven to 375°F. Brush bottom of baking dish with olive oil. Rub mushroom caps with lemon to prevent darkening. Brush caps with olive oil. Arrange rounded side down in single compact layer in baking dish. Fill mushrooms with pesto. Sprinkle tops with about 2½ tablespoons cheese. Drizzle small amount of olive oil over each. (*Can be prepared several hours ahead to this point. Cover dish tightly with plastic wrap and refrigerate.*) Bake until filling bubbles, 8 to 12 minutes. Sprinkle with remaining cheese and serve.

Fresh Basil Pesto

Make large quantities while fresh basil leaves are at their prime, and freeze the pesto in batches to be enjoyed year round.

Makes 1⅔ cups

2   cups packed fresh basil
    leaves
2   large garlic cloves
½   cup pine nuts
¾   cup freshly grated Parmesan
    or Romano cheese
⅔   cup olive oil

If using mortar and pestle, mince basil leaves finely. Transfer to mortar and crush to fine paste. Add garlic and work into paste. Gradually add pine nuts and crush until smooth. Blend in cheese. Add olive oil to mixture in slow steady stream, stirring constantly.

If using processor, combine basil and garlic in work bowl and blend to fine paste, scraping down sides of bowl as necessary. Add pine nuts and cheese and process until smooth. With machine running, pour olive oil through feed tube in slow steady stream and mix until smooth and creamy; if pesto is too thick, gradually pour up to ¼ cup warm water through feed tube with machine running.

Transfer pesto to jar. Cover surface of pesto with film of olive oil about ⅛ inch thick. Seal jar with tight-fitting lid. Refrigerate up to 3 months, or freeze. Stir oil into pesto before using.

BACON-WRAPPED CHUTNEY BANANAS

6 servings

2   bananas, peeled
    Fresh lemon juice
8   to 10 bacon slices
    (uncooked), halved
    crosswise
1   cup (about) mango chutney

Preheat oven to 375°F. Cut bananas into crosswise slices the same width as bacon strips. Roll in lemon juice. Wrap each banana piece in half bacon strip; secure with toothpick. Arrange on baking sheet. Bake until bacon is almost cooked, about 20 minutes. Meanwhile, place chutney in processor and mince finely using about 5 on/off turns, or mince by hand. Dip bacon-wrapped banana pieces into chutney to coat evenly. Return to baking sheet and continue baking until crisp, 5 to 10 minutes.

ZESTY BARBECUED FISH
(Ikan Bakr)

The fish can be cubed several hours ahead and marinated until ready to cook. This will intensify the flavor of the fish without altering texture.

Makes about 16 cubes

1   pound fillet of tuna,
    swordfish *or* similar firm
    fish, cut into ¾- to 1-inch
    cubes
¼   cup fresh lemon juice
2   tablespoons Sweet Soy
    Sauce (see following recipe)
1   tablespoon peanut oil *or*
    corn oil
½   teaspoon sugar
½   teaspoon salt
1   garlic clove, finely chopped

Combine fish, lemon juice, soy sauce, oil, sugar, salt and garlic in large bowl and mix well. Let mixture marinate for at least 15 minutes.

Preheat broiler or prepare charcoal grill. Broil or barbecue fish until firm, about 10 minutes. Arrange on platter. Serve warm or at room temperature.

Sweet Soy Sauce
(Kecap Manis)

Kecap Manis is an Indonesian seasoning that moves easily from Asian to American cooking. It can be purchased at Asian food stores but the homemade kind is far superior and can be refrigerated indefinitely.

Makes about 3 cups

1½ cups sugar
2   cups Chinese soy sauce
¼   cup water
3   to 4 lemongrass stalks*
    (about ten 1-inch pieces) *or*
    1 teaspoon sliced stalks
2   garlic cloves, crushed
2   whole star anise*

Rusks, Toasts, Croutons and Croûtes

The names may be different, but they all have one thing in common: They are all made from bread. In fact, a loaf of bread can be the handiest staple in the cupboard. It is the perfect base for creating an attractive array of appetizers with a minimum of time and effort. And if the schedule does not permit the home-baked version, just purchase an unsliced loaf with a fine tight crumb.

To streamline the preparation of hors d'oeuvres for a crowd, you can slice the loaves horizontally. Use chilled bread and a hot, sharp knife (preferably serrated) to make the task easier. When dinner is to follow the hors d'oeuvre, allow eight to ten rusks, toasts or croutons per person, or four or five croûtes or baskets. Double this amount for a party that offers only appetizers and cocktails. Here are the best ways to slice and prepare bread for hors d'oeuvres.

Melba Toast or Rusks

Browned and dried slowly in a low oven, these toasts make lovely companions to dips or pâtés and a sturdy base for hors d'oeuvres that must be made in advance. Stale baguettes are perfect for these tidbits. Slice vertically as thin as possible. Arrange on ungreased baking sheets and bake in 300°F oven until golden (time will vary depending on type of bread used). If wider loaves are used, trim crusts before cutting into desired size and shape. Melba toast stays fresh for 1 week in airtight container and can be frozen for up to 1 month.

Toasts

Trim crusts from fresh or day-old bread. Slice loaf as thin as possible. Cut into desired shape. Lightly brown both sides in toaster or broiler. These taste best straight from the oven. Enjoy with caviar, hot hors d'oeuvres or mayonnaise-based spreads and fillings.

Croutons

Trim crusts from fresh or day-old bread. Slice loaf ¼ inch thick. Shape into squares, rectangles, diamonds or the traditional heart pattern. Sauté on both sides in clarified butter or in mixture of butter and oil in large skillet over medium heat until crisp (mustard, garlic or herbs can be added to butter before sautéing for additional flavor). Use as a scoop for dips or as a base for first courses such as escargots, poached eggs or creamed vegetables.

Baskets or Croûtes

Like tartlet shells, these bread cups hold purees, creamed forcemeats or quiche fillings. Brush muffin tin with melted butter. Trim crusts from fresh or day-old bread. Slice loaf vertically as thin as possible. Using fluted cutter, inverted glass or clean, dry, canned food tin, cut out bread circles that are larger than cups in muffin tin. Brush rounds with melted butter. Ease into tin, buttered side up, pressing gently to form baskets. Bake in 400°F oven until brown, about 10 to 12 minutes. Carefully loosen baskets from pan. Let cool on rack. Store in plastic bag or other airtight container until ready to use. Just before serving, carefully spoon filling into baskets (for best results, filling should be room temperature). Sprinkle with grated cheese if desired. Bake in 350°F oven until heated through, 10 minutes. Broil about 1 minute to brown if desired.

Great Hints

- Save crusts and trimmings and mix in processor or blender for breadcrumbs. Store in airtight container.
- For a different flavor, grill or deep fry croutons or croûtes.
- For an attractive presentation on appetizer tray, vary the shapes, garnishes, fillings and the types of bread.

Melt sugar in medium saucepan over low heat until completely dissolved and light caramel color. Gradually stir in soy sauce, water, lemongrass, garlic and star anise, blending well (mixture will bubble over if ingredients are added too quickly). Bring mixture to boil over low heat, stirring constantly, about 10 minutes. Cool 1 hour. Strain through several layers of cheesecloth into jar with tight-fitting lid. Refrigerate sauce until ready to use.

Available in oriental markets.

CHICKEN LIVERS NORMANDY

8 servings

- ½ cup all purpose flour
- 1 teaspoon dried dillweed
- ½ teaspoon salt
- ½ teaspoon dried tarragon
- ¼ teaspoon dried summer savory
- ¼ teaspoon freshly ground pepper
- 3 pounds chicken livers, trimmed and patted dry
- 6 thick slices bacon, diced
- 4 tablespoons (½ stick) butter
- 3 tart green apples, peeled, cored and thinly sliced (3 cups)
- ½ cup chicken stock, preferably homemade (see recipe, page 38)
- 6 tablespoons Calvados *or* applejack
- ¼ cup minced fresh parsley leaves
- ¼ cup minced fresh chives (optional)

Combine flour, dillweed, salt, tarragon, savory and pepper in plastic bag. Add livers and shake until completely coated.

Cook bacon in large skillet over medium-high heat until crisp, about 8 minutes. Drain on paper towels. Discard all but 1 tablespoon fat from skillet. Add 2 tablespoons butter. Place over medium-high heat, add apple slices and sauté until crisp-tender, about 5 minutes. Remove from skillet and set aside. Melt remaining 2 tablespoons butter in same skillet over medium-high heat. Add livers (in batches if necessary) and sauté until crisp outside but still pink inside, about 3 minutes. Reduce heat to medium, add stock, bacon, apples and Calvados and cook gently several minutes to blend flavors, scraping up any browned bits. Taste and adjust seasoning with salt and pepper. Transfer to heated platter. Sprinkle with parsley and chives. Serve immediately.

SOPES, CHALUPAS AND TORTILLAS

Sopes, chalupas and tortillas can be prepared up to 1 hour ahead and set aside.

Makes 12 to 15

Basic Masa Dough

- 2 cups instant masa mix*
- ¼ cup stone-ground cornmeal
- 1½ teaspoons sugar
- 1 teaspoon vegetable shortening
- 1 teaspoon baking powder
- 1 teaspoon salt
- 1 cup warm water, or more if necessary

Peanut oil (for deep frying)

For basic dough: Combine masa mix, cornmeal, sugar, shortening, baking powder and salt in processor. With machine running, pour 1 cup warm water through feed tube in slow steady stream. Stop machine and test: Mixture should be texture of stiff cookie dough. If too stiff,

continue mixing, adding 3 to 4 more tablespoons water one at a time until dough attains correct texture and forms loose ball. (*Can also be prepared with electric mixer.*) Pinch off walnut-size piece of dough, roll into ball, then form into desired shape (see shaping instructions below). If dough is too dry, it will crack and will be difficult to shape; if too moist, it will stick to plastic wrap or mold. Return test piece of dough to processor (or mixing bowl) and mix in small amounts of additional water or masa mix as necessary.

Remove dough and pat into ball. Cover tightly with plastic wrap. Let rest at room temperature at least 30 minutes or up to several hours.

For sopes: Pour oil into large saucepan or deep-fat fryer to depth of 2½ inches and heat to 375°F. Coat inside surfaces of 3½-inch diameter tart molds with nonstick vegetable oil spray. Press dough into molds to thickness of about ¼ inch; if dough becomes dry while working, moisten hands with water. Trim edges of dough flush with rims of molds. Using tongs, immerse each dough-lined mold in oil 1 at a time, then immediately pry sope gently from mold with tip of knife and continue frying, spooning oil over sope until browned on both sides, 1 to 2 minutes. Remove sope from pan using slotted spoon and drain on paper towels. Cut away puffed portions. If dough on bottom looks uncooked, return sope to oil briefly.

For chalupas: Follow instructions for sopes, substituting ⅓-inch-deep fish-shaped tartlet pans or ½-inch-deep oval tartlet pans with sloping sides.

For tortillas: Pour oil into large saucepan or deep-fat fryer to depth of 2½ inches and heat to 375°F. Lay piece of plastic wrap over saucer. Pinch off walnut-size piece of dough and roll into ball. Set ball in center of saucer. Top with another piece of plastic, then another saucer. Press down on saucer gently to flatten dough to 4½- to 5-inch circle. Peel plastic wrap away from dough (do not peel dough away from plastic or circle will crumble). Immerse dough in hot oil; immediately begin

spooning oil over top and cook until puffed and brown, about 1 minute. Remove from pan using slotted spoon and drain on paper towels. Repeat with remaining dough.

*Available in Mexican markets.

SOPES WITH SHREDDED PORK

12 servings

- 1 medium tomato
- ⅓ cup vegetable oil
- 1 pound pork tenderloin, trimmed of all fat and cut into 1-inch pieces
- 4 orange slices (about ½ large orange)
- 1 cup water
- 1 small onion, minced
- 1 garlic clove, minced
- 1 dried chili pod
- ½ teaspoon salt, or to taste
- 3 to 4 cilantro (coriander) sprigs, minced
- ⅓ cabbage head, thinly sliced (garnish)
- 12 sope shells (see preceding recipe)
- 10 radishes, thinly sliced (garnish)
  Avocado slices (garnish)
  Mexican Cream (optional; see following recipe)

Cut core end of tomato flat. Insert tomato cut side down in feed tube of processor fitted with Shredder, or in food mill, compressing if necessary to fit. Process using firm pressure to extract pulp and juice. Discard any skin. Set tomato aside.

Heat oil in medium skillet over medium-high heat. Add pork and orange slices and sauté until browned on all sides, 8 to 10 minutes. Pour off excess fat; discard orange slices. Reduce heat to medium, add water and stir, scraping up any browned bits. Blend in onion and garlic with reserved tomato. Stem and seed chili pod. Open pod flat, then immerse pod pulp side down in broth over meat mixture. Cover and simmer for 15 minutes.

Remove chili from skillet. Using fork to hold chili, scrape pulp from skin with knife; discard skin. Stir pulp into meat mixture. Add more liquid as necessary to attain saucelike consistency. Season with salt to taste. Cover and continue cooking until pork is tender, about 2 to 3 minutes.

Transfer meat mixture to processor fitted with Steel Knife or to food mill and blend just until meat is coarsely shredded. (*Can be prepared 1 day ahead to this point and refrigerated.*) Return to skillet and keep warm over low heat.

To assemble, stir cilantro into pork mixture. Arrange bed of cabbage in sopes. Top evenly with pork mixture. Garnish with radishes. Transfer sopes to large platter. Garnish platter with avocado. Serve cream separately.

Filling Variations

Refried pinto beans, sautéed bulk Mexican chorizo, queso asadero *or* grated mozzarella, queso de Oaxaca *or* Monterey Jack cheese and avocado.

Refried pinto beans, grated long-horn or cheddar cheese, small chunks of grilled or fried beef, guacamole and strips of jalapeño pepper.

Shredded lettuce, shredded cooked chicken (mixed with enough chile salsa to moisten), guacamole and sour cream.

Mexican Cream

Makes about 1½ cups

- 1 cup sour cream
- ½ cup whipping cream
- 1 teaspoon fresh lime juice

Blend all ingredients well in medium bowl. Set aside at room temperature 2 hours to thicken. Refrigerate.

CHALUPAS WITH MEXICAN CRAB FILLING

14 servings

Crumb Mixture

- 2 tablespoons (¼ stick) butter
- 1 cup coarse fresh breadcrumbs
- ¼ cup cilantro (coriander) leaves, minced
- 3 tablespoons pine nuts *or* coarsely chopped almonds
- 15 chalupa shells (see recipe, page 9)
- 3 tablespoons vegetable oil
- 5 green onions, thinly sliced
- 2 large garlic cloves, minced
- 2 tomatoes, peeled and chopped
- 1 small red bell pepper, roasted, peeled and diced
- 20 large Mexican capers
- 12 stuffed green olives, sliced
- 2 tablespoons red wine vinegar
- 1 tablespoon caper juice
- 1 teaspoon pure ground chili powder
- ¼ teaspoon salt, or to taste
- 12 to 14 ounces cooked crabmeat, cut into bite-size pieces
- ¼ cup cilantro (coriander) leaves
- 2 hard-cooked eggs, crumbled or sliced (garnish)
  Cilantro (coriander) sprigs (garnish)
  Mexican Cream (see preceding recipe)

For crumb mixture: Melt butter in large skillet over medium-high heat. Add breadcrumbs, minced cilantro and pine nuts and stir constantly until golden brown, about 5 minutes. Remove from heat. Transfer ½ cup crumb mixture to small bowl. Crush 1 chalupa and add to bowl; set aside for topping. Transfer remaining mixture to medium bowl; set aside for filling.

Heat oil in same skillet over medium-high heat. Add onions and garlic and sauté until soft, about 1 minute. Add tomatoes, bell pepper, capers and olives and stir 2 minutes.

Blend in vinegar, caper juice, chili powder and salt. (*Can be prepared 1 day ahead to this point and refrigerated. Reheat before continuing.*) Gently stir in crab and cilantro with crumb mixture reserved for filling. Simmer until just heated through. Spoon into remaining chalupas. Sprinkle with remaining crumb mixture. Garnish with egg and cilantro. Serve immediately. Serve cream separately.

NAVAHO FRY BREAD WITH SALPICON

Salpicón *means bits and pieces of everything; here, it is a delicious way to use cooked chicken and pork.*

8 servings

Fry Bread

- 2 cups bleached all purpose flour
- 2½ teaspoons baking powder
- 1 teaspoon salt
- 1 tablespoon vegetable shortening
- ¾ cup plus 2 tablespoons warm water

  All purpose flour (for dredging)

Salpicón

- 2 cups chicken stock
- ½ pound cooked white meat of chicken, coarsely chopped
- ½ pound cooked pork, trimmed of all fat and coarsely chopped

Vinaigrette

- 2 garlic cloves, minced
- ¼ cup packed cilantro (coriander) leaves, minced
- 1 teaspoon pure ground chili powder
- 1 teaspoon salt
- ½ teaspoon dried oregano, crumbled
- ¼ teaspoon dry mustard
- ⅓ cup vinegar
- ¾ cup vegetable oil

- 2 poblano chilies, roasted, peeled, stemmed and seeded*

Peanut oil (for deep frying)

½ **pound queso añejo (enchilada cheese), crumbled** *or* **Monterey Jack, shredded**

½ **head of romaine lettuce, cut crosswise into ½-inch-thick slices**
 Green Chili Salsa (see following recipe) *or*
 Southwest Tomato Sauce (see recipe, page 115)
 Chopped fresh cilantro, also known as coriander (garnish)
 Mexican Cream (see recipe, page 10)

For bread: Combine flour, baking powder and salt in medium bowl. Cut in shortening until mixture resembles coarse meal. Add water and stir to moisten flour mixture; dough should be soft and slightly sticky. Knead with hands 3 to 4 times. Cover bowl with plastic. Let rest 15 to 20 minutes.

Divide dough into 8 equal portions. Dredge both sides of dough in flour. Shape into circles about 3 inches in diameter. Pierce hole in center with finger to prevent overpuffing when fried. Transfer to baking sheet. Cover with towel. Let rest at least 30 minutes.

For salpicón: Bring stock to boil in large saucepan. Remove from heat. Add chicken and pork and set aside 30 to 45 minutes, stirring mixture occasionally.

For vinaigrette: Combine garlic and cilantro in processor or blender. Add chili powder, salt, oregano and mustard and blend in vinegar. With machine running, add oil in thin steady stream and blend until smooth. Adjust salt. Transfer to jar.

Drain chicken mixture. Transfer to processor. Add chilies and mix using on/off turns just until coarsely shredded. Add just enough vinaigrette to moisten completely.

Pour oil into large saucepan or deep-fat fryer to depth of 2 to 3 inches and heat to 375°F. Meanwhile, place 1 piece of dough on lightly floured surface. Handling dough as little as possible, gently roll out into circle about 5½ inches in diameter; dough should be slightly

more than ¼ inch thick. Repeat with remaining dough.

Using tongs, immerse dough in hot oil and fry 30 seconds, being careful not to puncture dough while pushing down. Turn and brown on opposite side. Remove from oil and transfer to paper towel–lined baking sheet. Immediately top with cheese. Repeat with remaining pieces of dough.

Top each fry bread with about 3 tablespoons chicken mixture, several strips of lettuce and 2 tablespoons salsa. Garnish with cilantro. Serve immediately. Serve Mexican Cream separately.

* To roast chilies, preheat broiler. Cut small vertical slit in chili to avoid bursting. Arrange on baking sheet. Broil 4 inches from heat until blistered and charred on all sides, about 6 minutes, turning every few minutes.

To peel, immediately transfer chilies to plastic bag and seal. Freeze 10 minutes. (Chilies can be frozen six months. Thaw before continuing.) Skin, seed and stem chilies. Remove veins if desired (veins and seeds make chilies hot).

Green Chile Salsa

Tomatillos are a pale green fruit with a distinctive lemon flavor. They also tone down hot chilies. Salsa can be prepared 1 day ahead and refrigerated.

Makes about 2 to 2½ cups

6 **tomatillos, husks discarded and fruit quartered**
5 **green Anaheim** *or* **poblano chilies, roasted, peeled, stemmed and seeded (see footnote, preceding recipe)**
2 **unpeeled garlic cloves, roasted with the chilies and peeled**
½ **avocado, peeled**
1 **cup Mexican Cream (see recipe, page 10)**
¼ **cup loosely packed cilantro (coriander) leaves**
½ **to 1 teaspoon salt, or to taste**

Place tomatillos in medium skillet and cook over low heat until softened, 3 to 4 minutes. Transfer to processor or blender. Add chilies, garlic and avocado and mix until smooth. Add cream, cilantro and salt and puree until smooth. Serve warm or cold.

FLOUR TORTILLAS WITH BEEF FILLING

8 to 10 servings

1½ **tablespoons butter**
1½ **tablespoons vegetable oil**
1 **pound rib-eye steaks, cut into ¼ × ¼ × 3-inch strips, patted dry**
1 **large onion, halved from root end to stem end, then cut crosswise into thin strips**
8 **to 10 Flour Tortillas (see following recipe)**
 Green Chile Salsa (see preceding recipe)
2 **ripe tomatoes, peeled and diced**

Heat butter and oil in large skillet over medium-high heat. Add meat and sauté until browned on all sides. Remove from skillet using slotted spoon. Add onion to skillet and sauté until browned and softened. Return meat to skillet and stir just to heat through. Transfer filling to heated platter and serve with tortillas, salsa and tomatoes.

Flour Tortillas

Serve plain with butter or fill with meat, eggs or shredded cheese. Tortillas can be prepared up to 2 hours ahead. Wrap stacked tortillas in cloth, then wrap tightly in foil. Reheat in 275°F oven.

Makes 10 tortillas

2 **cups bleached all purpose flour**
1½ **teaspoons baking powder**
1½ **teaspoons salt**
5 **tablespoons lard** *or* **vegetable shortening**
¾ **cup hot water**
 Additional flour, if necessary

Combine flour, baking powder and salt in medium bowl. Using pastry blender, cut in lard until mixture resembles coarse meal. Add water and mix with fork until liquid is absorbed. Gently knead (in bowl) with hands 10 to 15 seconds; if dough feels too sticky, add 1 to 2 tablespoons more flour. Cover bowl with plastic wrap. Let dough rest about 15 minutes.

Divide dough into 10 golf ball–size rounds. Roll each in flour. Transfer to plastic bag and let rest 20 minutes.

Pat dough into 2- to 2½-inch circle (if dough is very moist, roll lightly in flour first). Let rest 5 minutes (if dough does not rest sufficiently, rolling will be difficult).

Using as little flour as possible, roll circle firmly 2 times in 1 direction, then make ¼ turn and roll 2 more times in same direction; *do not overwork dough.* (A small rolling pin helps to prevent overworking.) Repeat turning and rolling, forming as thin a circle as possible (about 7 inches in diameter). Slip tortilla under plastic wrap to prevent drying. Repeat with remaining pieces, lining up tortillas under plastic wrap in order of shaping.

Heat electric frying pan or seasoned griddle on highest setting.

Add first shaped tortilla and fry just until bubbles appear all over surface. Turn and lightly brown underside; do not press down on tortilla. (If overcooked, tortillas will be dry and will crack.) Drain on paper towels. Transfer tortilla to cloth-lined basket and cover to keep warm. Repeat with remaining tortillas, cooking each in order of shaping.

First Courses

❖ ❖ ❖ ❖ ❖ ❖ ❖ ❖ ❖ ❖ ❖ ❖ ❖ ❖

THAI STUFFED MUSSELS WITH BASIL

10 buffet servings

   8 **medium shallots**
   3 **medium garlic cloves**
   1 **½-inch piece fresh ginger**
   1 **fresh lemongrass stalk*** *or*
      ½ teaspoon grated lemon peel
   2 **tablespoons vegetable oil**
   2 **teaspoons shrimp paste (kapee)***
   1 **teaspoon chili powder, or to taste**
   ¾ **cup canned unsweetened coconut milk**
   3 **eggs, room temperature, beaten to blend**
   2 **teaspoons cornstarch**
      Salt and freshly ground white pepper
   3 **dozen mussels, scrubbed and debearded**
      Uncooked rice
   3 **dozen fresh basil leaves**

Grind shallots, garlic, ginger and lemongrass to fine paste in blender. Heat oil in wok or heavy large skillet over medium-high heat. Add shrimp paste, chili powder and shallot paste and sauté until mixture is brown and oil separates. Remove from heat. Beat coconut milk, eggs and cornstarch. Blend into shrimp paste mixture. Season generously with salt and pepper.

Add water to stockpot to depth of 2 inches and bring to boil. Add mussels, cover and steam until open, about 10 minutes. Remove open mussels from pot using slotted spoon. Continue cooking any remaining mussels up to 5 more minutes, discarding those that do not open. Strain cooking liquid. Remove mussels from shells and rinse shells in strained liquid to remove any sand. Reserve 3 dozen large half shells.

Preheat oven to 375°F. Line rimmed baking sheet with ½-inch layer of rice. Set reserved shells on rice. Top each shell with basil leaf, then 1 mussel. Cover with sauce. Bake 10 minutes. Reduce temperature to 350°F and continue baking until sauce is set, about 10 more minutes. Serve at room temperature.

*Available at oriental markets.

OYSTERS IN LEEKS AND PINE NUTS KOREAN STYLE

10 buffet servings

   ¾ **cup fine julienne of leek (white part only)**
   ¼ **cup white vinegar**
   2 **tablespoons light soy sauce**
   1 **tablespoon sugar**
   1 **teaspoon sesame oil**
      Small pinch of freshly ground white pepper
   2 **dozen oysters on the half shell***
   3 **tablespoons pine nuts, toasted** *or* **white sesame seed, toasted**

Bring leek, vinegar, soy sauce, sugar, oil and pepper to simmer over high heat in medium saucepan. Cool mixture to room temperature. *(Sauce can be prepared 1 day ahead and refrigerated. Allow to reach room temperature before using.)*

Preheat broiler. Arrange oysters on broilerproof platter. Run oysters under broiler to warm to room temperature; *do not cook.* Top each with about 1 teaspoon leek sauce. Sprinkle with toasted pine nuts and serve.

*Clams can be substituted for oysters. Steam clams to heat and open.

OYSTERS ON THE HALF SHELL WITH SPICY SAUSAGES

For greatest enjoyment, alternate an oyster with a bite of sausage. Serve with a very dry white wine.

6 servings

Sauce Mignonnette

- ½ cup tarragon vinegar
- 1 tablespoon minced shallot
  Freshly ground pepper

- 6 to 12 hot Italian sausages

- 36 oysters on the half shell

For sauce: Combine vinegar, shallot and pepper in small serving bowl.

Broil or sauté sausages until cooked. Drain on paper towels.

Cover 6 plates with cracked ice. Arrange oysters atop ice. Serve platter of sausages and sauce separately.

SPICY BEEF CREPES (Risoles)

Indonesians have placed their stamp on this French culinary idea by using their own unique blend of spices.

12 servings

- 2 teaspoons peanut oil *or* corn oil
- ¾ pound ground beef
- ¼ cup fresh or frozen peas (about ¼ pound unshelled)
- ½ teaspoon sugar
- ½ teaspoon salt
- ½ teaspoon freshly ground pepper
- ¼ teaspoon freshly grated nutmeg
- 2 teaspoons cornstarch dissolved in 2 teaspoons water

Crepes (see following recipe)
- ¼ cup clarified butter (see recipe, page 62), or more

Heat oil in heavy large skillet over medium-high heat. Add beef, peas, sugar, salt, pepper and nutmeg and stir-fry until beef is almost cooked through, about 3 minutes. Remove from heat. Stir in cornstarch mixture.

Arrange 2 tablespoons beef stuffing in center of cooked side of each crepe. Fold bottom edge over beef. Fold sides over, then roll up to enclose filling. Transfer to platter.

Heat ¼ cup clarified butter in large skillet over medium to medium-high heat. Add crepes (in batches if necessary; do not crowd) and fry on both sides until brown and crisp, adding more butter to skillet as necessary. Return to platter and serve immediately.

Crepes

Crepes can be prepared up to 4 days ahead, covered with plastic and refrigerated, or frozen several months.

Makes 12

- 1 cup all purpose flour
- ½ cup milk, room temperature
- ½ cup water
- 2 eggs, room temperature
- ½ teaspoon salt

- 1 tablespoon butter, or more

Combine flour, milk, water, eggs and salt in medium bowl and mix until smooth. Let batter stand at room temperature for 1 hour.

Melt 1 tablespoon butter in 6-inch skillet or crepe pan over medium-low heat. Ladle 3 tablespoons batter into corner of pan, tilting and swirling until bottom is covered with thin layer. Cook until underside of crepe is brown, shaking pan in circular motion to prevent sticking, about 1 minute. Turn crepe out onto kitchen towel. Cover with sheet of waxed paper. Repeat with remaining batter, adding more butter to skillet as necessary and stacking finished crepes between sheets of waxed paper.

PASTA RAMEKINS WITH GOAT CHEESE

6 servings

Pasta Ramekins

- 1½ cups all purpose flour
- 2 extra-large eggs, room temperature

Goat Cheese Filling

- 1 pound goat cheese
- ½ cup whipping cream
- 2 eggs
- 3 sun-dried tomatoes (optional), diced

- 4 tablespoons (½ stick) butter, melted (for ramekins and tops of pasta molds)
- ½ cup freshly grated Parmesan cheese
- 12 Garlic Croutons (see following recipe), garnish

For pasta: Mix flour and eggs in processor 30 seconds; do not let dough form ball (dough should appear moist and hold together when pinched). Divide dough in half. Knead 1 piece slightly in hand to form even ball; flatten slightly. Adjust pasta machine to widest setting. Run dough through machine 5 or 6 times to knead, folding dough in thirds (as for business letter) after each run. Wrap tightly in plastic. Repeat with remaining piece of dough. Let dough rest 15 minutes.

Adjust machine to next narrower setting. Run dough repeatedly through machine (do not fold), adjusting to next narrower setting after each run until dough is about ¹⁄₁₆ inch thick. Cut pasta into six 5-inch circles and six 3½-inch circles. Set aside.

For filling: Combine cheese and cream in large bowl until well blended; cheese should retain some texture. Mix in eggs and tomatoes.

Position rack in center of oven and preheat to 350°F. Butter six 5-ounce ramekins. Dust with Parmesan, shaking out excess. Bring large amount of salted water to rapid boil. Add pasta and cook until just tender to the bite (al dente), about 2 minutes (cooking time will depend on dryness of pasta). Drain well. Line ramekins with larger pasta circles. Add cheese mixture, filling molds ¾ full. Set smaller circles on top. Brush well with butter and sprinkle with Parmesan. Bake until molds are puffed and tops are brown and slightly crusty, 20 to 25 minutes. Transfer to individual plates. Unmold if desired. Garnish each with 2 croutons. Serve immediately.

Garlic Croutons

Makes 12

12 ½-inch-thick slices French bread from narrow baguette
6 tablespoons olive oil
1 garlic clove, halved

Preheat oven to 400°F. Brush both sides of bread slices with oil. Transfer to baking sheet. Bake until evenly browned, about 10 minutes per side. Very gently rub top of crouton with cut side of garlic to flavor lightly.

CAPELLINI WITH FRESH TOMATO AND BASIL SAUCE

6 servings

2 pounds fresh plum tomatoes, peeled, seeded and coarsely chopped
1 cup coarsely chopped fresh basil leaves
1 3¼-ounce jar capers, drained and rinsed
3 tablespoons Sherry vinegar
Salt and freshly ground pepper
1 pound capellini pasta*
¾ to 1 cup olive oil (preferably extra virgin)

Combine tomatoes and basil. Marinate at room temperature 1 to 2 hours or overnight in refrigerator.

Blend capers, vinegar, salt and pepper into tomato mixture. Bring large amount of salted water to rapid boil. Add pasta and cook until al dente; drain well. Transfer to platter. Add enough oil to coat. Mix in tomato sauce. Let stand 5 minutes before serving.

Angel hair pasta can be substituted.

RIGATONI DEL CURATO

Rigatoni "in the mode of a rustic priest"—who must have eaten well.

6 servings

2 ounces dried porcini mushrooms
3 cups cold water
1½ cups hot water

3 tablespoons butter
5 ounces sliced smoked bacon, blanched 3 minutes and minced (about 8 medium-thick slices)
1 large onion, minced
1 2-inch fresh rosemary sprig *or* pinch of dried, crumbled
5 fresh basil leaves *or* ¼ teaspoon dried, crumbled
1 pound fresh mushrooms, sliced
⅔ cup dry white wine
1 bay leaf
1¼ cups deglazed and reduced meat juices *or* 4 cups unsalted poultry stock *or* meat stock reduced to 1¼ cups

1 pound rigatoni pasta
2 tablespoons (¼ stick) unsalted butter

⅔ cup half and half *or* ⅓ cup whipping cream mixed with ⅓ cup milk
Salt and freshly ground pepper
2 cups (about) freshly grated Parmigiano-Reggiano cheese

Combine dried mushrooms and cold water and stir through once. Let sediment settle, then remove mushrooms with slotted spoon. Discard water. Combine mushrooms and hot water and set aside until soft, 20 to 30 minutes. Remove mushrooms (reserving liquid) and gently squeeze dry. Mince mushrooms, discarding hard core.

Melt butter in heavy large non-aluminum skillet over medium heat. Add bacon and onion with fresh rosemary and fresh basil (if using). Cook just until onion begins to color, about 5 minutes. Push mixture to

side, tip skillet and spoon off all but about 4 tablespoons fat. Discard fresh rosemary and fresh basil. Increase heat to medium high. Add fresh and dried mushrooms and sauté until fresh mushrooms begin to wilt, about 5 minutes. Add wine and bay leaf with dried rosemary and dried basil (if using) and boil until completely evaporated, about 7 minutes. Stir in 1 cup meat juices or reduced stock with reserved mushroom liquid and simmer slowly until liquid is reduced to thick glaze, stirring occasionally. Discard bay leaf. (*Mixture can be prepared up to 2 days ahead to this point and refrigerated.*)

About 1 hour before serving, bring large amount of salted water to rapid boil in large pot. Stir in pasta and cook until al dente. Drain well. (*Pasta can be cooked up to 1 day ahead. Drain in colander and rinse with warm water; redrain well. Transfer to bowl and toss with 2 tablespoons vegetable oil or butter. Cover and refrigerate. Bring to room temperature before using.*) Heat butter in large skillet over medium-high heat. Add mushroom mixture and cook until bubbling. Stir in remaining ¼ cup meat juices or reduced stock and boil until thick.

When ready to serve, bring to boil. Stir in half and half and boil 1 minute. Add pasta and toss gently until mixture is heated through and pasta is well coated, about 3 minutes. Season with salt and pepper to taste. Spoon into large soup bowls. Serve immediately with freshly grated cheese.

POACHED LEEKS IN SAUCE VERTE

Serve with thinly sliced black bread and a bowl of unsalted butter.

6 servings

Sauce Verte

2 eggs
1 egg yolk
1 tablespoon Dijon mustard
2 teaspoons white wine vinegar
¾ to 1 cup peanut oil

½ cup watercress leaves, blanched, drained and chopped

2 to 4 tablespoons minced fresh parsley (preferably Italian)

2 to 3 tablespoons cooked, drained, squeezed and chopped spinach

2 to 3 tablespoons minced fresh dill

2 to 3 tablespoons minced fresh chives
   Salt and freshly ground white pepper

12 leeks

12 slices ham (preferably smoked)
   Cherry tomatoes (garnish)
   Parsley sprigs (garnish)

For sauce: Combine first 4 ingredients in processor or blender and mix until smooth. With machine running, slowly add oil in thin steady stream until mixture resembles mayonnaise. Add next 5 ingredients with salt and pepper to taste and mix until smooth. Cover and chill until ready to serve.

Trim leeks, leaving 2 to 3 inches of greens. Carefully slit outer layer and remove; wash and set aside. Slit remaining layers lengthwise (leaving leeks intact) and wash thoroughly. Rewrap in outer layer and tie with string. Let stand in ice cold water 30 minutes.

Drain leeks well. Arrange in single layer in large saucepan. Add water to cover and season with salt. Bring just to boil over high heat. Reduce heat and simmer until leeks are just tender. Drain on paper towels. Carefully remove string.

Wrap each leek with ham and arrange seam side down on rectangular serving platter. Spoon sauce evenly over top. Garnish with tomatoes and parsley.

SOYBEAN CAKES
(Tahu)

An interesting textural comparison for soybean cakes: Poaching lends a firm and meaty texture, while the fried version is lighter and chewier.

12 servings

1 quart water
4 Chinese soybean cakes (dowfu)*

2 tablespoons peanut oil *or* corn oil
   Sweet and Sour Sauce (see following recipes)
   Hot Chili Paste (see following recipes)
   Java Peanut Dip (see following recipes)

Bring water to boil in large saucepan. Add 2 soybean cakes and cook 10 minutes, turning once. Remove with slotted spoon and drain on kitchen towel. Cut each cake into 9 cubes. Transfer to platter. Refrigerate until ready to use.

Gently pat remaining 2 soybean cakes dry with kitchen towel. Cut each cake into 9 cubes. Heat oil in wok or heavy large skillet over medium-high heat. Add cubes and fry until outside is brown and firm. Remove with slotted spoon and drain on paper towels. Arrange fried cubes on another platter. Accompany with Java Peanut Dip, Sweet and Sour Sauce and Hot Chili Paste.

*Japanese tofu can be substituted.

Sweet and Sour Sauce
(Colo Colo)

This sauce should be pungent but not too hot. Adjust salt and sugar according to personal preference.

Makes about ½ cup

2 shallots, sliced
2 tablespoons Sweet Soy Sauce (see recipe, page 7)
2 tablespoons peeled, seeded and chopped ripe tomato
2 tablespoons water
1 tablespoon fresh lime juice
1 teaspoon sliced fresh hot red chili pepper

½ teaspoon sugar
½ teaspoon salt

Combine shallots, soy sauce, tomato, water, lime juice, chili, sugar and salt in processor or blender and mix until smooth. Turn into serving bowl. Cover and refrigerate. Bring to room temperature before serving.

Hot Chili Paste
(Sambal Lombok)

This incendiary mixture is for those with adventurous palates. It can be toned down, however, by adjusting the amount of hot red chili used.

Makes about ⅓ cup

¼ cup sliced fresh hot red chili pepper
2 shallots, sliced
1 teaspoon sugar
1 teaspoon peanut oil *or* corn oil
1 teaspoon salt
¼ teaspoon shrimp paste (trassi)*

Combine chili, shallots, sugar, oil, salt and shrimp paste in processor or blender and mix to coarse paste. Transfer mixture to jar and refrigerate before serving.

*Available in oriental markets.

Java Peanut Dip
(Sambal Kacang)

Makes about 1 cup

½ cup crunchy peanut butter
¼ cup Sweet Soy Sauce (see recipe, page 7)
2 tablespoons hot water
1 tablespoon fresh lemon *or* lime juice
1 teaspoon sugar
1 teaspoon crushed fresh or dried hot red chili
1 garlic clove

Combine peanut butter, soy sauce, hot water, lemon juice, sugar, chili and garlic in processor or blender and puree coarsely using on/off turns. Transfer to serving bowl. Cover and refrigerate. Bring Java Peanut Dip to room temperature before serving.

2 ❖ Beverages

Hot Beverages

CAFE BRULOT

A Creole specialty: Strong chicory coffee is laced with brandy for an exciting taste.

8 servings

- 8 sugar cubes
- 5 whole cloves
- 2 cinnamon sticks, broken into 1-inch pieces
- 2 tablespoons minced orange peel
- 2 teaspoons minced lemon peel
- 1 bay leaf
- 1½ teaspoons coriander seed

- ¾ cup brandy
- ¼ cup Curaçao
- 4 cups freshly brewed dark-roast coffee with chicory

Heat sugar, cloves, cinnamon, citrus peels, bay leaf and coriander in chafing dish over medium flame. Mash together with back of spoon.

Pour brandy and Curaçao into corner of dish, heat briefly and ignite. When flame is high, stir in coffee. Cover to extinguish flame. Discard bay leaf. Serve immediately.

THAI TEA
(Nam Cha)

The 2 varieties of tea leaves grown in Thailand are red and black. Thai tea is brewed strong to accommodate the traditional addition of milk. When added to the red, a rich brick color results. When black tea is diluted with milk and becomes a muddy brown, Thais say that it is "Chao Phya water," named for the fast-flowing waters of the country's largest river. It is also good without milk, served with lime. To serve as iced tea, let cool to lukewarm. Fill each glass with crushed ice to 2 inches from top. Pour tea over ice. Spoon milk over and serve.

Makes 4 cups

- 4 cups water
- 7 tablespoons red or black Thai tea leaves
- 4 generous teaspoons sweetened condensed milk, or to taste

Bring water to rapid boil in medium saucepan over high heat. Fit paper coffee filter into 5- to 6-inch diameter strainer. Set strainer over top of 1½-quart measure. Place tea leaves in lined strainer. Quickly pour water over tea leaves in steady stream, then stir thoroughly. Brew tea 2 minutes. Discard leaves and filter. Pour tea into 4 tall glasses. Stir 1 generous teaspoon milk into each. Serve immediately.

HOT MULLED CIDER

8 servings

- 4½ cups apple cider *or* apple juice
- 1 small orange wedge (about ⅙ orange)
- 1 cinnamon stick
- ¾ cup rum
- ¾ cup applejack

Combine cider, orange and cinnamon stick in saucepan. Warm over low heat until mixture begins to simmer. Remove from heat. Stir in rum and applejack. Pour into heated mugs and serve immediately.

MARIA'S ESPRESSO

6 servings

- 6 tablespoons sugar
- 2 egg yolks
- 2¼ cups hot espresso

Combine sugar and yolks in small bowl of electric mixer and whip at medium speed until frothy, about 2 minutes. Fill 6 demitasse cups ¾ full with espresso. Top each serving with about 1 tablespoon egg mixture. Stir briefly and serve immediately.

MEXICAN COFFEE

6 servings

- 3¾ cups hot freshly brewed coffee
- ½ cup plus 1 tablespoon coffee liqueur
- 6 tablespoons tequila
- 1 cup whipping cream, whipped

Mix coffee, coffee liqueur and tequila. Divide among 6 mugs or heatproof glasses. Top with whipped cream and serve.

ALADDIN'S LAMP

6 servings

- ¾ cup brandy
- 6 tablespoons coffee liqueur
- 6 tablespoons orange liqueur
- 6 tablespoons whipped cream

Combine brandy and liqueurs in small saucepan and warm slightly. Divide evenly among heated cocktail glasses. Ignite briefly, then top each with 1 tablespoon whipped cream. Serve immediately.

Cold Beverages

MANGO-YOGURT COOLER
(Aam Lassi)

Makes about 1 quart

- 1 cup plain yogurt
- ½ cup fresh or canned mango (about 1 medium)
- ¼ cup cold water
- 3 tablespoons whipping cream
- 3 tablespoons honey *or* sugar
- 12 standard-size ice cubes

Mix yogurt, mango, water, whipping cream and honey in blender about 30 seconds. Add ice and blend until frothy, about 30 seconds. Serve immediately.

RUM SWIZZLE

12 servings

- 2¼ cups Jamaican rum
- 2¼ cups sweet vermouth
- Angostura bitters
- Freshly grated nutmeg

Pour rum and vermouth over ice in large pitcher and mix well. Add about 12 dashes of bitters and grated nutmeg to taste. Serve immediately.

KAPALUA BUTTERFLY

4 servings

- ½ cup dark rum
- 6 tablespoons pineapple juice
- 6 tablespoons fresh orange juice
- ¼ cup coconut syrup
- ¼ cup fresh lemon juice
- 2 teaspoons sugar
- 4 fresh pineapple chunks
- Dash of grenadine
- Crushed ice

Combine all ingredients in blender and mix until smooth. Pour into tall chilled glasses and serve.

DIFFERENT DRUMMER COCKTAIL

6 servings

- 3 cups fresh orange juice
- ¾ cup Jamaican rum
- ¾ cup coffee liqueur
- 24 ice cubes (about)
- 6 orange *or* lemon slices (garnish)

Combine orange juice, rum, liqueur and ice cubes in large jar with tight-fitting lid and shake well. Divide evenly among 6 cocktail glasses. Garnish each glass with orange or lemon slice. Serve immediately.

THE MANHATTAN FALCON

To salute the return of the peregrine falcons to their nest on The Manhattan Life Insurance Company's roof, head bartender Jimmy Zamanis of New York's St. Moritz On-the-Park created this cocktail.

1 serving

- 3 tablespoons (1½ ounces) vodka
- 1½ tablespoons (¾ ounce) applejack
- 1 teaspoon dark rum, or to taste

Combine all ingredients and serve well chilled over ice.

BOURBON FRUIT COOLER

Makes 6 cups

- 1 6-ounce can frozen pineapple juice concentrate
- 2 medium bananas (6 ounces each), peeled and cut into several pieces
- 1 cup ice cubes
- 2 tablespoons sugar
- 1½ cups club soda
- ⅔ cup bourbon

Combine frozen pineapple juice concentrate, bananas, ice cubes and sugar in processor or blender and mix until smooth. Transfer to chilled pitcher. Stir in soda and bourbon. Serve immediately.

CAJUN MARTINIS

Makes about 1 quart

- ¼ cup dry vermouth
- 1 fresh hot red pepper *or* jalapeño pepper, split lengthwise (stem intact)
- 4 cups (about) vodka *or* gin

Combine vermouth and pepper in 1-quart canning jar. Add vodka to top of jar. Cover with tight-fitting lid. Refrigerate 6 hours. Taste mixture to gauge strength of hot pepper flavor. Remove pepper at this point or continue steeping up to 6 more hours.

TORTOLA SUNRISE

2 servings

- ½ cup mixed vegetable juice
- ¼ cup tequila
- 2 tablespoons fresh grapefruit juice
- 2 tablespoons fresh orange juice
- Hot pepper sauce
- 2 lime wedges (garnish)

Blend all ingredients except lime in shaker or jar. Pour over ice cubes in 10-ounce glasses. Garnish with lime.

TROU CANARD

The custom of the trou normande, *in which a glass of Calvados is taken partway through a meal to "make a hole" for what is to follow, is reflected in this robust cocktail.*

1 serving

- ⅓ cup Calvados
- 2 dashes Angostura bitters
- 2 dashes orange bitters
- 1 sugar cube
- 1 thick apple slice

Combine all ingredients in cocktail shaker and shake until sugar is dissolved. Pour into glass and serve.

FRESH STRAWBERRY-CHAMPAGNE DRINK

4 servings

- 2 cups (1 pint) fresh strawberries
- ½ cup fresh orange juice
- ½ cup dry white wine
- ¼ cup sugar
- 1 750-ml bottle Champagne, chilled

Wash and stem strawberries. Reserve 4 for garnish; halve remaining strawberries. Combine halved strawberries, orange juice, wine and sugar in processor or blender and puree until smooth. Chill 1 hour.

Divide strawberry mixture among 4 large Champagne glasses. Fill with Champagne. Garnish each with 1 reserved whole strawberry and serve.

INDIA CUP

This is a reminder that not every Sunday brunch has to begin with a Ramos Gin Fizz or a Bloody Mary.

6 servings

- 3 tablespoons firmly packed dark brown sugar
- 3 tablespoons water
- 1½ cups pineapple juice
- 1 cup golden rum
- ⅓ cup fresh lime juice (3 to 4 limes)

Crushed ice
Lemon or lime peel spirals (garnish)

Combine brown sugar and water in pitcher and stir until sugar is dissolved. Add pineapple juice, rum and lime juice and mix well. Fill glasses with crushed ice and pour mixture over top. Garnish with citrus peel.

ABSINTHE SUISSESSE

Creamy and anise flavored, this French Quarter prebrunch drink is served straight from the blender.

6 servings

- ¾ cup Pernod
- ¾ cup half and half
- ¾ cup whipping cream
- 6 egg whites
- 2 tablespoons powdered sugar
- 3 cups crushed ice
   Freshly grated nutmeg (optional)

Blend Pernod, half and half, cream, egg whites and sugar in pitcher. Refrigerate until ready to use.

Pour half of mixture into blender. Add 1½ cups ice and blend at highest speed until frothy and smooth, 20 to 30 seconds. Pour into chilled goblets. Repeat with remaining mixture and ice. Sprinkle each serving with grated nutmeg.

BISCHOFSWEIN

This recipe makes enough Bischof, an orange and brandy base, to flavor ten bottles of wine. The resulting beverage is called Bischofswein. The base keeps well for future use.

- 6 large oranges
- 2½ cups plus 3 tablespoons sugar (¾ pound)
- 4 whole cloves
   Very small pinch of salt
- 1 750-ml bottle brandy

Alsatian Riesling *or* Crémant d'Alsace *or* brut Champagne (use 750-ml bottles)

Preheat oven to 200°F. Remove peel (orange part only) from oranges using vegetable peeler. Trim any white pith from peel and discard. Spread peel on baking sheet. Bake until brittle, about 45 minutes.

Transfer orange peel to processor. Add sugar and mix until peel is finely minced, about 5 minutes (or mince by hand). Transfer to large bowl. Squeeze enough oranges to yield about 3½ cups juice. Pour juice over sugar mixture. Add cloves and salt and stir until sugar is dissolved. Blend in brandy. Pour into tall jar with tight-fitting lid. Let stand in cool dark place for at least 1 week.

Strain Bischof through several layers of cheesecloth. Mix about ½ cup plus 2 tablespoons orange Bischof with every 750-ml bottle of wine or Champagne. Pour into wine glasses and serve immediately.

WINE AND CHAMPAGNE PUNCH

16 servings

- 5 kiwi fruit, peeled and sliced
- 3 pears, cored and cut into chunks
- 3 apples, cored and cut into chunks
- 16 large strawberries, hulled and halved
   Block of ice *or* decorative ice mold
- 8 750-ml bottles Fumé Blanc, well chilled
- 1 750-ml bottle late harvest Johannisberg Riesling, well chilled
- 1 750-ml bottle Champagne, well chilled
- ¾ cup pear brandy

Thread fruit evenly onto sixteen 6-inch bamboo skewers. Set ice in center of punch bowl. Add chilled wine, Champagne and brandy and mix gently. To serve, ladle into goblets. Garnish with skewered fruit.

ORANGE WINE

Drink chilled or use for added zest in compotes. Can be prepared 2 weeks before using.

Makes about 2 quarts

12 oranges

8 cups dry white wine
1 3- to 4-inch cinnamon stick
1 vanilla bean

1⅓ cups sugar
⅓ cup marc* (optional)

Remove strips of peel (colored part only) from oranges, using vegetable peeler (reserve oranges for another use). Arrange peel on racks. Let stand at room temperature until dry, 2 to 3 days.

Combine orange peel with wine, cinnamon and vanilla bean. Cover and let mixture stand in cool place 2 weeks.

Strain wine mixture, discarding solids. Heat 1 cup wine with sugar in small saucepan over low heat until sugar dissolves, swirling pan occasionally. Cool. Add marc and remaining wine. Chill.

*Also known as grappa (brandy made from the residue of grapes after pressing). Available in most liquor stores.

FISH HOUSE PUNCH

Makes about 5 quarts

3 quarts water
1 pound dark brown sugar
Juice and peel of 1 dozen lemons (about 3 cups juice)
4 cups Jamaican rum
4 cups brandy

Combine water and sugar in heavy large saucepan over medium-low heat and cook until sugar dissolves, shaking pan occasionally. Increase heat to medium high and boil syrup 2 minutes. Combine lemon juice and peel in large bowl. Pour hot syrup over. Let cool. Stir in rum and brandy. Strain before using. Serve over crushed ice.

TAHITIAN RUM PUNCH

Hibiscus is the usual floral garnish.

8 servings

4 cups pineapple juice
2 cups dark rum
1 cup Sugar Syrup (see following recipe)
4 medium limes, quartered
2 vanilla beans, split lengthwise
1 orange, peeled, seeded and very coarsely chopped
1 papaya, peeled, seeded and coarsely chopped
1 banana, peeled and coarsely chopped
1 mango, peeled, pitted and coarsely chopped
Fresh flowers (garnish)

Combine pineapple juice, rum and syrup in 3-quart container. Squeeze juice of limes into container, dropping in shells. Add vanilla beans. Stir in fruit. Refrigerate at least 4 hours. To serve, strain into 2-quart pitcher or punch bowl. Pour over ice in tall glasses. Garnish with flowers.

Sugar Syrup

Makes about 2 cups

2 cups sugar
1 cup water

Combine sugar and water in small saucepan and stir to dissolve. Cover and bring to boil over high heat. Uncover and boil 3 minutes. Cool before using. Store syrup in jar.

WATERMELON PUNCH

Makes about 2½ quarts

1 14-pound watermelon
4 cups (2 pints) strawberries, hulled
½ cup sugar
1 12-ounce can frozen lemonade concentrate, thawed
2 cups vodka (optional)

Fresh mint leaves (garnish)

Sketch basket design on watermelon. (If necessary, cut slice from bottom so melon stands upright.) Carve melon using long thin knife. Remove pulp with ice cream scoop.

Transfer pulp to processor or blender in batches and puree. Strain through sieve into large bowl until juice measures 7 cups. (Reserve any remaining pulp for another use.) Blend 3 cups strawberries with sugar in processor or blender until smooth. Stir strawberry puree, lemonade concentrate and vodka into watermelon juice. Refrigerate.

Just before serving, fill melon cavity with some of punch. Slice remaining strawberries; float atop punch. Garnish with mint. Refill basket with punch as necessary.

3 ❖ Soups

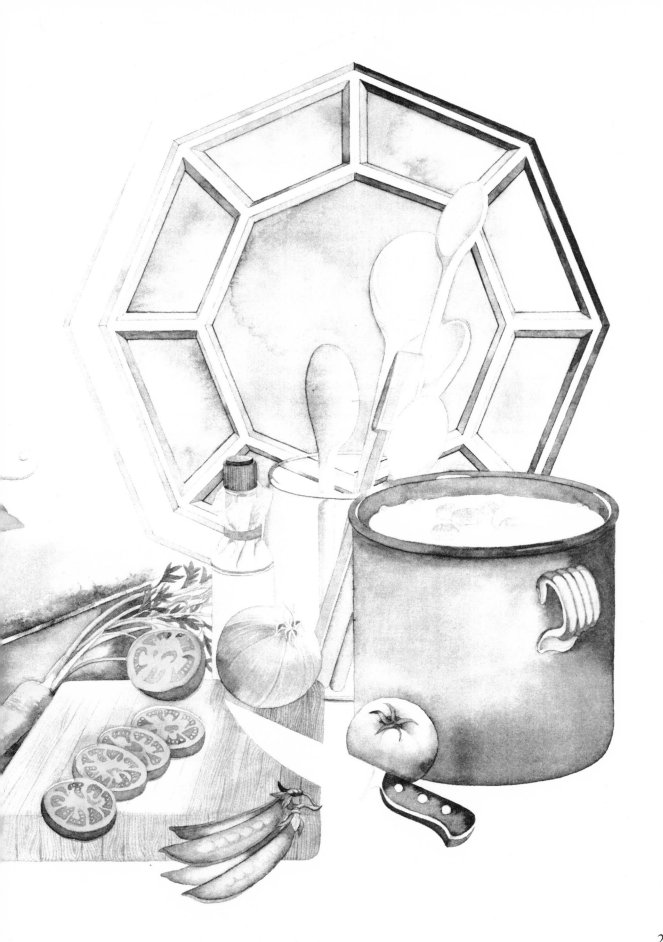

Hot Soups

CREAM OF ARTICHOKE SOUP

4 servings

- ½ cup plus 2 tablespoons (1¼ sticks) unsalted butter
- ½ cup chopped carrot
- ½ cup chopped celery
- ½ cup chopped onion
- ½ cup chopped mushroom

- ¼ cup unbleached all purpose flour
- 1 cup chicken stock
- 2 8½-ounce cans (drained weight) quartered artichoke hearts, juice reserved
- 1 bay leaf
- ¾ teaspoon salt
- ½ teaspoon freshly ground pepper
- ¼ teaspoon ground red pepper
- ¼ teaspoon dried thyme, crumbled *or* ¾ teaspoon minced fresh
- ¼ teaspoon dried oregano, crumbled *or* ¾ teaspoon minced fresh
- ¼ teaspoon ground sage
  Pinch of Hungarian sweet paprika

- 1 cup whipping cream

Melt 2 tablespoons butter in heavy large skillet over medium heat. Add carrot, celery, onion and mushroom and sauté until vegetables are soft and onion is translucent, about 15 minutes. Set aside.

Melt remaining butter in large stockpot over low heat. Add flour and cook, stirring constantly, 5 minutes. Stir in vegetables. Add stock in slow steady stream, stirring constantly. Add artichoke hearts with juice, bay leaf, salt, pepper, ground red pepper, thyme, oregano, sage and paprika and stir through. Increase heat to medium and simmer 30 minutes, stirring occasionally.

Beat cream in small bowl just until frothy. Blend into soup. Heat through; *do not boil*. Discard bay leaf. Adjust seasoning. Serve immediately.

FRESH TOMATO SOUP WITH CHEESE QUENELLES

6 servings

Cheese Quenelles

- 3 egg yolks
- 1½ tablespoons butter, melted and cooled
- ⅓ cup small curd cottage cheese
- ¼ cup white breadcrumbs
- ¼ teaspoon freshly grated nutmeg
  Pinch of dried tarragon *or* dried basil, crumbled
  Salt and freshly ground white pepper

Tomato Soup

- 1 slice bacon, finely diced
- 1 onion, finely chopped
- 1 small carrot, finely diced
- 1 celery heart, finely diced
- 1 garlic clove, unpeeled
  Pinch of dried thyme, crumbled
- 1 bay leaf
- 1 whole clove
- 1 sage leaf
  Pinch of fresh rosemary
- ½ cup tomato puree
- 2½ pounds fresh tomatoes, peeled, seeded and finely chopped
- 4 cups chicken stock

- 2 teaspoons (about) sugar
  Salt and freshly ground white pepper

For quenelles: Stir yolks and butter in medium bowl until smooth and frothy. Mix in remaining ingredients. Let stand at room temperature 3 hours.

For soup: Place bacon in heavy large skillet or Dutch oven over low heat. Cover and cook until fat is rendered, stirring occasionally, about 5 minutes. Add onion, carrot, celery heart, garlic, thyme, bay leaf, clove, sage and rosemary. Cover and cook until onion is translucent, stirring occasionally, about 10 minutes. Stir in tomato puree and cook 10 minutes. Add tomatoes and stock, increase heat and bring to boil. Reduce heat and simmer 35 minutes. Strain soup; set aside.

Just before serving, bring enough water to cover quenelles to rapid boil in deep skillet or large saucepan. Divide quenelle mixture into 6 equal portions. Form each quenelle into oval shape with moistened hands or by pressing between 2 spoons. Reduce heat so water simmers. Carefully immerse quenelles in simmering water. Let simmer until done, about 10 minutes. Meanwhile, add sugar to soup and rewarm over low heat. Season with salt and pepper. Ladle soup into bowls. Top with quenelles and serve.

*Clockwise from top: Soybean Cakes,
Spicy Beef Crepes, Zesty Barbecued Fish,
seashell filled with Hot Chili Paste*

*Counter clockwise from top: Schiacciata,
Crushed Chick-Peas with Coriander,
Caponata, Homemade Red Wine
Sausages, Warm Anchovy Butter with
Melted Onion and Garlic, Herbed
Roasted Red and Yellow Peppers on
Labna, Skewered Shrimp Wrapped in
Pancetta and Basil*

Clockwise from bottom left:
Chalupas with Mexican-Crab Filling,
Flour Tortillas with Beef Filling,
Navajo Fry Bread with Salpicon,
Fruit Empanadas, Bread Pudding,
Sopes with Shredded Pork,
Shrimp Huevos Rancheros

From top: White Wine Onion Soup with Gruyère Garlic Toast; Pear-Cranberry Crisp; Smoked Chicken, Apple, and Walnut Salad; Lemon-Mustard Dressing

*Clockwise from top:
Mozzarella, Tomato, and
Fresh Basil Pesto Salad;
Ravioli with Ligurian Walnut
Pesto; Mushrooms Stuffed
with Pesto and Cheese*

*Clockwise from top: Fresh Oranges
with Orange Zabaglione,
Ginger Coin Cookies,
Autumn Soup,
Sauce Verte*

MARIA LUNA'S BLACK BEAN SOUP

12 servings

- 1 pound dried black beans
- 1½ tablespoons salt
- ¼ teaspoon freshly ground pepper
  Large bouquet garni (large bay leaf, 2 fresh thyme sprigs, 4 fresh parsley sprigs, tied together in a cheesecloth bag)
  Pinch of dried oregano, crumbled

- 1½ cups chicken stock, preferably homemade (see recipe, page 38)

- ½ cup (1 stick) butter
- 1 cup sliced green onion
- 2 medium Anaheim chilies, split and seeded
- 2 medium garlic cloves, minced
- 1 cup dry vermouth
  Lemon slices (garnish)

Soak beans in cold water to cover at least 8 hours or overnight. Discard any that float. Drain beans and combine with 4 quarts water in stockpot. Bring to boil over high heat, skimming foam from surface. Add salt, pepper, bouquet garni and dried oregano. Reduce heat, cover and cook until beans are tender, about 3 hours, skimming foam from surface if necessary.

Strain off bean cooking liquid and reserve. Discard bouquet garni. Puree beans in processor or blender. Transfer to heavy large saucepan. Blend in stock and enough reserved bean cooking liquid (about half) to achieve medium-thick consistency.

Melt butter in heavy medium skillet over medium-low heat. Add green onion, chilies and garlic and cook until tender, stirring occasionally, about 15 minutes. Puree in processor or blender. Add to soup. Blend dry vermouth into soup. Cook over medium-low heat 15 minutes, adding more reserved bean cooking liquid if thinner consistency is desired. Season with salt and pepper. Ladle soup into bowls. Garnish with lemon slices and serve.

SWISS CHARD–BASIL SOUP

4 servings

- 2 heaping tablespoons pine nuts
- 2 tablespoons (¼ stick) butter
- 2 tablespoons olive oil
- 2 cups peeled and thinly sliced stalks from 1 bunch Swiss chard
- 1½ tablespoons minced shallot
- 1 small garlic clove, minced
- 4 cups (1 quart) chicken stock, preferably homemade (see recipe, page 38)
  Leaves from 1 bunch Swiss chard, cut into fine julienne (about 4 cups)
- ¾ to 1 cup packed fresh basil leaves,* cut into fine julienne
  Salt and freshly ground pepper

- 4 tablespoons (½ stick) butter
- ¼ cup *each* minced fresh chives, chervil and parsley (garnish)
  Freshly grated Parmesan cheese

Stir pine nuts in 4½-quart saucepan over medium-high heat until toasted, about 2 minutes. Remove nuts from pan and reserve. Place pan over medium-low heat. Add 2 tablespoons butter and oil and cook until butter is melted. Stir in Swiss chard stalks, shallot and garlic. Cover and cook, stirring occasionally, about 15 minutes. Increase heat, pour in stock and bring to boil. Reduce heat, add chard leaves and simmer until tender, about 5 minutes. Stir in basil and cook until wilted, about 3 minutes. Season with salt and pepper to taste.

To serve, divide remaining butter evenly among 4 heated soup plates. Ladle soup over butter and sprinkle evenly with chives, chervil, parsley and reserved pine nuts. Serve immediately with Parmesan cheese.

Use watercress if basil is not available.

MUSHROOM SOUP WITH SPINACH THREADS

8 servings

- 3 tablespoons butter
- 3 leeks (white part only), chopped (about 1½ cups)
- 2 medium onions, chopped
- 2 large garlic cloves, halved

- 2 pounds fresh mushrooms, 8 uniform mushrooms reserved and remainder chopped
- 2 teaspoons chopped fresh summer savory *or* ½ generous teaspoon dried, crumbled
- ¼ teaspoon dried oregano, crumbled
- ⅓ cup amontillado Sherry
- 9 cups homemade chicken stock (see recipe, page 38)
- 2 tablespoons tomato paste
- 1 bay leaf

  Salt and freshly ground pepper
- 8 to 10 young spinach leaves, stemmed and cut into fine shreds

Melt butter in heavy 5-quart saucepan over low heat. Add leeks, onions and garlic. Cover and cook 25 minutes, stirring mixture occasionally.

Stir in chopped mushrooms, savory and oregano. Increase heat to medium high and cook until mushrooms render liquid. Reduce heat to low and cook 5 minutes, stirring occasionally. Blend in Sherry and cook 1 to 2 minutes. Add stock, tomato paste and bay leaf. Bring to boil. Cover and simmer until richly flavored, about 45 minutes.

Strain soup through sieve, pressing on vegetables with spoon to extract all liquid. Cool. (*Soup can be prepared several days ahead to this point and refrigerated.*)

Just before serving, degrease soup. Bring to simmer. Season with salt and pepper. Stir in spinach and reserved whole mushrooms. Serve immediately.

Cream Soups and Veloutés

"Velouté" in French means velvety, a word that perfectly describes the textures of cream and velouté soups. Both are very popular in home and restaurant cooking in France because they are delicious and surprisingly easy to prepare.

While the terms "cream" and "velouté" are not really interchangeable, the soups themselves are very similar, the main difference being the basic sauce on which each is based. Cream soups begin as a thin béchamel, a classic white sauce of milk and a roux (butter and flour briefly cooked together). Velouté soups stem from the sauce of the same name, which is composed of stock thickened with roux.

The most traditional cream soups are made from a light béchamel combined with a pureed vegetable. And while the basic recipe can be adjusted to use virtually any vegetable, it is worth noting that a soup made with a vegetable high in starch—Green Pea Cream Soup (see recipe, page 35), for instance—does not need to be thickened with a roux. Also, instead of a béchamel, rice or potatoes can give a cream soup body. In this case, the milk is added later in the recipe.

Both cream and velouté soups can be enriched with cream, butter or egg yolks just before serving. In the classic tradition, velouté soups are finished with a mixture of both cream and egg yolks, which gives them a wonderful flavor and beautiful light yellow color. Now many cooks omit the yolks because of their tendency to curdle during reheating.

Vegetables, which are central to most of these soups, are easily pureed in a blender, food processor or food mill with a fine disc. For a very smooth, elegant texture, the soups can also be strained. Delicacy is characteristic of cream and velouté soups; therefore, extraneous flavorings are avoided in these recipes, allowing the principal ingredient to shine through.

Serve these exquisite soups in shallow bowls and top with a garnish that suggests the soup's flavor.

Most cream soups are as good chilled as they are hot, but veloutés should always be hot. And because cream and velouté soups are so sumptuous, they are best served in small portions as refined beginnings.

Tips for Perfect Cream and Velouté Soups

◆ Reheat soups over low heat, whisking or stirring frequently. Reheat a soup containing yolks in top of double boiler set over hot but not boiling water, stirring constantly. Remove soup as soon as it is warm.

◆ These soups will thicken on standing. After reheating, gradually add 1 or 2 tablespoons whipping cream, milk, broth, stock or water to thin soup to desired consistency.

◆ When serving cream soups chilled, do not add final butter enrichment because it will congeal and mar texture. Adjust seasoning before serving.

WHITE WINE ONION SOUP

6 servings

¼ cup (½ stick) butter
6 cups sliced Bermuda onion *or* Spanish onion (2½ pounds)
1 large garlic clove, minced
1 teaspoon sugar
2 tablespoons all purpose flour
5¾ cups chicken stock, preferably homemade (see recipe, page 38)
1¼ cups beef stock, preferably homemade (see recipe, page 37)
2 cups dry white wine
1 cup water
1½ cups 1 × ¼-inch carrot julienne
Freshly ground pepper
12 slices Gruyère Garlic Toast (see following recipe)
¼ cup chopped fresh parsley

Melt butter in heavy large saucepan over low heat. Add onion and garlic and stir to coat. Cover and cook 20 minutes, stirring occasionally. Sprinkle with sugar, increase heat to medium and cook uncovered until onion is deep amber color, about 30 minutes, stirring frequently. Reduce heat to low, blend in flour and stir 3 minutes. Add stocks, wine and water, increase heat and bring to boil, stirring constantly. Reduce heat to low, cover partially and simmer soup 20 minutes.

Stir in carrot julienne and simmer until tender, about 7 minutes. Season soup with pepper. Ladle into heated bowls. Top each with 2 slices Gruyère Garlic Toast. Sprinkle with parsley (or serve parsley separately) and serve immediately.

Gruyère Garlic Toast

Makes about 15 slices

1 10-ounce loaf Italian bread *or* French bread, cut into ½-inch slices

1 to 2 large garlic cloves, halved
3 tablespoons olive oil
½ pound sliced Gruyère*

Preheat oven to 425°F. Arrange bread in single layer on baking sheets.

Bake, turning once, until crisp and golden, about 5 minutes per side. (*Can be prepared up to 1 day ahead to this point. Cool completely. Store in airtight container.*)

About 15 minutes before soup is ready, preheat oven to 425°F. Line baking sheets with foil. Arrange toast on prepared baking sheets. Rub surfaces of toast with cut side of garlic clove. Drizzle with olive oil. Top with Gruyère. Bake until cheese is lightly browned, 5 to 7 minutes. Serve immediately.

* For stronger flavor, use ⅓ cup freshly grated Parmesan cheese instead of Gruyère. Sprinkle cheese evenly over each slice of toast before second baking.

SPICY PUMPKIN SOUP

This soup can also be served cold.

Makes about 1 quart

- 2 tablespoons (¼ stick) butter
- 2 celery stalks, diced
- 1 onion, chopped
- 1 tablespoon all purpose flour
- 1 teaspoon salt
- ⅛ teaspoon ground ginger
- ⅛ teaspoon freshly grated nutmeg
- 3 cups chicken stock
- 1½ pounds diced pumpkin *or* 1 16-ounce can
- 1 cup half and half *or* milk
  Chopped green onion (garnish)

Melt butter in large saucepan over medium heat. Add celery and onion and sauté until onion is golden, about 10 minutes. Blend in flour, salt, ginger and nutmeg and cook 3 minutes. Stir in chicken stock and pumpkin. Simmer mixture for 30 minutes. Transfer to processor or blender (in batches if necessary) and puree until smooth. Turn into large bowl. Stir in half and half, blending well. Ladle soup into bowls. Garnish with green onion and serve.

GREEN PEA CREAM SOUP

Soup can be prepared 1 day ahead. Cover and refrigerate.

4 servings

- 4 cups shelled fresh peas* (about 4 pounds unshelled)
- 2 cups water
  Salt and freshly ground pepper
- 2 cups whipping cream

Combine peas and 2 cups water in heavy medium saucepan. Season with salt and pepper. Bring to boil. Reduce heat, cover and simmer until just tender, about 7 minutes. Remove 2 tablespoons peas with slotted spoon and set aside for garnish. Continue cooking remaining peas until very tender, about 10 minutes.

Transfer peas and cooking liquid to blender and puree. With machine running, slowly add 1 cup cream and continue blending until smooth. Return soup to saucepan. Simmer over low heat 2 minutes, stirring frequently. Stir in remaining 1 cup cream. Bring to boil over medium-high heat, stirring constantly. Simmer until soup reaches desired consistency, about 5 minutes. Season with salt and pepper.

Just before serving, reheat reserved peas in small saucepan of boiling water 30 seconds; drain well. Ladle soup into bowls and garnish each with reserved peas.

* Two 10-ounce packages frozen peas can be substituted. Cook until just tender, about 5 minutes. Set aside 2 tablespoons for garnish. Continue cooking remaining peas until very tender, about 3 minutes.

MUSHROOM BROTH

6 servings

- 2 tablespoons (¼ stick) butter
- 8 large mushrooms, sliced (about 7 ounces total)
- ½ teaspoon dried chervil, crumbled
- ¼ teaspoon dried oregano, crumbled
- 6 cups rich beef stock, preferably homemade (see recipe, page 37)
  Salt and freshly ground pepper

Melt butter in small skillet over low heat. Add mushrooms and herbs and cook 5 minutes, stirring frequently. Bring stock to simmer over medium-high heat. Remove from heat and stir in mushroom mixture. Season with salt and pepper. Ladle into heated bowls and serve.

AUTUMN SOUP

This soup, which includes a bountiful array of autumn vegetables, takes its inspiration from the soups of Italy.

10 to 12 servings

- ¼ cup olive oil
- 2 onions, chopped
- 3 leeks (white part only), cleaned and thinly sliced
- 2 garlic cloves, minced
- 4 celery stalks, chopped
- 2 small turnips, peeled and chopped
- 2 carrots, peeled and chopped
- 2 parsnips, peeled and chopped
- 1 red bell pepper, seeded and chopped
- 1 green bell pepper, seeded and chopped
- 8 cups rich chicken stock
- 4 cups cooked small white beans
- 1 tablespoon chopped fresh basil *or* 1 teaspoon dried, crumbled
- 1 2-inch fresh rosemary sprig *or* large pinch of dried, crumbled
- 1 bay leaf
  Juice of ½ lemon
- 2 tablespoons olive oil
- 1 pound mild Italian sausage
- 2 cups shredded savoy cabbage *or* other green cabbage (½ small head)
- 1 cup shredded fresh spinach leaves (½ bunch)
  Salt and freshly ground pepper

¼ **minced fresh parsley**
Freshly grated Parmesan cheese
Sauce Verte (see following recipe)

Heat ¼ cup olive oil in large saucepan or Dutch oven over medium heat. Add onions, leeks, and garlic and cook, stirring frequently, until onion is soft and translucent, about 8 minutes. Add celery, turnips, carrots, parsnips and bell peppers and toss to coat with oil. Stir in stock, beans, basil, rosemary, bay leaf and lemon juice and bring to simmer. Reduce heat to medium low and simmer 10 minutes. Discard rosemary sprig and bay leaf. (*Soup can be prepared up to 2 days ahead to this point. Let cool, cover tightly and refrigerate.*)

Heat 2 tablespoons olive oil in large skillet over medium-high heat. Add sausage and sauté until cooked through. Drain on paper towels. Cut sausage into ½-inch-thick slices.

About 10 minutes before serving, bring soup to simmer. Add sausage and cabbage and simmer until cabbage is tender. Add spinach and simmer until wilted, about 3 minutes. Season soup with salt and pepper. Stir in parsley. Ladle into heated bowls. Serve with grated Parmesan and Sauce Verte.

Sauce Verte

Have guests stir a spoonful or two of this into their soup for more flavor. Sauce can be prepared up to 2 days ahead, covered and refrigerated. Allow to reach room temperature before serving.

Makes about ⅔ cup

½ **cup crumbled stale French or Italian bread**
1 **tablespoon red wine vinegar**
½ **cup chopped fresh parsley**
1 **hard-cooked egg, coarsely chopped**
2 **cornichons *or* tiny dill pickles, chopped**
1 **tablespoon chopped capers**
1 **anchovy fillet, chopped**
1 **garlic clove, halved**
2 **tablespoons olive oil**
¼ **teaspoon fresh lemon juice**

Place bread in processor or blender and sprinkle with vinegar. Add parsley, egg, pickles, capers, anchovy and garlic and mix until minced. With machine running, slowly add olive oil and lemon juice and blend thoroughly (sauce will be thick).

GENERAL LEE'S FAVORITE SOUP

12 servings

¼ **cup vegetable oil**
1 **medium onion, coarsely chopped**
1 **medium carrot, coarsely chopped**
1 **medium celery stalk, coarsely chopped**
1 **medium garlic clove, minced**
1 **cup dry Sherry**
2½ **pounds Italian plum tomatoes, halved and seeded**
¼ **cup tomato puree**
3 **quarts chicken stock, preferably homemade (see recipe, page 38)**
Salt and freshly ground white pepper

15 **to 20 small pearl onions or 1 cup diced onion**
1 **cup fresh corn kernels**
½ **cup diced carrot (¼ inch)**
½ **cup diced celery heart (¼ inch)**
1 **cup diced zucchini (¼ inch)**
1 **cup peeled, seeded and diced tomatoes (¼ inch)**

Heat oil in heavy 6-quart saucepan over medium-low heat. Add onion, carrot, celery and garlic. Cover and cook until tender, about 10 minutes, stirring occasionally. Tip pan and degrease thoroughly. Increase heat to medium high. Pour in Sherry and bring to boil, scraping up brown bits. Stir in plum tomatoes and tomato puree and return to boil. Stir 5 minutes. Add stock and return to

boil. Reduce heat and simmer until reduced to 8 cups, about 2½ hours. Season with salt and pepper to taste.

Strain soup through sieve, mashing vegetables with spoon, or use food mill. (*Can be prepared 2 days ahead up to this point.*)

Blanch pearl onions, corn, carrot and celery heart separately in boiling water until just crisp-tender. Rinse with cold water. Drain and set aside.

Just before serving, reheat soup. Stir blanched vegetables, zucchini and tomatoes into soup and bring to simmer. Ladle into individual serving bowls.

BEEF BARLEY SOUP

This soup is very peppery; decrease the amount of pepper to suit your own taste if you wish.

12 servings

8 **cups beef stock, preferably homemade (see recipe, page 37)**
1 **pound cooked beef, cubed**
1 **large potato (unpeeled), coarsely chopped**
1 **large onion, coarsely chopped (1 cup)**
3 **medium carrots, coarsely chopped (1 cup)**
3 **celery stalks, coarsely chopped (1 cup)**
¼ **pound green beans, trimmed and coarsely chopped (1 cup)**
1 **cup dry red wine**
⅓ **cup barley**
1 **tablespoon freshly ground pepper, or to taste**
1 **bay leaf**
2 **tablespoons (¼ stick) butter, room temperature**
2 **tablespoons all purpose flour**
Seasoned salt

Bring stock to boil in stockpot. Add beef, vegetables, ¾ cup wine, barley, pepper and bay leaf and boil until vegetables are cooked through, about 15 minutes. Blend butter and flour with fork to form paste. Whisk into soup with remaining ¼ cup wine and boil until slightly thickened, about 2 minutes. Discard bay leaf. Add seasoned salt and serve.

WINTER BORSCHT

The beef shin required for preparing the stock is ideal for this soup. Reserve remaining stock meat for another use, such as sandwiches. The borscht also is delicious served cold.

6 to 8 servings

- 3 quarts Beef Stock (see following recipe)
- 4 to 5 small beets, peeled and shredded (about 2½ cups)
- 4 large White Rose potatoes, peeled, halved lengthwise and cut into ⅛-inch-thick slices
- 2 large onions, coarsely chopped (about 2½ cups)
- 2 cups finely shredded cabbage
- ⅓ to ½ cup fresh lemon juice (about 2 lemons)
- 2 to 3 tablespoons sugar, or to taste
- 2 cups diced cooked beef (about ½ pound)
  Small boiled potatoes (optional)
  Sour cream (optional garnish)

Bring stock to boil in saucepan over high heat. Add beets and simmer 15 minutes, skimming as necessary. Add potatoes, onions, and cabbage and cook until soup is thickened, 35 to 40 minutes. Blend in lemon juice. Taste and add sugar. Stir in meat and heat through. Ladle into heated bowls and serve. Add 1 boiled potato to each bowl. Serve sour cream separately.

Beef Stock

Can be prepared several days ahead and refrigerated or frozen.

Makes 3 quarts

- 3 pounds beef bones (including marrow)
- 1 4- to 5-pound beef shin
- 1 large onion, peeled and studded with 2 whole cloves
- 2 garlic cloves
- 1 carrot, peeled
- 1 bay leaf
- 1 parsley sprig
- 1 tablespoon salt
- 1½ teaspoons dried thyme, crumbled

Preheat broiler. Arrange beef bones on broiler rack. Broil until browned, turning once, 7 to 8 minutes on each side. Transfer bones to 8-quart stockpot. Add remaining ingredients with enough water to cover. Bring to boil over high heat. Let boil 5 minutes, skimming surface as necessary. Reduce heat so water just simmers. Cover and cook until meat is tender, 2 to 2½ hours. Remove beef shin and meat from beef bones and let cool; refrigerate until ready to use. Return bones to pot and continue cooking for about 30 minutes to 1 hour (3 hours total). Discard bones. Strain stock through colander lined with several layers of moistened cheesecloth. Cool, then refrigerate overnight if desired.

Discard fat from surface of stock. Bring stock to simmer over high heat. Reduce heat and simmer gently until reduced to 3 quarts, 3 to 4 hours.

SAUSAGE GARBURE

Tradition dictates that you pour a splash of red wine from your glass into the garbure at table.

2 servings

- 3 cups water
- ¼ cup dried Great Northern beans *or* navy beans
- 1 1-pound smoked ham hock
- 1 small turnip, peeled and diced
- 1 medium carrot, sliced
- 1 medium celery stalk, sliced
- ½ small onion, sliced
- 2 garlic cloves, minced
- 1 parsley sprig
- ½ bay leaf
  Pinch *each* of dried marjoram, dried thyme and dried red pepper flakes
- ½ pound cabbage, shredded
- ½ cup peeled, diced boiling potato
- 4 ounces kielbasa, chorizo *or* cotechino sausage
- 4 ounces fresh fava beans (about 4), shelled, *or* 1 ounce shelled fava or lima beans
- 2 ounces fresh peas, shelled (2 to 3 tablespoons)
  Salt and freshly ground pepper

Croûtes (optional)

- 2 ¾- to 1-inch-thick slices French bread
- 1 tablespoon olive oil
- 2 tablespoons minced fresh parsley

Combine water and dried beans in large saucepan and bring to boil over high heat. Let boil 2 minutes. Remove from heat, cover and let stand 1 hour (or soak beans overnight without boiling). Add ham hock, turnip, carrot, celery, onion, garlic, herbs and pepper flakes and bring to boil. Reduce heat, cover partially and simmer 45 minutes. Add cabbage and potato and continue cooking until vegetables are tender, about 45 minutes. (*Can be prepared ahead to this point, cooled and refrigerated.*)

Prick sausage in several places with fork. Add to soup with fava beans and peas and cook 30 minutes, adding more water if soup is too thick. Season to taste with salt and pepper.

For croûtes: Preheat oven to 325°F. Arrange bread slices in single layer on baking sheet. Bake 15 minutes. Brush both sides with olive oil; turn slices over. Bake 15 minutes.

To serve, remove ham hock and sausage. Discard bone and tendon from hock; cut meat into bite-size pieces. Cut sausage into long diagonal slices. Discard bay leaf. Return meats to soup or serve separately on heated platter. Place 1 croûte in bottom of each heated bowl. Ladle soup over top. Sprinkle with parsley.

CREAM OF CHICKEN SOUP WITH APPLES

4 to 6 servings

  3 tablespoons butter
  2 cups chopped onion
  1 cup chopped carrot
  1 cup chopped celery
  1 tablespoon butter
  3 medium-size red apples (12 ounces), cored and sliced (4 cups)
4½ tablespoons all purpose flour
  2 tablespoons (¼ stick) butter
  5 cups chicken stock, preferably homemade (see recipe, this page)
  2 tablespoons applejack *or* Calvados
  ½ teaspoon dried marjoram, crumbled
  ½ teaspoon salt
      Freshly ground white pepper
  2 cups diced cooked chicken
  1 to 2 teaspoons cider vinegar (optional)

Melt 3 tablespoons butter in heavy large saucepan over high heat. Add onion and sauté 2 minutes. Reduce heat to medium low and cook, stirring occasionally, until transparent, about 4 minutes. Add carrot, celery and 1 tablespoon butter. Increase heat to medium high and sauté until vegetables are slightly tender, about 7 minutes. Add apples. Reduce heat to low, add flour and 2 tablespoons butter and stir 2 minutes. Blend in stock, applejack, marjoram, salt and pepper. Increase heat to medium and cook until soup thickens. Stir in chicken. Taste and adjust seasoning, adding vinegar if soup is too sweet. Serve hot.

COCK-A-LEEKIE SOUP

12 servings

  2 tablespoons pearl barley*
  3 quarts Chicken Stock (see following recipe)
  6 leeks, thinly sliced
2½ teaspoons salt
      Freshly ground pepper
  1 3- to 3½-pound chicken, cooked, skinned, boned and shredded
  3 tablespoons chopped fresh parsley

Soften barley by soaking for several hours in enough water to cover.

Combine undrained barley, stock, leek, salt and pepper in large saucepan and blend well. Cover partially and simmer 1 hour. Add chicken and parsley and simmer another 10 minutes.

*Rice may be substituted for barley. Cook soup for only 30 to 40 minutes before adding shredded chicken and parsley.

Chicken Stock

Makes 6 quarts

  5 pounds chicken wings
  3 pounds combined chicken necks and backs
  1 3- to 3½-pound chicken, trussed

  4 parsley sprigs (including stems)
  3 carrots, coarsely chopped
  2 leeks, quartered (including 2 inches of green part)
  2 celery stalks
  2 bay leaves
  1 onion, coarsely sliced
  1 turnip, quartered
  1 teaspoon salt
  1 teaspoon black peppercorns, crushed
  ½ teaspoon dried thyme, crumbled

Combine first 3 ingredients in large stockpot with enough water to cover, about 6 quarts. Bring to simmer over medium heat, skimming off foam as it rises to surface. Reduce heat and simmer uncovered for 30 minutes.

Add all remaining ingredients. Partially cover pot and simmer an additional 30 minutes or until whole chicken is cooked; remove and set whole chicken aside for another use. Continue simmering stock 2½ hours. Strain stock into bowl and let cool. Cover and chill overnight. When completely chilled, discard layer of fat that has formed on surface. Stock is now ready for use, or it can be tightly covered and frozen.

SOFT SHELL CRAB AND SWEET CORN CHOWDER

A favorite menu item at Pesca in New York.

10 servings

  2 tablespoons (¼ stick) butter
1¼ cups diced onion
  1 cup diced celery
  ⅓ cup diced carrot
  4 cups fresh corn kernels
  2 cups whipping cream
1½ cups milk
  1 cup chicken stock
  1 cup dry white wine *or* vermouth
  1 tablespoon paprika
  ¼ teaspoon ground mace
      Salt and freshly ground pepper
  5 jumbo soft shell crabs (aprons removed), cleaned and cut into 1-inch pieces
      Chopped Italian parsley (optional)

Melt butter in large saucepan over medium heat. Add onion, celery and carrot and sauté until tender, stirring frequently, about 5 minutes; *do not brown.* Stir in corn, cream, milk, stock, wine, paprika, mace and salt and pepper. Reduce heat to low and simmer until corn is not quite tender. Add crabs and continue simmering 10 minutes; *do not boil.* Ladle into bowls, garnish with parsley and serve immediately.

PROVENÇAL FISH SOUP

(*Bourride*)

6 servings

      Olive oil
  6 ¼-inch-thick slices French bread, cut into rounds to fit bottom of serving bowls

  2 tablespoons olive oil
  1 medium leek (about 1½ inches in diameter), sliced
  1 medium onion, sliced
  1 medium carrot, sliced
  2 garlic cloves, sliced

½ cup coarsely chopped fresh parsley
1 fennel bulb, coarsely chopped
1 fresh thyme sprig *or* ½ teaspoon dried, crumbled
2 3-inch strips fresh orange peel
1 bay leaf

3 to 4 pounds assorted fresh bass, cod, flounder and halibut steaks, 1 inch thick
2 cups water
1 cup dry vermouth

5 egg yolks
   Aïoli (see following recipe)

Preheat oven to 350°F. Brush olive oil over both sides of bread rounds. Arrange on baking sheet. Bake 4 minutes. Turn bread over and continue baking until toasted, about 4 more minutes. Set aside.

Heat 2 tablespoons olive oil in deep, heavy large skillet or Dutch oven over medium-high heat. Add leek, onion, carrot, garlic and parsley and sauté until onion is limp. Add fennel, thyme, orange peel and bay leaf and sauté until vegetables are limp, 5 minutes.

Arrange fish over vegetables in skillet in single layer. Pour in water and vermouth. Place over medium-high heat and bring to gentle simmer. Reduce heat to medium, cover partially and poach fish for 9 minutes. Transfer fish to heated platter. Strain broth. Ladle small amount of broth over fish to retain moistness. Cover to keep warm.

Whisk egg yolks with ½ cup Aïoli in heavy saucepan (off heat) until well blended, about 2 to 3 minutes. Whisk in ¼ cup broth 1 drop at a time. Gradually add remaining broth. Place over low heat and cook until sauce is thick enough to coat spoon.

Arrange croutons in heated individual bowls. Divide fish evenly among bowls. Pour sauce over fish and serve immediately. Serve remaining Aïoli separately.

Aïoli

This garlic-flavored mayonnaise is splendid as a sauce for fish or poultry, as a dip for crudités, as a dressing for boiled potatoes or as an accompaniment to hard-cooked eggs.

Makes 1⅔ cups

6 garlic cloves
½ teaspoon salt
½ cup fine fresh white breadcrumbs
2 tablespoons fresh lemon juice
2 egg yolks, room temperature
1 cup olive oil

If using mortar and pestle, combine garlic and salt in mortar and crush to paste. Add breadcrumbs and lemon juice and beat until smooth. Blend in egg yolks. Pour olive oil into mixture in slow steady stream, whisking constantly until Aïoli is thick and creamy.

If using processor, combine garlic and salt in work bowl and blend to fine paste, scraping down sides of bowl as necessary. Add breadcrumbs and lemon juice and process until smooth. Blend in egg yolks. With machine running, pour olive oil through feed tube in slow steady stream and mix until Aïoli is thick and creamy.

Refrigerate until ready to use.

Chilled Soups

THREE-MELON SOUP OF SUMMERTIME

6 servings

2 cups fresh orange juice
1½ cups finely chopped peeled cantaloupe
1½ cups finely chopped peeled crenshaw melon
⅓ cup fresh lime juice
¼ cup honey
2 tablespoons sugar
2 tablespoons minced fresh mint *or* 1 teaspoon dried, crumbled

2 cups Asti Spumante *or* other sparkling white wine
1 cup finely chopped seeded watermelon
   Fresh mint sprigs (garnish)

Puree orange juice, cantaloupe, crenshaw melon and lime juice in processor or blender (in batches if necessary). Mix in honey, sugar and mint. Pour puree into nonmetal container. Add wine and watermelon. Cover and refrigerate several hours or overnight. Garnish each serving with mint sprigs.

PINEAPPLE PRINCESS SOUP

4 to 6 servings

1 large ripe pineapple

1 papaya, peeled, halved, seeded and coarsely chopped
2 tablespoons tequila
1 tablespoon fresh lime juice
1 tablespoon sugar

1 kiwi fruit, peeled and sliced
1 papaya, peeled, halved, seeded and sliced (reserve 2 tablespoons seeds)

2 tablespoons tequila
1 tablespoon fresh lime juice
1 tablespoon sugar

Nasturtiums (garnish)

Slice pineapple in half lengthwise through crown. Cut around inside of each half and along core with serrated knife. Cut fruit from both sides of core (in as large a piece as possible), being careful not to pierce shell. Set aside. Remove core and discard. Transfer any juice or pulp remaining in shells to blender. Freeze pineapple shells with crown attached until ready to use.

Set aside half of pineapple. Chop remainder coarsely and transfer to blender. Add chopped papaya and puree until smooth, stopping once to scrape down sides of container. Add tequila, lime juice and sugar and blend well. Taste and adjust flavoring. Transfer puree to medium bowl. Cover and refrigerate for at least 2 hours.

Slice reserved pineapple into bite-size pieces. Transfer to large bowl. Add kiwi fruit and sliced papaya. Mix remaining tequila, lime juice and sugar in small bowl. Pour over fruit, tossing gently to coat well. Refrigerate mixture at least 2 hours, stirring occasionally.

To serve, arrange frozen pineapple shells on large platter. Spoon puree evenly into shells. Drain fruit and arrange over puree. Sprinkle with papaya seeds. Ladle mixture at table into glass bowls or goblets and garnish each with nasturtiums.

COLD CORN AND ZUCCHINI SOUP

Serve with cornsticks or corn bread.

8 servings

4 ears fresh corn (2 cups kernels)

¼ cup (½ stick) butter
2 tablespoons olive oil
1 large onion, minced
2 garlic cloves, minced

4 fresh tomatoes, peeled, seeded and finely chopped *or* 2 cups canned Italian plum tomatoes with liquid, processed through food mill
4 cups beef stock
4 thin zucchini, cut into 1-inch slices
3 tablespoons minced fresh basil *or* 1 tablespoon dried, crumbled
3 tablespoons freshly grated Parmesan cheese
1 small dried hot chili pepper *or* ¼ teaspoon dried red pepper flakes
Salt
1 cup whipping cream

Cook corn in boiling water until tender, about 5 minutes. Drain and cool. Cut kernels off cobs.

Melt butter with oil in heavy large saucepan over low heat. Add onion, cover and cook until just beginning to color, about 10 minutes, stirring occasionally. Add garlic and cook 2 minutes, stirring frequently. Stir in tomatoes, stock, zucchini, basil, cheese and pepper and cook until zucchini is crisp-tender. Blend in about ¾ of corn. Taste and season with salt. Puree mixture in batches in processor or blender. Transfer to bowl. Cover and refrigerate several hours or overnight. Blend in cream. Garnish each serving with some of remaining corn kernels.

CHILLED RED PEPPER SOUP

4 servings

4 red bell peppers
2 tablespoons (¼ stick) butter
3 medium shallots *or* green onions *or* 1 medium onion, finely chopped
1 28-ounce can Italian plum tomatoes
1 cup dry red wine
1 teaspoon sugar
Salt and freshly ground pepper
1 cup tomato juce

Preheat broiler. Arrange peppers on broiler pan. Roast 6 inches from heat

source, turning until blackened on all sides. Transfer to plastic bag and steam 10 minutes. Peel peppers, discarding veins and seeds. Rinse if necessary; pat dry with paper towels. Puree 2 peppers or chop very finely by hand. Slice remaining 2 peppers into very fine julienne; reserve for garnish.

Melt butter in large saucepan over medium heat. Add shallots and cook until softened and beginning to color, 3 to 5 minutes. Puree tomatoes (and liquid) in food mill set over shallot mixture. Blend in wine, sugar, salt, pepper and pureed peppers. Bring to boil. Reduce heat and simmer 20 minutes, stirring occasionally. Remove from heat. Stir in tomato juice. Let cool. Cover and refrigerate several hours or overnight. Garnish each serving with reserved red pepper julienne.

ICED PUREE OF VEGETABLES AND HERBS

8 servings

2 tablespoons (¼ stick) butter
1 pound leeks, cut into 1-inch slices
½ cup coarsely chopped celery (including leaves)
3 tablespoons fresh lemon juice

1 cup shelled fresh green peas
1 cup finely shredded fresh spinach *or* Swiss chard
1 cup finely shredded lettuce
5 cups chicken stock
2 cups half and half
Salt and freshly ground pepper
1 tablespoon minced fresh parsley
1 tablespoon minced fresh mint leaves *or* 1 teaspoon dried, crumbled

Melt butter in heavy large saucepan over low heat. Add leeks, celery and lemon juice and cook until leeks are tender, about 15 minutes, stirring mixture occasionally.

Stir in peas, spinach and lettuce. Add stock, increase heat and bring to boil. Reduce heat and simmer until all vegetables are tender, about 10 minutes. Blend in half and half. Puree soup in batches in blender. Strain soup through fine sieve. Season with salt and pepper to taste. Refrigerate several hours or overnight. Stir in parsley and mint just before serving.

COUNTRY-STYLE JERUSALEM ARTICHOKE SOUP

4 servings

- 1 **pound Jerusalem artichokes (also called sunchokes), peeled**
- ¼ **cup fresh lemon juice**
- 2 **tablespoons salt**
- 2 **cups half and half, or more**

- 1 **tablespoon butter**
- 1 **tablespoon olive oil**
- 2 **strips lean bacon, chopped into ¼-inch pieces**
- 1 **cup chopped peeled tomato**
- 1 **garlic clove, minced**
  Salt and freshly ground white pepper
- ½ **cup minced celery leaves**
- ¼ **cup minced green onion**

Cut artichokes into ½-inch slices. Transfer to medium saucepan and cover with water. Add lemon juice and salt. Place over high heat and bring to boil. Reduce heat and simmer until fork tender, 15 to 20 minutes. Drain well. Puree in blender with 2 cups half and half. Strain mixture if desired.

Heat butter and oil in large skillet over medium heat. Add bacon and cook until crisp, 5 to 7 minutes. Drain fat from skillet. Add tomato and garlic and cook 5 minutes. Transfer bacon mixture to large bowl. Blend in artichoke puree. Stir in more half and half if thinner soup is desired. Season with salt and pepper. Refrigerate several hours or overnight. Sprinkle each serving with celery leaves and onion.

GOLDEN MUSTARD SQUASH SOUP

6 servings

- ¼ **cup (½ stick) butter**
- 1 **cup chopped onion**
- 1 **medium carrot, chopped**
- 1 **celery stalk, chopped**
- 3 **cups rich chicken stock**
- 2 **cups rich beef stock**
- 1½ **pounds yellow summer squash, diced**
- 1 **6- to 8-ounce White Rose potato, peeled and diced**

- ¾ **cup whipping cream**
- 1½ **tablespoons Dijon mustard**
- ½ **teaspoon freshly grated nutmeg**
  Salt and freshly ground white pepper
  Grated carrot and snipped fresh chives (garnish)

Melt butter in heavy large saucepan over low heat. Add onion, carrot and celery. Cover and cook until onion is translucent, about 10 minutes, stirring occasionally. Add chicken and beef stock, squash and potato. Increase heat to high and bring to simmer. Simmer until mixture is very tender, about 30 minutes.

Transfer mixture to processor or blender in batches and puree until smooth. Pour into bowl. (For finer texture, strain soup.) Stir in cream, mustard and nutmeg with salt and pepper to taste. Cover and refrigerate. Taste and adjust seasoning. Garnish with carrot and chives just before serving.

COLD BEET SOUP WITH SHRIMP

8 servings

- 8 **cups light chicken stock, preferably homemade (see recipe, page 38)**
- 1¼ **pounds trimmed beets, peeled and coarsely chopped**
- 1 **medium onion, chopped**
- 3 **medium shallots, chopped**

- 2 **tablespoons red wine vinegar**
- 1 **tablespoon fresh lemon juice**
  Salt and freshly ground white pepper
- ⅓ **cup Crème Fraîche, lightly whipped (see following recipe)**
- ½ **cup cooked tiny shrimp (garnish)**
  Dill sprigs (garnish)

Bring stock, beets, onion and shallots to boil in large saucepan. Cover and simmer until tender, about 25 minutes. Strain through fine sieve, reserving beets for another use. Cool liquid. Mix in vinegar, lemon juice and salt and pepper. Refrigerate until well chilled.

Just before serving, taste soup and adjust seasoning. Ladle into individual bowls. Top with dollop of Crème Fraîche. Garnish with shrimp and dill.

Crème Fraîche

- 2 **cups whipping cream**
- 1 **tablespoon buttermilk**

Mix cream and buttermilk in covered jar and shake 2 minutes. Let stand at room temperature until thick, about 8 hours. Refrigerate.

4 ❖ Entrées: Meat

Beef and Veal

❖ ❖ ❖ ❖ ❖ ❖ ❖ ❖ ❖ ❖ ❖ ❖ ❖ ❖ ❖

POLYNESIAN FLANK STEAK

Accompany with a composed salad of white rice, fresh green peas and mint.

4 to 6 servings

- 2 tablespoons (¼ stick) butter
- 1 bunch green onions, minced
- 1 cup dry breadcrumbs
- 1 papaya, peeled, seeded and coarsely chopped
- 1 banana, mashed
- ½ cup unsalted peanuts, coarsely chopped
- 2 teaspoons soy sauce
- 1 teaspoon fresh lemon juice
- ½ teaspoon dried tarragon, crumbled
- 1 2- to 2½-pound (about) flank steak, well dried, fat trimmed

- ¾ cup papaya nectar
- ¼ cup dry white wine
  Safflower oil

Melt butter in large skillet over medium-high heat. Add green onion and sauté until soft but not brown. Stir in breadcrumbs, papaya, banana, peanuts, soy sauce, lemon juice and tarragon. Remove from heat. Score meat lightly on both sides. Spread stuffing evenly over meat. Roll up jelly roll style, securing with string several times in both directions.

Preheat oven to 300°F. Combine papaya nectar and wine. Heat oil in large flameproof casserole or Dutch oven over medium-high heat. Add meat and brown on all sides. Pour nectar mixture over. Cover tightly, transfer to oven and roast until tender, about 1 hour, turning occasionally. Transfer to heated platter and let stand 15 minutes. Slice into serving pieces. Spoon small amount of sauce over and serve. Serve remaining sauce separately.

MEAT LOAF WITH THREE CHEESES

12 servings

  Breadcrumbs

- 2 pounds ground beef
- 1 large onion, finely chopped
- 1 garlic clove, finely chopped
- 2 cups fresh spinach (stems discarded), washed, dried and finely chopped
- ½ cup freshly grated Parmesan cheese
- 2 tablespoons finely chopped fresh parsley *or* 1 teaspoon dried, crumbled
- 2 eggs, beaten to blend
- 3 slices French, Italian *or* homemade white bread, soaked in ½ cup milk 5 minutes, drained and squeezed dry
- 2 teaspoons salt
  Freshly ground pepper

- 1 cup finely cubed mozzarella cheese
- 1 cup slivered Gruyère
  Butter

Generously butter 12 × 4 × 2½-inch baking pan. Sprinkle with breadcrumbs, shaking out excess.

Combine meat, onion, garlic, spinach, Parmesan, parsley, eggs, bread, salt and pepper in large bowl and blend well.

Preheat oven to 350°F. Divide mixture into 3 portions. Pat ⅓ of mixture into bottom of prepared pan (be sure meat touches sides of pan). Sprinkle mozzarella cubes over top. Add another ⅓ meat mixture and cover with Gruyère slivers. Add remaining ⅓ meat mixture, patting in place to edge of pan. Sprinkle with breadcrumbs and dot with butter. Bake until cooked through, about 1 hour. Remove from pan using large spatula. Transfer to large platter. Serve hot or cold.

STEAKS WITH ZESTY TARRAGON BUTTER

6 servings

- 2 medium shallots
- 2 tablespoons chopped fresh parsley
- 4 teaspoons tarragon vinegar
- ½ teaspoon dried tarragon, crumbled
- ½ teaspoon freshly ground pepper
- ½ cup (1 stick) chilled butter, cut into small pieces

- 6 beef tenderloin steaks

Combine shallots, parsley, vinegar, tarragon and pepper in processor and mince using several on/off turns. Add butter and blend well. Transfer to waxed paper and form into cylinder. Refrigerate or freeze until firm.

Grill, broil or pan-fry steaks to desired doneness. Transfer to individual plates. Slice butter evenly into 6 rounds (or thinner if desired). Set atop steaks and serve immediately.

LAZY TEXAS BRISKET

12 servings

- 1 large garlic clove, minced
- 1 4- to 5-pound beef brisket
- 1 tablespoon chili powder
- 1 teaspoon paprika
- 1 teaspoon salt
- ½ teaspoon ground cumin
- ½ teaspoon dried sage, crumbled
- ½ teaspoon sugar
- ½ teaspoon dried oregano, crumbled
- ¼ teaspoon ground red pepper
- ¼ teaspoon freshly ground pepper
  Broncbuster's Barbecue Sauce (see following recipe)

Preheat oven to 200°F. Rub garlic into both sides of brisket. Combine remaining seasonings in small bowl and mix well. Rub into brisket. Set brisket fat side up on large piece of foil and wrap tightly. Transfer to shallow roasting pan. Bake until tender, about 8 hours. Serve hot or cold with sauce.

Broncbuster's Barbecue Sauce

Makes 2 cups

- 2 tablespoons (¼ stick) butter
- 1 medium onion, chopped
- ½ cup water
- ½ cup prepared chili sauce
- ½ cup catsup
- ¼ cup cider vinegar
- 2 tablespoons fresh lemon juice
- 2 tablespoons firmly packed brown sugar
- 2 tablespoons Worcestershire sauce
- 1 tablespoon molasses
- 2 teaspoons salt
- 2 teaspoons dry mustard
- ½ teaspoon freshly ground pepper
- ½ teaspoon paprika

Melt butter in large skillet over medium-low heat. Add onion. Cover and cook until translucent, about 10 minutes, stirring occasionally. Blend in remaining ingredients. Bring sauce to boil. Reduce heat and simmer gently, uncovered, 30 minutes, stirring occasionally. Serve at room temperature.

BOILED BEEF GERMAN STYLE (*Tellerfleisch*)

A flavorful entrée which is low in fat and calories.

6 servings

- 2 carrots
- 1 onion, studded with 6 cloves
- 1 small celery root, quartered
- 1 leek (about ¾ pound), trimmed
- 2 teaspoons salt
- 10 peppercorns
- 10 allspice berries
- 3 garlic cloves
- 2 bay leaves
- 2 tablespoons red wine vinegar
- 2 tablespoons sugar
- 1 3-pound beef brisket

Combine all ingredients except brisket in 8- to 10-quart saucepan or Dutch oven with enough water to cover and bring to boil over high heat. Reduce heat, cover and simmer 30 minutes. Add brisket and enough water just to cover. Return to simmer. Cover partially and cook until meat is fork tender, about 3 hours, skimming surface as necessary after first 15 minutes. (*Brisket can be prepared several hours ahead to this point. Set aside in cooking liquid at room temperature.*) Transfer to heated platter. Pour several spoonfuls of liquid over and serve.

GRILLED STEAK WITH CREOLE SAUCE

Accompany with hot buttered grits.

6 servings

- ¼ pound thick-cut bacon, diced
- 2 tablespoons vegetable oil
- 2 cups thinly sliced onion
- 2 6-ounce bunches green onions, trimmed and sliced into ¼-inch rounds
- 4 medium celery stalks, cut into ¼-inch slices
- ¼ pound smoked ham, diced
- 1 green bell pepper, seeded and cut into ¼-inch strips
- 1 red bell pepper, seeded and cut into ¼-inch strips
- 4 large, firm, ripe tomatoes, peeled, seeded and coarsely diced
- 2 teaspoons firmly packed brown sugar
- 1 10-ounce package frozen sliced okra, thawed and drained
- 2 large garlic cloves, minced
- 2 teaspoons red wine vinegar
- 1 teaspoon dried thyme, crumbled
- 1 teaspoon salt
- ¼ teaspoon ground allspice
- ⅛ teaspoon ground red pepper
  Freshly ground pepper

- 6 6-ounce rib eye steaks

Sauté bacon in heavy large skillet over medium-high heat until fat is rendered and bacon begins to turn golden brown. Discard all but 2 tablespoons fat. Add vegetable oil to skillet and reheat over medium-high heat. Mix in onions, celery, ham and peppers and stir with wooden spoon until vegetables soften and begin to color, 8 to 10 minutes. Increase heat to high. Add tomatoes and brown sugar and simmer until tomato juices evaporate, stirring occasionally, about 5 minutes. Blend in remaining ingredients except steaks and cook until mixture bubbles. Reduce heat to medium low, cover partially and simmer until sauce is thick, 25 to 30 minutes. Adjust seasoning. Remove from heat. (*Sauce can be prepared 1 day ahead and refrigerated. Reheat thoroughly before serving.*)

Prepare charcoal grill or preheat broiler. Season steaks with salt and pepper. Cook to desired doneness. Transfer steaks to platter. Top with sauce and serve immediately.

BEEF WITH PANCETTA AND GORGONZOLA

This sauce is also superb with liver.

6 servings

- 2 tablespoons (¼ stick) butter
- 2 tablespoons olive oil
- 2 red onions, sliced into ¼-inch rings
  Salt and freshly ground pepper

- 1 cup whipping cream
- 2 tablespoons cornstarch
- 4 ounces Gorgonzola cheese

- 6 slices pancetta, about ⅛ inch thick
- 2 tablespoons (¼ stick) butter
- 6 1-inch-thick tenderloin, rib or sirloin steaks (about 1½ pounds total), patted dry

- 2 tablespoons minced fresh parsley

Melt butter with oil in heavy medium skillet over medium-low heat. Stir in sliced onions. Season with salt and pepper. Cover and cook, stirring frequently, until onions are tender, 10 to 12 minutes. Keep warm.

Gradually blend cream into cornstarch in heavy small saucepan. Bring to boil over low heat, stirring constantly. Remove from heat. Add cheese and stir until smooth. Season with salt and pepper to taste. Set sauce aside at room temperature until ready to use.

Cook pancetta slices in heavy large skillet over medium heat until edges begin to curl; *do not cook until crisp.* Remove with slotted spoon. Melt butter in same skillet over medium-high heat. Add steaks, searing and browning on one side. Turn and sprinkle with salt and pepper. Continue cooking to desired doneness, 3 to 5 minutes for medium rare. Just before steaks are done, spoon 2 tablespoons sauce over each, then cover skillet so cheese melts quickly. Remove from heat.

To serve, set steaks on pancetta slices. Surround with onions. Sprinkle with minced parsley. Reheat remaining sauce over very low heat or in top of double boiler over simmering water. Serve sauce separately.

STANDING RIB ROAST OF BEEF WITH MADEIRA SAUCE

10 servings

- 2 teaspoons salt
- 1 teaspoon dried thyme, crumbled
- 1 teaspoon freshly ground pepper
- 1 10-pound standing rib of beef (4 ribs), trimmed, fat scored, chine removed and tied onto roast

Sauce

- ⅔ cup water
- 1½ tablespoons butter
  Juice of ½ lemon
- ¼ teaspoon salt
- ½ pound small white mushrooms, trimmed (sliced or halved if desired)

- ¼ cup (½ stick) butter
- ½ cup minced shallot
- 1 cup beef stock
- ½ cup Madeira
- 1 tablespoon tomato paste
  Salt and freshly ground pepper

Combine salt, thyme and pepper in small bowl and blend well. Rub into roast, covering entire surface. Transfer meat to rack in large roasting pan. Let stand at room temperature 1 hour.

For sauce: Combine water, butter, lemon juice and salt in nonaluminum medium saucepan and bring to boil over medium-high heat. Reduce heat to low and stir in mushrooms. Cover and cook gently about 5 minutes. Uncover and set aside. (*Can be prepared several hours ahead to this point. Let stand at room temperature until ready to use.*)

Preheat oven to 500°F. Roast meat 10 minutes. Reduce oven temperature to 350°F and continue roasting until meat thermometer inserted in thickest portion of meat (without touching bone) registers 130°F (for rare), about 17 minutes per pound; do not baste. Transfer roast to heated serving platter. Tent with foil and keep warm.

Discard as much fat as possible from roasting pan. Add ¼ cup butter to pan and melt over medium-high heat. Stir in shallot and sauté until tender. Drain mushroom cooking liquid into measuring cup and add water, if necessary, to equal 1 cup. Pour into roasting pan with beef stock, Madeira and tomato paste and blend well. Reduce heat to low and cook, stirring up any browned bits, until liquid is reduced to 2 cups. Stir in mushrooms and cook just until heated through. Season with salt and pepper to taste. Transfer to heated sauceboat. Carve roast at table and serve immediately with sauce.

PHYLLO-WRAPPED VEAL ROLL

Can be assembled ahead and refrigerated overnight. Bake just before serving.

6 servings

- 2 tablespoons olive oil
- 1 medium onion, minced
- 1½ pounds ground veal
- 1 medium tomato, peeled, seeded and chopped
- 1 tablespoon chopped fresh thyme *or* 1 teaspoon dried, crumbled
- 1 teaspoon cinnamon

- 4 tablespoons (½ stick) butter
- 3 tablespoons all purpose flour
- 1 cup milk
- 1 egg, room temperature, beaten to blend

- ¼ cup pine nuts (1¼ ounces)

- 2 tablespoons olive oil
- 1 garlic clove, minced
- 6 ounces stemmed fresh spinach, chopped
- ¼ teaspoon freshly grated nutmeg
  Salt and freshly ground pepper

½ cup freshly grated Romano
cheese

10 phyllo pastry sheets (do not
use ultra-thin)

⅓ cup unsalted butter, melted

Heat 2 tablespoons olive oil in heavy
large skillet over medium-low heat.
Add onion and cook until soft, about
10 minutes. Add meat and cook,
breaking up meat with fork and
spooning off excess liquid as it accu-
mulates, until only a few traces of
pink remain, 5 to 8 minutes. Add
tomato, thyme and cinnamon. Cover
and simmer 20 minutes, stirring
occasionally.

Meanwhile, melt 3 table-
spoons butter in heavy small saucepan over low heat. Add flour and
stir 3 minutes. Pour in milk, increase
heat to medium high and stir until
sauce boils and thickens. Remove
from heat. Whisk in egg. Place over
medium heat and continue stirring
2 minutes. Set sauce aside.

Melt remaining 1 tablespoon
butter in heavy small skillet over
medium heat. Add pine nuts and stir
until golden brown. Remove from
skillet and drain on paper towels.

Heat 2 tablespoons olive oil in
heavy large skillet over medium-high
heat. Add garlic and sauté just until
it begins to release fragrance. Blend
in spinach, cover and cook just until
wilted, about 1 to 2 minutes. Season with nutmeg, salt and pepper.

Stir sauce, pine nuts and grated
cheese into meat. Add salt and pepper. Let cool. (*Can be prepared ahead
to this point.*)

Preheat oven to 350°F. Lightly
grease rimmed large baking sheet.
Cover work surface with kitchen
towel. Place 2 phyllo sheets on towel
with long edge nearest you. Brush
generously with melted butter.
Repeat 4 more times, brushing each
double layer with butter. Spread
cooled meat mixture on phyllo,
leaving 1¾-inch border. Arrange
spinach in lengthwise strip along
center of meat. Using towel as aid,
roll phyllo up lengthwise. Transfer
seam side down to prepared baking
sheet. Bake until crisp and golden,
about 1 hour. Let roll stand for 10
to 15 minutes before slicing.

VEAL ROULADES WITH WILD RICE STUFFING AND MUSTARD SAUCE

6 servings

1⅔ cups water

6 tablespoons wild rice

3 tablespoons butter

3 tablespoons all purpose
flour

3 cups hard cider, or more

1½ tablespoons Dijon mustard

6 tablespoons (¾ stick)
unsalted butter

½ cup chopped onion

½ cup chopped seedless or
seeded green grapes
Salt and freshly ground
pepper

12 medium veal scallops (about
2 pounds total), pounded ¼
inch thick

2 tablespoons Calvados

½ cup chopped fresh parsley
Watercress sprigs (garnish)

Bring water to boil in heavy small
saucepan. Stir in rice. Reduce heat
to medium low, cover and simmer
until rice is tender but crunchy and
water is absorbed, about 30 minutes.

Melt butter in heavy medium
saucepan over medium-low heat.
Add flour and stir 3 minutes, then
gradually add 3 cups cider. Increase
heat to medium high and stir until
sauce boils and thickens enough to
coat back of spoon (if sauce is too
thick, add more cider). Remove from
heat. Whisk in mustard. Taste and
adjust seasoning.

Melt 2 tablespoons butter in
heavy medium skillet over medium-
high heat. Add onion and stir until
soft but not brown, about 5 minutes. Let cool. Mix in rice, grapes
and 1 tablespoon sauce. Season with
salt and pepper.

Preheat oven to 350°F. Grease
8 × 12-inch baking dish. Place
heaping tablespoon of stuffing in
center of each veal scallop. Spread
evenly, leaving small border. Roll veal
up and tie securely. Melt 4 table-

spoons butter in heavy large skillet
over medium-high heat. Add roulades and brown on all sides. Transfer roulades to baking dish. Discard
fat from skillet. Deglaze pan with
Calvados and pour over roulades.
Top with sauce. Bake until veal is
tender and juices run clear when
roulade is pierced with skewer, 20
to 25 minutes.

Place 2 roulades in center of
individual plate. Spoon some sauce
over each. Top with parsley. Garnish with watercress. Serve remaining sauce separately.

BRAISED VEAL SHANK WITH WINE AND HERBS

A succulent dish from Lombardy.

4 servings

2 tablespoons (¼ stick)
unsalted butter

2 tablespoons olive oil

1 2½- to 3-pound veal shank*

2 large fresh sage leaves *or* 2
small dried, crumbled

1 2-inch fresh rosemary sprig
or ¼ teaspoon dried,
crumbled

2 cups dry white wine, or
more

1 cup poultry stock, *or* meat
stock

Salt and freshly ground
pepper

Fresh rosemary sprigs *or*
Italian parsley sprigs
(optional garnish)

Heat butter and oil in 12 × 8 × 3-
inch enameled cast-iron or heavy
aluminum flameproof roasting pan
over medium-high heat. Add veal
and fresh sage and fresh rosemary
(if using). Reduce heat to medium
and cook slowly until veal is browned
on all sides (including ends), about
30 minutes. Stir in dried sage and
dried rosemary (if using). Add 1 cup
wine and simmer until reduced by
half, about 20 minutes, turning veal
occasionally.

Preheat oven to 300°F. Cover pan tightly with aluminum foil. Transfer to oven and braise veal 40 minutes. Add another ¼ cup wine and ¼ cup stock. Re-cover pan loosely and continue cooking until veal is caramel color, maintaining ¼-inch depth of wine in pan and basting often, about 1½ to 2 hours. (*Veal shank can be prepared up to 1 hour ahead to this point. Reheat in 350°F oven before continuing with recipe.*)

Transfer veal to serving platter. Tent platter with aluminum foil to keep veal warm. Discard fresh herbs. Remove as much fat from pan juices as possible. Place pan over high heat, add about ¼ cup wine with remaining ¾ cup stock and bring to boil, scraping up any browned bits. Let boil until sauce is reduced to about ⅔ cup. Season with salt and pepper to taste. Keep warm over low heat until ready to serve.

Either at table or in kitchen, slip meat from bone. Slice meat thinly across grain. Overlap slices on serving platter. Garnish with fresh rosemary or Italian parsley sprigs. Serve sauce separately.

* Veal shank, preferably cut from hind quarter, can be ordered from your butcher. If 1 large veal shank is unavailable, 2 smaller shanks can be substituted.

VEAL CHOPS WITH CAPERS AND CREAM

Chicken breasts can be substituted for veal.

6 servings

- 6 veal loin chops, about ¾ inch thick
- 2 tablespoons (¼ stick) butter
- 2 tablespoons olive oil
  Salt and freshly ground pepper
- 2 tablespoons minced shallot
- ½ cup beef stock
- ¼ cup dry vermouth
- 1 tablespoon fresh lemon juice, or to taste
- ½ cup whipping cream
- 2 tablespoons capers, rinsed and drained
- 2 tablespoons minced fresh parsley

Preheat oven to 200°F. Pat veal dry with paper towels. Melt butter with oil in heavy large skillet over medium heat. Add veal (in batches if necessary; do not crowd) and brown on one side, about 7 minutes. Turn chops over. Season with salt and pepper. Continue cooking until just springy to touch and pink in center, about 7 minutes. Transfer to heated platter. Cover and place in oven, leaving door ajar.

Pour off all but 2 tablespoons fat in skillet. Add shallot and stir 2 minutes. Add stock, vermouth and lemon juice and boil until reduced by half, scraping up any browned bits. Stir in cream and capers. Simmer until thickened to saucelike consistency. Adjust seasoning. Pour sauce over veal. Sprinkle with parsley and serve.

ROLLED VEAL SCALLOPS WITH PROSCIUTTO, SAGE AND FONTINA

Turkey breast scallops can be substituted for veal.

12 servings

- 1 cup (2 sticks) unsalted butter, room temperature
- ¼ cup minced fresh parsley
- 1 tablespoon fresh sage leaves, minced *or* 1 teaspoon dried, crumbled
- 1 large garlic clove, minced
  Grated peel of 1 lemon
- 12 veal scallops, pounded and halved (2½ pounds total)
- 12 paper-thin slices prosciutto (about 4 ounces), halved and cut to about same size as veal
- 12 paper-thin slices Italian Fontina cheese (about 6 ounces), halved and cut to about same size as veal

  Olive oil
  Fresh mint leaves (garnish)
  Lemon slices (garnish)
  Mustard Marsala Aïoli (see following recipe)

Blend butter, parsley, sage, garlic and lemon peel in small bowl. Spread herbed butter evenly over veal scallops. Top each scallop with prosciutto slice, then cheese. Starting at short ends, roll up each scallop. Tie closed with string and thread lengthwise onto 9- to 10-inch skewer. Refrigerate for at least 3 hours or overnight.

Preheat broiler or preheat oven to 400°F. Thread rolls evenly onto four 12-inch skewers. Balance ends of skewers on sides of broiler pan. Brush rolls with olive oil. Broil, basting frequently with drippings, until golden brown, 8 to 10 minutes. (Or, roast in oven 10 to 12 minutes.) Remove skewers (if desired) and strings. Arrange rolls on platter. Garnish with mint and lemon slices. Serve hot or at room temperature with aïoli.

Mustard Marsala Aïoli

Makes about 2 cups

- 2 medium garlic cloves
- ½ teaspoon salt
- 1 tablespoon Dijon mustard
- 2 egg yolks, room temperature
- ¾ cup vegetable oil
- ¾ cup olive oil
- 2 tablespoons fresh lemon juice
- 1 tablespoon dry Marsala

Combine garlic and salt in processor and mince well. Add mustard and yolks and mix until smooth. With machine running, add oils in slow steady stream (sauce should be thick and satiny). Blend in lemon juice and wine. Turn into jar with tight-fitting lid. Refrigerate sauce until ready to serve.

*From top: Chocolate and Chestnut-topped La Mystere,
Oysters on the Half Shell with Spicy Sausages,
Braised Lamb with Garlic and Herbs*

Clockwise from top:
Asparagus Salad with Soy-Lemon
Dressing, Spring Carrots with
Rice, Saute of Lamb with
Garlic and Basil, Frozen Moka
Mousse with Jamaican
Chocolate Sauce

Clockwise from top:
Endive, Bacon and Pecan Salad;
Hot Brownie Souffle; Steaks with
Zesty Tarragon Butter and Baked
Potato Chips; Smoked Trout
Mousse with Rye Heart Toast

Baked Ham surrounded by (clockwise from top):
Honey Shallot Sauce, Minted Spinach Sauce,
Spicy Red Wine Sauce with Glazed Apples,
Pumpernickel Mustard Sauce, Pear and Shallot Confit
with Grapes, Green Sauce, Apricot Scallion Sauce

Sardinian Pork Steaks

STUFFED VEAL MEDALLIONS WITH TALEGGIO SAUCE

Sautéed red peppers and zucchini are a lovely accompaniment for this.

6 servings

   1   **cup whipping cream**
   2   **tablespoons cornstarch**
   ¼   **pound Taleggio cheese, grated or sliced**
        Salt and freshly ground pepper

   6   **1-inch-thick veal medallions from tenderloin (about 18 ounces total)**
   3   **ounces prosciutto, finely chopped**
   2   **large garlic cloves, pureed**
   2   **tablespoons minced fresh Italian parsley**

        All purpose flour
        Salt and freshly ground pepper
   1   **egg**
   1   **tablespoon water**
   1   **tablespoon oil**
   ½   **cup fresh breadcrumbs**
   ½   **cup hazelnuts, skinned, finely chopped and toasted**

   6   **tablespoons (¾ stick) butter**
        Parsley sprigs (garnish)

Gradually blend cream into cornstarch in heavy small saucepan. Bring to boil over low heat, stirring constantly. Remove from heat. Add cheese and stir until smooth. Add salt and pepper. Set sauce aside at room temperature until ready to use.

Make horizontal slit in side of each veal medallion, cutting ⅔ way through to form pocket. Combine prosciutto, garlic and parsley. Fill each pocket with mixture and press to close.

Season flour with salt and pepper. Blend egg, water, oil and salt and pepper in small bowl. Mix breadcrumbs and hazelnuts. Flour each medallion, shaking off excess. Brush each evenly with egg mixture, then coat with crumbs.

Melt butter in heavy large skillet over medium-high heat. Add veal and brown quickly on each side. Sprinkle with salt and pepper. Top with sauce. Cover and cook until cheese is melted and meat is done, about 7 minutes. Transfer veal to platter. Garnish with parsley sprigs and serve.

VEAL WITH CUCUMBERS AND MORELS

(Les Noisettes de Veau aux Concombres et Morilles)

Serve with wild rice and braised celery or sautéed carrot and zucchini.

6 servings

Champagne Sauce with Morels

   1   **cup dried morels (1½ ounces)**
   2   **tablespoons (¼ stick) butter**
   1½ **tablespoons minced shallot (about 1 large)**
        Salt and freshly ground white pepper

   2¼ **cups dry white wine**
   1½ **cups unsalted chicken stock**
   ¾   **cup chopped mushrooms *or* mushroom trimmings**
   6   **medium shallots, minced**
   ¼   **cup plus 2 tablespoons dry Sherry**
        Large pinch of dried thyme, crumbled
   4½ **cups whipping cream**

   1   **English cucumber, peeled**
   2   **tablespoons (¼ stick) butter**
   1½ **cups unsalted chicken stock**

   2   **pounds boneless veal loin, cut into 12 even slices**
        All purpose flour
   3   **tablespoons vegetable oil**
   2   **tablespoons (¼ stick) butter**

For sauce: Combine morels in medium bowl with just enough lukewarm water to cover. Let stand until water is clear, changing water about 5 times, about 1 hour total. Drain well. Pat dry. Trim off tough ends of stems. Cut each morel into halves or quarters, depending on size. Melt 2 tablespoons butter in large skillet over low heat. Add morels and 1½ tablespoons minced shallot and cook until morels are lightly glazed, stirring occasionally, about 10 minutes. Season with salt and white pepper. Reserve 24 uniform pieces of morel for garnish. Set remainder aside.

Combine wine, 1½ cups stock, mushrooms, remaining shallots, Sherry and thyme in large saucepan. Place over medium heat and cook until reduced to about 3 tablespoons. Add cream and cook until thickened, stirring occasionally. Strain through fine sieve set over bowl. Return sauce to large saucepan. Add morels. Place over medium-high heat and bring to simmer. Reduce heat and simmer gently 10 to 15 minutes. Season to taste with salt and white pepper. Set sauce aside.

Cut cucumber crosswise into six 1½-inch-wide pieces. Cut each piece lengthwise into 4 slices. Melt 2 tablespoons butter in large skillet over medium-high heat. Add cucumber and sauté until just beginning to brown, about 4 minutes. Season with salt and white pepper. Add 1½ cups stock, reduce heat and poach gently until cucumber is lightly glazed. Set aside.

Season veal slices on both sides with salt and white pepper. Lightly dredge in flour, shaking off excess. Heat oil in heavy large skillet over medium heat. Add veal in batches (do not crowd) and cook until just beginning to color, about 1 minute. Add small amount of butter to skillet, adjusting heat to prevent butter from burning. When butter just begins to color light brown, turn veal with spatula. Continue cooking until veal is slightly firm when pressed with finger, about 3 minutes, watching carefully to prevent overcooking. Arrange veal on plates. Spoon sauce around veal. Garnish with reserved morels and poached cucumber slices. Serve immediately.

SPIT-ROASTED STUFFED VEAL WITH THYME BUTTER

The boneless veal roast is filled with sun-dried tomatoes, mushrooms, Herbes de Provence and garlic.

10 servings

Stuffing

1 ounce shiitake mushrooms *or* other dried black mushrooms (about 1 cup)
2 tablespoons (¼ stick) unsalted butter
2 tablespoons chopped shallot
1 small garlic clove, minced
¾ cup dried French breadcrumbs
½ cup (1 stick) unsalted butter, melted
½ cup sun-dried tomatoes packed in olive oil, drained and sliced (reserve oil)
2 teaspoons Herbes de Provence
Salt and freshly ground pepper

1 8-pound veal sirloin *or* rump roast, boned
1 tablespoon Dijon mustard
2 teaspoons Herbes de Provence
¼ teaspoon salt
Freshly ground pepper

Thyme Butter

1 cup (2 sticks) butter, room temperature
1 tablespoon fresh lemon juice
1 teaspoon minced fresh thyme *or* ¼ teapoon dried, crumbled
1 teaspoon chopped fresh parsley

Chopped fresh parsley (garnish)

For stuffing: Cover dried mushrooms with warm water in small bowl. Let stand until softened, about 30 minutes. Drain well and pat dry. Slice mushrooms into ½-inch-wide strips, discarding hard cores.

Melt 2 tablespoons butter in large skillet over medium heat. Add shallot, garlic and mushrooms and stir until shallot is limp, about 2 minutes. Transfer to large bowl. Add breadcrumbs, melted butter, toma-toes, 2 teaspoons herbs, salt and freshly ground pepper to taste.

Open boned veal on work surface. Season lightly with salt and pepper. Spoon stuffing evenly down center. Roll veal up around stuffing and tie firmly at 1½-inch intervals; *do not tie too tightly or stuffing will come out of ends.* Mix mustard, remaining Herbes de Provence, salt and pepper with reserved tomato oil in small bowl. Rub mixture over entire surface of veal. Skewer veal and arrange on rotisserie. (Veal can also be roasted in 350°F oven.) Roast until veal is slightly pink, juices run clear when pricked with fork and meat thermometer inserted in thickest part of meat registers 160°F, about 1½ hours.

For butter: Mix butter, lemon juice, thyme and 1 teaspoon parsley in small bowl. Roll into cylinder, refrigerate and cut into pats, or pack into individual ramekins. Serve butter at room temperature.

Let veal stand 20 minutes before carving. Arrange on serving platter. Top with parsley and serve with thyme butter.

Lamb

APRICOT-STUFFED LAMB CHOPS

2 servings

4 dried apricots, halved
2 tablespoons thinly slivered onion
2 double-thick (2 ribs each) loin lamb chops (about 8 ounces each), pocket cut horizontally through center to bone
¼ cup parsley sprigs

2 teaspoons olive oil
1 teaspoon Herbes de Provence
1 garlic clove
2 to 3 tablespoons fresh lemon juice
Grated peel of 1 lemon

Fresh mint sprigs and lemon wedges (optional garnish)

Insert 4 apricot halves and 1 table-spoon slivered onion into pocket of each lamb chop. Press firmly to close. Mix parsley sprigs, olive oil, herbs, garlic, lemon juice and peel in processor or blender to coarse paste. Rub evenly over both sides of each chop. Cover and set aside at room temperature 2 hours.

Grease broiler pan and set about 5 inches from heat source. Preheat broiler. Transfer lamb chops to heated pan. Broil until chops are crusty and brown outside but still pink inside, about 7 minutes on each side. Transfer to individual plates. Garnish with mint sprigs and lemon wedges and serve.

MUSTARD-GINGER LAMB CHOPS WITH VEGETABLE GARNISH

Serve with steamed snow peas, potatoes and grilled tomatoes.

4 servings

- 4 garlic cloves, crushed
- 1 2-inch piece fresh ginger, peeled and coarsely chopped
- 2 teaspoons dry vermouth
- 2 teaspoons fresh lime juice
- 2 teaspoons White Wine Thyme Vinegar (see following recipe)
- ¼ teaspoon crushed red peppercorns
- ¼ teaspoon crushed green peppercorns
  Pinch of salt
- 1 cup (scant) extra-strong Dijon mustard
- 1 teaspoon unrefined orange blossom honey

  Salt and freshly ground pepper
- 16 New Zealand lamb chops *or* 8 small American chops, trimmed of all fat and gristle
- 6 to 8 slices whole wheat bread, toasted, mixed in blender and served
- 8 tablespoons (1 stick) butter, melted and clarified (see recipe, page 62)
- ⅓ cup chopped fresh parsley
- ⅓ cup chopped shallot

Combine garlic, ginger, vermouth, lime juice, thyme vinegar, peppercorns and salt in small saucepan and cook over medium-high heat until reduced by half. Add mustard and honey and bring to boil, stirring constantly, until slightly reduced, about 5 to 8 minutes (mixture will be sticky). Strain through cheesecloth into jar with tight-fitting lid and seal tightly. Refrigerate until ready to use. (*Can be prepared up to 6 weeks ahead.*)

Lightly sprinkle salt and pepper over both sides of lamb chops. Spread 1½ to 2 teaspoons mustard mixture over all sides of each chop (if using American lamb, use 2 to 3 teaspoons per chop). Dip all sides into breadcrumbs, covering completely and patting gently so breadcrumbs adhere.

Heat 4 tablespoons butter in large skillet over medium-high heat until foam subsides. Add half of chops and brown on both sides (be careful not to burn; chops should be medium rare). Transfer to platter and keep warm. Repeat with remaining chops. Blend parsley and shallot, sprinkle lightly over top of each lamb chop and serve.

White Wine Thyme Vinegar

Makes 2 to 3 tablespoons

- ¼ cup white wine vinegar
- 1 teaspoon dried thyme

Combine vinegar and thyme in small saucepan and bring to simmer over medium heat. Let simmer 5 minutes. Strain through fine sieve.

LAMB SHANKS PROVENÇAL

4 servings

- 4 lamb shanks (about ¾ pound each)
- 4 medium garlic cloves, slivered
- ⅓ cup olive oil
- 2 medium onions, chopped
- 4 carrots
- 2 celery stalks, including leaves
- 2 cups canned, drained Italian plum tomatoes
- 1 cup dry red wine
- 1 cup beef bouillon
- 1 lemon, halved and seeded
  Bouquet garni (bay leaf, parsley sprig and rosemary sprig tied in a cheesecloth bag)
- 1 teaspoon salt
  Freshly ground pepper

Trim excess fat from lamb shanks and discard. Make small slits in shanks and insert garlic (1 clove per shank). Heat olive oil in large skillet over medium-low heat. Add onions. Cover and cook until translucent, stirring occasionally, about 10 minutes. Remove onions with slotted spoon and set aside. Increase heat to high. Add shanks to skillet and brown evenly on all sides, about 10 minutes. Return onions to skillet. Add remaining ingredients, except salt and pepper, in order listed and bring to boil. Reduce heat to low, cover and simmer until shanks are fork tender, about 1 to 1½ hours. Transfer shanks to heated ovenproof serving platter and keep warm while preparing sauce.

Preheat oven to 425°F. Place same skillet over high heat and boil until sauce is slightly thickened and reduced to 3 cups. Discard lemon halves and bouquet garni. Transfer sauce to processor or blender and puree. Add salt and pepper to taste. Ladle some of sauce over shanks. Transfer remaining sauce to sauceboat and keep warm. Bake lamb shanks until glaze forms over top, about 15 to 20 minutes. Serve immediately with remaining sauce.

LAMB WITH WILD MUSHROOM SAUCE

To cut a lamb loin into medallions, buy a double lamb loin (about 3¼ pounds) from back of lamb. Have the butcher split this in two, crack the chine bone and saw halfway into remaining flat bone 1 to 2 inches apart along bone. You can then have the butcher continue the procedure or do it at home yourself as follows: Remove the tenderloins from the loins by slicing with wide, even strokes. Remove the chine bone and flat bone attached to the loin and break them up; reserve for sauce. Trim meat of excess fat and the fell. Cut loins into 1-inch-wide medallions. Cut the tenderloins into 2-inch-wide medallions, then butterfly by cutting ⅔ through; open to form round pieces.

6 servings

- 8 dried morels
- 8 dried cèpes
- 2 cups warm water

1 tablespoon vegetable oil
11 ounces lamb bones and trimmings (see above)
¼ pound lamb stew meat
5¼ cups veal stock, heated

2 tablespoons (¼ stick) unsalted butter
1 tablespoon chopped shallot

6 tablespoons (¾ stick) unsalted butter
1 double lamb loin (about 3¼ pounds), cut into medallions (see above)
Salt and freshly ground pepper

Fresh lemon juice
2 tablespoons whipping cream
1 teaspoon unsalted butter

Soak morels and cèpes separately in warm water 30 minutes. Strain morel liquid through several layers of moistened cheesecloth and reserve. Discard cèpe liquid. Rinse morels and cèpes separately in strainer under cold running water until all grit is removed; discard any twigs. Slice morels thinly; discard stems. Set mushrooms aside.

Heat oil in heavy large skillet over medium-high heat. Brown lamb bones and trimmings and stewing meat on all sides, turning occasionally. Remove bones, trimmings and stew meat; pour off fat. Add 1 cup hot stock to skillet, stirring to scrape up any browned bits. Add 4 cups hot stock and continue cooking, whisking occasionally.

Melt 2 tablespoons butter in heavy small skillet over medium-high heat. Add morels, cèpes and shallot and toss 2 minutes. Add to reducing stock with reserved morel liquid. Reduce heat to medium and continue cooking until sauce is reduced to 1 cup.

Melt 3 tablespoons butter in each of 2 heavy medium skillets over medium-high heat. Brown lamb medallions on both sides. Reduce heat slightly and cook to desired doneness, about 5 minutes total for medium-rare. Season with salt and pepper. Deglaze skillets with re-maining ¼ cup stock and add liquid to sauce.

Taste sauce and adjust seasoning with salt, pepper and lemon juice (be careful not to mask smoky flavor). Whisk in cream. Remove from heat and stir in remaining 1 teaspoon butter. Arrange lamb on plates. Top with some sauce. Serve remaining sauce separately.

BRAISED LAMB WITH GARLIC AND HERBS

Serve this dish with rice or orzo.

6 servings

¼ cup olive oil
3 to 4 pounds boneless lamb shoulder, cut into 1½-inch cubes
Salt and freshly ground pepper
14 medium garlic cloves, unpeeled
3 medium shallots, finely chopped
4 medium fennel bulbs, tough outer layer discarded, strings peeled off, cored and coarsely chopped
1 cup dry vermouth *or* dry white wine
1 cup beef stock

2 tablespoons fresh lemon juice
6 juniper berries, crushed *or* 2 tablespoons gin
½ teaspoon dried thyme, crumbled

1 tablespoon minced fresh parsley *or* fresh mint sprig
1 lemon, thinly sliced (garnish)

Heat oil in Dutch oven over medium-high heat. Pat lamb dry. Add to pan in batches (do not crowd) and brown on all sides. Remove lamb and season lightly with salt and pepper. Reduce heat to medium. Add garlic, shallots and half of fennel to pan and stir frequently until just beginning to soften, about 5 minutes. Pour in vermouth and stock. Increase heat to high and stir, scraping up any browned bits. Return lamb to Dutch oven with lemon juice, juniper berries and thyme and bring to boil. Reduce heat, cover and simmer gently until lamb is tender, about 1 to 1½ hours, adding remaining fennel 15 minutes before end of cooking time. Skim fat from surface.

Remove lamb and fennel from pan with slotted spoon. Remove garlic cloves and place in strainer. Press with back of spoon, returning pulp to pan. Bring liquid to boil. Cook until reduced to saucelike consistency. Adjust seasoning. Return lamb and fennel to pan and heat through. Turn into serving dish. Garnish with parsley or mint and lemon slices and serve.

SLICED LAMB WITH HOT SPICE
(Shaptak)

This recipe can be doubled.

2 servings

2 tablespoons corn oil *or* peanut oil
¼ cup finely chopped onion
2 tablespoons minced garlic
2 tablespoons minced fresh ginger
½ teaspoon five-spice powder
¼ teaspoon salt
¾ pound lamb from leg or chop, sliced into thin 2-inch strips
1½ 5-inch fresh green chilies, seeded and sliced into ½-inch pieces
2 tablespoons hot water
2 tablespoons light soy sauce
1 teaspoon sugar

Heat oil in wok or heavy medium skillet over high heat. Add onion, garlic, ginger, five-spice powder and salt and stir 3 minutes. Add lamb and stir 1 minute. Blend in chilies, hot water, soy sauce and sugar and stir about 1 minute or until lamb reaches desired doneness and serve.

SOUR CREAM AND HERB BARBECUED LAMB

6 servings

1 6-pound leg of lamb, boned and butterflied (fell trimmed)
1 cup sour cream
3 garlic cloves, minced
2 tablespoons chopped fresh parsley
1 teaspoon dried rosemary, crumbled
1 teaspoon dried oregano, crumbled
1 teaspoon salt
½ teaspoon coarsely ground pepper

Place lamb on baking sheet. Combine all remaining ingredients and blend well. Spread over all surfaces of lamb. Cover loosely with waxed paper. Refrigerate at least 4 hours or up to 2 days. (Bring to room temperature before continuing.)

Prepare barbecue or preheat broiler. Barbecue or broil lamb until instant-reading thermometer inserted in thickest part of meat registers 130°F to 140°F for rare or 160°F for medium (thinner parts of meat will cook more quickly). Let rest at room temperature 10 minutes. Cut into thin slices across grain of meat. Arrange lamb on platter and serve immediately.

SPINACH-STUFFED LEG OF LAMB

(Arni Psitó Ghemisto)

Leg of lamb is the traditional main course for celebrations and Sunday dinners in Greek homes. For an extra timesaving step, the leg of lamb can be stuffed, rolled and tied the evening before the dinner, covered lightly with waxed paper and refrigerated. This version also includes oven-roasted potatoes, baked with the lamb and basted with the accumulated drippings.

10 servings

Spinach Stuffing

2 pounds fresh spinach (about 2 large bunches), stemmed, rinsed and lightly shaken
1 tablespoon salt

⅓ cup olive oil
1 cup thinly sliced green onion
¼ cup chopped fresh parsley
¼ cup dry breadcrumbs
1 egg, beaten to blend
¼ teaspoon dried dillweed
¼ teaspoon dried oregano, crumbled
⅛ teaspoon freshly ground pepper

Lamb

1 7-pound leg of lamb, trimmed, boned and patted dry
¼ cup olive oil
3 tablespoons fresh lemon juice
2 large garlic cloves, minced
2 teaspoons dried oregano, crumbled
2 teaspoons salt
½ teaspoon freshly ground pepper
¼ pound feta cheese, cut into ¾-inch cubes (about 1 cup)

2 cups hot water, or more
4 to 5 large potatoes, peeled and quartered lengthwise

For stuffing: Slice spinach very thinly. Squeeze dry. Transfer to colander and sprinkle with 1 tablespoon salt. Let stand 1 hour. Squeeze again to remove all remaining moisture.

Heat oil in large skillet over medium-high heat. Add onion and sauté until soft, about 10 minutes. Add spinach and parsley and sauté about 2 more minutes. Remove from heat and cool 5 minutes. Stir in breadcrumbs, egg, dillweed, oregano and pepper.

For lamb: Preheat oven to 400°F. Place lamb skin side down on work surface. Flatten slightly. Combine ¼ cup oil, lemon juice, garlic, oregano, salt and pepper in small bowl and beat well with fork. Rub half of oil mixture over top of lamb. Spread spinach mixture over. Arrange feta cubes over spinach. Starting at shank end, fold ⅓ of meat over, then fold leg portion over top (as for business letter). Tie with string, starting at thicker end and using slipknots, to form roll enclosing stuffing. Close cavities at ends with threaded larding needle. Rub outside thoroughly with remaining oil mixture.

Transfer meat to large roasting pan. Add 1 cup hot water. Roast 30 minutes. Reduce oven temperature to 350°F and continue roasting, basting frequently, until meat thermometer inserted into thickest part of meat registers desired doneness (about 2 hours for medium) and adding more hot water to pan as necessary to prevent drippings from burning. Approximately one hour before meat is done, arrange potatoes around lamb and baste with pan drippings.

Transfer lamb to serving platter and let stand several minutes before carving. Arrange potatoes around roast. Discard any fat from pan. Add 1 cup hot water to drippings, scraping up any browned bits. Place pan over medium-high heat and warm through. Strain drippings and ladle sauce over meat.

GARLIC AND CUMIN SCENTED BROILED LEG OF LAMB

(Bhonao Raan)

Perfect for barbecuing too.

6 to 8 servings

1 5- to 6-pound leg of lamb, boned and butterflied
¼ cup plain yogurt
¼ cup minced onion
2 tablespoons fresh lemon juice
1 tablespoon minced garlic
1 tablespoon grated fresh ginger
1 tablespoon cumin seed, crushed
2 teaspoons black peppercorns, cracked
Coarse salt

Indian Clarified Butter (see following recipes) *or* vegetable oil (for basting)

Pineapple Chutney (see following recipes)
Creamy Mint Dressing (see following recipes)

Trim all fat from lamb. Pound meat to even thickness (scoring thickest part of meat first facilitates pounding). Prick meat well with fork. Transfer to shallow roasting pan large enough for meat to lie flat. Mix yogurt, onion, lemon juice, garlic, ginger, cumin and peppercorns with salt to taste in medium bowl. Rub marinade over both sides of meat. Cover and set aside at room temperature 4 hours or refrigerate overnight (let stand at room temperature 2 hours before cooking).

Preheat broiler. Brush rack set in broiler pan with clarified butter or oil. Arrange meat on rack. Broil 2 inches from heat source to desired doneness, about 8 minutes on each side for medium-rare, 10 minutes for medium and 12 minutes for well done, brushing frequently with clarified butter or oil. Let rest on carving board 5 minutes. Cut meat across grain into thin slices and serve. Serve Creamy Mint Dressing and Pineapple Chutney separately.

Indian Clarified Butter (Usli Ghee)

Makes about 1/3 cup

½ cup (1 stick) unsalted butter

Melt butter in small saucepan over low heat. Increase heat to medium and simmer until foam subsides, about 10 minutes, then stir constantly until solids turn brown. Remove from heat and let brown residue settle to bottom. Let cool. Pour off clear liquid to use for basting. (*Indian Clarified Butter can be stored in covered jar in refrigerator up to four months.*)

Pineapple Chutney

Makes about 2 cups

1½ cups sugar
 1 medium pineapple, peeled, cored and minced or pureed
   Juice of 1 medium lemon (about 2½ to 3 tablespoons)
 1 tablespoon coarse salt

1½ teaspoons cumin seed
1½ teaspoons fennel seed
 1 teaspoon black peppercorns (optional)
 ¾ teaspoon ground red pepper
 ¾ teaspoon freshly ground pepper

Cook sugar, pineapple puree, lemon juice and salt in nonaluminum medium saucepan over medium-high heat until thickened to jamlike consistency, about 30 minutes, stirring occasionally. Cool mixture to room temperature.

Coarsely grind cumin and fennel seed in spice grinder or mortar. Mix into cooled pineapple mixture with remaining ingredients. Cover chutney and let stand for 1 week before serving.

Creamy Mint Dressing (Podina ka Raita)

Almost any type or combination of chilies can be used, such as jalapeño, yellow or hot green Indian peppers.

Makes about 1¾ cups

 1 cup thinly sliced Spanish onion
 1 cup plain yogurt
 ½ cup sour cream
 ¼ cup minced fresh mint leaves
 2 large mild fresh green chilies, seeded and minced
   Salt

Bring 3 to 4 cups water to boil in small saucepan. Add onion, remove from heat and let stand 15 seconds. Drain and rinse in cold water. Drain again. Transfer onion to serving bowl. Add remaining ingredients and mix well. Let stand 15 minutes before serving.

SAUTE OF LAMB WITH GARLIC BASIL SAUCE

Fresh basil is essential to this dish. When it is in season, look for young plants in nurseries or garden shops. To keep last-minute effort to a minimum, bone lamb and prepare sauce one day in advance.

4 servings

 2 racks of lamb (4 pounds total)
 1 chicken leg with thigh attached *or* 4 chicken wings, skinned
 2 tablespoons clarified butter (see recipe, this page) *or* vegetable oil, or more
 1 large onion, chopped
 1 small celery stalk with leaves, chopped
 ½ cup full-bodied dry white wine
 3 cups rich homemade beef stock *or* veal stock
 1 tablespoon chopped fresh basil *or* 1 teaspoon dried, crumbled
 1 teaspoon tomato paste
 ¼ teaspoon dried savory, crumbled
 1 large garlic clove, crushed
 4 whole black peppercorns
 2 whole cloves
 1 bay leaf

 ½ cup whipping cream
16 medium garlic cloves
 1 to 3 tablespoons water

 2 to 3 tablespoons butter

 1 cup full-bodied dry white wine
 8 to 10 large basil leaves, minced
   Salt and freshly ground pepper
   Spring Carrots with Yellow Rice (see recipe, page 137)
   Fresh basil sprigs (garnish)

To bone racks, trim off all fat. Depending on how racks are butchered, there may be piece of shoulder blade at 1 end of rack; trim meat from above blade and reserve for sauce. Remove blade and set aside. Run knife along ribs, easing meat away from bones. Using knife, release meat at base of rack. Trim rib eyes, reserving meat scraps. Divide each rib eye into 8 even rounds (noisettes). Wrap noisettes loosely in paper towels and refrigerate until ready to use. Discard any remaining fat on bones. Reserve bones and any meat scraps for preparing sauce.

Using heavy cleaver, chop bones from 1 rack into large chunks (reserve bones of second rack for use in stocks or sauces). Chop chicken to about same size as bones. Heat butter in heavy large skillet over medium-high heat. Add bones and chicken and brown until crusty and dark, about 12 minutes, turning often and adjusting heat so any bits on bottom of pan do not burn. Transfer bones and chicken to 2½- to 3-quart heavy saucepan. Add meat scraps to skillet and brown well, about 10 minutes, adding more butter to skillet if necessary. Add to bones. Add onion and celery to skillet, reduce heat to medium and cook until browned. Pour in ½ cup wine and stir, scraping up any browned bits, until reduced to glaze. Add to bone mixture. Blend in stock, basil, tomato paste, savory, 1 garlic clove, peppercorns, cloves and bay leaf. Increase heat to medium high and bring to simmer. Cover sauce partially and cook until reduced by about half, about 3 hours.

Meanwhile, combine cream, 16 garlic cloves and water with ¼ cup simmering sauce in small saucepan over medium-low heat. Cover and simmer until garlic can easily be mashed with back of spoon, about 40 minutes, stirring occasionally.

Uncover garlic mixture and cook until thick, stirring frequently, about 8 minutes. Press mixture through fine sieve (you should have about ½ cup thick puree). Cool; refrigerate until ready to use. (*Can be prepared 1 day ahead.*)

Strain sauce through fine sieve, pressing on bones and vegetables with spoon to extract all liquid; degrease. Return to saucepan and continue simmering until reduced to ¾ cup. (*Sauce can be prepared up to 1 day ahead.*)

Melt butter in heavy large skillet over medium-high heat; do not burn. Arrange half of lamb pieces in skillet, spacing evenly (do not crowd) and cook to desired degree of doneness, about 1 minute on each side for rare. Transfer to platter. Tent with foil to keep warm. Repeat with remaining lamb.

Pour off all fat from skillet. Add remaining wine and boil, scraping up any browned bits, until liquid just covers bottom of pan; *do not reduce to glaze.* Stir in sauce and garlic puree and simmer 1 minute to blend. Add minced basil and simmer 1 minute. Season with salt and pepper. Mound Spring Carrots with Yellow Rice in center of individual heated dinner plates. Arrange four pieces of lamb around each mound. Nap lamb with sauce. Garnish with basil and serve.

RACK OF LAMB WITH THYME
(Le Carré d'Agneau Rôti à la Fleur de Thym)

Serve with souffléed potatoes, lightly sautéed cherry tomato halves, carrots, zucchini and asparagus tips.

4 servings

   2 **racks of lamb (about 2 pounds each), trimmed (blade bones and trimmings reserved)***
   ½ **cup water**

   8 **medium plum tomatoes, diced (about 12 ounces)**
   2 **medium carrots, diced**
   2 **medium celery stalks, diced**
   1 **medium onion, diced**
   5 **large garlic cloves, halved (about 4 teaspoons)**
   2 **bay leaves**
   1 **tablespoon chopped fresh thyme *or* 1 teaspoon dried, crumbled**
   1 **teaspoon dried rosemary, crumbled**
   6 **black peppercorns**
      Salt
   1 **teaspoon chopped fresh thyme *or* ⅓ teaspoon dried, crumbled**

   2 **to 3 tablespoons vegetable oil**
   ½ **teaspoon dried thyme, crumbled**
      Salt and freshly ground pepper
      Watercress sprigs (garnish)

Preheat oven to 400°F. Combine reserved bones and trimmings in roasting pan. Roast until well browned, about 45 minutes, stirring occasionally. Transfer bones and trimmings to stockpot. Degrease pan. Place over medium-high heat and stir in water, scraping up any browned bits. Pour deglazed juices into stockpot.

Combine tomatoes, carrots, celery, onion, garlic, bay leaves, 1 tablespoon fresh or 1 teaspoon dried thyme and rosemary in large skillet over medium-high heat and cook until juices have evaporated, about 8 minutes. Add vegetable mixture to stockpot. Add peppercorns with enough water to cover. Place over medium heat and bring to simmer. Reduce heat to low, cover partially and simmer gently 3 to 4 hours, skimming frequently. Strain stock into bowl; let cool. Discard fat from surface. Pour stock into saucepan and cook over high heat until reduced to ½ cup. Season with salt. Stir in 1 teaspoon fresh or ⅓ teaspoon dried thyme. Set sauce aside; keep warm.

Preheat oven to 450°F. Coat large roasting pan with 2 to 3 tablespoons vegetable oil. Rub lamb with dried thyme, salt and pepper. Wrap exposed bones tightly in aluminum foil. Arrange lamb meat side down in prepared pan. Transfer to oven and immediately reduce temperature to 400°F. Roast 2 to 3 minutes. Turn lamb over and continue roasting until tender, 25 to 27 minutes for medium rare. Discard foil. Let lamb stand 5 to 8 minutes. Slice racks into individual chops. Transfer chops to plates. Garnish plates with watercress sprigs and serve. Accompany with sauce.

*If racks are purchased already trimmed, ask butcher for an additional 2 pounds of lamb bones and trimmings for sauce.

Pork

HOMEMADE RED WINE SAUSAGES

If you do not have a meat grinder with a sausage stuffing horn, use a pastry bag fitted with a ½-inch or larger tip or a funnel to fill the sausage casing.

16 to 18 servings

  2 pounds pork from Boston butt, boned, trimmed of gristle and connective tissue and cubed
 18 ounces bacon *or* salt pork, blanched in boiling water 5 minutes, drained and cubed
 12 ounces beef chuck, trimmed of gristle and connective tissue and cubed
  1 cup coarsely chopped onion
  2 tablespoons minced fresh Italian parsley
  4 teaspoons salt
2½ teaspoons coarsely chopped garlic
  2 teaspoons freshly ground pepper
  2 teaspoons Hungarian sweet paprika
  ½ teaspoon sugar
  ⅛ teaspoon *each* ground cloves and allspice
  ⅛ teaspoon freshly grated nutmeg
  1 cup full-bodied dry red wine

    Sausage casing (about 3½ yards)*

  1 750-ml bottle dry white wine
  2 cups meat stock *or* chicken stock (preferably homemade)

    Parsley sprigs (garnish)

Combine pork, bacon and beef chuck and freeze for 30 minutes.

Puree onion, parsley, salt, garlic, pepper, paprika, sugar and spices in processor. Mix in ¼ of meat mixture using on/off turns until medium

coarse. Turn into large bowl. Repeat with remaining meat mixture in 3 batches. Combine mixture with hands. Gradually blend in 1 cup red wine. Cover loosely and refrigerate overnight. (*Can be prepared up to 2 days ahead.*)

Wash salt off casing by slipping one end over faucet and running warm water through. (If there are holes in casing, tie closed or cut off.) Soak in tepid water 1 hour. Cut into 2-foot lengths.

Fit meat grinder with coarsest plate. Place stuffing horn on grinder. Wring out casing and place one end over attachment. Gradually push all of casing onto horn, leaving 2-inch overhang. Tie knot in overhanging end. With right hand, feed meat mixture into grinder. Meanwhile, anchor casing on top of horn with left thumb, allowing casing to unroll as mixture is extruded. Stop occasionally to mold meat. Pierce any air bubbles with needle. Do not pack too full or sausage will burst as it cooks. Remove sausage; knot casing.

Form into links by knotting 3-inch pieces of string around sausage at 5- to 6-inch intervals or twist 1 measured link clockwise and next one counterclockwise. Repeat with remaining casing. Hang sausages at room temperature or refrigerate overnight to dry.

Bring white wine and stock to simmer in heavy large skillet. Add sausages, cover and poach until juices run clear when sausages are pricked, about 20 minutes. To retain plumpness, cool sausages in cold water. (*Can be prepared 1 day ahead and refrigerated.*)

Prepare barbecue or preheat broiler. Grill sausages over hot coals or in broiler pan several inches from heat until brown. Arrange on platter, garnish with parsley and serve.

*Available in specialty markets and butcher supply stores. Natural casing is packed in salt and can be stored in refrigerator 1 year.

SAUSAGES WRAPPED IN BUCKWHEAT CREPES
(Galettes aux Saucisses)

Serve these sausages with hard cider.

Makes 18 to 20

Sausages

1½ pounds pork butt, trimmed and cut into 1-inch cubes
  8 ounces fresh unsalted pork fatback, cut into 1-inch cubes
  4 ounces slab bacon (rind removed), cut into 1-inch cubes
  2 chicken livers, cut into 1-inch pieces
  3 large shallots, minced
  2 medium garlic cloves, crushed
  2 tablespoons applejack
  1 tablespoon freshly ground pepper
1½ teaspoons ground coriander seed
  ½ teaspoon ground fennel seed
  ¼ teaspoon dried thyme, crumbled

    Salt
 10 feet sausage casing*

Buckwheat Crepes

  2 tablespoons dried currants
  2 tablespoons applejack

  1 cup buckwheat flour**
1½ tablespoons all purpose flour
  2 eggs
  1 tablespoon firmly packed brown sugar
  ¼ teaspoon salt
  ¼ teaspoon Quatre-Epices (see recipe, page 5)
1⅔ cups milk
  5 tablespoons corn oil

Vegetable oil

1 **cup water**
Apple slices (optional garnish)

For sausages: Place first 4 ingredients in glass bowl. Mix in shallots, garlic, applejack, pepper, coriander, fennel and thyme. Marinate in refrigerator 24 hours, stirring occasionally.

Wash salt off casing by slipping one end over faucet and running warm water through. (If there are holes in casing, tie closed or cut off.) Soak in tepid water 1 hour.

Grind meat mixture with coarse blade of meat grinder. Mix in salt. To check seasoning, fry small piece of mixture until cooked through. Taste, then adjust seasoning of uncooked portion if necessary. Fit meat grinder or heavy-duty mixer with sausage horn. Squeeze all water from sausage casing. Tie knot at 1 end. Pull casing over horn until knot touches tip. Grind sausage mixture directly into casing. (Casing can also be stuffed using pastry bag or funnel with ¾- to 1-inch opening.) Tie end of casing. Twist and tie sausage at 3½- to 4-inch intervals; cut apart.

For crepes: Soak dried currants in applejack at least 1 hour, stirring occasionally.

Mix buckwheat flour, all purpose flour, eggs, brown sugar, salt and Quatre-Epices in large bowl. Gradually add milk, stirring until smooth. Blend in oil. Let batter rest 30 minutes.

Mince currants and add to batter with soaking liquid. Heat 7-inch crepe pan or heavy skillet over medium-high heat. Grease with paper towels soaked in oil. Remove from heat. Working quickly, add about 3 tablespoons batter to pan, tilting until bottom is covered with thin layer of batter. Pour any excess batter back into bowl. Cook crepe until bottom is lightly browned, loosening edges with knife. Turn crepe over and cook second side. Slide onto plate. Repeat with remaining batter, oiling pan as necessary. (*Crepes can be prepared 1 day ahead, wrapped in foil and refrigerated. Reheat in 350°F oven for about 15 minutes.*)

Pour 1 cup water into large skillet. Prick sausages and add to skillet. Bring to simmer and cook,

turning occasionally, until sausages have rendered fat and browned on both sides, about 25 minutes. Drain on paper towels. Wrap each sausage in 1 crepe. Garnish with apple slices if desired and serve.

*Available in specialty markets and butcher supply stores. Natural casing is packed in salt and can be stored in refrigerator 1 year.

**Available at natural foods stores.

ROASTED SPARERIBS WITH HOISIN-HONEY GLAZE

Serve with a good Mexican beer.

6 to 8 servings

1 **12-ounce bottle beer**
¾ **cup hoisin sauce**
¾ **cup honey**
¾ **cup soy sauce**
¾ **cup minced green onions**
3 **tablespoons minced fresh ginger *or* 1 tablespoon ground**
9 **pounds lean spareribs**

Combine all ingredients except ribs in medium saucepan over low heat and cook 5 minutes to blend flavors. (*Glaze can be prepared ahead to this point, cooled, covered and refrigerated. Reheat before proceeding with recipe.*)

About 2 hours before serving time, position racks in upper and lower thirds of oven and preheat to 350°F. Brush ribs with glaze. Arrange on racks set in 2 large roasting pans. Roast until well browned, 1½ to 1¾ hours, turning ribs every 30 minutes and basting with glaze. Transfer to work surface and cut between ribs. Arrange on heated platter and serve immediately.

ALSATIAN SMOKED BACON (Tranches de Lard Fumé)

In France, bacon is cooked slowly until lightly browned on the outside and still soft inside. Bacon can be crisped American style if desired.

6 servings

1 **1½-pound slab bacon, rind discarded**

2 **tablespoons (¼ stick) butter**
⅓ **cup Alsatian Riesling *or* other dry Riesling**
Freshly ground pepper
Salt (if necessary)

Cut bacon into ⅙-inch slices. Place in large saucepan of cold water and bring to boil over high heat. Reduce heat and simmer 3 minutes. Drain well; pat dry.

Melt butter in heavy large skillet over low heat. Add bacon and cook until still soft but golden on both sides, degreasing skillet frequently and watching carefully so bacon does not crisp. Transfer bacon to heated platter. Add wine to skillet and stir, scraping up any browned bits. Season generously with freshly ground pepper. Taste and season with salt if necessary. Pour over bacon and serve immediately.

PORK CHOPS NORMANDY

4 servings

1 **small tart apple, cored and cut into paper-thin slices**
4 **double-thick (about 1½ inches) lean loin pork chops (about 8 ounces each), pocket cut horizontally through center to bone**
4 **teaspoons fresh lemon juice**
2 **tablespoons plus 2 teaspoons tarragon mustard**
2 **tablespoons fresh lemon juice**
4 **teaspoons minced fresh parsley**
2 **teaspoons vegetable oil**
2 **small garlic cloves, minced**
1½ **teaspoons dried thyme, crumbled**

Apple-Onion Puree (see following recipe)
Fresh tarragon and thyme sprigs (optional garnish)

Divide apple slices into 4 equal portions. Lightly pound chops to flatten slightly and increase size. Stuff pockets of chops with apple slices. Pat chops dry and rub each with ½ teaspoon lemon juice. Arrange in single layer in baking dish. Mix remaining ingredients except garnish and Apple-Onion Puree to coarse paste. Rub over both sides of chops. Set aside 1 to 2 hours.

Grease broiler pan and position about 4 inches from heat source. Preheat pan and broiler. Transfer chops to heated pan. Cook until inside is juicy, outside is charred and crusty and thermometer inserted in thickest part of chop (without touching stuffing or bone) registers 170°F; turn occasionally and brush during last several minutes with any mixture remaining in dish. Transfer chops to individual plates. Divide puree evenly among plates. Garnish with tarragon and thyme and serve.

Apple-Onion Puree

Can be prepared up to 1 day ahead and reheated.

4 servings

   4 teaspoons unsalted butter
   2 Golden Delicious apples, cored and coarsely diced
   2 medium onions, coarsely diced
   4 teaspoons firmly packed light brown sugar
      Pinch of salt
   2 tablespoons Sherry vinegar

Heat butter in heavy or nonstick large skillet over medium-high heat. Add apples and onions and cook until glossy and heated through, 3 to 4 minutes. Sprinkle with sugar and salt. Reduce heat to very low, cover and cook until mixture is almost tender, about 30 minutes, stirring frequently. Stir in vinegar. Continue cooking, uncovered, until mixture is very soft and beginning to color. Transfer to processor and mix using on/off turns just until coarsely pureed; *do not overprocess.* Serve immediately.

SARDINIAN PORK STEAKS

Although Italian sweet peppers are preferable for this dish, bell peppers can be substituted. Round out the meal with salad and a chilled bottle of Corvo.

6 servings

   2 ounces salt pork, diced
   2 tablespoons full-bodied olive oil
   3 pounds pork steaks cut from shoulder, loin or leg
      Salt and freshly ground pepper
   2 large sweet red peppers, cut into thin strips (about 2 × ¼ inches)
   1 large sweet yellow pepper *or* ½ green bell pepper, cut into thin strips
   1 large onion, cut into thin strips (about 2 × ¼ inches)
   1 small green bell pepper, cut into thin strips
   1 large garlic clove, minced
   1 to 2 small dried hot red peppers, rinsed, partially seeded and cut into thin strips, *or* 1 long mildly hot red pepper, cut into thin strips
   ½ cup Veal Stock, preferably homemade (see following recipe) *or* chicken stock (see recipe, page 38), or more
   1 large tomato, peeled, seeded and chopped
   ½ cup oil-cured black olives, pitted and coarsely chopped
   2 tablespoons capers, rinsed and drained

Blanch salt pork in boiling water 5 minutes; drain, rinse and pat dry.

Combine olive oil with blanched salt pork in heavy large skillet and cook over medium heat until pork begins to color.

Sprinkle steaks lightly on both sides with salt and pepper. Push salt pork to one side of skillet and increase heat to medium high. Add steaks in batches so sides do not touch and brown on all sides. Remove steaks and set aside.

Increase heat to high. Add red and yellow peppers, onion and green pepper and toss constantly until vegetables begin to color. Sprinkle lightly with salt and pepper. Add garlic and hot pepper and stir-fry briefly. Stir in stock and tomato. Return pork steaks to skillet and baste generously with sauce. Reduce heat, cover and simmer 45 minutes,

adding more stock if necessary (mixture should be moist with small amount of liquid). (*At this point dish can be refrigerated 1 to 2 days.*)

Twenty minutes before serving, add olives and capers and reheat, stirring several times. Adjust seasoning. Make bed of pepper and onion mixture on heated platter and arrange pork steaks over top. Moisten with sauce and sprinkle with any olives and capers left in skillet.

Veal Stock

Stock can be prepared ahead. Store in refrigerator several days or freeze.

Makes about 3 quarts

  10 to 15 pounds veal bones
   4 to 5 medium carrots, diced
   3 to 5 medium onions, diced
   3 to 4 medium celery stalks, diced
   2 to 3 leeks (green part only), diced (optional)
   1 garlic head, cloves separated and halved (about ⅓ cup)
   2 cups water
   7 cups tomato puree
   4 to 5 bay leaves
   2 teaspoons dried thyme, crumbled
   8 to 10 black peppercorns

Preheat oven to 400°F. Place veal bones in large roasting pan. Roast until medium brown, about 1 hour, turning once. Transfer bones to 8-quart stockpot. Degrease roasting pan. Add vegetables and garlic; roast until lightly browned, 10 to 12 minutes. Add mixture to stockpot. Place roasting pan over medium-high heat and stir in 2 cups water, scraping up any browned bits. Add pan juices to stockpot. Add remaining ingredients with enough water to cover. Place over medium heat and bring just to simmer. Skim surface. Reduce heat to very low, cover partially and simmer gently at least 12 hours (preferably 24), skimming occasionally and adding water as necessary. Strain stock through colander, pressing on vegetables to extract all liquid; discard bones and vegetables. Strain stock through fine sieve. Let cool. Degrease surface.

COLD BRAISED CITRUS PORK

A citrus marinade and gentle oven braising leave the pork moist and succulent. You may find it helpful to order the meat ahead if pork tenderloin is hard to find in your area.

6 servings

1 cup Sherry
1 cup fresh orange juice
½ cup fresh lemon juice
½ cup olive oil
2 teaspoons grated lemon peel
2 teaspoons dried marjoram, crumbled
1 teaspoon cumin seed
1 teaspoon ground ginger
2 bay leaves
2 boneless pork tenderloins (3 to 3½ pounds total)

Salt and freshly ground pepper
2 tablespoons (¼ stick) butter

1 to 2 tablespoons red currant jelly
1 to 2 teaspoons Dijon mustard

Combine first 9 ingredients in large dish or plastic bag. Add pork and marinate 2 to 3 hours in refrigerator, turning pork over frequently.

Preheat oven to 325°F. Pat pork dry with paper towels (reserve marinade). Sprinkle with salt and pepper. Melt butter in Dutch oven or heavy roasting pan over medium heat. Add pork and brown on all sides, about 20 minutes. Add reserved marinade. Cover and bake, basting often, until thermometer inserted in thickest part of meat registers 165°F to 170°F, about 1¼ hours. Remove pork from cooking liquid and cool to room temperature. Wrap tightly in foil and refrigerate up to 2 days. Strain cooking liquid. Transfer to small saucepan and refrigerate.

Just before serving, discard fat from surface of cooking liquid. Bring to simmer over medium heat. Stir in currant jelly and mustard. Remove from heat. Slice chilled pork and arrange on platter. Pour warm sauce over and serve.

PORK STEAKS WITH CARDAMOM AND FRESH GRAPES

A robust country dish that is best mellowed overnight before serving.

8 servings

3 tablespoons vegetable oil, or more
8 well-marbled pork steaks *or* cutlets from sirloin or leg, cut to thickness of about 1 inch (3½ pounds total)

4 medium onions, thinly sliced
2 large garlic cloves, minced
Seeds of 16 cardamom pods, ground (1½ teaspoons ground)
¼ teaspoon whole coriander seed, ground
¼ cup brandy
1 tablespoon cider vinegar *or* wine vinegar
1 cup dry red wine
1 cup rich meat stock *or* poultry stock, preferably homemade

Salt and freshly ground pepper
½ cup red grapes, halved and seeded
1 tablespoon minced chives *or* green onion (garnish)

Heat 3 tablespoons oil in heavy nonaluminum large skillet over medium-high heat. Brown pork steaks in batches (do not crowd), adding oil as necessary. Remove pork from skillet.

Pour off all but about 2 tablespoons fat from skillet. Reduce heat to low, add onions, cover and cook until softened, about 10 minutes, stirring occasionally. Increase heat to medium and stir until browned, 5 to 7 minutes. Stir in garlic, cardamom and coriander and cook 2 minutes; do not brown. Pour in brandy and vinegar and boil, scraping up any browned bits, until reduced to glaze. Add wine and boil 4 minutes. Blend in stock and bring to simmer. Add pork and spoon liquid over. Cover and simmer gently

until pork is tender, approximately 45 minutes.*

Skim fat from surface. (*Can be prepared 1 day ahead to this point, cooled and refrigerated. Reheat pork gently in simmering liquid before continuing.*) Transfer pork to serving platter. Simmer liquid until thickened to saucelike consistency. Season with salt and pepper. Stir in grapes and heat through. Pour sauce over pork. Top with chives and serve.

If preparing ahead, slighty undercook pork at this point.

BASIC BAKED HAM

The serving size recommended, about ½ pound of bone-in ham per person, is quite generous and will probably yield "dividend" dishes.

16 to 28 servings

1 8- to 14-pound half or whole partially or fully cooked ham (bone in)
1 to 2 quarts dry white wine
1 bay leaf
½ teaspoon freshly ground pepper

Place ham in very large stockpot. Pour wine over, then add enough water to cover. Add bay leaf and pepper. Bring to boil over high heat, skimming any foam that rises to surface. Reduce heat and simmer 30 to 45 minutes.

Preheat oven to 350°F. Transfer ham to work surface; reserve about 2 cups cooking liquid (remaining liquid can be used for preparing soup). Using sharp knife, trim off fat, leaving ¼- to ⅛-inch layer all around. Set ham on rack in heavy large roasting pan. Slash large decorative crisscross pattern in fat atop ham to allow fat to melt while baking. Spoon reserved liquid over ham. Bake, basting occasionally, until thermometer inserted in thickest part of meat (without touching bone) registers 140°F for fully cooked ham or 160°F for partially cooked ham, about 11 minutes per pound.

Cool ham 10 minutes. To carve, start at rounded end (not bone end) and cut ham straight down bone into slices. Then cut horizontally along top of bone to release slices. Transfer to platter and serve.

5 ❖ Entrées: Poultry

Chicken

CHICKEN SAUTE WITH RED WINE

4 servings

    8 ounces thickly sliced bacon,
      cut crosswise into ¼-inch
      strips
   24 uniform-size pearl onions,
      peeled
    2 tablespoons (¼ stick) butter
    8 ounces mushrooms,
      quartered
      Salt and freshly ground
      pepper

    1 3- to 3½-pound chicken,
      cut into 9 pieces

    3 tablespoons butter

    4 teaspoons all purpose flour

    2 garlic cloves, minced
    2 cups dry red wine
   1⅓ cups chicken stock,
      preferably homemade (see
      recipe, page 38)

      Large pinch of sugar
      (optional)

Cook bacon in heavy large skillet over medium low heat until fat begins to render. Increase heat to medium high, add onions and sauté until bacon is brown. Transfer bacon to paper towels using slotted spoon. Continue to sauté onions, turning carefully, until browned on all sides, about 5 more minutes. Transfer onions to paper towels. Discard all but 1 tablespoon fat from skillet. Add 1 tablespoon butter and melt over medium heat. Add mushrooms and

salt and pepper and brown lightly. Transfer to paper towels using slotted spoon.

Pat chicken dry. Sprinkle lightly on all sides with salt and pepper. Melt 1 tablespoon butter in same skillet over medium-high heat. Add chicken pieces (in batches if necessary; do not crowd) and brown thoroughly on all sides, transferring chicken pieces to plate as they are browned. Return legs, thighs and onions to skillet. Scatter mushrooms over top. Arrange breast and wing pieces over mushrooms. Pour juices remaining on plate over chicken. Reduce heat to low, cover and cook gently until juices run clear when chicken is pricked with fork.

Meanwhile, mash remaining butter in cup. Add flour and mix to form paste.

Transfer breast pieces to platter using slotted spoon. Cover and keep warm. Continue cooking remaining chicken and vegetables until tender, about 10 minutes. Using slotted spoon, transfer mushrooms and onions to medium bowl. Add drained bacon.

Skim off as much fat as possible from juices in skillet. Reheat juices until very hot, scraping up any browned bits. Add garlic to skillet and stir over low heat 30 seconds. Pour in wine and bring to boil. Let boil 3 minutes. Add stock and boil, stirring and skimming fat frequently, until sauce is reduced to about 1½ cups. Pour sauce into heavy medium saucepan and bring to simmer. Gradually add butter mixture to simmering sauce, whisking constantly, then bring to boil, whisking.

Return vegetable-bacon mixture to sauce. Reduce heat to low and cook 2 minutes to blend flavors. Adjust seasoning; if flavor is too tart, add pinch of sugar. Spoon sauce and vegetable-bacon mixture over chicken and serve.

CHICKEN SAUTE WITH MUSHROOMS, SHALLOTS AND HERBS

4 servings

    1 3- to 3½-pound chicken,
      cut into 9 pieces
      Salt and freshly ground
      pepper
    1 tablespoon vegetable oil
    1 tablespoon butter
    4 ounces mushrooms, sliced

    4 teaspoons finely minced
      shallot

    ½ cup dry white wine
    ⅔ cup Tomato-flavored Brown
      Sauce (see following recipe)
    4 teaspoons Cognac
    2 teaspoons chopped fresh
      tarragon *or* ½ teaspoon
      dried
    2 teaspoons chopped fresh
      parsley

Pat chicken dry. Sprinkle lightly on all sides with salt and pepper. Heat oil and butter in heavy large skillet over medium-high heat. Add chicken pieces (in batches if necessary; do not crowd) and brown thoroughly on all sides. Transfer to plate using slotted spoon. Add mushrooms to skillet and brown.

Reduce heat to low. Return all chicken to skillet with juices remaining on plate. Cover and simmer until breast pieces are tender and juices run clear when breast is pricked with fork, about 15 minutes.

Transfer breast pieces to platter using slotted spoon. Cover and keep warm. Add shallot to skillet. Continue cooking remaining chicken until tender, about 10 minutes. Transfer to same platter, leaving vegetables in skillet.

Skim off as much fat as possible from mixture in skillet. Reheat until very hot. Pour in wine and bring to boil. Let boil, stirring and skimming frequently, until reduced by about half. Reduce heat to medium, add brown sauce and 2 teaspoons Cognac and continue simmering, stirring frequently, until sauce is thick enough to coat spoon. Stir in tarragon and remaining Cognac. Adjust seasoning. Spoon mushrooms and sauce over chicken. Top with parsley and serve.

Tomato-flavored Brown Sauce

Sauce can be prepared ahead and in larger quantities to be used in recipes that call for brown sauce. Store in refrigerator several days or freeze.

Makes ⅔ cup

- 2 teaspoons vegetable oil
  Wing tips and neck of 1 chicken, chopped into several pieces
- ½ onion, diced
- ½ carrot, diced
- 1 cup chicken stock, preferably homemade (see recipe, page 38)
- 2 fresh tomatoes *or* canned plum tomatoes, coarsely chopped
  Pinch of dried thyme, crumbled
- ½ small bay leaf

- 2 tablespoons cold water
- 1 teaspoon tomato paste
- 1 teaspoon potato starch, arrowroot *or* cornstarch

Heat oil in heavy medium saucepan over medium-high heat. Add wing tips, neck, onion and carrot and sauté just until well browned. Stir in stock, tomatoes, thyme and bay leaf. Bring to boil, stirring constantly. Reduce heat to very low and simmer, uncovered, for about 45 minutes.

Strain stock into another medium saucepan, pressing on vegetables to extract all liquid. Skim as much fat as possible from surface. Simmer over medium heat until reduced to ⅔ cup. Blend cold water into tomato paste in small bowl. Add potato starch and whisk to form smooth paste. Gradually whisk mixture into simmering sauce. Return to boil, whisking constantly until thickened. Remove from heat.

CHICKEN COACHELLA

4 to 6 servings

- ½ cup dried currants
- 1 cup water
- ¼ cup Cognac

- ¼ cup (½ stick) unsalted butter
- 2 tablespoons olive oil
- 2 pounds skinned, boned chicken breasts, cut lengthwise into ½-inch-wide strips
- 3 tablespoons minced shallot
- 1½ cups whipping cream
- 2¼ teaspoons minced fresh thyme *or* ¾ teaspoon dried, crumbled
- 2¼ teaspoons minced fresh marjoram *or* ¾ teaspoon dried, crumbled
  Salt and freshly ground pepper
- 2 medium-size pink grapefruit, peeled and segmented

Bring currants and water to boil in small saucepan over medium-high heat. Reduce heat and simmer 3 minutes. Drain and rinse under cold water. Add currants to Cognac.

Heat butter and oil in heavy large skillet over medium-high heat. Add chicken and sauté only until

opaque, 3 to 5 minutes. Remove from skillet using slotted spoon. Add shallot to skillet and sauté until softened. Remove currants from Cognac using slotted spoon. Increase heat to medium-high. Stir Cognac into skillet, scraping up any browned bits. Add cream and boil until reduced by about half. Blend in currants, thyme and marjoram with salt and pepper to taste. Stir in chicken and grapefruit and heat until warmed through. Serve immediately.

CHICKEN IN SILKY ALMOND SAUCE (Murghi dil Bahasht)

8 servings

- 2 3- to 3½-pound chickens, each cut into 8 pieces, skinned (wing tips discarded)
- 2 tablespoons vegetable oil

- ½ cup vegetable oil
- 5 cups thinly sliced onions (about 5 medium)
- 6 tablespoons blanched slivered or ground almonds
- 3 tablespoons ground coriander
- 2 tablespoons chopped fresh ginger
- 2 teaspoons ground cardamom
- 2 teaspoons ground red pepper
- 1 teaspoon ground cumin
- ½ teaspoon ground fennel seed

- 2 cups plain yogurt
- 1 cup water
  Coarse salt
  Cilantro (coriander) leaves (garnish)

Pat chicken dry. Heat 2 tablespoons oil in heavy-bottomed large skillet or Dutch oven over medium-high heat. Add chicken in batches and cook on all sides just until no longer pink (do not brown). Remove from skillet using slotted spoon.

Heat remaining oil in skillet. Add sliced onions and fry until wilted and pale brown, stirring constantly to color evenly, about 12 minutes. Stir in almonds, coriander, ginger, cardamom, ground red pepper, cumin and fennel and cook 3 to 5 more minutes. Remove mixture from heat.

Transfer half of mixture to processor or blender. Puree with 1 cup yogurt and ½ cup water. Repeat with remaining onion mixture, yogurt and water. Pour almond sauce back into skillet and add chicken. Place over medium-high heat and bring to boil. Reduce heat, cover and simmer until chicken is tender and sauce is thickened, about 45 minutes (oil will begin to separate from sauce and thin glaze will form over chicken). Remove from heat. Season with salt. Let stand at room temperature at least 30 minutes (preferably 1 hour, or refrigerate overnight). Rewarm over very low heat. Transfer to serving dish. Garnish with cilantro and serve immediately.

CHEVRE AND MUSHROOM STUFFED CHICKEN LEGS

6 servings

- 5 ounces fresh goat cheese, such as Bûcheron or Montrachet
- 4 thin slices salami, minced
- 2 tablespoons minced green onion *or* fresh chives
- 1 teaspoon minced fresh parsley
- 6 large chicken legs with thighs attached
- 6 dried morel mushrooms
- 1 heaping tablespoon dried cèpes *or* porcini mushrooms
- 3 tablespoons unsalted butter
- 1 tablespoon vegetable oil
- ½ cup minced shallot
- 1 garlic clove, minced
- 2 tablespoons Sherry vinegar
- 4 cups rich homemade unsalted chicken stock (see recipe, page 38), reduced to 2 cups

- ¼ teaspoon fresh thyme leaves *or* pinch of dried, crumbled Salt and freshly ground pepper
- 1 teaspoon fresh tarragon *or* ¼ teaspoon dried, crumbled
- 2 tablespoons tomato puree Onion-steamed Broccoli with Lemon Dill Butter (see recipe, page 128)

Blend cheese, salami, onion and parsley in small bowl. (*Can be prepared up to 3 days ahead to this point and refrigerated.*)

To bone chicken, place 1 chicken leg, skin side down, on work surface. Make slit along side of thighbone, continuing slit down center of drumstick. Holding hip end of thigh in one hand, gradually release thigh by scraping meat off bone on all sides. Remove thigh by cutting through socket where it articulates with drumstick, being careful to avoid piercing skin. Cut around head of drumstick to free it, then bone out completely, according to instructions for thigh. Cut out cartilage, again not piercing skin. Remove each tendon by holding onto end and scraping off meat as you pull it out. Arrange boned leg with meat side up. Repeat with remaining chicken legs.

Divide stuffing among chicken legs. Fold over sides to enclose completely. Sew edges together using thick cotton thread and long needle.

Rinse all dried mushrooms under cold water. Transfer to small bowl. Cover with hot water and let soften 40 minutes. Rinse morels inside and out to remove sand and slice thinly. Remove cèpes, squeeze dry (reserve soaking liquid) and chop. Strain liquid through sieve lined with dampened paper towel; set liquid aside.

Heat 1 tablespoon butter with oil in nonaluminum heavy large skillet over medium-high heat. Add half of chicken and brown on all sides, turning with wooden spatula to avoid piercing skin. Drain on paper towels. Repeat with remaining chicken.

Pour off all fat from skillet. Melt remaining 2 tablespoons butter in

same skillet over medium heat. Add shallot and stir until soft, 2 to 3 minutes. Stir in garlic and mushrooms and cook until aromatic, about 1 minute. Add vinegar and reduce to glaze, scraping up any browned bits. Pour in reserved soaking liquid and reduce by about half. Add stock, thyme and salt and pepper. Arrange chicken legs in skillet seam side up. Bring liquid to gentle simmer. Cover and cook until ends of thighs are firm and juices run clear when chicken is pricked with fork, about 25 minutes.

Transfer chicken to platter. Degrease sauce. Add tarragon and bring to boil. Cook until thickened and reduced by about ⅔. Meanwhile, remove thread from chicken. Stir tomato puree into sauce. Adjust seasoning. Pour sauce over chicken. Surround with broccoli and serve immediately.

CHICKEN LEGS WITH WILD MUSHROOM STUFFING

8 servings

- 16 to 24 chicken drumsticks (2 to 3 per serving)

Stuffing

- 1 cup warm water
- ½ ounce dried wild mushrooms (cèpes, morels or porcini)
- 2 tablespoons (¼ stick) butter
- 3 ⅛-inch-thick slices prosciutto (about 4 ounces), diced
- 3 medium garlic cloves, minced (about 1½ teaspoons)
- 2 shallots, chopped (about ¼ cup)
- 1 pound fresh mushrooms, thinly sliced (about 7 cups) Grated peel of ½ lemon
- ½ cup chopped fresh parsley

  Salt and freshly ground pepper
  All purpose flour (about ½ cup)

¼ **cup (½ stick) butter**
½ **cup Cognac**
2 **to 3 cups warmed chicken stock, preferably homemade (see recipe, page 38)**

2 **tablespoons (¼ stick) butter**
¼ **cup chopped fresh parsley**
1 **medium garlic clove, minced**

To bone each drumstick, cut meat and sever tendons around bone at large end of leg using small sharp knife. Loosen meat around bone with fingers, then scrape all meat down bone using knife. Pull pocket of skin and meat off bone, cutting skin at joint if necessary to separate. Turn pocket inside out. Set aside until ready to fill.

For stuffing: Combine water with wild mushrooms in small bowl. Set aside until softened, about 30 minutes. Drain well, reserving liquid. Remove and discard any woody stems; chop mushrooms. Strain liquid through several layers of moistened cheesecloth.

Melt 2 tablespoons butter in heavy large skillet over low heat. Add prosciutto, 3 minced garlic cloves, shallots and sliced mushrooms. Cook until shallots are softened and mushrooms begin to render liquid, about 6 minutes, stirring occasionally. Add chopped wild mushrooms and lemon peel. Stir in reserved mushroom liquid. Increase heat to medium high and cook until almost all liquid is evaporated. Mix in ½ cup chopped parsley.

Fill each drumstick with as much stuffing as possible (about 1 tablespoon). Set remaining stuffing aside. Sew end of drumstick closed with 3 to 6 stitches of thread or unwaxed dental floss. Season chicken with salt and pepper. Dredge in flour, shaking off excess.

Melt ¼ cup butter in heavy large skillet over medium-high heat. Add chicken in 4 batches and sauté until well browned on all sides, about 8 minutes. Remove chicken from skillet. Pour off any burned butter. Return skillet to medium-high heat. Add Cognac and stir, scraping up any browned bits. Boil until reduced by half. Remove from heat. Return chicken to skillet in single layer and add enough warm stock to come halfway up chicken. Place over medium-high heat and bring to boil. Cover surface of chicken with foil. Cover skillet tightly. Reduce heat to low and simmer until juices run clear when chicken is pricked with fork, about 20 to 25 minutes, turning chicken once.

Transfer chicken to heated platter and cover to keep warm. Increase heat to high and cook until sauce thickens and coats back of spoon. Taste and season with salt and pepper if desired. Whisk in 2 tablespoons butter. Blend in parsley, garlic and remaining stuffing. Remove thread from chicken and discard. Pour sauce evenly over chicken and serve immediately.

VINEYARD CHICKEN

Serve with sautéed mushrooms and crisp pan-roasted potatoes.

4 servings

2 **tablespoons all purpose flour**
¼ **teaspoon dried basil, crumbled**
¼ **teaspoon dried tarragon, crumbled**
¼ **teaspoon paprika**
 Salt and freshly ground white pepper
4 **chicken breast halves, boned and skinned**
1 **tablespoon safflower oil**
1 **tablespoon butter**
2 **small garlic cloves, minced**
½ **cup dry white wine**
1 **cup red grapes, halved and seeded**
½ **cup chicken stock, preferably homemade (see recipe, page 38)**
1 **teaspoon fresh lemon juice**
1 **tablespoon finely chopped fresh parsley (garnish)**

Mix flour, basil, tarragon, paprika and salt and pepper in large bowl. Add chicken and toss gently to coat. Heat oil with butter in heavy large skillet over medium-high heat. Stir in garlic. Add chicken and sauté on both sides until golden brown. Pour in wine. Cover and cook just until chicken is done, about 3 minutes. Add grapes, broth and lemon juice and continue cooking until heated through. Transfer chicken and grapes to heated serving platter using slotted spoon. Continue cooking sauce until reduced by half. Pour sauce over chicken. Top with parsley and serve.

SOUTHERN FRIED CHICKEN

2 servings

2 **small chicken legs**
2 **small chicken thighs**
1 **small whole chicken breast, split**
1 **cup buttermilk**

½ **cup all purpose flour**
1 **teaspoon salt**
½ **teaspoon ground sage**
¼ **teaspoon paprika**
¼ **teaspoon freshly ground pepper**
2 **eggs, lightly beaten with 1 tablespoon water**
1 **cup fine dry breadcrumbs**

 Oil (for deep frying)

Rinse chicken pieces and pat dry. Arrange in shallow dish. Pour buttermilk over chicken, coating evenly. Marinate at room temperature 30 minutes, turning occasionally.

Combine flour, salt, sage, paprika and pepper in paper bag. Add chicken to bag in batches and shake to cover with flour mixture. Dip chicken into egg mixture, then roll in breadcrumbs. Let stand on rack 15 minutes.

Pour oil into 10-inch skillet or electric frypan to depth of 1 inch and heat to 375°F. Add chicken legs and thighs and fry, turning frequently with tongs, until browned, about 12 minutes. Fry breasts about 8 minutes. As chicken pieces are cooked, transfer to paper towels and drain well. Serve chicken hot or at room temperature.

❖

DOUBLE-FRIED CHICKEN WITH GINGER AND SESAME OIL
(Kara-age)

6 servings

- 1   2½- to 3-pound frying chicken
- ¼   cup Japanese soy sauce
- ¼   cup saké *or* dry Sherry
- 1   1-inch piece fresh ginger, minced
- 1   garlic clove, minced

- ½   cup all purpose flour
- ½   cup cornstarch
  Salt
  Kona sansho* (Japanese fragrant pepper) *or* freshly ground pepper

  Oil (for deep frying)
  Sesame oil
  Lemon wedges (garnish)

Cut chicken into 12 pieces, quartering breast and halving thighs crosswise. Combine soy sauce, saké, ginger and garlic in shallow baking dish. Add chicken, turning to coat all sides. Let chicken marinate at room temperature 30 minutes, turning frequently.

Combine flour, cornstarch, salt and kona sansho or pepper in shallow bowl. Dredge chicken in flour mixture, shaking off excess. Transfer chicken to waxed paper. Let stand until chicken is not completely white, 10 minutes.

Heat oil in wok or deep fryer to 360°F, adding a few drops of sesame oil. Add chicken to oil in batches and fry just until lightly colored, about 45 seconds to 1 minute. Drain well on paper towels. Reduce oil temperature to 325°F. Return chicken to oil in batches and fry until coating is brown and chicken is cooked through, about 6 to 10 minutes. Drain on paper towels. Serve at room temperature with wedges of lemon.

*Available in oriental markets.

BAKED HONEY CHICKEN
(Jasha)

4 servings

- 1   3-pound chicken, cut up
- 3   tablespoons finely chopped onion
- 2   tablespoons honey
- 2   tablespoons dark soy sauce
- 1   tablespoon minced fresh ginger
- 1   teaspoon minced garlic

- ¼   cup thinly sliced green onion (green part only)

Arrange chicken in 9 × 13-inch baking dish. Combine onion, honey, soy sauce, ginger and garlic in small bowl and spoon over chicken. Marinate for 1 hour, turning pieces once.

Preheat oven to 425°F. Bake chicken 30 minutes. Turn pieces over and sprinkle with green onion. Continue baking until chicken is tender and juices run clear when chicken is pricked with fork, 10 to 15 minutes. Serve immediately.

INDONESIAN SPICED CHICKEN

Perfect for parties or picnics.

10 buffet servings

- 2   cups minced onion
- ½   cup dark soy sauce
- ¼   cup fresh lemon juice
- 3   medium garlic cloves, minced
- 5   teaspoons grated fresh ginger
- 1   tablespoon ground cumin
- 1   tablespoon ground coriander
- 1   tablespoon sugar
- 1   teaspoon salt
  Freshly ground pepper
- 2   3-pound chickens, each cut into 10 serving pieces

Preheat oven to 400°F. Combine onion, soy sauce, lemon juice, garlic, ginger, cumin, coriander, sugar, salt and pepper in large bowl. Rub each piece of chicken thoroughly with mixture. Arrange chicken, skin side up, on baking sheet. Bake until

chicken is golden brown and juices run clear when pierced with fork, about 45 minutes, basting once with onion mixture (turning chicken is unnecessary). Serve chicken at room temperature.

BUTTERFLIED DEVILED CHICKEN

6 servings

- ½   cup prepared hot mustard (preferably English, German or Chinese)
- 1   large shallot
- 3   tablespoons cider vinegar
- 2   teaspoons honey
  Generous pinch of freshly ground pepper
- 2   3-pound frying chickens, butterflied*

- ¼   cup (½ stick) melted butter
  Parsley sprigs (garnish)

Combine mustard, shallot, vinegar, honey and pepper in processor or blender and mix until smooth. Reserve ¼ cup of mixture for basting and refrigerate. Transfer remaining mixture to small bowl. Loosen skin from flesh of chicken breast, thighs and drumsticks with fingers (being careful not to puncture skin). Using fingers, spread mustard mixture between meat and skin. Pull any extra skin over breast and fasten with small skewer. Refrigerate until ready to roast.

Preheat oven to 375°F. Arrange chicken skin side up on rack in shallow roasting pan. Brush with melted butter and reserved mustard mixture. Roast about 20 minutes. Turn chicken over; repeat basting. Roast another 20 to 25 minutes. Turn chicken again and continue roasting, basting as necessary, until tender, about 15 to 20 minutes. To serve, cut chicken into quarters and arrange on heated platter. Garnish with fresh parsley sprigs.

*To butterfly chicken, cut down middle of backbone, then loosen meat by scraping down each side of backbone with boning knife, keeping knife against bone. Turn chicken over, skin side up, and flatten by pounding with palm of hand. Turn again and slip out breast bones with sharp small knife, being careful to keep skin intact.

ENGLISH ROAST CHICKEN WITH HERBED ORANGE STUFFING

6 servings

Herbed Orange Stuffing

1½ pounds ground veal
2 tablespoons (¼ stick) unsalted butter
1 large onion, minced
2 carrots, finely diced
4 cups fresh white breadcrumbs
¾ cup whipping cream, or slightly more
½ cup minced fresh herbs (such as tarragon, parsley and thyme)
½ cup dried currants soaked in ⅓ cup fresh orange juice 30 minutes
½ cup chopped walnuts
1 teaspoon dried marjoram, crumbled
1 teaspoon salt
　Freshly ground pepper
　Freshly grated nutmeg

1 5- to 6-pound roasting chicken
¾ cup (1½ sticks) unsalted butter, room temperature
1 tablespoon minced fresh parsley
1 tablespoon honey
　Grated peel of 1 lemon
　Grated peel of 1 orange

　Fresh watercress sprigs (garnish)

For stuffing: Sauté veal in nonstick large skillet over medium-high heat until just beginning to lose pink color, about 3 minutes. Transfer to large bowl. Melt 2 tablespoons butter in same skillet over medium-high heat. Add onion and carrots and sauté until softened and just beginning to color. Blend into veal. Add breadcrumbs, ¾ cup cream, minced herbs, undrained currants, walnuts, marjoram, salt, pepper and nutmeg and toss gently. Mixture should just hold together; add small amount of cream if necessary.

Preheat oven to 375°F. Season main cavity of chicken with salt. Stuff main and neck cavities loosely. Truss chicken, then secure wings and legs with string. Cream together butter, parsley, honey, lemon peel and orange peel. Rub most of flavored butter over entire surface of chicken. Set chicken on rack in roasting pan. Tent with greased parchment paper. Roast 1 hour.

Baste chicken with pan juices and brush with remaining flavored butter. Continue roasting, basting frequently, until skin is rich golden brown, leg moves easily and juices run clear when chicken is pricked with fork, about 1 hour.

Let stand 15 minutes on heated platter. Garnish platter with watercress. Nap chicken with pan juices and serve.

HARISSA-ROASTED CHICKEN

The chickens are butterflied and partially boned before cooking.

16 to 18 servings

½ cup fresh orange juice
¼ cup cider vinegar
2 tablespoons grated orange peel
2 tablespoons vegetable oil
1 tablespoon Harissa (see following recipes)
2 teaspoons sugar

3 3-pound chickens

¾ cup whole blanched almonds, toasted
3 small red onions, sliced into thin rings
　Piquant Orange-Mustard Sauce (see following recipes)

Combine orange juice, cider vinegar, orange peel, oil, Harissa and sugar in small bowl. Let mixture stand at room temperature for at least 2 hours.

To prepare chickens: Remove wings at second joint. Cut along both sides of backbone with sharp knife or poultry shears and remove. Open chicken, skin side up. Press hard on breast area with heel of hand to snap breast bone. Turn chicken over and remove breast and rib bones with small sharp knife; do not cut skin. Carefully cut through joints between legs and thighs. Cut away pelvic bones and run knife along thigh bones, scraping away meat. Twist off thigh bones to free from leg joints. Pat chicken into butterfly form and spread on large platter. Spoon about ⅓ of Harissa mixture over meat side. Turn and loosen skin over breast at neck with fingertips. Gradually loosen skin over breast and thighs, being careful not to tear skin. Spoon some of Harissa mixture under thigh and breast skin. Pour remaining mixture over chickens. Cover with plastic wrap and refrigerate 3 to 4 hours.

Preheat oven to 450°F. Pour about 1 cup water into large broiler pan. Position flat rack over pan and arrange chickens, skin side up, on rack. Roast 10 minutes. Turn chickens over and roast 10 minutes. Baste and turn. Reduce oven temperature to 350°F and continue roasting, basting occasionally, until juices run clear when flesh is pricked and thermometer inserted in thickest portion of leg without touching bone registers 160°F, about 25 minutes. If skin is not crisp, broil chickens several minutes. Cool chickens to room temperature in pan.

To serve, divide each chicken into 4 pieces by separating legs and thighs and halving breasts. Slice each thigh crosswise into 5 to 6 pieces. Cut each breast half into 8 pieces. Arrange pieces to resemble oversized butterflied bird and garnish with legs. Scatter almonds over and surround with red onion rings. Serve sauce separately.

Harissa

If covered with thin film of oil, this will keep in refrigerator two months.

Makes about ⅔ cup

8 to 10 large dried red chilies (mild or hot)
　Hot water
1 large garlic clove

¾ teaspoon caraway seed
¾ teaspoon cumin seed
¾ teaspoon coriander seed
　Pinch of cinnamon
2 teaspoons (about) olive oil

Soak chilies in hot water about 1 hour to soften. Drain, seed, devein and mince. Transfer to mortar. Add remaining ingredients except oil and mash to paste with pestle. Stir in enough olive oil to loosen slightly. Pack into small jar. Cover with thin film of olive oil. Refrigerate. Stir before using.

Piquant Orange-Mustard Sauce

For best results, all ingredients should be at room temperature. This sauce can be prepared up to 3 days ahead.

16 to 18 servings

5 tablespoons coarse French mustard
3 egg yolks
3 tablespoons fresh lemon juice
2 tablespoons minced sweet onion
1 tablespoon grated orange peel

1½ cups vegetable oil
2 tablespoons orange juice
1 tablespoon Harissa, or to taste (see previous recipe)
　Salt and freshly ground pepper

Blend mustard, yolks, lemon juice, onion and orange peel in processor or blender using on/off turns until creamy and smooth. With machine running, pour in oil, then orange juice, in slow, steady stream; sauce should be thick. Turn into bowl. Blend in Harissa. Season with salt and pepper. Refrigerate. Let stand at room temperature for 1 hour before serving.

Turkey

TURKEY MOLE

2 servings

2 tablespoons oil
2 small turkey thighs (about 12 ounces *each*)
　Chicken stock (preferably homemade) *or* salted water
1 to 2 dried ancho chilies,* rinsed, stemmed, seeded and coarsely torn

1 medium tomato, peeled, seeded and chopped
6 blanched almonds
½ corn tortilla, chopped
2 tablespoons minced onion
1 teaspoon toasted sesame seed
¼ to ½ teaspoon dried red pepper flakes, or to taste
⅛ teaspoon aniseed
　Pinch *each* of cinnamon and ground cloves

¼ ounce unsweetened chocolate
　Salt and freshly ground pepper

1 tablespoon toasted sesame seed

Garnishes

1 medium tomato, peeled, seeded and chopped
½ cup sliced radish
¼ cup minced fresh cilantro (coriander) *or* parsley
¼ cup chopped green chilies
1 lime, cut into wedges

Heat oil in medium skillet over medium-high heat. Add turkey and brown on all sides, 4 to 5 minutes each side. Transfer to saucepan just large enough to accommodate (do not clean skillet). Add enough stock or salted water to saucepan to cover turkey. Bring to boil over high heat. Reduce heat to low, cover and simmer gently 1 hour. Meanwhile, combine ancho chilies in bowl with enough hot water to cover. Soak until well softened, 1 hour.

Drain turkey well, reserving cooking liquid. Transfer turkey to baking dish. Drain chilies, discarding soaking liquid; pat dry. Transfer chilies to blender. Add tomato, almonds, tortilla, onion, 1 teaspoon toasted sesame seed and spices and mix to coarse puree.

Heat skillet in which turkey was cooked over medium-high heat. Add chili puree, immediately reduce heat and simmer 5 minutes, stirring constantly. Blend in 1 cup reserved turkey and cooking liquid with chocolate and stir until chocolate is melted. Season sauce with salt and pepper. Pour evenly over turkey. (*Can be prepared ahead to this point, covered and refrigerated.*)

Preheat oven to 325°F. Cover dish and bake until turkey is tender when pierced with fork and sauce is consistency of whipping cream, about 1 hour (if sauce is too thick, thin with small amount of reserved turkey cooking liquid). Sprinkle turkey with 1 tablespoon toasted sesame seed.

To serve, place garnishes in individual small bowls. Arrange around turkey and select as desired at table.

*Also called chili pods.

ROAST TURKEY WITH CORNMEAL

Cornmeal and butter spread under the turkey skin crisps the skin. Busy cooks note: The bird is done in just three hours because it is not stuffed.

12 servings

- 2 cups (4 sticks) unsalted butter *or* 1 pound pork lard, room temperature
- 1⅓ cups whole-grain yellow cornmeal*
- 1 18- to 20-pound turkey
- 2 large onions, coarsely chopped
- 4 medium garlic cloves
- 1 bay leaf
- 6 fresh thyme sprigs *or* 1½ teaspoons dried, crumbled
  Salt and freshly ground pepper
- 2 quarts turkey or chicken stock (preferably homemade)
- 2½ tablespoons cornstarch

Mash half of butter with cornmeal into paste. Chop turkey neck into 1-inch pieces and reserve. Pat cavity and outside of bird dry. Loosen breast skin by gently sliding hand under neck flap and down between breast meat and skin, being careful not to tear skin. Spread cornmeal mixture evenly over breast under skin. Place onion, garlic, bay leaf and thyme in main cavity of turkey. Truss turkey. Sprinkle outside with salt and pepper. Rub remaining 1 cup butter all over turkey.

Preheat oven to 350°F. Lightly butter roasting pan. Heat pan in oven until hot, about 5 minutes. Place turkey on side in hot roasting pan. Roast 40 minutes. Turn turkey onto other side and roast 40 minutes longer, basting occasionally. Turn turkey breast side up. Add chopped neck bones to pan. Continue roasting, basting frequently, until meat thermometer inserted in thickest part of thigh (without touching bone) registers 170°F to 175°F, about 1 hour and 40 minutes more.

Transfer turkey to heated serving platter. Let rest while preparing sauce. Remove onion, garlic, bay leaf and thyme from cavity. Add to neck bones. Bake until onions are lightly colored, about 15 minutes. Pour off drippings, reserving 2 tablespoons. Add 1 quart broth to pan. Place over medium heat, scraping up all browned bits with wooden spoon. Strain liquid into heavy 3-quart saucepan. Add remaining 1 quart broth. Bring to boil, skimming fat from surface, and reduce by ⅓ (to 5 cups). Mix reserved turkey drippings and cornstarch to paste. Reduce heat, and when liquid stops boiling, slowly whisk in cornstarch. Stir until sauce is clear and slightly thickened. Strain into sauceboat.

Carve roasted turkey at table, passing warm sauce separately.

*Available at natural foods stores.

Duck and Goose

❖ ❖ ❖ ❖ ❖ ❖ ❖ ❖ ❖ ❖ ❖ ❖ ❖ ❖ ❖

DUCK WITH PLUM SAUCE

Excellent with wild rice, watercress salad and a cool white Zinfandel.

4 to 6 servings

- 2 3-pound (about) ducks
- 1 cup plus 2 tablespoons plum wine
- 2 tablespoons (¼ stick) butter
- 1 tablespoon powdered sugar
- 4 firm fresh plums, halved
- 2 fresh nectarines *or* firm fresh peaches, peeled and quartered

- 1½ cups Duck Stock (see following recipe)
- 2 tablespoons raspberry vinegar *or* red wine vinegar
- 3 tablespoons orange liqueur
- 1½ teaspoons cornstarch
  Watercress sprigs (garnish)

Preheat oven to 425°F. Arrange duck breasts and legs on rack in shallow large pan (reserve carcasses for Duck Stock). Roast until tender, turning once, about 35 minutes for breasts and 40 minutes for legs. Transfer to serving platter and keep warm.

Boil ½ cup plum wine in medium skillet over medium-high heat until reduced to 3 tablespoons. Set aside. Melt butter in heavy large skillet over medium-high heat. Stir in powdered sugar. Add fruit and sauté until glazed but still firm, about 4 minutes. Spoon glazed fruit around duck; keep warm.

Degrease roasting pan. Place pan over medium-high heat, add ½ cup plum wine and stir, scraping up any browned bits. Add to reduced wine in skillet. Pour in 1½ cups stock with vinegar. Place over medium-high heat and bring to boil. Cook sauce, stirring constantly, until reduced to 1 cup. Blend remaining 2 tablespoons plum wine with liqueur and cornstarch. Stir cornstarch mixture into sauce. Cook until thickened, about 3 more minutes. Pour sauce over duck. Garnish with watercress and serve immediately.

Duck Stock

- 1 to 2 duck carcasses, halved (with wings and all giblets except liver)
- 2 carrots, quartered
- 1 onion, quartered
- 1 celery stalk, quartered
- ½ teaspoon dried thyme, crumbled

Combine all ingredients in stockpot with enough water to cover. Place over high heat and bring to boil. Reduce heat, cover and simmer for 2½ hours, skimming surface frequently. Strain into container. (*Can be prepared ahead and stored in refrigerator up to 1 week or frozen up to 3 months.*) Discard fat from surface of stock before using.

BREAST OF DUCK WITH LINGONBERRY SAUCE AND ONION MARMALADE

Shredded red cabbage sautéed in butter with salt and pepper can be substituted for onion marmalade.

2 servings

Glace de Canard

- 1 5- to 5¼-pound duck
- 2 to 3 tablespoons oil
- 1 tablespoon juniper berries
- 1 tablespoon whole black peppercorns
- 2 tablespoons clarified butter (see recipe, page 62)

Lingonberry Sauce

- 1½ tablespoons raspberry vinegar
- 3 tablespoons honey-sweetened wild lingonberry conserve*
- 2 teaspoons whipping cream
- 1½ teaspoons glace de canard Freshly ground pepper Pinch of salt

Onion Marmalade

- 2 medium-size white onions, thinly sliced
- 1 cup Gamay wine
- ½ cup strawberry vinegar (see following recipe)
- 1 tablespoon unrefined honey
- 1 tablespoon rosehips Freshly ground pepper

For glace de canard: Remove breast meat from duck in 2 segments. Cover and refrigerate. Cut remaining duck into large pieces. Heat oil in large skillet over medium-high heat. Add duck pieces and brown well on all sides. Transfer to large stockpot using slotted spoon. Drain fat from skillet. Deglaze skillet with 1 cup water, scraping up any browned bits, and add to stockpot. Add juniper berries, peppercorns and enough water to cover. Place over medium-high heat and bring to boil. Reduce heat to low and simmer until liquid is reduced to 1 cup, about 6 hours. Strain well; transfer liquid to small saucepan and cook over medium-high heat until reduced to 1 to 1½ tablespoons. Pour into small bowl.

Heat butter in large skillet over medium-high heat. Add duck breasts and sauté until golden but still rare, about 5 to 6 minutes. Transfer to platter; discard skin. Return breasts to skillet skinned side down and cook another 1 to 2 minutes. Transfer to ovenproof platter and keep warm in 200°F oven.

For sauce: Discard butter from skillet. Add vinegar and deglaze. Add all remaining ingredients for sauce and cook over medium heat until reduced by half. Set sauce aside.

For marmalade: Combine all ingredients in medium saucepan over medium-high heat and cook, stirring frequently, until liquid is absorbed, about 1 hour. Transfer to processor or blender and mix using on/off turns until consistency of marmalade, 10 seconds.

To assemble, spoon onion marmalade into center of serving platter. Thinly slice duck breasts and arrange over marmalade. Top with lingonberry sauce and serve.

*Available at natural foods stores.

Strawberry Vinegar

Makes about 1½ cups

- 2 cups hulled strawberries
- 1½ cups Champagne vinegar

Combine strawberries and vinegar in medium bowl. Cover and refrigerate 2 days. Transfer to nonaluminum medium saucepan and bring to boil over medium-high heat. Strain into jar.

DUCK WITH CRANBERRY AND LEMON SAUCE (*Canard aux Baies d'Hiver et au Citron*)

Traditionally made with red currants, this recipe calls for more readily available fresh cranberries.

6 servings

- 2 tablespoons (¼ stick) butter
- 3 5-pound ducks (about), wing tips and necks chopped into 1½-inch pieces
- 1 quart veal stock, preferably homemade (see recipe, page 66)

- 1½ cups fresh cranberries
- 1 teaspoon grated lemon peel

- 1 cup (scant) water
- 3 tablespoons currant jelly, or more

- ¼ cup ruby Port Fresh lemon juice Salt and freshly ground pepper Peel of 2 lemons, cut into fine julienne and blanched 10 minutes Watercress sprigs (garnish) Brussels Sprouts with Grilled Almonds (see recipe, page 137)

Melt butter in heavy large saucepan over medium-high heat. Add duck wings and necks and sauté until deep golden. Discard butter from skillet. Add veal stock and bring to boil. Reduce heat to low and simmer until reduced to 1 to 1¼ cups, about 1½ hours. (*Duck essence can be prepared* several days ahead and refrigerated, or frozen for several months.)

Preheat oven to 325°F. Crush 12 cranberries. Place 4 crushed cranberries and pinch of lemon peel into cavity of each bird. Truss birds. Set on rack in large roasting pan. Roast until juices run clear when pricked with fork, about 2 to 2½ hours, tilting ducks at regular intervals to drain juice from cavities into roasting pan.

Meanwhile, combine remaining cranberries in medium saucepan with water and 3 tablespoons currant jelly. Cook over low heat until just tender, about 3 minutes. Reserve 18 uniform berries for garnish. Return remainder to heat and continue cooking berries until completely softened, about 7 minutes. Press mixture through fine sieve to remove skins. (*Cranberry puree can be prepared several days ahead to this point and refrigerated.*) Blend about ⅓ cup cranberry puree, or to taste, into reserved duck essence. Set aside.

Remove ducks from roasting pan and keep warm. Degrease pan. Place over medium-high heat, add Port and stir, scraping up any browned bits. Blend pan juices into sauce. Puree sauce in blender or processor until smooth. Strain into small saucepan. Taste and adjust seasoning with currant jelly, lemon juice, salt and pepper. Stir in lemon peel julienne. Reheat sauce. Arrange 1 leg and half of duck breast on side of each heated plate. Spoon sauce over. Garnish with watercress and reserved berries. Spoon brussels sprouts onto plate and serve.

GARLIC- AND PEAR-SCENTED ROAST GOOSE

Anyone with a passion for garlic will love this Renaissance-inspired recipe. Though the garlic-pear stuffing is discarded, it imparts a delicious flavor to the bird. Serve with Lemon–Pine Nut Sauce and Pears Cooked in Verjuice (see recipe, page 141).

8 to 10 servings

- 12 ounces *unpeeled* garlic, rinsed
- 2 large ripe pears, stemmed, cored and halved
- 1 10- to 12-pound goose
- ¼ cup red wine vinegar
  Salt and freshly ground pepper
- 1½ cups dry white wine
- 1 cup medium dry Sherry
- 2 cups (about) chicken or veal stock

  Evergreen sprigs (optional)
  Lemon–Pine Nut sauce (see following recipe)

Coarsely chop garlic and pears in processor using 5 to 6 on/off turns, or chop by hand. Set aside. (*Stuffing can be prepared 1 day ahead, covered and refrigerated.*)

Preheat oven to 325°F. Remove goose neck, giblets and wing tips and set aside for Lemon–Pine Nut Sauce; reserve liver for stuffing. Pat goose dry. Trim fat from neck and tail. Rub outside of goose with vinegar. Prick leg, back and breast skin with fork; *do not pierce meat.* Season outside and cavity with salt and pepper. Set liver in center of cavity and surround with garlic-pear stuffing. Using thick thread, sew neck and cavity closed.

Set goose, breast side up, on rack over large roasting pan. Pour 2 cups water into pan. Cover loosely with foil. Roast 45 minutes. Blend wine and Sherry and baste goose with ⅓ of mixture. Cover and continue roasting 45 minutes, adding stock to pan as juices evaporate. Skim fat from pan juices. Turn goose and baste with ⅓ of wine mixture. Roast 45 minutes. Baste with remaining wine mixture; uncover and roast until juices run clear when thigh is pierced with fork, about 30 minutes.

Set goose on ovenproof platter and tent completely with foil. Let rest 15 to 30 minutes before carving.

To serve, remove trussing threads. Discard stuffing, reserving liver. Thinly slice liver. Surround goose with evergreen sprigs. Serve with sliced liver and Lemon–Pine Nut Sauce.

Lemon–Pine Nut Sauce

Thickening sauces with nuts is a technique that came to Europe with the Saracens. Begin sauce as soon as goose goes into the oven and finish it while the bird rests before carving.

8 to 10 servings

Stock

- 3 cups water
- 1 cup dry white wine
- 1 carrot, chopped
- 1 onion, chopped
- 1 celery stalk with leaves, chopped
- 1 tablespoon white wine vinegar
- ⅛ teaspoon whole cumin seed, crushed
  Goose neck, giblets and wing tips

Enrichment

- 3 tablespoons pine nuts, ground to paste
- 2 tablespoons pine nuts
- 2 tablespoons minced fresh parsley
- 1 to 1½ tablespoons fresh lemon juice
  Salt and freshly ground pepper

For stock: Bring all ingredients to simmer in stockpot. Cover partially and simmer 3 hours, skimming occasionally. Add water if necessary to keep ingredients covered. Strain through fine sieve into clean saucepan, pressing on ingredients with back of spoon to extract liquid. Cook stock over high heat until reduced by half.

For enrichment: When goose is transferred to platter, skim all fat from pan juices. Bring juices to boil in roasting pan over medium-high heat. Add reduced stock and boil 5 minutes, stirring to scrape up any browned bits. Whisk in nut paste and boil 1 minute. Stir in pine nuts, parsley, lemon juice and salt and pepper. Pour juices accumulated on serving platter into sauce. Transfer to sauceboat and serve.

Game Birds

❖ ❖ ❖ ❖ ❖ ❖ ❖ ❖ ❖ ❖ ❖ ❖ ❖ ❖

ROASTED CORNISH GAME HENS WITH CITRUS SAUCE

8 servings

Glacéed Citrus Peel

 1 medium Valencia orange
 1 medium grapefruit
 1 cup water
 ½ cup sugar
 ⅛ teaspoon fresh lemon juice

 8 1-pound (about) Cornish game hens* (preferably fresh), wing tips cut off and reserved for stock with necks, gizzards and hearts

Stock

 4 cups water
 3 celery tops
 1 leek top
 ¼ large carrot
 ¼ medium onion
 ½ bay leaf
 3 whole peppercorns
 1 fresh thyme sprig *or* pinch of dried, crumbled
   Several parsley stems

Marinade

 2 cups dry red wine
 2 medium Valencia oranges
 2 medium grapefruit
 2 teaspoons firmly packed brown sugar
   Salt and freshly ground pepper

 8 tablespoons (1 stick) butter

Sauce

 2 tablespoons (¼ stick) butter
 ¼ cup minced shallot
 3 tablespoons beurre manié**
 ¼ cup orange liqueur
   Salt and freshly ground pepper
 2 tablespoons (¼ stick) unsalted butter

For glacéed peel: Remove peel (colored part only) of orange and grapefruit with vegetable peeler; reserve fruit for marinade. Cut into very fine, long julienne. Transfer to small saucepan. Cover with cold water and bring to boil. Drain and repeat. Drain well. Combine 1 cup water with ½ cup sugar and lemon juice in small saucepan. Place over low heat and cook, swirling pan gently, until sugar is dissolved. Increase heat slightly and bring syrup to simmer. Reduce heat, add fruit peel julienne and simmer very gently until peel is softened and sugar is absorbed, about 30 minutes; *do not boil.* Turn out onto waxed paper, separating strands with knife tip. Cool completely. *(Glacéed citrus peel can be prepared several months ahead and refrigerated in airtight container.)*

For stock: Combine reserved wing tips, necks, gizzards and hearts with remaining stock ingredients in 6-quart saucepan and bring to boil over medium-high heat. Reduce heat, cover partially and simmer, skimming frequently, until liquid is reduced to 2 cups. Strain into bowl, pressing on vegetables with back of spoon to extract all liquid. Let cool. Degrease surface of stock. Set aside. *(Stock can be prepared several days ahead and refrigerated or frozen.)*

For marinade: Pour wine into large nonaluminum bowl. Holding fruit over wine, remove peel from 2 oranges and 2 grapefruit. Squeeze enough orange and grapefruit juice to measure 2 cups, using reserved fruit if necessary. Strain and add juice to wine mixture. Stir in brown sugar, blending well. Season with salt and pepper. Add game hens. Cover and refrigerate overnight, turning occasionally.

Preheat oven to 400°F. Pat birds dry (reserve marinade) and truss. Season with salt and pepper. Rub 1 tablespoon butter over each bird. Arrange birds breast side down on rack in large roasting pan. Roast, turning breast side up, then breast side down every 10 to 15 minutes, until tender and browned and juices run clear when flesh is pricked with fork, about 40 to 45 minutes. Meanwhile, pour reserved marinade into large saucepan. Place over high heat and reduce to 2 cups; set aside for sauce. Pour any juices that have accumulated in cavities of birds into roasting pan. Transfer birds to heated serving platter breast side down. Cover and keep warm.

For sauce: Degrease pan juices and set pan aside. Melt 2 tablespoons butter in large skillet over low heat. Add shallot and cook until soft. Blend in reduced marinade, reserved stock and pan juices. Increase heat to medium high and cook until reduced to about 2 cups. Whisk in 1½ tablespoons beurre manié, blending well. Add remaining beurre manié if necessary to thicken sauce. Stir in liqueur. Season with salt and pepper to taste. Whisk in unsalted butter 1 tablespoon at a time.

To serve, glaze top of each bird with sauce. Garnish tops with small mound of glacéed citrus peel. Serve immediately with remaining sauce.

*Four 2-pound (about) hens can be substituted. Rub each bird with 2 tablespoons butter and roast at 400°F for about 1 hour. To serve, cut birds in half down center.

**For beurre manié, whisk together 1½ tablespoons butter (room temperature) with 1½ tablespoons all purpose flour.

GAME HENS WITH CABBAGE AND SAUSAGE

Marinate hens overnight to develop a wild game flavor. Serve with mustard, cornichons and French bread.

4 to 6 servings

4   Cornish game hens, cut in half and backbones removed
    Salt and freshly ground pepper
2   tablespoons Herbes de Provence (or other aromatic herb mixture)
1   medium onion, thinly sliced
8   parsley sprigs
6   whole cloves
4   tablespoons brandy
5   cups (about) dry red wine

1   2-pound cabbage, quartered and cored

10 ounces salt pork, blanched 5 minutes and sliced into ¼-inch-wide strips
1   medium onion, chopped
2   large carrots, chopped
3   medium garlic cloves, crushed
1   pound fully cooked Polish sausage (kielbasa), sliced ¼ inch thick
¾   cup chicken stock, preferably homemade (see recipe, page 38)
½   cup dry white wine
2   tablespoons brandy
8   juniper berries *or* 3 tablespoons gin
½   teaspoon dried thyme, crumbled
    Bouquet garni (3 parsley sprigs and 1 bay leaf, tied together in cheesecloth bag)

Place half of hens in bottom of deep nonaluminum pot. Sprinkle lightly with salt and pepper. Season with 1 tablespoon Herbes de Provence, half of sliced onion, half of parsley, 3 cloves and 2 tablespoons brandy. Cover with remaining hens and repeat seasoning. Cover with red wine. Marinate in refrigerator for 12 to 24 hours.

Cook cabbage in boiling salted water 10 minutes. Drain and squeeze dry, then chop coarsely. Set aside.

Remove hens from marinade and pat dry. Stir salt pork in heavy large skillet over medium heat until brown and crisp. Transfer to paper towels to drain, using slotted spoon. Increase heat to medium high. Add hens to skillet (in batches if necessary; do not crowd) and brown well on both sides, shaking pan occasionally to prevent sticking. Remove hens. Reduce heat to medium low. Add cabbage, onion, carrots and garlic and cook, stirring frequently, until vegetables soften, about 8 minutes. Stir in salt pork. Add hens and remaining ingredients. Season with salt and pepper. Baste hens with liquid in pan. Reduce heat, cover and simmer until hens are just tender, about 30 minutes, basting occasionally. (*Game hens can be prepared several hours ahead to this point.*)

Preheat broiler. Using slotted spoon, arrange vegetables and sausage in shallow broilerproof baking dish large enough to accommodate hens in single layer. Pat hens dry and place atop vegetables. Broil 4 to 6 inches from heat source until skin is crisp, about 10 minutes. Meanwhile, degrease cooking juices and strain into sauceboat. Place hens on large platter. Surround or top with sausage and vegetables. Serve immediately with sauce.

ROAST SQUAB WITH HONEY SAUCE
(*Pigeonneau Rôti au Miel*)

2 servings

2   15-ounce squab
    Salt and freshly ground pepper

2   tablespoons oil
2   teaspoons butter

1   teaspoon chopped shallot
¼   cup Port
¼   cup dry red wine
2   teaspoons honey vinegar *or* cider vinegar
1½ cups veal stock, preferably homemade (see recipe, page 66)

½   teaspoon cornstarch mixed with 1 to 2 tablespoons Port (optional)

1   teaspoon raw honey
    Cognac to taste
    Salt and freshly ground pepper

Discard giblets from squab. Cut off wings and reserve. Rinse squab thoroughly and pat dry. Tie legs to breast with string. Sprinkle squab and wings with salt and pepper and set aside.

Preheat oven to 450°F. Heat oil and butter in large ovenproof skillet over medium-high heat until very hot. Add squab and wings and cook until crisp and deep brown, turning frequently. Arrange squab in skillet breast side up. Transfer to oven and roast about 15 minutes (for medium rare). Transfer squab and wings to heated platter. Reduce oven temperature to 350°F.

Discard ¾ of fat from skillet. Return skillet to medium heat, add shallot and sauté about 5 *seconds; do not burn*. Add Port, red wine, vinegar and squab wings and cook until liquid is reduced by half. Add veal stock and continue cooking until liquid is reduced to ⅔ cup (if sauce is too thin, blend in cornstarch mixture and cook until sauce reaches desired consistency).

Slice squab, adding to sauce any juices that have accumulated on platter. Arrange slices in center of platter with wings on either side. Return squab to oven for 2 minutes to heat through.

Stir honey and Cognac into sauce. Season with salt and pepper. Place over medium heat and cook until hot; *do not boil*. Pour sauce over squab and serve immediately.

❖

6 ❖ Entrées: Seafood

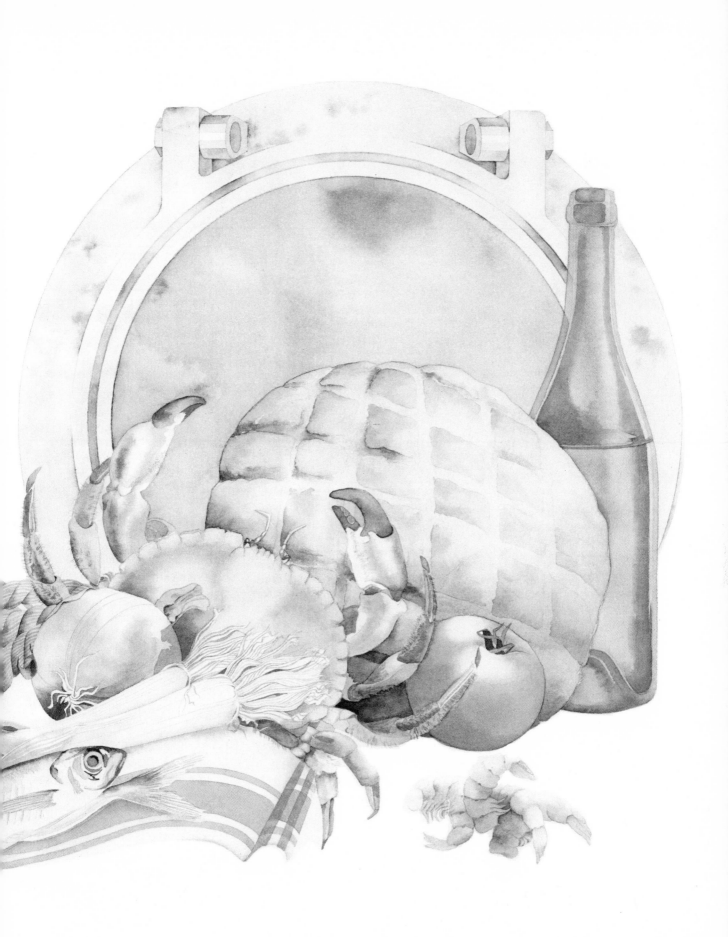

Fish

STEAMED BASS FILLETS WITH CHIVE SAUCE

6 servings

    1 cup Fish Stock (see
       following recipe)
 ½ cup dry white wine
    2 tablespoons (¼ stick) butter
    2 pounds 6 ounces sea bass
       fillets, boned, side belly
       trimmed off and discarded
       and fish cut into 6 equal
       portions

 ½ cup whipping cream
    2 tablespoons snipped fresh
       chives
       Salt and freshly ground
       pepper

Combine stock and wine in steamer. Spread 1 tablespoon butter over rack. Set rack in steamer. Arrange fish on rack. Dot fish with remaining butter. Cover, place over high heat and steam until fish is just cooked, 7 to 8 minutes per inch thickness of fillets.

Remove fish from steamer. Peel off any skin. Arrange on heated platter; keep warm. Continue boiling steaming liquid until reduced to 1 cup. Add cream and boil until thickened and reduced to about 1 cup. Stir in chives. Pour any liquid from fish into sauce. Season with salt and pepper. Spoon sauce over fish and serve.

Fish Stock

Stock can be prepared 2 days ahead and refrigerated.

Makes 5 cups

    2 tablespoons (¼ stick)
       unsalted butter
    1 large onion, thinly sliced
    3 celery stalks, thinly sliced
       Pinch of ground mace
    3 pounds fish bones (from
       nonoily fish)
    1 small bay leaf

Melt butter in heavy 6-quart saucepan over low heat. Add onion, celery and mace. Cover and cook until softened, about 15 minutes, stirring frequently. Mix in bones and bay leaf. Add water just to cover. Increase heat and bring to boil. Let boil 3 minutes, skimming foam from surface as necessary. Reduce heat and simmer 40 minutes. Line strainer with moistened tea towel and set over 3-quart saucepan. Pour stock through strainer. Place over medium-high heat and boil until reduced to 5 cups.

BLUEFISH EN PAPILLOTE NICOISE

For a delicious summertime variation, use foil for the papillotes and grill the packets on the barbecue.

6 servings

    2 tablespoons (¼ stick) butter
 1½ pounds tomatoes, peeled,
       seeded and chopped

 ½ cup (1 stick) butter, room
       temperature
    2 tablespoons chopped fresh
       basil
    1 large garlic clove, crushed
       and minced
    1 teaspoon grated lemon peel
       Salt and freshly ground
       pepper

    2 pounds 6 ounces bluefish,
       boned, belly trimmed off
       and discarded and fish
       divided into six 6-ounce
       portions
    6 anchovy fillets (optional)

       Lemon slices and Italian
       parsley (garnish)

Melt 2 tablespoons butter in small skillet over high heat. Add tomatoes and cook until liquid evaporates and tomatoes thicken into saucelike consistency, about 20 minutes, stirring frequently; tomatoes should measure about ¾ cup. Pour tomatoes onto plate and cool completely.

Cream ½ cup butter in large bowl of electric mixer until fluffy. Gradually beat in tomatoes. Stir in basil, garlic and lemon peel. Season generously with salt and pepper. Divide tomato butter into 6 equal portions. (*Can be prepared 1 day ahead and refrigerated.*)

Fold 15-inch-wide piece of parchment or foil in half. Trace half heart shape starting at folded end; heart should be 11½ inches long and 8 inches wide at widest part. Cut out heart. Repeat 5 more times. Unfold hearts. Oil inside of each, leaving 1-inch border all around.

Center 1 portion of fish on 1 side of each heart. Top with 1 portion tomato butter, then 1 anchovy. Fold other side over top and seal edges tightly (use paper clip if necessary). (*Papillotes can be prepared 6 hours ahead to this point and refrigerated.*)

Preheat oven to 400°F. Arrange papillotes on 2 baking sheets. Bake 15 minutes. Switch pans to opposite racks and continue baking 10 minutes. Serve papillotes immediately, garnished with lemon slices and parsley.

HALIBUT ESPAGNOL

6 servings

- 6 tablespoons (¾ stick) chilled unsalted butter
- 2 tablespoons chopped fresh basil
- 2 tablespoons chopped fresh parsley
- ¼ teaspoon saffron threads, crushed
- 6 ½-inch-thick halibut fillets (about 2¼ pounds total)
- ½ cup fish stock (see recipe, page 84), room temperature
- ½ cup dry white wine
- 2 dozen mussels, cooked and shucked

Beat butter in small bowl until smooth. Blend in basil, parsley and saffron. Set herb butter aside.

Arrange halibut in single layer in large skillet. Pour in stock and wine. Place over low heat, cover and simmer gently until just firm and opaque, about 7 to 8 minutes per inch thickness. Transfer halibut to heated platter using slotted spatula. Cover with foil and keep warm.

Transfer liquid to small heavy saucepan. Increase heat and boil until reduced to ¼ cup, stirring frequently to prevent browning. Add any liquid released from halibut and reduce again to ¼ cup. Reduce heat to low. Gradually whisk in herb butter. Add mussels and heat through; *do not boil*. Spoon herb sauce and mussels around halibut and serve immediately.

SOLE QUENELLES WITH PEARS AND LEEK SAUCE

8 servings

Sole Quenelles

- 1½ pounds well-chilled fillet of sole, halibut *or* scrod
- 2 egg whites
- 2 teaspoons salt
- ½ teaspoon freshly ground white pepper
  Pinch *each* of ground ginger and freshly grated nutmeg
  Small pinch of ground red pepper

Leek Sauce

- ¼ cup (½ stick) butter
- 1 large leek or 2 medium (white part only), quartered or halved lengthwise and very thinly sliced (2½ cups)
- 1 tablespoon all purpose flour
- 2 cups heated Fish Stock (see following recipe)
- 2 cups pear nectar
- 1 tablespoon honey
- ¼ teaspoon ground ginger
  Pinch *each* of freshly grated nutmeg and ground red pepper
- 1 tablespoon fresh lemon juice
  Salt and freshly ground white pepper
- 1½ to 1¾ cups chilled whipping cream
- 2 tablespoons (¼ stick) butter
- 3 Anjou pears
- 2 tablespoons (¼ stick) butter
  Dash of fresh lemon juice
- 2 tablespoons snipped fresh chives (garnish)

For quenelles: Puree fish in processor. Add whites, salt, white pepper, ginger, nutmeg and red pepper and mix until smooth. Refrigerate puree in processor bowl (with knife intact) until well chilled, about 30 minutes.

For sauce: Melt ¼ cup butter in heavy large skillet over low heat. Add leek, cover and cook until very soft, about 15 minutes, stirring frequently to prevent browning.

Whisk flour into leek mixture, blending well. Cook 3 minutes, stirring. Whisk in hot fish stock and pear nectar. Blend in honey, ginger, nutmeg and red pepper. Increase heat to high and bring mixture to boil, whisking constantly. Transfer to blender and mix until smooth. Return sauce to skillet. If necessary, place over medium-high heat and cook until sauce thickens and coats back of spoon. Blend in lemon juice. Season with salt, white pepper and red pepper to taste. Set sauce aside at room temperature.

Return chilled work bowl containing quenelle mixture to base. With machine running, pour 1½ cups cream through feed tube in slow steady stream, blending until thoroughly incorporated and mixture is just creamy; do not overprocess or quenelles will not hold shape. Add remaining cream if necessary (mixture will be slightly sticky). Taste and adjust seasoning.

Preheat oven to 350°F. Butter shallow baking dish. Bring large amount of salted water to rapid boil. Reduce heat so water is just shaking. Using serving spoons, form quenelle mixture into egg shapes in batches of 4, gently dropping into simmering water as formed. Poach until firm to touch, 5 to 8 minutes, turning once. Remove quenelles from water using slotted spoon and drain on paper towels. Repeat with remaining quenelle mixture. Transfer to prepared dish. Reheat sauce, whisk in 2 tablespoons butter and pour over top. Bake 10 minutes. (*Sauced quenelles can be prepared ahead and kept warm in 250°F oven 10 minutes or refrigerated overnight and gently rewarmed in low oven.*)

Meanwhile, peel pears. Cut each pear into 6 wedges; discard cores. Heat 2 tablespoons butter in large skillet over medium-high heat. Add pears and lemon juice and sauté until tender. Surround quenelles with pears. Sprinkle with chives. Serve immediately.

Fish Stock

Can be prepared several days ahead and refrigerated, or frozen for up to 2 months.

Makes about 2 cups

- 12 ounces fish trimmings and bones
- 2 cups water
- 2 cups dry white wine
- 1 celery top
- 1 leek top
- ½ onion
- 1 parsley sprig
- 1 fresh thyme sprig *or* pinch of dried, crumbled
- ¼ bay leaf

Combine all ingredients in large saucepan and bring to boil over high heat, skimming foam from surface as necessary. Reduce heat to low, cover partially and simmer until liquid is reduced by half, about 45 minutes, skimming occasionally. Strain stock through colander lined with several layers of moistened cheesecloth. Set aside.

SCALLOP-FILLED SALMON MEDALLIONS WITH LETTUCE SAUCE

6 servings

- 8 ounces fresh scallops, well chilled
- 1 egg white
- ½ teaspoon fresh lemon juice
- ½ teaspoon salt
  Pinch *each* of ground red pepper and freshly grated nutmeg
- ½ cup whipping cream, well chilled
- 6 fresh 5 × 7-inch salmon fillets, ½ inch thick, skinned
- 1 cup dry white wine
- ½ cup water
- 1 shallot, minced
- 1 bay leaf
- 3 whole peppercorns
- ¼ teaspoon dried tarragon

- 2 tablespoons (¼ stick) butter
- 1 head butter lettuce *or* Boston lettuce (11 ounces), rinsed, dried and cut julienne
- 1 cup whipping cream
  Salt and freshly ground pepper

Puree scallops, egg white, lemon juice, salt and red pepper and nutmeg in blender or processor until smooth, stopping as necessary to scrape down sides of container. Transfer to bowl set in ice. Stir in chilled cream 1 drop at a time, making sure liquid is absorbed before adding more. Cover and refrigerate for 2 hours.

Spread salmon fillets evenly with scallop mixture, leaving 1-inch border. Starting at narrow end, roll fillets up and fasten with wooden picks. (*Can be prepared several hours ahead to this point, covered and refrigerated.*)

Combine wine, water, shallot, bay leaf, peppercorns and tarragon in large skillet. Add salmon rolls and bring just to simmer. Cover and cook, adjusting heat so liquid is barely shaking, until scallop mixture is just set when tested with fork, about 10 minutes.

Melt butter in heavy skillet over low heat. Add lettuce, cover and cook until wilted, about 5 minutes, stirring occasionally. Puree in blender or processor until smooth.

Remove salmon from skillet using slotted spatula and set aside.

Strain salmon cooking liquid. Return to skillet and boil until reduced to ¼ cup. Add cream and continue boiling until sauce is thickened. Stir in lettuce puree. Season with salt and pepper.

Slice salmon rolls into ½-inch-thick rounds. Divide sauce among 6 heated plates. Arrange medallions atop sauce. Serve immediately.

SALMON TROUT FILLETS WITH RED WINE SAUCE
(Filets de Truite Saumonée au Pinot Noir d'Alsace)

6 servings

- 1¾ pounds shallots
- 6 salmon trout (3¼ to 3½ pounds total), filleted, backbones and heads reserved
- 1 750-ml bottle Pinot Noir d'Alsace, Zinfandel *or* Côtes du Rhône
  Small bouquet garni (1 small parsley sprig, 1 small fresh thyme sprig and 1 bay leaf tied in cheesecloth bag)
  Salt and freshly ground pepper
- 16 tablespoons (2 sticks) butter
- ¾ teaspoon anchovy paste
- 2 tablespoons all purpose flour
  Salt and freshly ground pepper
  Fresh Parsley Noodles (see recipe, page 142)
  Chopped fresh parsley (garnish)

Mince 10 medium shallots. Transfer to 2-quart saucepan. Add fish bones and heads, wine, bouquet garni and small pinch of salt and pepper. Place mixture over high heat and bring to boil. Reduce heat and simmer 35 minutes, pressing on bones to extract all flavor.

Strain mixture through fine sieve set over bowl. Return liquid to saucepan. Place over medium-high heat and reduce to ¾ cup. Increase heat to high and bring to rapid boil. Add 12 tablespoons butter to center of pan 1 tablespoon at a time, whisking constantly; sauce will be light. Blend in anchovy paste. Taste and season with salt* and ground pepper. Set sauce aside.

Bring large amount of salted water to rapid boil in heavy deep skillet. Add remaining shallots and blanch 3 minutes. Drain well. Pat dry. Melt 2 tablespoons butter in skillet over low heat. Add shallots and cook until tender and golden, stirring occasionally, about 40 minutes. Stir shallots into sauce (shallots will reheat sauce). Add several tablespoons sauce to skillet and stir, scraping up any browned bits. Blend skillet juices back into sauce.

Combine flour and salt and pepper on large plate. Melt 2 tablespoons butter in skillet over medium-high heat. Lightly dredge fillets in flour, patting off excess. Add fillets to skillet and sauté on both sides until just opaque, about 2 minutes on each side. Divide Fresh Parsley Noodles among individual plates. Top each serving with 2 fillets. Spoon sauce over top. Sprinkle with parsley and serve immediately.

*If sauce is too acidic, add small amount of anchovy paste or concentrated meat extract for seasoning instead of salt.

STUFFED SWORDFISH ITALIAN STYLE

6 servings

Leek Stuffing

 2 tablespoons (¼ stick) butter
 2 medium leeks (white part only), quartered and sliced ⅛ inch thick (about 1½ cups)
 2 tablespoons chopped fresh basil
 2 tablespoons chopped fresh parsley
 Salt and freshly ground pepper

 6 1-inch-thick swordfish steaks (about 2½ pounds total)
 6 ¼-inch-thick slices mozzarella cheese, cut ½ inch smaller than perimeter of steaks (about 6 ounces total)

Beurre Blanc

 ½ cup fish stock (see recipe, page 84)
 ½ cup minced shallot
 ¼ cup white wine vinegar
 ¼ cup dry white wine

 1 cup (2 sticks) chilled unsalted butter, cut into ½-inch pieces
 2 tablespoons (¼ stick) butter, melted

For stuffing: Melt 2 tablespoons butter in large skillet over medium-high heat. Add leeks and sauté until cooked through and liquid is evaporated, about 6 minutes; *do not brown.* Let cool. Blend in basil and parsley. Season to taste with salt and pepper. (Filling should measure about ¾ cup.)

To cut pockets in fish, slice steaks horizontally through center to about ½ inch from edge. Insert cheese into pockets. Spread filling evenly over cheese. Secure fish with toothpicks to prevent stuffing from falling out during cooking. (*Can be prepared 1 day ahead to this point and refrigerated.*)

For beurre blanc: Combine stock, shallot, vinegar and white wine in heavy small saucepan over medium-high heat and boil until liquid is reduced to 2 tablespoons, watching carefully to prevent complete evaporation. Remove pan from heat. Add 2 pieces of butter and whisk quickly until just incorporated. Place over very low heat and whisk in remaining butter 1 piece at a time; sauce should be thick and emulsified. Season with salt and pepper. Strain through fine sieve. (*Beurre blanc can be kept warm for several hours in vacuum bottle.*)

Preheat broiler. Brush broiler pan with 1 tablespoon melted butter. Arrange fish on pan. Brush top of fish with remaining melted butter. Broil until fish is opaque and top is golden brown, turning once, about 3 minutes on each side. Transfer to platter. Spoon sauce over and serve.

TROUT VERONA

6 servings

 6 boned fresh trout (2¼ to 3 pounds total)
 ¼ cup all purpose flour seasoned with salt and freshly ground pepper

 ¼ cup olive oil
 ½ cup dry white wine
 1 tablespoon fresh lemon juice
 8 ounces fresh small shrimp, shelled and deveined
 2 to 3 teaspoons coarsely chopped fresh rosemary
 3 to 4 tablespoons chilled butter

Pat fish dry. Dredge fish in seasoned flour, shaking off excess. Heat 2 tablespoons oil in heavy large skillet (preferably black steel or cast iron) over medium-high heat until very hot. Add half of fish and fry until outside is crisp and golden brown, turning once, about 4 minutes on each side. Transfer to heated serving platter. Heat remaining 2 tablespoons oil in skillet and repeat with remaining fish. (Fish can be fried simultaneously in 2 skillets.)

Heat wine and lemon juice in small saucepan over medium-high heat. Add shrimp and rosemary and cook until shrimp just turn pink, 2 to 3 minutes. Remove shrimp from pan using slotted spoon and arrange atop fish. Continue cooking until liquid is reduced to 2 tablespoons. Remove from heat and whisk in butter 1 tablespoon at a time. Pour over fish and serve.

MESQUITE-GRILLED FRESH TUNA

Tuna steaks can be broiled rather than grilled if you wish.

8 servings

 8 1½-inch-thick tuna steaks (about 2⅔ pounds total)
 Juice of 1 large lemon
 8 tablespoons (1 stick) butter
 Salt and freshly ground pepper
 Tomato-Basil Sauce (see following recipe)

Prepare outdoor grill, heating coals until almost white. Top charcoal with 3 mesquite chunks and heat through.

Arrange tuna in shallow pans. Squeeze lemon juice over. Dot each with 1 tablespoon butter. Season with salt and pepper. Set pan on hot grill rack, but not over hottest part of fire. Cover and cook until opaque, about 25 minutes, depending on fire and thickness of fish. Top with sauce and serve.

Tomato-Basil Sauce

Makes 2 cups

Fish Fumet

 1 tablespoon unsalted butter
 1 medium onion, sliced
 1 small carrot, sliced
 2½ pounds fish bones and heads (from nonoily fish)
 ¼ cup mushrooms stems
 1 quart water
 1 cup dry white wine
 1 bouquet garni (2 parsley sprigs, 2 thyme sprigs and 1 bay leaf tied in cheesecloth bag)
 ¼ teaspoon salt
 5 white peppercorns

 ¼ cup (½ stick) unsalted butter
 4 medium shallots, minced
 4 tablespoons chopped fresh basil
 8 parsley stems
 3 tablespoons tomato paste
 1½ cups whipping cream
   Salt and freshly ground pepper

For fumet: Melt 1 tablespoon butter in heavy 4-quart saucepan over low heat. Add onion and carrot, cover and cook until onion is translucent, stirring occasionally, about 10 minutes. Add fish bones and mushroom stems. Cover and cook until bones fall apart, about 10 minutes. Blend in water, wine, bouquet garni, ¼ teaspoon salt and peppercorns and bring to boil. Reduce heat, cover partially and simmer until reduced to 2 cups. Strain. Measure 1½ cups fumet; reserve rest for another use. *(Fumet can be refrigerated for several days, or frozen several months.)*

Melt ¼ cup butter in heavy large skillet over low heat. Add shallots, cover and cook until limp, about 5 minutes. Add 1½ cups fumet and 2 tablespoons basil with parsley stems. Increase heat to medium high and reduce mixture by half, about 8 minutes, stirring occasionally. Reduce heat to medium. Blend in tomato paste and cook 2 minutes. Stir in cream and cook until reduced to 2 cups, about 15 minutes (sauce should be consistency of creamy vinaigrette). Discard parsley. Add remaining basil. Season with salt and pepper. Serve warm.

LEMON FISH WITH VEGETABLES AND PARSLEY SAUCE

A superb entrée in the Greek style.

12 servings

 ¾ cup fresh lemon juice
 2 generous teaspoons dried oregano, crumbled
   Salt and freshly ground pepper
 1 8-pound or two 4-pound whole fish (such as cod, sea bass, sea trout *or* pike)

 2 cups dry white wine
 ½ cup olive oil
 1 garlic clove, minced
 10 medium-size new potatoes, peeled and cut into 1½-inch slices
 8 to 12 medium carrots, peeled and cut into 1-inch slices
 1½ pounds pearl onions, peeled
 1 celery stalk, cut into 1-inch slices

 1 tablespoon cornstarch diluted with ½ cup water
 20 green Greek olives (garnish)
   Lemon wedges and fresh dill sprigs (garnish)
   Parsley Sauce (see following recipe)

Blend lemon juice, oregano, salt and pepper in container large enough to hold fish. Add fish and marinate at room temperature 2 hours, turning fish over occasionally.

Bring 1 cup wine, oil and garlic to boil in fish poacher over medium-high heat. Add potatoes, carrots, onions and celery. Cover and cook until vegetables are tender; check frequently and add water to poacher as necessary. Remove each vegetable as it is done.

Arrange fish on piece of cheesecloth that is several times width of fish. Pour marinade into poacher. Blend in remaining wine with enough water to cover fish. Holding sides of cheesecloth, lower fish into poacher. Place over medium-high heat and bring to boil. Reduce heat so liquid is just shaking, cover partially and poach until fish is tender, turning once, about 9 minutes total per inch of thickness.

Transfer fish to platter. Increase heat and reduce poaching liquid to 1½ cups. Whisk in cornstarch mixture and cook until thickened to desired consistency; do not boil. Strain liquid. Pour over fish. Arrange vegetables around fish. Garnish with olives, lemon and dill. Serve chilled or at room temperature with sauce.

Parsley Sauce

This sauce can double as a dip. Simply add slightly more oil to the running processor or blender and mix until thickened.

Makes 3 generous cups

 12 ⅜-inch-thick slices white bread, crusts trimmed
 2 bunches parsley, stemmed
 ¼ cup fresh lemon juice
 1 very small onion
 2 tablespoons vinegar
   Salt
 3 cups corn oil
 4 egg yolks, room temperature
 ¼ cup milk
   Freshly ground pepper

Soak bread in water, then squeeze dry. Transfer to processor or blender. Add parsley, lemon juice, onion and vinegar with salt to taste and mix until creamy. With machine running, add oil in slow steady stream until sauce is consistency of thin mayonnaise. Mix in yolks. Blend in milk. Add pepper to taste. Refrigerate 4 to 5 hours. Serve chilled. Sauce will thicken on standing.

*Minted Zucchini and Sweet Corn Salad (top left),
Rice Salad with Braised Broccoli, Harissa-Roasted
Chicken with Piquant Orange Mustard Sauce*

Clockwise from top:
Lemon Praline Tart, Chevre and
Mushroom-stuffed Chicken Legs
surrounded by Onion-steamed
Broccoli with Dill, baked new
potatoes, Shrimp Mousse with
Peas and Green Herb Sauce

*Clockwise from top:
Vietnamese Cold Noodles
surrounded by complementary
toppings, Thai Stuffed Mussels
with Basil, Oysters in Leeks
and Pine Nuts, Indonesian
Spiced Chicken Pieces*

Clockwise from top:
Salad of Roasted Peppers,
Broccoli with Sautéed Pine Nuts,
Gorgonzola cheese with fresh pears,
Braised Veal Shank with Wine
and Herbs, Rigatoni del Curato

*From bottom:
Duck with Cranberry and
Lemon, Brussels Sprouts with
Grilled Almonds, Bread and
Onion Sausage, Pear Brandy
Gratin, Brown Sugar Crown Cake
with fresh currants*

SNAPPER WITH GINGER AND LIME

(Blanc de Snapper à la Julienne de Gingembre et au Citron Vert)

4 servings

- 2 limes

  Butter (for parchment)

- ¼ cup (½ stick) butter
- 1 heaping tablespoon minced shallot
- 1⅓ cups dry vermouth
- 5 teaspoons finely slivered ginger
- 4 8-ounce red snapper fillets
  Salt and freshly ground white pepper
- ¾ cup whipping cream
- 1 egg yolk, room temperature

  Very fine lime peel julienne and chopped fresh chives (garnish)

Peel limes in long strips with vegetable peeler. Cut peel into very fine slivers. Remove white pith from fruit using sharp knife and discard. Carefully segment fruit. Transfer peel to small saucepan and cover with water. Place over high heat and bring to boil. Immediately drain and rinse with cold water. Pat dry. Set aside.

Preheat oven to 400°F. Cut piece of parchment to fit ovenproof large skillet. Butter 1 side of paper. Set aside.

Melt ¼ cup butter in same skillet. Stir in shallot. Add vermouth, ginger and lime peel. Season fish with salt and white pepper. Arrange fish in skillet. Cover with parchment circle, buttered side down. Bake until fish is opaque, about 7 to 10 minutes.

Whip ¼ cup cream in small bowl until just beginning to thicken and almost consistency of thin mayonnaise. Gently blend in yolk. Measure exactly ¼ cup and set aside.

Transfer fish to heated platter and cover to keep warm. Place skillet over medium-high heat and reduce liquid to ¾ cup. Add remaining cream and boil 1 minute. Pour any juices that have accumulated on fish platter into skillet and boil about 30 seconds. Add reserved ¼ cup cream mixture and swirl skillet gently to blend. Strain sauce. Pour around fish. Arrange lime segments in flower-petal pattern over top. Sprinkle lime peel julienne atop fish. Sprinkle with chives and serve.

Shellfish and Crustaceans

❖ ❖ ❖ ❖ ❖ ❖ ❖ ❖ ❖ ❖ ❖ ❖ ❖ ❖

MUSSELS IN MUSTARD SAUCE

Serve these steamed mussels in wide, shallow bowls. Accompany with a salad of escarole and curly endive.

4 servings

- 3 tablespoons butter
- 3 shallots, chopped
- 2 leeks, cleaned and finely sliced (white part only)
- 6 cups dry vermouth
- 6 pounds fresh mussels, scrubbed and debearded

- ¼ cup (½ stick) butter, cut into pieces
- ¼ cup all purpose flour
- 1 cup whipping cream
- 3 egg yolks, beaten
- ¼ Lemon Mustard (see following recipe)
  Salt and freshly ground white pepper

Melt 3 tablespoons butter in large saucepan over medium-high heat. Add shallot and leek and sauté until limp. Pour in vermouth and bring to boil. Add mussels, cover and steam until shells open, about 10 minutes. Transfer mussels to tureen using slotted spoon; set aside and cover to keep warm.

Strain mussel liquid through fine sieve set over bowl. Measure 2 cups and pour into saucepan. Place over high heat and cook until reduced by half. Remove from heat. Mix butter with flour until well blended. Return mussel liquid to high heat and gradually stir in butter mixture, blending thoroughly. Reduce heat to medium high, add cream and cook until thickened. Remove from heat. Whisk in egg yolks and mustard. Place over medium-low heat and stir until thick and creamy. Season sauce with salt and pepper.

To serve, divide mussels evenly among bowls. Serve sauce separately.

Lemon Mustard (Moutarde au Citron)

Makes about 1 cup

- 1 cup Dijon mustard
- 1 tablespoon fresh lemon juice
- 1 teaspoon honey
  Grated peel of 1 lemon

Whisk all ingredients in medium bowl. Transfer to jar with tight-fitting lid. Store in cool, dark place.

❖

SHELLFISH WITH RED PEPPER SAUCE

6 servings

 2 cups dry white wine
 ¼ cup (½ stick) butter
 ¼ cup minced fresh parsley
 ¼ cup minced shallot
 1 bay leaf
   Salt and freshly ground
   pepper
 30 mussels, scrubbed and
   debearded

 1 pound whole bay scallops *or*
   quartered sea scallops
 3 large red bell peppers,
   seeded, deveined and cut
   into large pieces
 1 tablespoon butter, room
   temperature
   Freshly ground pepper

 Parsley sprigs (garnish)

Combine wine, ¼ cup butter, parsley, shallot, bay leaf and salt and pepper in large saucepan and bring to boil over high heat. Let boil 2 minutes. Add mussels. Cover tightly and cook 3 minutes, shaking pot vigorously every 60 seconds. Remove opened mussels using slotted spoon. Continue cooking unopened mussels 2 or 3 more minutes, shaking pot every 60 seconds. Discard any remaining unopened mussels.

Discard mussel shells. Line strainer with several layers of dampened cheesecloth. Strain cooking liquid twice. Transfer to large saucepan and bring to gentle simmer over medium heat. Add scallops and poach just until opaque, about 1 minute. Remove scallops using slotted spoon. Increase heat and cook liquid until reduced to 1 cup.

Place red pepper in processor and puree 5 *full* minutes. Transfer to heavy medium saucepan. Place over lowest possible heat and cook, stirring frequently, until nearly dry, about 20 to 25 minutes. Return to processor and puree 2 minutes. Press puree through fine strainer. Reheat

reserved cooking liquid. Stir in pepper puree and butter. Season generously with pepper.

Divide mussels and scallops evenly among individual plates. Spoon sauce over. Garnish with parsley and serve.

STUFFED CRAB

4 servings

 ¼ cup (½ stick) butter
 ¾ cup chopped onion
 ½ cup chopped green onion
 1 hard-cooked egg, mashed
 2 cups cooked crabmeat
 ½ cup half and half
 ¼ cup minced fresh parsley
 3 garlic cloves, minced
 ½ teaspoon salt
 ¼ teaspoon freshly ground
   pepper
   Hot pepper sauce
 ½ cup seasoned breadcrumbs
 2 tablespoons Sherry
 4 teaspoons fresh lemon juice
   Butter

Preheat oven to 400°F. Melt butter in large skillet over medium heat. Add onion and green onion and cook until soft. Remove from heat and add egg, crab, half and half, parsley, garlic, salt, pepper, hot pepper sauce and half the breadcrumbs and stir well. Return to heat and cook about 5 minutes. Adjust seasoning. Remove from heat and stir in Sherry. Stuff into 4 crab shells (or divide among ramekins). Sprinkle with remaining breadcrumbs and lemon juice. Top each with pat of butter. Bake until tops are golden brown, about 10 to 15 minutes. Serve hot or cold.

SOFT SHELL CRABS LOUISIANA STYLE

6 servings

 18 fresh soft shell crabs (about
   2 pounds)

 ½ cup olive oil
 1¼ cups finely diced onion
 2 medium garlic cloves,
   crushed

 1 tablespoon fresh thyme
   leaves *or* 1 teaspoon dried,
   crumbled
 ½ teaspoon firmly packed
   grated lemon peel
 2 pounds tomatoes, peeled,
   seeded and chopped
   Salt and freshly ground
   pepper
 1 tablespoon finely crushed
   sassafras leaves

 **Italian parsley sprigs
   (garnish)**

To clean crabs, place on back and remove triangular apron. Lift flaps on each end and remove spongy lungs, exposing cartilage. Using scissors, cut off head just behind eyes. Squeeze body to release sack and discard.

Heat ¼ cup olive oil in heavy 2-quart saucepan over medium heat. Add onion and garlic and cook until onion is translucent, about 6 minutes, stirring frequently; *do not brown*. Add thyme and lemon peel and cook 2 minutes, stirring occasionally. Blend in tomatoes. Reduce heat and simmer until reduced to 3 cups, about 20 minutes, stirring occasionally. Remove from heat. Season with salt and pepper. Stir in sassafras leaves. (*Sauce can be prepared 1 day ahead and refrigerated.*)

Heat remaining ¼ cup oil in 12- to 14-inch skillet over medium heat. Add 6 crabs and fry until bottom side turns pink, about 3 minutes. Turn and repeat. Remove from skillet using slotted spoon; keep warm. Repeat with remaining crabs. Add sauce to skillet. Increase heat and bring to boil. Let boil until reduced to medium-thick consistency. Pour sauce onto serving platter. Arrange crabs in sauce. Garnish with parsley and serve.

❖

FLORIDA LOBSTER WITH ORANGE BUTTER

4 servings

6 tablespoons dry white wine
¾ cup whipping cream
32 tablespoons (4 sticks) butter, room temperature
Salt and freshly ground pepper
1 cup frozen orange juice concentrate, thawed

4 Florida lobsters (2 to 2½ pounds total) *or* 4 small lobster tails (about 7½ ounces each), cooked
¾ cup (about) dry white wine
¼ cup (½ stick) butter
3 medium carrots, 3 medium leeks and 2 small turnips, cut into large julienne and blanched 2 minutes

12 peeled orange sections

Reduce 6 tablespoons wine in medium saucepan over medium heat by about ¾. Add cream and reduce until thickened. Whisk in 2 cups butter 1 tablespoon at a time, incorporating each piece completely before adding another. Remove from heat and season with salt and pepper. Reduce orange juice concentrate in small saucepan over medium heat by half. Whisk into butter mixture. Set aside and keep warm.

Cut lobsters in half and remove meat from tail. Cut each tail into 5 slices. Transfer to 10-inch skillet, keeping each tail together. Add enough wine to cover bottom of skillet. Cover with foil and warm lobster over low heat. Melt ¼ cup butter in small skillet over low heat. Add vegetable julienne and stir until warmed through.

Transfer lobster to plates. Top each with sauce and 3 orange sections. Garnish with vegetable julienne and serve immediately.

FIREWORKS SHRIMP

4 servings

1 pound medium shrimp, shelled and deveined
3 garlic cloves, minced
⅓ to ½ teaspoon minced fresh ginger
1 tablespoon chili paste with garlic
3 tablespoon tomato sauce *or* tomato puree
2 tablespoons dry Sherry
1 tablespoon oyster sauce
1 tablespoon light soy sauce
1 teaspoon red wine vinegar
1 teaspoon sesame oil
½ teaspoon sugar

2 tablespoons peanut oil

4 ounces snow peas, trimmed
4 bok choy (Chinese cabbage) stalks, cut diagonally into 1½-inch pieces
3 green onions, cut diagonally into 3-inch pieces

2 tablespoons cornstarch mixed with 3 tablespoons cold water

Cut shrimp in half lengthwise and set aside. Combine minced garlic, ginger and chili paste in small bowl and set aside. Blend tomato sauce, Sherry, oyster sauce, soy sauce, vinegar, sesame oil and sugar in another bowl.

Heat wok to very hot over high heat. Add 1 tablespoon peanut oil and roll around sides of wok. When oil just begins to smoke, add shrimp and stir-fry only until translucent. Tip shrimp out onto plate and cover with wok top.

Immediately return wok to high heat. Add remaining peanut oil and roll around sides of wok. Add garlic mixture, snow peas, bok choy and green onion pieces and stir-fry until snow peas turn bright green.

Pour sauce around sides of wok. Return shrimp to wok. Stir in small amount of cornstarch solution to thicken. Taste and adjust seasoning. Serve immediately.

SKEWERED SHRIMP WRAPPED IN PANCETTA AND BASIL

16 to 18 servings

6 large shallots, minced
1 cup dry vermouth
½ cup olive oil (preferably extra virgin)
¼ cup cider vinegar
¼ cup fresh lemon juice
¼ cup tightly packed minced fresh basil *or* 4 teaspoons dried, crumbled
1 tablespoon minced fresh savory *or* 1 teaspoon dried, crumbled
⅛ teaspoon freshly ground pepper
5 pounds (about 65) jumbo shrimp, shelled and deveined

75 fresh large basil leaves
14 ounces thinly sliced pancetta

Mix first 8 ingredients in large bowl. Stir in shrimp. Refrigerate overnight.

Soak 20 to 25 bamboo skewers in water (this will prevent burning). Drain shrimp; pat dry. Wrap each with basil leaf, then cover entirely with pancetta slice. Thread 3 shrimp through tail and head onto each skewer. Cover with plastic wrap and refrigerate until ready to cook.

Prepare barbecue or preheat broiler. Grill skewers over medium-hot coals (if coals are too hot, shrimp will be tough) or in broiler pan 3 to 4 inches from heat source until shrimp are just pink and opaque; *do not overcook*. Arrange shrimp on platter and serve.

7 ❖ Entrées: One-dish Meals

Meat

RAGOUT DE LA GIRONDE

Much of the charm of this dish is its flexibility. Almost any meat can go into it and your own seasoning preferences will give it a stamp of individuality. The cooking method is unique: Half of the ingredients are arranged in the pot, cooked slowly in the oven, cooled and then refrigerated overnight. This first batch, rich with concentrated flavors, acts as a "starter" when the remaining ingredients are added the next day. The flavor will be richer if stew is prepared several days ahead and then refrigerated to mellow.*

6 to 8 servings

    8   ounces bacon *or* salt pork
        slices
    8   carrots, thinly sliced
    2   to 3 bay leaves, or to taste
    1   small bunch parsley,
        chopped
    ¼   cup chopped fresh thyme *or*
        2 teaspoons dried thyme,
        crumbled
    3   garlic cloves, minced
    8   fresh or dried figs, halved
    6   onions, sliced
    2   pounds beef stew meat, cut
        into 2-inch cubes
        Salt and freshly ground
        pepper
    2   pounds boneless pork, cut
        into 2-inch cubes
    1   pound mushrooms,
        stemmed

    ½   cup brandy
        Dry red wine (about two
        750-ml bottles)

Preheat oven to 325°F. Grease Dutch oven or large casserole. Arrange enough bacon or salt pork slices in bottom to cover. Layer with about half of carrots and 2 to 3 bay leaves. Add layer of chopped parsley, thyme and garlic. Arrange figs over seasonings and 2 sliced onions over figs. Top with half of beef and refrigerate remainder. Add another layer of 2 sliced onions. Sprinkle with salt and pepper. Top with half of pork and refrigerate remainder. Arrange half of mushrooms over and sprinkle lightly with salt and pepper.

Warm brandy in small saucepan. Ignite and pour over ragout, shaking pan gently until flame subsides. Add enough red wine to cover all ingredients. Cover and bake until wine is reduced by half, about 2 to 3 hours, adjusting oven temperature as necessary so ragoût is just bubbling slightly. Set aside to cool. Refrigerate overnight.

Bring ragoût back to room temperature. Preheat oven to 325°F. Season remaining beef and pork with salt and pepper. Layer remaining carrots, beef, onion, pork and mushrooms over top of ragoût. Pour in enough wine to barely cover all ingredients. Cover and bake until wine is reduced by half (ragoût should be bubbling slightly). Discard bay leaves. Ladle ragoût into bowls and serve.

*Half of stew can be reserved to use as base for next Ragoût de la Gironde. Fill pot with layers of same ingredients (or substitute ham, lamb, sausage, chicken or turkey for beef and pork). Add enough wine just to cover all ingredients. Cover and cook until wine is reduced by half. Remember that new ingredients are on top and concentrated sauce is at bottom, so be sure to include some rich sauce from bottom with each serving.

DIJON AND COGNAC BEEF STEW

As with most stews, this country-style dish is even better the second day. Serve with boiled new potatoes, sautéed green beans and a Pinot Noir. Follow with a refreshing Belgian endive salad.

4 to 6 servings

    4   ounces salt pork, blanched 5
        minutes (rind removed and
        reserved), cut into small
        dice
    1   large onion, chopped
    3   large shallots, chopped
    2   pounds lean beef chuck,
        trimmed and cut into
        1-inch cubes
        All purpose flour
        Butter

    ¼   cup Cognac
    2   cups beef stock, preferably
        homemade (see recipe, page
        37)
    1   tablespoon Dijon mustard
    1   tablespoon coarse French
        mustard
    2   large carrots, cut into
        bite-size pieces
        Salt and freshly ground
        pepper

    2   tablespoons (¼ stick) butter
    7   ounces small fresh
        mushrooms, halved
    ¼   cup full-bodied red wine
    1   tablespoon coarse French
        mustard

Cook salt pork in heavy nonaluminum large skillet over medium heat until golden. Remove with slotted spoon and transfer to 4-quart saucepan or Dutch oven. Add onion and shallots to skillet and brown quickly over high heat. Transfer to saucepan using slotted spoon. Coat beef cubes with flour, shaking off excess. Add butter to same skillet if necessary and melt over medium heat. Add meat in three batches and brown well on all sides; *do not allow cubes to touch or they will steam rather than brown.* Adjust heat so that particles in pan do not burn. Transfer meat to saucepan.

Pour Cognac into hot skillet and cook until only a thin glaze of liquid remains. Stir in stock and bring to boil, scraping up any browned bits clinging to pan. Add to beef along with Dijon mustard, 1 tablespoon coarse mustard and reserved pork rind. Bring to simmer, cover partially and cook until beef is barely tender, about 2 to 3 hours. Add carrot and cook until fork tender. Season to taste with salt and pepper. (*Stew can be prepared up to this point and stored in refrigerator two to three days, or in freezer up to three months.*)

Just before serving, bring stew to simmer. Heat remaining butter in medium skillet over medium-high heat. Add mushrooms and brown well. Add wine and remaining mustard and boil about 20 seconds. Stir mixture into stew and let simmer for 5 minutes.

CARBONNADE FLAMANDE

Beer is used to braise the meat for this classic Belgian beef stew. Steamed new potatoes make a delicious accompaniment.

8 servings

- 2 cups cold water
- 2 ounces salt pork *or* fatback, cut into ¼-inch cubes

- 3 tablespoons vegetable oil
- 2 garlic cloves, halved
- 4 pounds lean beef stew meat, cut into 1½-inch cubes
- 1 tablespoon all purpose flour
- ¼ teaspoon freshly ground pepper

- 2 12-ounce bottles dark beer
- ¼ cup red wine vinegar
- 3 tablespoons Dijon mustard
- 3 bay leaves
- ½ teaspoon dried thyme, crumbled
- 2 tablespoons (¼ stick) unsalted butter
- 4 large onions, sliced into ¼-inch-thick rings
- 8 medium carrots, cut into ½-inch cubes.

  Fresh parsley (garnish)

Bring water to boil with salt pork in medium saucepan over medium-high heat. Reduce heat and simmer 5 minutes. Drain and rinse salt pork under cold water. Pat dry. Transfer salt pork to deep, heavy Dutch oven.

Heat oil in heavy large skillet over medium heat. Add garlic and cook until golden brown, stirring occasionally. Discard garlic. Pat beef dry. Add beef to skillet in batches and brown well on all sides. Remove from skillet using slotted spoon and add to salt pork. Return beef to skillet with salt pork. Sprinkle with flour and stir to blend. Season with pepper. Cook 3 minutes, stirring occasionally. Return mixture to Dutch oven using slotted spoon.

Degrease skillet. Place over medium-high heat, add beer and stir, scraping up any browned bits. Blend in vinegar, mustard, bay leaves and thyme. Pour beer over meat mixture. Melt butter in same skillet over medium-high heat. Add onions and sauté until golden brown, about 7 minutes. Mix onions into meat. Bring stew to simmer. Reduce heat to low, cover and cook until meat is tender, skimming fat as necessary, 1½ to 1¾ hours; add carrots during last 30 minutes of cooking time. If stew is too dry, add more water or beef broth as necessary. If too liquid, remove beef and vegetables using slotted spoon. Cook liquid uncovered until reduced to desired consistency. Discard bay leaves. Garnish with fresh parsley and serve. (*Stew can be prepared 2 to 3 days ahead and gently rewarmed over low heat.*)

SAVORY VEAL ONE-POT (*Eingemachtes Kalbfleisch*)

4 to 5 servings

- 1¾ pounds stewing veal (cut from shoulder or breast), trimmed and cut into 1¼-inch cubes
- 2 tablespoons (¼ stick) butter
- 1 small onion, finely chopped
- ¾ cup water
- 7 to 8 peppercorns, finely crushed
- 3 ¼-inch-wide strips lemon peel
- 1 small bay leaf
- ½ teaspoon salt
  Pinch of sugar

- 3 tablespoons butter
- 8 ounces fresh small mushrooms, trimmed
- 3 leeks (with some of green), cut into ¾-inch lengths
- 1 cup fresh cauliflower florets

Sauce

- 1 tablespoon butter
- 1 tablespoon all purpose flour
- 1 egg yolk, lightly beaten
- 2 tablespoons whipping cream
- 1 tablespoon chopped capers
  Juice of ½ lemon
  Salt

- 1½ teaspoons chopped fresh parsley (garnish)
  Lemon wedges (garnish)

Combine veal in 3-quart Dutch oven or flameproof casserole with enough water to cover. Place over medium heat and bring to boil. Let boil 5 minutes. Drain veal well. Rinse out Dutch oven and return to medium heat. Add 2 tablespoons butter and stir until melted. Blend in onion and cook 3 to 4 minutes. Add water and veal. Stir in peppercorns, lemon peel, bay leaf, salt and sugar and bring to boil. Reduce heat to low, cover and simmer 1 hour.

Melt 3 tablespoons butter in medium skillet over medium-high heat. Add mushrooms and cook 3 to 4 minutes; set aside (do not wipe out skillet). Remove lemon peel and bay leaf from broth and discard. Layer mushrooms, leeks and cauliflower in Dutch oven. Cover and cook until vegetables are tender, about 15 minutes.

For sauce: About 5 minutes before vegetables are done, melt 1 tablespoon butter in same skillet over medium heat. Stir in flour and mix until smooth. Cook about 2 minutes. Gradually drain broth from Dutch oven into flour mixture and stir until sauce is smooth. Combine egg yolk and cream in small bowl. Slowly stir ¼ cup sauce into egg mixture. Gradually add egg mixture to sauce, stirring constantly. Mix in capers and lemon juice. Remove from heat. Taste and season with salt. Transfer veal and vegetables to serving dish. Pour sauce over top. Garnish with chopped parsley and lemon wedges and serve immediately.

DEVONSHIRE LAMB HASH

6 servings

- 6 slices bacon, cut into ½-inch-wide strips (about 6 ounces)
- 2 tablespoons (¼ stick) unsalted butter
- 2 cups coarsely chopped onion
- 1 teaspoon firmly packed brown sugar
- 6 medium carrots, cut into ¼-inch dice
- 2 medium garlic cloves, minced
- 1 teaspoon dried rosemary, crumbled
- 1 teaspoon salt
- ½ teaspoon dried thyme, crumbled
- ½ teaspoon ground mace
  Freshly ground pepper
- 1 tablespoon all purpose flour
- ½ cup lamb or beef stock (preferably homemade)

- ½ cup dry English hard cider
- 2 tablespoons (¼ stick) unsalted butter
- 6 slices firm home-style white bread, crusts trimmed, cut into 3-inch circles
- ¼ cup (½ stick) butter
- 1½ pounds (5 cups) cooked shoulder or leg of lamb, trimmed of fat and cut into ½-inch dice (about 4 pounds uncooked lamb with bone)
- 1½ pounds boiling potatoes, cooked, peeled and coarsely chopped
- ½ cup minced fresh parsley
- 6 poached eggs (optional)

Sauté bacon in heavy large skillet over medium-high heat until fat is rendered and bacon begins to crisp. Discard all but 1 tablespoon bacon fat. Add 2 tablespoons butter to skillet. Add onion and stir 5 minutes. Sprinkle with sugar and continue stirring until onion is almost translucent and just beginning to color, about 5 minutes. Reduce heat to medium, add carrots and garlic and stir until carrots are softened, 8 to 10 minutes. Blend in rosemary, salt, thyme, mace and pepper and stir until vegetables are colored, about 10 minutes. Reduce heat to low. Stir in flour and cook 3 minutes. Pour in stock and cider and cook, stirring, until sauce thickens, about 5 minutes. Set aside.

Melt 2 tablespoons butter in heavy large skillet over medium-high heat. Fry bread rounds until crisp and golden, turning once. Drain thoroughly.

Melt ¼ cup butter in same skillet over medium-high heat. Add lamb and potatoes and sauté until lightly golden brown. Stir into vegetable mixture. Cook over medium-high heat until bottom is crusty and edges are crisp.

Serve hash directly from skillet or turn out onto platter. Surround with bread and sprinkle with chopped parsley. Top with poached eggs if desired.

PORK RAGOUT WITH CITRUS AND LIME-CURRANT GLAZED ONIONS

Serve with noodles or rice pilaf.

4 servings

- 2 tablespoons raisins
- 3 tablespoons warm water

Pork Ragoût

- 2 pounds pork shoulder, trimmed of fat and cut into 1½-inch cubes
- 2 tablespoons all purpose flour
- 2 tablespoons (¼ stick) unsalted butter, or more
  Salt and freshly ground pepper
- 1 teaspoon unsalted butter
- ½ cup minced fresh parsley
- 3 garlic cloves, minced
- ½ cup fresh orange juice
- ½ cup veal stock, preferably homemade (see recipe, page 66)

Lime-Currant Glazed Onions

- 1 pound pearl onions, peeled
- 1 tablespoon butter
- ⅓ cup veal stock, heated
- 2 tablespoons fresh lime juice
- 2 tablespoons currant jelly
- 1½ teaspoons grated orange peel
- 1½ teaspoons grated lime peel
- ¾ teaspoon freshly grated nutmeg
- 1 teaspoon freshly grated nutmeg
- 4 3-inch strips orange peel
- 3 2-inch strips lime peel

Soak raisins in warm water about 30 minutes.

For ragoût: Pat meat dry. Flour lightly and shake off excess. Melt 2 tablespoons butter in heavy large skillet over medium heat. Add half of pork and brown, 15 to 20 minutes. Season with salt and pepper. Transfer to plate. Repeat with remaining pork, adding more butter to skillet as necessary. Set aside.

Melt 1 teaspoon butter in same skillet. Add parsley and garlic and toss 1 minute. Add orange juice, stirring with wooden spoon to scrape up any browned bits. Blend in stock and heat briefly. Return pork to skillet and stir to coat. Place aluminum foil, shiny side down, over pork, pushing down into sides of skillet. Cover skillet. Reduce heat to low and cook 10 minutes.

For onions: Cover onions with water in large saucepan and bring to boil. Cook until onions are barely tender, about 5 minutes; drain. Melt 1 tablespoon butter in same saucepan over medium-high heat. Add onions and season with salt and pepper. Add hot stock and lime juice. Drain raisins and add to saucepan with 1 tablespoon currant jelly. Stir until jelly melts, about 2 minutes. Reduce heat to medium and cook, tossing occasionally, until liquid is almost evaporated and onions are glazed, about 15 minutes.

Mix grated orange and lime peels into pork. Return foil and lid to skillet and continue cooking until pork is tender and juices run clear when pork cube is cut in half, about 5 minutes. Mix in ¾ teaspoon freshly grated nutmeg.

Add remaining 1 tablespoon currant jelly to onions and stir until jelly melts. Adjust seasoning.

Mound pork ragoût in center of large platter. Sprinkle remaining 1 teaspoon nutmeg over pork. Arrange onions around pork. Alternate orange and lime peels over onions and serve.

SAUSAGE, LEEK AND MUSHROOM PIE IN CHEDDAR CRUST

6 servings

Cheddar Cheese Crust

2½ cups all purpose flour
  1 teaspoon salt
  1 teaspoon dry mustard
  ¾ cup finely grated sharp cheddar cheese
  6 tablespoons chilled lard, cut into 1-inch pieces
  ¼ cup (½ stick) chilled unsalted butter, cut into 1-inch pieces
  6 tablespoons (about) ice water

Sausage, Leek and Mushroom Filling

1½ pounds fresh link sausage, such as English bangers *or* Italian sweet sausages
  5 medium leeks, trimmed, halved lengthwise and washed
2½ cups water
  2 tablespoons (¼ stick) unsalted butter
  1 pound button mushrooms, halved
  1 tablespoon fresh lemon juice
1½ cups whipping cream
  ¼ cup (½ stick) unsalted butter
  6 tablespoons all purpose flour
  4 egg yolks, room temperature
1½ tablespoons grated lemon peel
  2 teaspoons prepared horseradish
1½ teaspoons salt
  ¾ to 1 teaspoon fennel seed, crushed in mortar
  ¼ teaspoon freshly grated nutmeg
  Freshly ground white pepper

  Poached eggs (optional)

For crust: Sift flour, salt and dry mustard together twice into large bowl. Stir in cheese. Cut in lard and butter until mixture resembles coarse meal. Sprinkle on just enough water to gather dough into ball. Flatten into 6-inch round. Wrap dough in plastic and refrigerate at least 1 hour or overnight.

For filling: Place sausages in heavy large skillet and barely cover with water. Simmer over medium heat 10 minutes. Cool in liquid. Discard skins. Slice sausages into ½-inch pieces.

Cut leeks crosswise into 1-inch chunks. Transfer to large saucepan.

Add water and bring to boil over high heat. Reduce heat to medium and cook just until tender, 5 to 6 minutes. Drain, reserving 2 cups leek stock.

Melt 2 tablespoons butter in heavy large skillet over medium-high heat. Add mushrooms and sauté until lightly browned, about 3 minutes. Increase heat to high, add lemon juice and cook until liquid is absorbed and mushrooms are golden brown, 2 to 3 minutes. Add sausages and stir until heated through. Taste and adjust seasoning. Cool to room temperature.

Heat reserved leek stock and cream in medium saucepan over medium heat. Melt ¼ cup butter in heavy deep saucepan over medium-low heat. Add flour and stir 3 minutes. Increase heat to medium high. Whisk hot stock mixture into flour until sauce thickens. Remove from heat. Whisk in yolks one at a time. Place sauce over low heat and stir several minutes to thicken; *do not boil.* Remove sauce from heat. Stir in remaining ingredients except poached eggs.

Lightly butter deep 2-quart terrine (preferably oval) or oven-proof baking dish. Blend leeks, mushroom-sausage mixture and sauce. Pour into dish.

Position rack in center of oven and preheat to 425°F. Roll dough out to ¼-inch thickness on lightly floured surface. Moisten edges of terrine with water. Cover terrine with dough, then trim, leaving ½-inch overhang. Flute edges. Reroll scraps and cut out decorations such as leaves or flowers. Moisten undersides of decorations with water and affix to dough. Cut several holes or slits in top to allow steam to escape. (*Can be prepared ahead to this point and refrigerated overnight.*)

Bake pie until pastry is rich golden brown, about 30 minutes. Cover crust with foil and continue baking 15 minutes to ensure pie is heated through. Cool 15 to 20 minutes. Accompany with poached eggs if desired.

TOURTE OF SAUSAGE AND WINTER FRUITS

Tourte can be prepared one day ahead and reheated before serving.

6 to 8 servings

- ½ cup water
- ½ cup sour cream
- 2 tablespoons (¼ stick) unsalted butter
- 2 teaspoons sugar
- 2 teaspoons dry yeast

- 1 egg
- 1 teaspoon salt
- ½ teaspoon freshly ground white pepper
- 4 cups (about) unbleached all purpose flour

- 1 12-ounce package mixed dried pitted fruit, finely chopped
- 1 cup dry white wine

- 1 tablespoon butter
- 1 large onion, chopped
- 2 tablespoons Cognac
- 2 Granny Smith or Newtown apples, cored and finely chopped
- 1 pound kielbasa sausage, cooked, skinned and coarsely chopped
- 12 ounces Gruyère, shredded Salt and freshly ground pepper

- 1 egg beaten with 1 teaspoon cold water

Grease large bowl and set aside. Combine water, sour cream, butter and sugar in small saucepan over low heat and warm to 100°F. Remove from heat and let cool to about 60°F. Stir in yeast. Let stand until bubbly and proofed, about 10 minutes.

Transfer yeast mixture to processor. Add egg, 1 teaspoon salt and ½ teaspoon pepper and mix until blended. Mix in enough flour to make soft, slightly sticky dough. Continue mixing until dough is smooth and elastic. Transfer to prepared bowl, turning to coat entire surface. Cover and let stand at room temperature until more than doubled, about 1½ hours. Punch dough down and let rise again.

Meanwhile, combine mixed fruit and wine in medium bowl and set aside.

Melt butter in large skillet over medium-high heat. Add onion and sauté until browned. Drain wine from fruit and pour into skillet. Increase heat to high, add Cognac and boil, stirring constantly, until reduced to thin glaze. Remove from heat and stir in fruit, apples and sausage. Let cool. Blend in Gruyère. Season with salt and pepper.

Generously grease 11 × 1-inch tart pan with removable bottom. Punch dough down and transfer to lightly floured work surface. Remove ⅔ of dough and roll into 15-inch circle. Press circle into bottom of prepared pan, leaving generous overhang. Spoon fruit filling into pan. Roll out remaining dough as thinly as possible and trim to 13-inch circle (reserve scraps). Moisten edges of both pieces of dough with water. Arrange 13-inch circle over tourte, pinching edges to seal. Fold edges under to form thick coil of dough around tourte. Cut remaining scraps into long thin strips and decorate top of tourte in crisscross pattern. Cover with towel and let rise until doubled, 1 hour.

Position rack in bottom third of oven and preheat to 375°F. Brush tourte with beaten egg. Bake until golden, about 50 minutes. Cool 20 minutes in pan, then carefully unmold onto wire rack. Serve warm.

Poultry

❖ ❖ ❖ ❖ ❖ ❖ ❖ ❖ ❖ ❖ ❖ ❖ ❖ ❖ ❖

MURGHI MASALAM

A subtly seasoned and very mild curry—for more heat, add more red pepper. By Indian standards, the long list of spices is not unusual.

2 servings

- 1 whole chicken breast, skinned and boned
- 2 chicken legs, skinned and boned
- 2 chicken thighs, skinned and boned
- ½ cup plain yogurt
- 1½ teaspoons salt
- 1 garlic clove, minced
- ½ teaspoon minced fresh ginger
- ¼ teaspoon turmeric
- ¼ teaspoon crushed dried red pepper flakes, or to taste
- ⅛ teaspoon ground red pepper

Masala

- 4 tablespoons clarified butter (see recipe, page 62)
- 1 large onion, chopped
- ¼ cup shredded coconut
- 1½ teaspoons ground almonds
- 1½ teaspoons ground cumin
- ½ teaspoon ground coriander
- ¼ teaspoon mustard seed
- ⅛ teaspoon freshly grated nutmeg
- ⅛ teaspoon ground mace
- 1½ teaspoons ground cardamom
- ¼ teaspoon cinnamon
- ¼ teaspoon ground cloves

- ½ cup warm water

- 1 tablespoon milk
- ⅛ teaspoon ground saffron
- ¼ cup chopped cilantro (coriander) leaves (optional) Fresh lemon juice

Halve chicken breast lengthwise, then crosswise to make 4 pieces.

Pierce all chicken pieces with fork. Combine yogurt, salt, garlic, ginger, turmeric, crushed red pepper and ground red pepper in small bowl. Rub mixture into chicken pieces. Transfer to platter. Let stand at room temperature 2 hours.

For masala: Heat 2 tablespoons clarified butter in heavy large skillet over medium-low heat. Add onion and cook until soft and golden, about 5 to 6 minutes. Remove onion using slotted spoon and set aside to cool (do not clean skillet). Combine coconut, almonds, cumin, coriander, mustard seed, nutmeg and mace in heavy-bottomed small pan. Place over medium-low heat and toast, stirring occasionally, 2 to 3 minutes; *do not burn.*

Combine cooled onion and toasted coconut-spice mixture in processor or blender and grind to fine paste. Transfer to small bowl. Add cardamom, cinnamon and cloves, mixing well.

About 45 minutes before serving time, add remaining 2 tablespoons clarified butter to skillet in which onion was cooked. Arrange chicken pieces in skillet, scraping off excess yogurt mixture and reserving. Place skillet over medium heat and brown chicken on all sides, about 6 minutes. Spoon reserved yogurt mixture and masala over chicken and mix well. Stir in water. Cover and simmer over low heat until tender, about 30 to 40 minutes.

Warm milk in very small pan over low heat. Mix in saffron. Stir into chicken mixture and cook 2 minutes. Transfer mixture to serving dish. Sprinkle with chopped cilantro leaves and several drops of lemon juice. Serve immediately.

CHICKEN FRICASSEE WITH SPRING VEGETABLES

4 servings

1½ **pounds asparagus (tips cut off diagonally and reserved), stems trimmed, peeled and cut diagonally into 1½-inch pieces**

1 **cucumber, peeled, halved, seeded and cut into balls with small melon baller**
  Peel of 2 lemons, cut into ⅛-inch julienne
1 **cup shelled fava beans (1 pound unshelled) *or* 4 ounces green beans, trimmed**

3 **tablespoons unsalted butter**
1 **small leek (white part only), thinly sliced**
1 **cup shelled fresh peas (1 pound unshelled)**
  Pinch of sugar (optional)
1 **tablespoon fresh lemon juice**
  Salt and freshly ground pepper

2 **tablespoons (¼ stick) butter**
2 **tablespoons oil**
1 **2½- to 3-pound chicken, cut up and patted dry**
  Salt and freshly ground pepper
1 **tablespoon minced fresh tarragon *or* 1 teaspoon dried, crumbled**
1 **bay leaf**
1 **cup dry white wine *or* dry vermouth**
3 **cups (about) chicken stock, preferably homemade (see recipe, page 38)**

6 **egg yolks, room temperature**
1 **cup whipping cream**
1 **tablespoon fresh lemon juice**

1 **tablespoon butter**
1 **tablespoon *each* minced fresh parsley, chervil and tarragon (garnish)**
4 **fluted lemon slices (garnish)**

Bring large pot of salted water to boil over medium-high heat. Add asparagus pieces and cook until almost tender when pierced with knife, about 3 to 5 minutes. Add tips and cook until tender, about 2 minutes. Remove with slotted spoon and plunge into ice water to stop cooking process. Pat dry with paper towels. Repeat with cucumber, cooking about 2 minutes; lemon peel, cooking about 10 minutes; and fava beans, cooking about 5 min-

utes (4 minutes for green beans). Remove husks from fava beans.

Melt 3 tablespoons butter in medium skillet over low heat. Add leek, cover and cook 15 minutes, stirring occasionally. Add peas, cover and cook 10 minutes. Add sugar if desired. Stir in fava beans and cook until vegetables are tender, about 5 minutes. Remove from heat. Add asparagus, cucumber and 1 tablespoon lemon juice. Season to taste with salt and pepper.

Preheat oven to 325°F. Melt 2 tablespoons butter with oil in large skillet over medium-high heat. Add chicken and sauté on all sides until lightly browned. Sprinkle with salt and pepper. Transfer chicken to flameproof baking dish, arranging white meat on top. Add tarragon, bay leaf, wine and enough stock to cover chicken completely. Partially cover dish, place over low heat and bring to simmer. Cover and bake 15 minutes. Remove white meat and bake remaining pieces 5 minutes longer. Transfer chicken to platter using slotted spoon and set aside.

Discard fat from dish. Place over medium-high heat and cook until liquid is reduced to 2 cups. Discard bay leaf. Add chicken. (*Chicken and vegetables can be prepared ahead to this point and refrigerated.*)

Place dish over medium-low heat and bring mixture to simmer. When chicken is heated through, transfer to serving plate. Tent with foil to keep warm.

Whisk egg yolks and cream in large bowl. Slowly whisk heated stock into yolk mixture, then return to dish. Place over medium heat and stir with wooden spoon until mixture thickens and finger drawn across coated spoon leaves a path; *do not boil or yolks will curdle.* Stir in 1 tablespoon lemon juice and season with salt and pepper to taste.

Melt 1 tablespoon butter in medium saucepan over medium-high heat. Add vegetables and reheat. Divide chicken and sauce evenly among heated soup plates. Spoon vegetables over chicken. Sprinkle with parsley, chervil and tarragon. Garnish with lemon peel and fluted lemon slices. Serve immediately.

ROSEMARY BREAD WITH CHICKEN AND PROSCIUTTO

8 servings

Bread

¼ cup olive oil
1 tablespoon minced fresh rosemary *or* 1 teaspoon dried, crumbled
2¼ to 2½ cups warm water (105°F to 115°F)
1 tablespoon sugar
1 envelope dry yeast
6 cups unbleached all purpose flour
1 teaspoon salt
Additional unbleached all purpose flour (for kneading)

Filling

4 large whole chicken breasts, skinned, boned and halved
⅓ cup olive oil
3 tablespoons fresh lemon juice
1 teaspoon crushed peppercorns

1 tablespoon unsalted butter
1 tablespoon olive oil
4 ounces prosciutto, coarsely chopped
2 medium onions, chopped
3 small carrots, chopped
2 large celery stalks, chopped
3 medium garlic cloves, minced
2 chicken livers, trimmed and coarsely chopped
1 cup dry red wine
Coarse salt and freshly ground pepper

1 egg blended with 1 teaspoon water (glaze)
Sun-dried tomatoes (optional)

For bread: Combine ¼ cup olive oil and rosemary in small saucepan over medium-low heat and sauté rosemary until it begins to turn golden. Cool. Blend ¼ cup warm water with sugar in medium bowl. Sprinkle with yeast. Let stand until foamy, about 5 minutes. Mound flour on work surface and make well in center. Add salt, yeast mixture and rosemary-oil mixture to well. Using fingertips, gradually draw flour from inner edge of well into center until all flour is incorporated; add enough of remaining 2¼ cups water to bind dough. Lightly flour work surface and hands. Knead until smooth and elastic, about 5 minutes, adding more flour as necessary. Grease large bowl. Add dough, turning to coat entire surface. Cover with plastic wrap. Let rise in warm draft-free area until doubled in size, about 1 hour. (*Can be prepared 1 day ahead and refrigerated before rising. Dough will double in refrigerator in about 6 hours. Punch dough down, cover and leave in refrigerator until ready to proceed.*)

For filling: Marinate chicken in ⅓ cup olive oil, lemon juice and crushed peppercorns for 2 to 8 hours in nonaluminum bowl in refrigerator.

Melt 1 tablespoon butter with 1 tablespoon olive oil in heavy large skillet over medium-low heat. Add prosciutto, onions, carrots, celery and garlic. Cover and cook, stirring occasionally, until onions are translucent, about 10 minutes. Add chicken livers. Remove chicken from marinade and arrange over vegetables. Cover with round of waxed or parchment paper. Place lid on skillet and simmer until chicken just turns opaque, about 30 seconds. Transfer chicken mixture to large bowl. Deglaze skillet with wine, scraping up any browned bits. Boil until wine is reduced to about ¼ cup. Pour over chicken mixture. Season with salt and pepper. Cool.

To assemble, position rack in center of oven and preheat to 400°F. Punch dough down and knead 1 minute. Roll dough out on lightly floured surface into 18- to 20-inch round. Roll up onto rolling pin and transfer to heavy baking sheet. Spread half of vegetables in center of dough, leaving 6-inch border. Place chicken atop vegetables. Cover with remaining vegetables. Lift edges of dough over filling and gather together in center, pleating to keep circular shape. Squeeze edges to seal, then twist into topknot. Brush bread with egg glaze. Bake until golden, about 50 minutes. Place bread on rack for at least 30 minutes to cool. Serve warm or at room temperature. (*Do not hold at room temperature for more than 2 hours.*) Accompany with tomatoes if desired.

CHICKEN AND PORK ADOBO

Serve with rice and a green salad.

6 servings

2½ pounds chicken legs and thighs
1½ pounds lean boneless pork, cut into 1-inch cubes
¾ cup red wine vinegar
¾ cup water
¼ cup soy sauce
8 whole peppercorns
4 garlic cloves, minced (about 1 tablespoon)
1 bay leaf

2 tablespoons vegetable oil

Minced fresh parsley (garnish)

Arrange chicken pieces and pork in shallow 9 × 13-inch baking dish. Combine vinegar, water, soy sauce, peppercorns, garlic and bay leaf in medium bowl and blend well. Pour over meat. Cover dish and refrigerate 1 hour, turning chicken and pork occasionally.

Remove chicken and pork from marinade using slotted spoon and set marinade aside. Pat meat dry. Heat oil in heavy Dutch oven or flame-proof casserole (not cast iron) over medium-high heat. Add chicken in batches and brown well on all sides. Remove from pot. Add pork to same pan and brown well, adding more oil if necessary. Pour reserved marinade over pork. Bring to boil. Reduce heat, cover and simmer 15 minutes. Return chicken to pot. Cover and simmer until chicken and pork are tender, about 30 minutes more. Transfer chicken and pork to serving platter. Cover with foil and keep warm.

Skim any fat from sauce. Discard bay leaf. Boil sauce over high heat until reduced to about ¾ cup. Spoon over chicken and pork. Garnish with parsley and serve.

Seafood

❖ ❖ ❖ ❖ ❖ ❖ ❖ ❖ ❖ ❖ ❖ ❖ ❖ ❖

RAGOUT OF LOBSTER WITH MORELS
(Ragoût de Homard aux Morilles)

6 first-course servings

10 to 12 quarts (about) Court Bouillon (see following recipes)

3 1½- to 1¾-pound whole live unshelled lobsters

Beurre Blanc

3 cups Fish Fumet (see following recipes)

1½ cups dry white wine

½ cup mushroom stems or trimmings

2½ tablespoons Champagne vinegar

2 tablespoons minced shallot (about 1 large)

1 bay leaf
  Small pinch of fresh thyme

4 cups whipping cream

2 tablespoons roux* *or* thick velouté (optional enrichment)

½ cup (1 stick) chilled unsalted butter, cut into ¼-inch slices
  Salt and freshly ground white pepper

Lobster Sauce

2 tablespoons vegetable oil

¼ cup Cognac

2 medium onions, diced

2 medium carrots, diced

2 medium celery stalks, diced

2 teaspoons chopped fresh tarragon

2 bay leaves
  Pinch of chopped fresh thyme

1 pound plum tomatoes, peeled, seeded and chopped

3 cups dry white wine

⅓ cup dried morels (½ ounce)

2 teaspoons butter

1 teaspoon minced shallot
  Salt and freshly ground pepper

2 tablespoons (about) butter, melted

1 tablespoon (about) Cognac

6 tablespoons sliced leek, poached in chicken stock (garnish)
  Additional beurre blanc (optional garnish)

Bring enough Court Bouillon to cover lobsters to rapid boil in large stockpot. Add lobsters head first. Return court bouillon to boil. Cook lobsters until bright red and tender, about 10 minutes. Plunge lobsters into ice water; let stand 30 minutes to stop cooking process. Crack shells; do not cut meat. Cut through tail lengthwise. Holding lobsters over large bowl to catch juice, remove all shells, discarding head. Reserve meat, shells and juice.

For beurre blanc: Combine Fish Fumet, wine, mushrooms, vinegar, shallot, bay leaf and thyme in heavy large saucepan and bring to boil over high heat. Let boil until reduced to about ½ cup. Add cream and boil until reduced by half, whisking occasionally. Whisk in roux or velouté if desired. Remove from heat and whisk in 2 slices of butter. Place over very low heat and whisk in remaining butter 1 slice at a time. (If at any time sauce starts to break down, remove from heat and whisk in 2 slices of butter.) Strain sauce through fine sieve. Season with salt and white pepper. Set aside at room temperature.

For lobster sauce: Heat oil in large skillet over medium-high heat. Stir in reserved lobster shells. Pour Cognac into corner of skillet, heat briefly and ignite, shaking skillet gently until flames subside. Add onions, carrots, celery, tarragon, bay leaves and thyme and sauté 5 min-

utes. Stir in tomatoes, wine and reserved lobster juice and cook until liquid is reduced by about half, about 20 minutes. Strain mixture through fine sieve or chinois set over bowl, pressing firmly with back of spoon to extract all liquid. Transfer liquid to saucepan. Place over medium-low heat and cook until reduced to ½ to ¾ cup. Blend in beurre blanc. Set aside.

Combine morels in small bowl with just enough lukewarm water to cover. Let stand until water is clear, changing water about 5 times, about 1 hour total. Drain well; pat dry. Trim off tough ends of stems. Melt 2 teaspoons butter in small skillet over low heat. Add shallot and morels and cook until morels are lightly glazed, stirring occasionally, about 10 minutes. Season with salt and pepper. Set aside for garnish.

Preheat oven to 300°F to 325°F. Arrange lobster in shallow baking dish. Brush with melted butter. Sprinkle with about 1 tablespoon Cognac. Transfer to oven and heat through, about 3 to 4 minutes. Meanwhile, gently reheat sauce in top of double boiler over low heat, whisking constantly. Spoon lobster sauce onto heated individual plates. Arrange lobster decoratively on sides of plates. Garnish each serving with morels and leek. Fill 2 plastic squeeze bottles fitted with narrow tips with additional beurre blanc. Pipe sauce onto plates in decorative pattern. Serve ragoût immediately.

*Make roux from equal parts butter and flour. Heat butter in heavy saucepan until foam almost disappears. Remove pan from heat and whisk in flour. Return pan to medium-low heat, whisking constantly until mixture resembles a honeycomb and is pale straw color, about 2 minutes.

Fish Fumet
Makes 1½ quarts

1 tablespoon butter

1 large onion, sliced

½ small carrot, sliced
½ cup mushroom stems and pieces
4 pounds fish heads and bones
quarts water
2 cups dry white wine
1 very small bouquet garni (thyme, bay leaf and parsley stems tied in cheesecloth bag)
½ teaspoon salt
6 white peppercorns

Melt butter in large saucepan over medium-high heat. Add onion and carrot and sauté 5 minutes. Stir in mushrooms. Blend in fish heads and bones. Reduce heat to low, cover and cook until bones fall apart, about 15 minutes. Increase heat to high, stir in water and wine and bring to brisk boil. Reduce heat to medium, add bouquet garni and salt and cook, uncovered, 35 minutes, adding peppercorns during last 10 minutes. Strain before using.

Court Bouillon

Makes about 3 quarts

1½ quarts water
1½ quarts dry white wine
4 cups fresh parsley (about 1 bunch)
2 medium onions, diced
2 medium carrots, diced
2 medium celery stalks, diced
6 to 8 ¼-inch-thick lemon slices
4 teaspoons salt
2 bay leaves
2 tarragon sprigs *or* large pinch of dried, crumbled
2 thyme sprigs *or* large pinch of dried, crumbled

Combine all ingredients in 6- to 8-quart stockpot and bring to boil over medium-high heat. Let boil 15 minutes. Strain bouillon before using.

DEEP-DISH SEAFOOD PIZZA

Manufactured from the same high temperature clay as the baking stone, the deep-dish pizza pan ensures a crisp crust for Sicilian-style pizzas and other doughs baked in it. A stoneware pie pan or cast-iron skillet can, however, be substituted. To adjust filling proportions for another pan, measure the amount of dried beans it will contain, then use the same volume of ingredients. Any combination of fish and shellfish can be used. Estimate the size of crust needed by measuring the diameter and depth of pan.

4 to 6 first-course or 3 to 4 main-course servings

Basic Pizza Dough for 14-inch pizza (see recipe, page 120)

2 pounds tomatoes (preferably Italian pear tomatoes), peeled, seeded, juiced and finely chopped
2 teaspoons salt
2 to 3 teaspoons minced fresh garlic
Freshly ground pepper

8 to 12 ounces squid, cleaned, trimmed and cut into ½-inch rings (separate tentacles)
2 tablespoons olive oil
½ to ¾ teaspoon minced fresh oregano *or* basil *or* ⅛ teaspoon dried, crumbled

1 pound (¾ inch thick) halibut *or* other fresh white-fleshed fish, boned and skinned*
¼ cup olive oil
1½ teaspoons minced fresh oregano *or* basil *or* ½ teaspoon dried, crumbled

8 ounces medium shrimp, shelled and deveined
5 to 6 ounces whole bay scallops *or* halved or quartered sea scallops
3 tablespoons olive oil
¾ teaspoon minced fresh oregano *or* basil *or* ¼ teaspoon dried, crumbled

Cornmeal
1 egg white, lightly beaten

10 clams, scrubbed**

2 tablespoons minced shallot

4 ounces *each* freshly grated mozzarella cheese (preferably whole milk) and Italian Fontina or bel paese cheese, combined (1 cup)
Salt and freshly ground pepper
3 tablespoons freshly grated Parmesan cheese

1 tablespoon fresh lemon juice
1 tablespoon minced fresh chives
1 tablespoon minced fresh parsley
Lemon wedges (garnish)

Prepare basic dough and set aside to rise.

Place tomatoes in colander. Sprinkle with salt and let drain at least 30 minutes. Squeeze until completely dry (potato ricer works well). Roll in cheesecloth or kitchen towel to remove any remaining moisture. Transfer to bowl. Add garlic and pepper and mix well.

Combine squid, 2 tablespoons olive oil and ½ to ¾ teaspoon fresh oregano in small bowl, mixing well.

Cut halibut into ¾-inch squares. Transfer to another bowl. Add ¼ cup olive oil and 1½ teaspoons fresh oregano, mixing well. Set aside in refrigerator until ready to use.

Combine shrimp and scallops in medium bowl. Add 3 tablespoons olive oil and remaining ¾ teaspoon fresh oregano, mixing well. Set aside in refrigerator until ready to use.

Position rack in center of oven and preheat to 500°F. Shape pizza dough into 14-inch circle following Basic Pizza Dough directions. Sprinkle bottom of 10-inch deep-dish pan with cornmeal. Fit dough into dish, trimming so dough extends ½ inch beyond rim, then fold back on itself and crimp or flute decoratively. Brush dough with egg white. Reduce oven temperature to 425°F. Bake 10 minutes.

Meanwhile, add water to heavy large pot to depth of ½ inch. Bring to boil over high heat. Add clams. Cover, reduce heat to medium high and steam, stirring occasionally, until clams open, about 5 to 7 minutes.

If any clams remain shut after 7 minutes, remove opened clams and continue steaming remainder; discard any clams that do not open. Return clams to pot. Cover and remove from heat.

Sprinkle partially baked dough with shallot, half of mozzarella mixture and all of tomatoes. Drain squid thoroughly; season with salt and pepper. Arrange over crust. Bake 8 minutes. Drain halibut and season with salt and pepper. Arrange on pizza and top with remaining cheese mixture. Bake 4 more minutes. Drain shrimp and scallops well. Season with salt and pepper. Place over pizza. Sprinkle with Parmesan cheese. Bake just until shrimp turn pink, about 3 minutes.

With bulb baster, remove any liquid released from tomatoes and fish during cooking. Sprinkle pizza with lemon juice, chives and parsley. Arrange clams in half shells over top. Garnish with lemon wedges. Serve hot.

*If fish used is less than ³/₄ inch thick, adjust cooking time accordingly, using guideline of about 9 minutes cooking per inch thickness.

**Mussels can be substituted for clams or used in addition to clams.

SCANDINAVIAN SEAFOOD STEW

This full-flavored dish needs only a green salad, Swedish rye bread and a dry Chablis to make a party dinner.

8 servings

 1 pound tiny onions, peeled*
 2 large leeks (white part only), cleaned and chopped
 2 medium carrots, finely chopped
 3 tablespoons butter
 1 teaspoon dried thyme *or* 1 tablespoon minced fresh
 1 teaspoon dried dillweed *or* 1 tablespoon minced fresh dill
 ¼ teaspoon dried savory *or* ³/₄ teaspoon minced fresh
   Generous pinch of ground cardamom

 1½ pounds new potatoes, peeled and cut into small cubes
 7 cups Spiced Fish Stock (see following recipe)
 ½ cup whipping cream
 1½ pounds clams *or* mussels, soaked in cold water with 1 teaspoon salt for 1 hour, rinsed, scrubbed and debearded
 1 pound medium shrimp, shelled and deveined
 1 pound cod fillet, cut into bite-size pieces
 1 pound haddock fillet, cut into bite-size pieces
 ¼ to ½ teaspoon salt
 ¼ teaspoon freshly ground pepper
 ½ cup minced green onion tops (garnish)
 1 tablespoon minced fresh dill (optional garnish)

Combine onions, leeks, carrots, butter, herbs and cardamom in heavy, nonaluminum 6-quart pan. Cover and cook over low heat until vegetables are wilted, about 20 minutes. Add potato and stock and simmer until onions and potato are tender. (*Can be prepared a day ahead up to this point and chilled.*)

About 15 minutes before serving, bring to gentle simmer. Stir in cream. Add clams or mussels, cover and cook very gently until shells *begin* to open. Add shrimp and cook until barely firm, about 1 minute longer. Stir in cod and haddock and season with salt and pepper. Ladle into bowls. *Do not allow the fish to overcook as it continues to cook in the stock.* Discard any clams or mussels that have not opened and sprinkle each serving with some of the onion tops and dill. Serve immediately.

*For ease in peeling tiny onions, drop them into boiling water and boil one minute. Drain in colander. Rinse with cold water until cool, then trim off tops and bottoms. Make a slit in skin and slip off.

Spiced Fish Stock

This recipe produces a more robust stock than most. It adds much to Scandinavian Seafood Stew and to almost any fish sauce or stewed creation as well. Although trimmings from white-fleshed fish (turbot, sole or flounder) are preferred, you may use whatever is available. Collect the trimmings over a period of time and store them in the freezer. When five or six pounds have accumulated, it is time to make stock. Stock can be made 1 to 2 days ahead and refrigerated, or frozen up to 3 months.

Makes about 3 quarts

 5 to 6 pounds fish trimmings (bones, heads, tails), preferably from white-fleshed fish (thaw if frozen)
 2 large onions, sliced
 1 large carrot, sliced
 26 whole white peppercorns
 4 unpeeled garlic cloves
 4 whole allspice berries
 3 whole cardamom pods
 2 parsley sprigs
 1 whole clove
 ½ teaspoon dried thyme
   Salt
 1 bottle (750 ml) dry white wine (Fumé Blanc, Chardonnay *or* Chablis)
 2 quarts water

Place fish trimmings in heavy, nonaluminum 8-quart stockpot. Add onions, carrot, peppercorns, garlic, allspice, cardamon, parsley, clove, thyme and salt. Cover and cook over medium-low heat until fish has released its juices, about 15 minutes, watching carefully to avoid burning. Add wine and water and slowly bring to simmer, skimming off any foam that rises to surface. Partially cover and simmer gently 45 minutes. Strain through several layers of dampened cheesecloth.

❖

8 ❖ Entrées: Eggs and Vegetables

Eggs

❖ ❖ ❖ ❖ ❖ ❖ ❖ ❖ ❖ ❖ ❖ ❖ ❖ ❖

TIMBALE RUSTICA

Ham or prosciutto can be substituted for pork sausage in this tasty timbale. Serve hot or at room temperature.

4 servings

   2 **small green bell peppers (7 ounces total)**
   2 **large red bell peppers (10 ounces total)**

   1 **pound fennel (fronds removed, minced and reserved for garnish)** *or* **stalks from 2 Swiss chard bunches**
   2 **tablespoons (¼ stick) butter**
   2 **tablespoons olive oil**
   2 **small leeks (white part only) cut into ⅛-inch julienne (about 1 cup)**

   1 **tablespoon butter**
   1 **tablespoon oil**
   1 **precooked smoked pork sausage, halved lengthwise and cut into ⅛-inch slices**

   2 **tablespoons hot water**
1½ **teaspoons saffron threads, crushed in mortar**
   8 **eggs, room temperature, beaten**
   1 **small garlic clove, minced**
   1 **cup whipping cream**
   ½ **cup freshly grated Parmesan cheese**
   1 **teaspoon salt**
   ¾ **teaspoon minced fresh thyme** *or* **marjoram** *or* **¼ teaspoon dried, crumbled**
   ¼ **teaspoon freshly ground pepper**

   Tomato Coulis (see following recipe)

Preheat broiler. Arrange peppers on broiler pan and broil 6 inches from heat source, turning with tongs until charred on all sides, about 15 to 20 minutes. Transfer to plastic bag and seal tightly. Let steam 10 minutes. Peel peppers and cut in half. Discard cores and seeds. Rinse under cold water. Pat dry and cut into ⅛-inch julienne.

Peel strings off fennel bulbs with knife and discard any tough outer leaves. Core and slice into ¼-inch julienne (or peel Swiss chard stalks and slice into ¼-inch julienne). Heat 2 tablespoons each butter and oil in heavy 10-inch skillet over medium-low heat. Add fennel and leeks. Cover and cook, stirring occasionally, about 15 minutes. Add roasted peppers. Cover and cook until leeks are tender, about 5 minutes. Turn into large mixing bowl. Let cool at least 10 minutes.

Preheat oven to 325°F. Butter 2-quart loaf pan. Line with parchment paper; butter paper. Melt 1 tablespoon butter with oil in small skillet over medium heat. Add sausage and sauté until lightly browned on all sides, about 3 minutes. Add to pepper mixture.

Pour 2 tablespoons hot water into small bowl. Add saffron and stir until dissolved. Blend into pepper mixture with eggs, garlic, whipping cream, Parmesan, salt, thyme or marjoram and pepper. Taste and adjust seasoning, adding more crushed saffron threads if deeper golden color is desired.

Pour mixture into prepared loaf pan. Cover with buttered parchment paper, buttered side down. Set in deep large pan. Add enough simmering water to come within 1 inch of top of loaf pan. Bake until faint line of shrinkage appears around sides of timbale and tester inserted in center comes out clean, about 1 to 1¼ hours. Remove loaf pan from water and let stand 15 minutes. Discard parchment paper. Gently pour off any liquid that has accumulated. Run tip of sharp thin knife around inside edge of pan and unmold onto warm serving platter. Spoon Tomato Coulis around mold and garnish with reserved fennel fronds.

Tomato Coulis

Can be prepared ahead and reheated slowly just before serving.

Makes about 1½ cups.

   2 **tablespoons olive oil**
   1 **tablespoon minced shallot**
   2 **pounds tomatoes, peeled, cored, seeded, juiced (juice reserved) and coarsely chopped**
      Salt and freshly ground pepper
      Sugar (optional)
   1 **tablespoon butter**

Heat olive oil in heavy large saucepan over medium-high heat. Add shallot and sauté until translucent, about 3 minutes. Strain reserved tomato juice into pan. Add chopped tomatoes. Reduce heat to medium low, cover and cook, stirring occasionally, until liquid has evaporated and tomatoes are soft enough to puree with back of spoon, about 30 to 40 minutes. (Toward end of cooking time, reduce heat and stir tomatoes frequently to avoid burning.) Season with salt and pepper to taste. Add sugar if desired. Reduce heat to low and whisk in butter.

CURRIED ROLLED SOUFFLE

6 to 8 servings

Soufflé Roll

- 2 tablespoons (¼ stick) butter
- 2 tablespoons all purpose flour
- 1 cup milk
- ½ teaspoon salt
- 5 eggs, separated (room temperature)

Filling

- 2 tablespoons (¼ stick) butter
- 1 tablespoon curry powder
- 1½ tablespoons all purpose flour
- ¾ cup hot chicken stock, preferably homemade (see recipe, page 38)
- 1 teaspoon fresh lemon juice
- 1 cup cooked slivered crab, shrimp *or* chicken breast
- ¼ cup whipping cream
  Salt and freshly ground white pepper
- 2 tablespoons (¼ stick) butter, melted
  Fresh Mint Chutney (see following recipe)

For soufflé roll: Preheat oven to 350°F. Butter 11 × 17-inch jelly roll pan. Line with waxed or parchment paper; butter paper. Melt 2 tablespoons butter in medium saucepan over low heat. Add flour and cook, stirring constantly, 3 minutes; *do not brown.* Remove from heat and stir in milk and salt. Place over medium-high heat and stir until mixture thickens. Remove from heat and whisk in yolks one at a time. Beat whites in large bowl until stiff but not dry. Stir ⅓ of whites into milk mixture, then gently fold in remaining whites. Spread mixture in prepared pan. Bake until soufflé is puffed and light golden, about 20 minutes.

For filling: Melt butter in medium saucepan over low heat. Stir in curry powder and simmer gently 2 minutes. Add flour and stir 3 minutes. Whisk in stock and lemon juice. Increase heat to medium and cook until thick. Stir in shellfish or chicken. Add cream and heat through. Season with salt and white pepper. (*Can be prepared up to 2 days ahead and refrigerated. Bring to room temperature before continuing.*)

Remove soufflé from oven; do not turn off oven. Dampen nonterry kitchen towel in hot water and wring dry. Pull tautly over pan. Top with cutting board or baking sheet. Turn pan over, letting soufflé invert onto towel; peel off waxed paper. Let cool several minutes. Spread filling evenly over soufflé, leaving 1-inch border on all sides. Using towel as aid, roll soufflé up lengthwise. Transfer to baking dish. Drizzle with melted butter. Return roll to oven and bake until puffed and golden, 10 to 12 minutes. Serve immediately with Fresh Mint Chutney.

Fresh Mint Chutney

Makes about ¾ cup

- 2 ounces fresh mint leaves
- 2 to 3 tablespoons chopped onion
- 1 tablespoon chopped green chilies
- 1 teaspoon chopped fresh ginger
- 1 teaspoon sugar
  Salt
- 1 tablespoon cider vinegar

Combine mint, onion, chilies, ginger, sugar and salt in processor or blender and mix to paste. With machine running, gradually add vinegar. Transfer to small container with tight-fitting lid and refrigerate up to 2 days.

❖

SHRIMP HUEVOS RANCHEROS

In this variation on a favorite Tex-Mex dish, puffy corn tortillas are stuffed with a savory shrimp and egg filling.

12 servings

- 5 to 6 tablespoons butter
- 24 small to medium shrimp, halved horizontally *or* 1½ cups lobster or langostino, sliced
- 8 green onions (with 1½ inches green), thinly sliced
- 4 fresh green chilies (Anaheim or poblano), roasted, peeled, seeded (see footnote to recipe, page 11) and cut into ½ × 1-inch strips
- 8 eggs, beaten to blend
- 1 teaspoon salt, or to taste
- 6 tablespoons sour cream, room temperature
- 12 masa tortillas (see recipe, page 9)
  Sliced green onions (garnish)
  Southwest Tomato Sauce (see following recipe)

Melt butter in medium skillet over medium-high heat. Add shrimp, onions and chilies and sauté just until shrimp turn pink, about 1½ minutes. Reduce heat to medium low, add eggs and gently scramble until just set. Season with salt. Stir in sour cream. Remove from heat. Using sharp knife, cut slit in side of tortilla, forming pocket. Spoon in egg mixture, dividing evenly. Transfer to platter. Sprinkle with green onions. Pass sauce separately.

Southwest Tomato Sauce

Makes about 1 quart

- 4 to 5 large tomatoes *or* one 28-ounce can Italian plum tomatoes, broken up with fork
- ¼ cup vegetable oil *or* olive oil
- 1 medium onion, minced
- ½ green bell pepper, minced
- 2 garlic cloves, minced
- ½ cup red wine vinegar
- 6 tablespoons tomato paste

6   medium basil leaves *or* 4 to
5 cilantro (coriander) sprigs
1   teaspoon salt
Freshly ground pepper
¾   cup loosely packed fresh
parsley *or* cilantro leaves,
minced

Cut out stem end of tomatoes (do not core). Broil tomatoes 4 inches from heat source until skin is softened, turning occasionally. Transfer to processor or blender and puree until smooth.

Heat oil in medium skillet over medium-high heat. Add onion, bell pepper and garlic and sauté until beginning to soften, 3 to 4 minutes. Add tomatoes and blend well. Stir in vinegar, tomato paste, basil, salt and pepper. Simmer until sauce is medium-thick, 8 to 10 minutes. Stir in parsley. Serve sauce warm or at room temperature.

Vegetables

❖   ❖   ❖   ❖   ❖   ❖   ❖   ❖   ❖   ❖   ❖   ❖   ❖   ❖

PARSNIP STEW WITH SMOKING DAY BISCUITS

A cross between an early New England chowder and stew that features a variety of winter vegetables, this stew can be prepared several days ahead and refrigerated, or frozen up to 3 months. The biscuits were meant to use up those bits of deep-smoked country bacon from last year's porker. This hearty combination needs only fruit and cheese to follow.

4 to 6 servings

12   ounces lean salt pork, cut into small dice
2   medium carrots, diced
1   large onion, finely chopped
3   large or 5 small parsnips, peeled, cored if necessary and diced
1   cup tightly packed chopped green cabbage
1   medium-size potato, peeled and diced
5   cups rich chicken stock, preferably homemade (see recipe, page 38)
1   bay leaf
Pinch of ground cloves
Generous pinch of dried thyme *or* ¼ teaspoon minced fresh
Salt and freshly ground pepper

Smoking Day Biscuits (see following recipe)

Blanch salt pork by dropping into boiling water for 5 minutes. Drain well and rinse. Sauté salt pork in heavy 4- to 5-quart saucepan over medium heat until golden. Remove with slotted spoon and set aside. Pour off all but about 2 tablespoons fat from pan. Add carrots and onion and sauté until onion is soft. Add salt pork and remaining ingredients (except biscuits) and bring to simmer. Cook uncovered until vegetables are crisp-tender, about 10 minutes. Serve from tureen and accompany with biscuits.

Smoking Day Biscuits

Makes about 2 dozen

1   cup all purpose unbleached flour
1   cup cake flour (do not use self-rising)
4   teaspoons baking powder
½   teaspoon salt
¼   cup (½ stick) chilled unsalted butter, cut into 4 pieces
2   slices bacon, cooked crisp, drained and crumbled
2   small green onions, minced
⅔   to ¾ cup cold milk

Unsalted butter
Honey

Preheat oven to 425°F. Grease baking sheet and set aside. Combine dry ingredients in deep bowl and mix well. Cut in butter with pastry blender until mixture resembles coarse meal. Toss in bacon and green onions using fork. Add enough milk to make dough moist but not wet, tossing with fork until just blended; *do not overwork dough.*

Turn onto floured board and knead *only* once or twice. Gently shape into rectangle ½ inch thick. Cut into squares and place ⅛ to ¼ inch apart on baking sheet. Bake until puffed and golden, 15 to 18 minutes. Serve immediately with unsalted butter and honey.

EGGPLANT "CREPES" SORRENTO

A hearty meatless do-ahead dish that can be doubled easily or even tripled for a party. An escarole and curly endive salad and a Zinfandel or Valpolicella are the perfect complements.

6 to 8 servings

4   medium eggplants, cut into ¼-inch-thick ovals from stem end to bottom (about 6 to 7 slices per eggplant)
Salt

Olive oil

Mushroom-Cheese Filling

1   tablespoon olive oil
1   large onion, minced
12   ounces fresh mushrooms, sliced
¼   cup (about) dried mushrooms (preferably cèpes), soaked in ½ cup warm water 30 minutes and drained well (reserve liquid)

Salt and freshly ground
pepper
12 ounces ricotta cheese
½ cup *each* freshly grated
Parmesan and Romano
cheeses, preferably imported
(about 2½ ounces each)
3 green onions, chopped
1 egg
1 tablespoon chopped fresh
basil leaves *or* ¾ teaspoon
dried, crumbled
½ teaspoon chopped fresh
oregano *or* ⅛ teaspoon
dried, crumbled
½ teaspoon fresh mint leaves
or ⅛ teaspoon dried,
crumbled

Tomato-Basil Sauce

2 tablespoons olive oil
1 large onion, minced
1 large garlic clove, minced
1½ teaspoons chopped fresh
basil leaves *or* generous ½
teaspoon dried, crumbled
Generous pinch of dried
oregano, crumbled
3 cups tomato puree
1 tablespoon tomato paste
Salt and freshly ground
pepper

6 ounces mozzarella or
scamorza* cheese, shredded

Place eggplant in colander and
sprinkle lightly with salt. Set aside
30 minutes to drain. Rinse under
running water; pat dry.

Preheat oven to 475°F. Brush
large baking sheet with olive oil.
Lightly brush 1 side of eggplant
slices with oil. Arrange about ¼ of
eggplant slices oiled side down on
prepared baking sheet. Bake in
batches until softened, about 5 minutes. (This can also be done on baking sheet lined with oiled aluminum
foil; while 1 batch is baking, next
can be arranged on another piece of
foil.) If time allows, spread baked
slices on paper towels. Top with
more paper towels, then weight with
heavy chopping board. Let stand
overnight to drain thoroughly and
flatten slightly.

For filling: Heat olive oil in
heavy nonaluminum large skillet
over very low heat. Add onion, cover
and cook slowly to mellow flavor,

about 30 minutes, stirring occasionally. Increase heat to high, add
fresh mushrooms and sauté until
lightly browned. Add dried mushrooms with liquid and cook until
moisture has evaporated. Let cool.
Season to taste with salt and pepper.
Combine ricotta, Parmesan, Romano, green onions, egg, basil,
oregano and mint in large bowl and
beat well. Blend in cooled mushroom mixture. (*Filling can be prepared 1 day ahead and refrigerated.*)

For sauce: Heat olive oil in
heavy nonaluminum large skillet over
very low heat. Add onion, cover and
cook slowly to mellow flavor, about
30 minutes, stirring occasionally. Uncover, increase heat to medium, add
garlic, basil and oregano and stir
30 seconds. Blend in tomato puree
and tomato paste with salt and pepper
to taste. Bring to boil. Let boil until thickened slightly, about 5 minutes. (*Sauce can be prepared 2 months
ahead and frozen.*)

Grease shallow large baking
dish. Spread about 1 tablespoon
filling over each piece of eggplant,
leaving 1-inch border at thicker end.
Starting at narrower end, roll eggplant up jelly roll style. Transfer to
prepared baking dish. (*Can be prepared up to 1 day ahead to this point.
Cover tightly with plastic wrap and
refrigerate.*)

Preheat oven to 375°F. Spread
sauce over rolls. Sprinkle with
shredded cheese. Bake until sauce is
bubbling and cheese begins to color,
about 45 minutes. Serve immediately.

**A mild, chewy, slightly salty dried mozzarella
traditionally made from water buffalo milk.
Available at Italian markets and many specialty
foods stores.*

ZUCCHINI LASAGNE WITH CACIOCAVALLO CHEESE

2 servings

Sauce

3 tablespoons olive oil
½ cup finely chopped onion

1 celery stalk, finely chopped
1 garlic clove, finely chopped
1 pound fresh tomatoes,
chopped *or* one 1-pound
can whole tomatoes,
drained and chopped
2 tablespoons minced fresh
parsley
1 tablespoon tomato paste
1 tablespoon minced fresh
basil *or* 1 teaspoon dried,
crumbled
Salt and freshly ground
pepper

Filling

2 tablespoons (¼ stick) butter
1 small zucchini (about 4
ounces), cut into ¼-inch
slices
4 ounces mushrooms,
stemmed and cut into
¼-inch slices
¼ cup whipping cream
2 tablespoons freshly grated
Parmesan cheese

2 lasagne noodles
4 ounces caciocavallo cheese,
coarsely grated (provolone
can be substituted)
¼ cup freshly grated Parmesan
or Romano cheese

For sauce: Heat olive oil in large skillet over medium heat. Add onion,
celery and garlic and cook until
softened, about 5 minutes. Stir in
tomatoes, parsley, tomato paste and
basil and simmer 20 to 25 minutes,
breaking up tomatoes as sauce
cooks. Puree sauce in food mill or by
pressing through strainer. Season
to taste with salt and pepper (be
careful; caciocavallo can be salty).

For filling: Melt butter in small
skillet over high heat. Add zucchini
and mushrooms and sauté until
lightly browned around edges. Stir
in cream and continue cooking until
cream is reduced to smooth, syrupy
consistency. Let cool. Blend in 2
tablespoons Parmesan. Season with
salt and pepper.

Bring large saucepan of salted
water to rapid boil over high heat.
Add noodles and cook just until
tender, about 10 to 15 minutes.
Drain well; pat dry with paper towels. Cut noodles in half crosswise.
Cover bottoms of 2 individual grat-

in dishes with thin layer of tomato sauce. Lay 1 piece of noodle in each dish, trimming or tucking in any excess. Spoon ¼ of filling over each. Sprinkle with half of caciocavallo. Repeat layers of tomato sauce, pasta, filling and cheese. Top with remaining tomato sauce. Sprinkle with grated Parmesan or Romano. (*Can be prepared ahead to this point, covered tightly with foil or plastic and refrigerated or frozen. Bring to room temperature before baking.*)

Preheat oven to 450°F. Bake until lasagne is bubbly and cheese is lightly browned, about 10 to 15 minutes. Let lasagne stand 5 minutes before serving.

Savory Pies

WHITE CHEESE TART
(Tarte au Fromage Blanc)

6 servings

Pastry

- 1¼ cups sifted all purpose flour
- ½ cup (1 stick) well-chilled butter, cut into ¼-inch pieces
- ½ teaspoon Quatre-Epices (see recipe, page 5)
- 1 egg, beaten to blend
- ½ teaspoon salt

Filling

- 6 tablespoons (¾ stick) butter, room temperature
- 4 ounces cream cheese, room temperature
- 2 tablespoons all purpose flour
- 4 ounces creamed small curd cottage cheese
- ⅓ cup sour cream
- 2 eggs
- 2 tablespoons chopped fresh parsley, or to taste
- 1 medium garlic clove, mashed
  Pinch of dried thyme, crumbled
  Salt and very coarsely ground pepper

For pastry: Place flour in large bowl. Cut in butter and spice mixture using pastry blender. Quickly work together with fingertips until mixture resembles coarse meal; *do not overwork or pastry will be tough.* Add beaten egg and salt and quickly work into dough. Flatten dough into disc. Wrap tightly in plastic and refrigerate at least 1 hour. (*Can be prepared 1 day ahead and refrigerated.*)

For filling: Blend butter and cream cheese in large bowl of electric mixer until smooth. Mix in flour. Combine cottage cheese, sour cream and eggs in blender and mix at low speed until completely smooth, about 30 seconds. Gradually blend cottage cheese mixture into butter mixture. Mix in parsley, garlic and thyme. Season with salt and pepper to taste. (*Filling can be prepared 1 day ahead and refrigerated.*)

Preheat oven to 425°F. Roll dough out on lightly floured surface into circle ⅙ inch thick. Fit dough into 8- to 9-inch ceramic pie dish. Prick dough with fork. Line dough with foil. Fill with dried beans or pie weights. Bake until crust is well set, about 12 minutes. Remove foil and weights and continue baking until light brown. Let cool on wire rack until ready to use.

Position rack at lowest level of oven and preheat to 375°F. Pour filling into baked pastry. Bake 18 minutes. Set tart on highest oven rack and continue baking until top is puffed and golden brown, 17 to 22 minutes. Let tart cool about 1 hour before serving.

SPINACH, MUSHROOM AND GRUYERE CHEESECAKE

Serve with homemade tomato sauce.

12 servings

- 1 tablespoon unsalted butter (for pan)
- 1⅓ cups fine breadcrumbs, toasted
- 5 tablespoons unsalted butter, melted

- 1½ pounds cream cheese, room temperature
- ¼ cup whipping cream
- ½ teaspoon salt
- ¼ to ½ teaspoon freshly grated nutmeg
- ¼ teaspoon ground red pepper
- 4 eggs
- 4 ounces Gruyère, shredded
- 1 10-ounce package frozen chopped spinach, thawed and squeezed dry
- 2½ tablespoons finely chopped green onion

- 3 tablespoons unsalted butter
- 8 ounces mushrooms, finely chopped
  Salt and freshly ground pepper

Preheat oven to 350°F. Butter 9-inch springform pan. Mix breadcrumbs and melted butter. Press mixture firmly onto bottom and sides of pan. Bake until set, 8 to 10 minutes. Cool.

Mix cream cheese, cream, salt, nutmeg and red pepper in blender or processor until smooth. Blend in eggs. Divide mixture evenly between 2 medium bowls. Stir Gruyère into one half. Mix spinach and onion into remainder. Pour spinach filling into pan.

Preheat oven to 325°F. Melt remaining butter in large skillet over medium-high heat. Add mushrooms and cook until all moisture is evaporated, about 10 minutes, stirring frequently. Season with salt and pepper. Spoon mushrooms over spinach filling. Carefully pour cheese filling over top. Set pan on baking sheet. Bake 1¼ hours. Turn oven off and cool cheesecake about 1 hour with door ajar. Transfer to rack. Remove springform. Cool to room temperature before serving.

GOAT CHEESE PIZZA WITH PROSCIUTTO AND SAGE

Makes one 12-inch pizza

Basic Pizza Dough for 12-inch pizza (see recipe, page 120)

1 **large tomato (about 8 to 9 ounces), peeled, seeded, juiced and diced**
¾ **teaspoon salt**

4 **ounces chèvre (Montrachet, Pyramide, Banon, Crottin de Chavignol *or* Lezay), trimmed**
1½ **cups whole milk ricotta (about 12 ounces)**
2 **ounces prosciutto, minced (about ½ cup)**
¼ **cup freshly grated Parmesan cheese**
½ **teaspoon fresh sage, minced *or* ⅛ teaspoon dried, crumbled**
   Freshly ground pepper

   Olive oil
2 **tablespoons pine nuts**

   Olive oil
   Sage leaves (garnish)

Prepare dough. Set aside to rise.

Place tomato in colander. Sprinkle with salt and let drain at least 30 minutes. Squeeze until completely dry (potato ricer works well). Roll tightly in cheesecloth or kitchen towel to remove any remaining moisture.

Mash goat cheese in medium bowl using fork. Stir in ricotta, prosciutto, Parmesan, sage and tomato, blending well. Season with pepper to taste.

Position rack in center of oven and arrange baking stone or quarry tiles over top. Preheat oven to 425°F for 30 minutes. Shape pizza dough into 12-inch circle following directions for Basic Pizza Dough. Brush with olive oil. Spread cheese mixture evenly over dough, leaving ½-inch border. Sprinkle with pine nuts. Bake until crust browns, about 15 to 20 minutes.

Brush rim of pizza with olive oil. Divide pizza into serving pieces with pizza cutter, scissors or serrated knife. Garnish each piece with fresh sage leaf. Arrange bouquet of sage leaves in center. Serve pizza immediately.

PIZZA PIPERADE

Makes one 12-inch pizza

Basic Pizza Dough for 12-inch pizza (see recipe, page 120)

3 **medium-size red bell peppers (about 11 ounces total)**
2 **medium-size green bell peppers (about 8 ounces total)**
1 **large tomato (about 8 to 9 ounces)**

2 **tablespoons olive oil**
1 **small onion, sliced**
1 **large garlic clove, minced**
1½ **teaspoons minced fresh thyme, marjoram *or* basil *or* ½ teaspoon dried, crumbled**
   Salt and freshly ground pepper

   Olive oil

2 **tablespoons *each* freshly grated Parmesan and Romano cheese**

4 **ounces freshly grated Gruyère *or* Emmenthal cheese (about 1 cup)**
2 **ounces Bayonne ham, diced (about ½ cup)**

   Olive oil
2 **tablespoons *each* freshly grated Parmesan and Romano cheese**
2 **tablespoons minced fresh chervil *or* parsley**
   Niçoise olives (optional garnish)

Prepare dough. Set aside to rise.

Preheat broiler. Arrange red peppers, green peppers and tomato in broiler pan. Roast 6 inches from heat source, turning until blackened on all sides. Transfer to plastic bag and steam 10 minutes. Peel peppers, discarding veins and seeds. Rinse, if necessary, and pat dry with paper towels. Slice into julienne. Peel tomato, cut in half and squeeze out juice and seeds. Chop coarsely and squeeze until completely dry (potato ricer works well). Roll in cheesecloth or kitchen towel to remove any remaining moisture.

Heat 2 tablespoons olive oil in heavy small skillet over low heat. Add onion. Cover and cook, stirring occasionally, until translucent, about 10 minutes. Increase heat to medium, add peppers and cook, uncovered, 5 more minutes, stirring occasionally. Stir in garlic and thyme. Season with salt and pepper. Cool at least 10 minutes.

Position rack in center of oven and arrange baking stone or quarry tiles over top. Preheat oven to 425°F for 30 minutes. Shape pizza dough into 12-inch circle following Basic Pizza Dough directions. Brush with olive oil. Sprinkle with 2 tablespoons *each* Parmesan and Romano. Add Gruyère and tomato to peppers, mixing well. Spread over pizza, leaving ½-inch border. Bake 15 minutes. Sprinkle ham over. Bake until crust browns, about 5 minutes.

Brush rim of pizza with olive oil. Divide pizza into serving pieces with pizza cutter, scissors or serrated knife. Sprinkle with remaining 2 tablespoons Parmesan cheese, Romano cheese and chervil. Top with olives. Serve hot.

Pizza Primer

Equipment

Your homemade pizzas will be best if you cook them on a ceramic baking stone. Available at cookware stores or through mail order, these porous trays simulate old-fashioned brick ovens. While they may not attain the high temperatures of Neapolitan furnaces manufactured from Mount Vesuvius's black volcanic rock, they retain enough heat to draw out the dough's moisture and produce a delicious crackling crust. Marketed in 12- and 16-inch rounds, a 14 × 16-inch rectangle and a 10-inch deep-dish pan for Sicilian pies, baking stones can also be utilized for bread, cookies and tart shells.

Although less expensive half-inch-thick unglazed quarry tiles can be substituted for baking stones, they do not produce a crust as crisp as one made on a baking stone, and their seams make it difficult to slide pizzas on and off them. A long-handled wooden baker's peel facilitates this task. (A plywood board or flat cookie sheet will work but they don't *feel* as professional.)

Ingredients

No matter what their ethnicity, fresh uncooked ingredients give pizza the most pizzazz. Anything that exudes liquid should be thoroughly dried before cooking; if liquid still escapes, remove it with a bulb baster or drain it through a slit cut in the crust. When layering ingredients, place some of the cheese on the bottom to keep the crust crisp. Foods that need to be moistened while cooking—fish and onions, for example —should be placed under tomatoes; foods requiring the most heat, such as sausage, should be put on top. Mozzarella, particularly the skim milk variety, gives pizza its characteristic long strands, but its rubbery texture can be modified by substi-

tuting some Italian Fontina, bel paese or other good melting cheese. Another alternative is to use buffalo milk mozzarella: Its clean tart flavor adds a superb touch.

Topping ingredients, like those for stir-fry, can be cut and readied ahead to simplify assembly.

Any leftover uncooked dough can be baked for bread, or it can be added to the next batch of homemade pizza dough.

BASIC PIZZA DOUGH

Pizza dough can be prepared several days ahead and allowed to rise before being punched down and refrigerated until two or three hours before shaping and baking. If dough rises before it is needed, punch down and let rise again, or refrigerate up to two days. Bring to room temperature at least two hours before using. When making 14-inch or 16-inch pizzas, increase topping proportions by about ⅛ and ¼ respectively.

Dough for 12-inch pizza

4 first-course or 2 main-course servings

- 1½ **cups bread flour *or* all purpose flour**
- ½ **teaspoon salt**
- ¾ **teaspoon dry yeast**
- ½ **cup to ½ cup plus 1 tablespoon warm water (105°F to 115°F)**
- 1 **tablespoon olive oil**

  Rice flour *or* all purpose flour

  Cornmeal

Dough for 14-inch pizza

6 to 8 first-course or 3 to 4 main-course servings

- 2 **cups bread flour *or* all purpose flour**
- ¾ **teaspoon salt**
- 1 **teaspoon dry yeast**

- ⅔ **cup to ⅔ cup plus 1 tablespoon warm water (105°F to 115°F)**
- 1 **tablespoon olive oil**

  Rice flour *or* all purpose flour

  Cornmeal

Dough for 16-inch pizza

8 to 10 first-course or 4 to 5 main-course servings

- 2½ **cups bread flour *or* all purpose flour**
- 1 **teaspoon salt**
- 1½ **teaspoons dry yeast**
- ¾ **cup to ¾ cup plus 2 tablespoons warm water (105°F to 115°F)**
- 2 **tablespoons olive oil**

  Rice flour *or* all purpose flour

  Cornmeal

Mixing

Here is the point where you can begin giving the pizza your own personal touch. Most of our basic recipes use ¼-inch crust thickness as a general guide, but alter the dough to suit individual preference. For a thinner, crisper crust, make the dough drier and shape to ⅛-inch thickness, trimming off excess. Increase oven temperature to 475°F or 500°F and bake until brown, about 15 minutes. For a thicker crust, make dough moister and softer. Let rise again 30 minutes before topping.

By hand: Mix flour and salt on work surface or in bowl. Make 5-inch well in center, distributing flour evenly around sides so water does not run out. Sprinkle yeast into well. Pour about 2 tablespoons water into well and mix with fingertips until yeast is dissolved. Pour in remaining water with olive oil. Starting from inside of circle, gradually brush flour into liquid with fingers. When all flour is incorporated, gather dough into ball. Knead until smooth and elastic, occasionally slapping dough forcefully on surface, about 7 to 10 minutes. If any dry particles remain, sprinkle with drops of water. If dough is too sticky, knead in additional flour. Dough should be soft and easy to knead; however, dough becomes softer as it rises and if too soft, it will be difficult to shape.

With food processor: Mix flour and salt in work bowl using several on/off turns. Sprinkle yeast over water and stir until dissolved. Add olive oil to yeast mixture. With machine running, add yeast mixture through feed tube and continue processing until dough is smooth, moist and well mixed, about 7 seconds; *dough should not form ball.* Turn dough out onto work surface and knead until silken, about 3 minutes.

With heavy-duty mixer: Combine flour and salt in large bowl of electric mixer fitted with dough hook. Sprinkle yeast over water and stir until dissolved. Add olive oil to yeast mixture. With machine running at low speed, gradually pour yeast mixture into flour and knead according to manufacturer's instructions until dough has massed on hook and becomes smooth and silken, about 15 to 20 minutes (if dough does not cling to hook after about 5 minutes, beater height may need adjustment; check instruction booklet). If dough starts to climb onto head of mixer, sprinkle with additional 1 to 2 tablespoons flour to prevent sticking.

Rising
Forming dough into circle for rising makes eventual shaping of pizza easier. To do so, hold dough with left hand while stretching dough towards you and tucking ends underneath with right hand. Turn dough slightly and repeat folding and tucking until ball forms. Pat sides of dough to even ball. Sprinkle ball and baking sheet with rice flour. (Rice flour is preferred because it is not readily absorbed.) Arrange dough tucked side down on sheet. Cover dough completely with plastic wrap to prevent crust from forming, but allow enough space between dough and wrap for dough to expand. Transfer to cold oven and let rise until dough doubles to triples in size, about 1½ to 2 hours.

Shaping
Pizza can be shaped successfully with or without tossing. Tossing may seem awkward to the beginner on first try, but it is easily mastered.

To shape without tossing: Flour hands lightly. Make 2 fists and fit together under center of dough, forming flat surface for dough to rest on. Gradually pull fists apart, turning them simultaneously, to stretch dough. If dough sticks, flour hands again. As center becomes thin, move fists farther apart to stretch sides of dough. Repeat as necessary, being careful not to make dough too thin in center. Thin out edge by pulling dough between rounded thumb and first finger. Dough should be about ¼ inch thick.

To shape by tossing: Flour hands lightly. Make 2 fists and cross wrists closely together under center of dough. In one smooth motion, stretch dough by pulling fists outward and uncrossing wrists in twisting motion to give dough spin while tossing upward. Catch dough on fists. Flour hands again if dough sticks. Cross wrists lower on forearms (fists will be farther apart so sides of dough will be stretched when tossed). Repeat toss; do not toss more than twice or dough will be too thin in center. Thin out edge by pulling dough between rounded thumb and first finger. Dough should be about ¼ inch thick.

Baking
When baking several pizzas and only one oven is available, prepare the second pizza on another peel to go into the oven when the first one comes out.

Thirty minutes before shaping dough, position rack in center of oven and line with baking stone or quarry tiles. (If using optional steaming method, see additional instructions following.) Preheat oven to 425°F.

Meanwhile, flatten dough into as wide a circle as possible by repeatedly pushing down and out in rocking motion with fingertips (avoid using rolling pin, which compresses dough). If dough is sticky, lightly flour dough and work surface. Turn dough over and repeat procedure on other side until dough measures 8 to 9 inches in diameter.

Sprinkle peel or thin wooden board with cornmeal. Place dough on peel. Shape to correct size. Pinch ends up to form thick edge. Just before baking, place topping on pizza (if added sooner, pizza will be soggy). Shake peel back and forth. If pizza does not move freely, slide long, flexible-blade spatula under dough to loosen. Sprinkle preheated baking stone or quarry tiles with cornmeal. Starting from back of baking stone, tip peel and ease far edge of pizza out onto baking stone, then pull peel quickly out from under pizza, leaving pizza on stone. When pizza is cooked, slip peel under crust and transfer to serving board.

Optional Steaming Method
To further simulate a baker's oven, steam can be added when cooking pizza. Fill broiler pan half full with water and set aside. Place firebrick on floor of oven at same time baking stone is preheated. When oven is ready, set broiler pan on opened oven door. Carefully transfer firebrick to prepared broiler pan using fireplace tongs. Set pan on floor of oven. Close door and let steam develop for several minutes before adding pizza.

TOMMASO'S CALZONE WITH RICOTTA, MOZZARELLA AND PROSCIUTTO

Tommaso's, named for Tomas "Tommaso" Chan, its former Chinese proprietor, offers an incredible calzone (pizza turnover) which the current owners, the Crotti family, bake in an ancient wood-burning brick oven. Pizza was so unknown in America that in 1937 this venerable San Francisco haunt was described as a spot where you won't ". . . eat anything you have eaten before."

2 to 4 main-course servings

　　Basic Pizza Dough for 12-
　　inch pizza (see recipe, page
　　120)

　1　medium tomato (about 6 to
　　7 ounces), seeded, juiced
　　and diced
　¾　teaspoon salt

　3　ounces mushrooms

1¼　cups whole milk ricotta
　　cheese

　3　ounces *each* freshly grated
　　mozzarella cheese
　　(preferably whole milk) and
　　Italian Fontina cheese (½
　　cup)
　¼　cup freshly grated Parmesan
　　cheese
　2　ounces prosciutto, minced*
　　(about ½ cup)
　1　medium garlic clove,
　　minced
　1　tablespoon fresh basil *or*
　　oregano, minced, *or* 1
　　teaspoon dried, crumbled
　　Olive oil

　2　tablespoons freshly grated
　　Parmesan cheese

Prepare dough. Set aside to rise.
　　Place tomato in colander. Sprinkle with salt and let drain at least 30 minutes. Squeeze until completely dry (potato ricer works well). Roll tightly in cheesecloth or kitchen towel to remove any remaining moisture.

Clean mushrooms with damp paper towel; *do not rinse or pizza will be soggy.* Slice thinly, then extract liquid by squeezing one handful of mushrooms at a time in potato ricer or dishcloth.
　　Position rack in center of oven and arrange baking stone or quarry tiles over top. Preheat to 425°F for 30 minutes. Combine ricotta, mozzarella, Fontina, ¼ cup Parmesan, prosciutto, garlic, basil, tomato and mushrooms in medium bowl and mix well. Shape pizza dough into 12-inch oval following Basic Pizza Dough directions. (Calzone is formed into an oval instead of circle so filling will fit in corners when dough is folded over.) Brush dough with olive oil. Mound ricotta filling on half of dough, leaving ½-inch border. Brush edges of dough with water. Fold other half of dough over to form turnover, pressing edges together with fingers and fork tines to seal. Flute decoratively. Brush outside of dough with olive oil. Make 3 steam vents in top of turnover with tip of knife. Bake 30 minutes; if dough becomes too brown, cover with foil for last 10 minutes.
　　Brush crust with olive oil. Let rest 5 minutes before cutting to prevent dough from cracking. Using pizza cutter, scissors or serrated knife, slice dough in half horizontally, then into 4 sections vertically. Sprinkle with remaining 2 tablespoons Parmesan cheese. Serve immediately.

*Two to 3 ounces sweet Italian sausage can be substituted for prosciutto. Before using, sauté until barely done, then cool and slice.

GOAT CHEESE AND GREEN ONION PITHIVIERS

Attractive double-crust puff pastry pies with a savory cheese filling.

8 servings

Puff Pastry*

　1　pound (about 3¼ cups) all
　　purpose flour
1½　teaspoons salt
2½　cups (5 sticks) chilled
　　unsalted butter
　¾　cup ice water, or more
　1　tablespoon fresh lemon
　　juice

Filling

　2　tablespoons (¼ stick)
　　unsalted butter
24　green onions (including
　　several inches of green
　　tops), cut into fine julienne

　1　egg
　1　egg yolk
　½　cup whipping cream
　1　tablespoon Dijon mustard
　½　cup fresh French or Italian
　　breadcrumbs
　4　ounces goat cheese
　¼　teaspoon freshly grated
　　nutmeg
　　Salt and freshly ground
　　pepper

　1　egg blended with 1
　　tablespoon water

For pastry: Set ¼ cup flour aside; place remainder in work bowl of processor fitted with Steel Knife. Add salt. Cut ½ cup chilled butter into small pieces; distribute over flour. Mix using on/off turns until mixture resembles coarse meal, about 4 to 5 seconds. Combine ¾ cup ice water with lemon juice. With machine running, pour liquid through feed tube in steady stream and blend 30 seconds. (If dough does not form ball, add 1 more tablespoon ice water.) Remove dough from work bowl and divide in half. Return half of dough to work bowl and process until very smooth, about 1½ to 2 minutes. Remove; repeat with remaining dough (can be done all at once in large-capacity processor). Combine halves, wrap in plastic and chill thoroughly.
　　Place remaining 2 cups chilled butter in heavy plastic bag with reserved ¼ cup flour. Pound and work mixture with rolling pin until blended. Shape into 6-inch square and chill thoroughly.
　　Lightly flour work surface. Dust chilled dough lightly with flour. Roll out into 14-inch square. Set butter square in center of dough and fold over edges to enclose butter completely, pinching edges to seal. Sprinkle with flour. Turn dough over.

(If kitchen is warm, return dough to refrigerator for 30 minutes.) Shape into rectangle. Sprinkle lightly with flour. Using heavy rolling pin, roll from center of dough away from you, stopping 1 inch from far end. Move pin down 1 inch below center and continue rolling in same direction. Repeat until you have begun rolling 1 inch from edge nearest you. Gently even sides of dough. Roll thicker top and bottom edges until dough forms rectangle about 8 × 20 inches; do not puncture any air bubbles that form during rolling. *If dough resists rolling, return to refrigerator. If at any time butter can be seen between layers, rechill until butter is firm.*

Brush excess flour from dough. Fold ends of rectangle to meet in center. Roll lightly. Again brush off excess flour. Fold together again, as though closing a book, to form 4 layers. Chill dough for 30 minutes.

Place dough on floured surface with narrow end nearest you. Roll into 8 × 20-inch rectangle, brush off

flour and fold as before. Repeat rolling and folding 3 more times, chilling at least 30 minutes between each. Chill dough at least 3 hours after last folding.

For filling: Melt butter in heavy large skillet over very low heat. Add onions, cover and cook 30 minutes, stirring occasionally. Cool filling completely.

Beat whole egg and yolk in medium bowl to blend. Whisk in cream and mustard. Stir in cooled onions and breadcrumbs. Crumble in goat cheese. Season with nutmeg and salt and pepper. (*Filling can be prepared 1 day ahead, covered and refrigerated.*)

Cut chilled puff pastry dough in half. Roll 1 portion into 12 × 22-inch rectangle, being careful not to roll over edges of dough. Cut out eight 5-inch circles. Repeat with remaining half of dough. Refrigerate circles 30 minutes. (*Dough circles can be made ahead to this point and refrigerated several days or frozen.*)

Arrange 8 dough circles on baking sheets. Prick all over with

fork. Divide filling among centers of circles, leaving 1½-inch border. Brush border with cold water. Immediately top each with second dough circle, stretching gently to fit over filling. Press edges firmly to seal. Cut tiny hole in center of top pastry layer to allow steam to escape during baking. Freeze 20 minutes.

Preheat oven to 450°F. Invert custard cup slightly smaller than pastry over 1 Pithiviers. To form decorative border, make ridges by pressing back of knife vertically into pastry from outer edge toward cup every ¼ inch. Remove cup. Repeat with remaining Pithiviers.

Paint Pithiviers with egg glaze. Cut decorative swirls in top of dough using small sharp knife. Bake until puffed and golden brown, about 15 to 20 minutes. Turn off oven and let pastries cool in oven 5 minutes. Serve immediately.

Commercial puff pastry can be substituted for homemade. Four sheets, about 10 × 10 inches each, will be needed.

Pasta

SPAGHETTINI PRIMAVERA

Serve with a bowl of grated Parmesan and crusty French bread.

4 to 6 servings

- 4 tablespoons olive oil
- 1 pound sweet Italian sausage
- 2 dried hot chili peppers
- 1 28-ounce can Italian plum tomatoes, drained and chopped
- 1 cup minced fresh parsley (preferably Italian)
- 2 large garlic cloves, minced
- 3 red bell peppers, roasted, peeled and thinly sliced
- 1 sprig fresh oregano *or* 1 teaspoon dried

Salt and freshly ground pepper

- 12 ounces imported spaghettini
- 3 tablespoons minced fresh parsley
- 3 tablespoons freshly grated Parmesan cheese

Heat 2 tablespoons oil in heavy large skillet over medium heat. Add sausage, cover partially and cook until well browned on all sides, about 20 minutes. Transfer to cutting board and reserve.

Discard all but 1 tablespoon fat from skillet. Increase heat to medium high and add remaining 2 tablespoons oil. Add chili peppers and sauté until skins turn black. Remove peppers and discard.

Add tomatoes, parsley and garlic to skillet and bring to simmer. Reduce heat and add red pepper, oregano and salt and pepper. Cover and simmer gently 15 minutes, watching carefully and stirring occasionally to prevent burning (there is not much liquid in sauce).

Cut sausage into thin slices and add to skillet. Turn heat to low and cover partially.

Bring large quantity of salted water to boil. Add spaghettini and cook until al dente. Immediately add 2 cups cold water to stop cooking process. Drain well. (Spaghettini can be held covered for 10 to 15 minutes before serving if necessary.) Add to skillet and toss thoroughly with sauce. Sprinkle with parsley and Parmesan and serve from skillet.

RAVIOLI WITH LIGURIAN WALNUT PESTO

4 servings

Filling

2 pounds Swiss chard, heavy white stems removed
8 ounces ricotta cheese
⅓ cup freshly grated Parmesan cheese
¼ cup (½ stick) butter, melted
1 egg
½ teaspoon freshly grated nutmeg

Pasta

4 cups all purpose flour
4 eggs, room temperature
2 teaspoons olive oil
Pinch of salt

1 cup Ligurian Walnut Pesto (see following recipe)
Ground walnuts (optional garnish)
Freshly grated Parmesan cheese

For filling: Bring small amount of water to boil in large saucepan fitted with rack or steamer tray. Add chard and steam just until tender. Drain well. Mince chard. Transfer to large bowl. Add ricotta, Parmesan, butter, egg and nutmeg and mix well.

For pasta: Mound flour on work surface and make well in center. Break eggs into well. Add oil and salt to eggs and beat lightly with fork. Slowly incorporate flour into eggs, starting at inner edge of well, until all flour is blended into eggs and mixture forms loose crumbly mass; sprinkle small amount of water into dough if necessary. Knead dough with heel of hand until smooth and elastic, about 8 to 10 minutes, adding several drops of water if dough is too firm. Set dough aside to rest for 5 minutes.

Scrape up any bits of dough on work surface and discard; reflour lightly. Roll dough into thin sheet. Using pastry wheel, cut dough into 2 × 4-inch rectangles. Spoon filling into centers. Fold in half, forming 2-inch squares. Press edges to seal, moistening with small amount of water if dough is too dry. Dust ravioli with flour. Transfer to baking sheet lined with lightly floured waxed paper; do not overlap ravioli. Set aside for 20 to 30 minutes.

Bring large amount of salted water to rapid boil. Add ravioli, stirring vigorously, and cook until ravioli rise to surface and are al dente, about 4 to 5 minutes. Remove with slotted spoon and drain well. Transfer ravioli to buttered heated platter. Thin pesto with 2 to 3 tablespoons pasta cooking water. Pour pesto over ravioli and toss lightly until pasta is well coated with sauce. Sprinkle with ground walnuts. Serve immediately with cheese.

Ligurian Walnut Pesto

If you use young oregano, this pesto will stay sweet and delicious in the refrigerator for up to one month. Otherwise, make the pesto just before serving to prevent any bitterness.

Makes about 2 cups

1 cup packed fresh oregano *or* marjoram leaves
4 small garlic cloves
1 cup walnut halves
½ cup freshly grated Parmesan *or* Romano cheese
6 tablespoons warm water
6 tablespoons whipping cream
½ cup virgin olive oil

If using mortar and pestle, combine oregano or marjoram and garlic in mortar and crush to fine paste. Gradually add walnut halves and work into paste. Add cheese and blend well. Slowly add water, cream and olive oil to mixture one at a time, stirring constantly until blended. Serve at room temperature.

If using processor, combine oregano or marjoram and garlic in work bowl and blend to fine paste, scraping down sides of bowl as necessary. Add walnut halves and blend to paste. Add cheese and mix well. Blend in water and cream. With machine running, pour olive oil through feed tube in slow steady stream and process until smooth. Serve at room temperature.

TONNARELLI WITH LOBSTER SAUCE (Tonnarelli col Sugo di Aragosta)

Tonnarelli originated in the Abruzzi region of Italy, where the pasta is known as maccheroni alla chitarra *(guitar-string spaghetti) because the dough is cut on a wooden frame strung with wires. These long, square-shaped noodles are rolled thick and are made with semolina flour (from durum hard wheat), which contributes to their firm and chewy texture. If dough is sticky while kneading with pasta machine, dust with all purpose flour.*

4 servings

Tonnarelli

2 cups semolina flour
3 eggs, room temperature

Lobster Sauce

¼ cup olive oil
2 anchovy fillets, minced
2 medium garlic cloves, chopped
⅓ small hot red or green chili (optional)
1 28-ounce can Italian plum tomatoes, drained (liquid reserved) and seeded in food mill or fine strainer
1 12- to 14-ounce lobster tail

1 teaspoon minced fresh parsley
1 teaspoon minced fresh oregano leaves *or* ½ teaspoon dried, crumbled
Pinch of dried marjoram, crumbled
Salt and freshly ground pepper

Butter

For tonnarelli: Mix, knead and shape dough sheets according to instructions for Basic Egg Pasta Dough (page 125), progressively narrowing rollers until machine is set on *third* narrowest setting. Transfer dough sheets to kitchen towels. Repeat process with remaining pieces of dough. Dry dough according to recipe for Basic Egg Pasta Dough.

Pasta Primer
Basic Egg Pasta Dough
Instructions
See individual pasta recipes for proportions of specific ingredients.

To Mix and Knead Dough
Mound flour on work surface and make well in center. Break eggs into well and blend with fork. Gradually draw small amount of flour from inner edge of well into eggs with fork, stirring constantly until all flour is incorporated. Gather dough into loose mass and set aside. Scrape any hard bits of flour from work surface and discard. Lightly flour work surface and hands. Knead dough until smooth and elastic, 10 to 12 minutes. Insert finger in center of dough: if dry, dough is ready for pasta machine; if sticky, sprinkle dough lightly with flour and continue kneading until dough reaches the correct consistency.

To Knead and Shape Dough in Pasta Machine
Cut off 1 egg-size piece of dough. Store remaining dough in plastic wrap or dry towel to prevent drying; set aside. Flatten piece of dough with heel of hand, then fold in half. Turn pasta machine to widest setting and run dough through. Continue folding and kneading process with pasta machine until dough is smooth and velvety, at least 2 more times (number of times will depend on how vigorously dough was kneaded by hand). Dust dough lightly with more flour as necessary.

Adjust pasta machine to next narrower setting. Run dough through machine *without folding,* dusting lightly with flour if sticky. Repeat, narrowing rollers after each run until machine is on second to narrowest setting; pasta should be less than $\frac{1}{16}$ inch thick.

For Stuffed Pasta
The first dough sheet must be cut and shaped before forming remaining sheets or dough will become too brittle. Knead each piece of dough slightly before running through pasta machine.

For Flat Pasta and Noodles
Knead and shape remaining dough into sheets, kneading each egg-size piece of dough slightly before running through machine. Set aside until sheets look firm and leathery and edges begin to curl up slightly but are not brittle. This will take 10 to 30 minutes depending on dryness of dough and temperature and humidity of kitchen. *Pasta must be cut at this point or dough will become too brittle.*

After cutting, pasta can be arranged on kitchen towel to dry until ready to cook; overlap as little as possible. *(Unstuffed pasta can be left overnight to dry completely in cool dry place. Stuffed pasta can be assembled 1 day ahead, covered with kitchen towel and refrigerated.)*

To Cook Pasta
Fill pasta cooker or stockpot ¾ full with salted water and bring to rapid boil over high heat. Stir in 1 tablespoon oil. Add pasta and stir vigorously to prevent sticking. Cook until just firm but tender to bite (al dente), about 5 to 20 seconds for freshly made pasta and up to 3 minutes for that which has thoroughly dried. Taste often to prevent overcooking. Drain.

Tips and Techniques
- The fresher, moister and thinner the pasta, the shorter the cooking time. Freshly made pasta usually needs only 5 to 20 seconds cooking time.
- Humidity and size of eggs you use will influence amount of flour required to make pasta. Be flexible and make adjustments according to conditions.
- When rolling out pasta dough by hand, be sure to roll over the edges as they are likely to be thicker than the middle.
- When pasta dough is dry enough for shaping, the edges will be slightly curled.

To shape tonnarelli, run dough sheet through narrow blades of pasta machine. Arrange noodles on kitchen towels, overlapping as little as possible. Repeat with remaining dough.

For lobster sauce: Heat oil in medium saucepan over medium-low heat. Add anchovies, garlic and hot chili and stir until anchovy is melted. Add tomatoes and lobster. Cover and cook 5 minutes, stirring occasionally. Remove lobster from saucepan using slotted spoon. Increase heat to medium high and continue cooking until tomato mixture is reduced to saucelike consistency, about 15 to 30 minutes. Shell lobster and cut meat into small pieces.

Add lobster to saucepan. Stir in parsley, oregano and marjoram. Reduce heat to medium low and cook 5 minutes. Add salt and pepper. Set aside.

Cook pasta according to instructions for Basic Egg Pasta Dough. Butter heated serving platter. Transfer pasta to platter and toss lightly. Place sauce over high heat and simmer, stirring, just until heated through; do not boil. Pour lobster sauce over pasta and mix gently. Serve immediately.

9 ❖ Vegetables and Side Dishes

Vegetables and Fruit

❖ ❖ ❖ ❖ ❖ ❖ ❖ ❖ ❖ ❖ ❖ ❖ ❖ ❖

BROCCOLI WITH PINE NUTS

6 servings

> 2 **pounds broccoli, peeled and cut into long stalks**
> 2 **tablespoons (¼ stick) butter or reserved fat from Braised Veal Shank with Wine and Herbs (see recipe, page 47)**
> 2 **tablespoons pine nuts**
> 1 **tablespoon fresh lemon juice**
> **Salt and freshly ground pepper**

Fit large saucepan with steamer. Pour in enough water to come just below steamer and bring to rapid boil. Add broccoli, cover and steam until crisptender, about 8 to 10 minutes depending on thickness of broccoli stalks. Rinse under cold water to stop cooking process. (*Broccoli can be cooked up to 1 day ahead and refrigerated at this point.*)

About 10 minutes before serving, melt butter or reserved fat in large skillet over medium heat. Add pine nuts and cook 3 minutes, stirring constantly. Add broccoli and cook until stalks begin to color slightly, turning occasionally and increasing heat if necessary. Transfer to serving platter. Sprinkle with lemon juice. Season with salt and pepper. Serve immediately.

For variation, steam broccoli leaves with stalks. Quickly sauté leaves in butter. Arrange leaves in single layer on serving platter and top with lightly steamed broccoli.

GLAZED MATCHSTICK BEETS

8 servings

> 2½ **cups pear nectar**
> 2½ to 3½ **cups water**
> 3 **tablespoons butter**
> 1½ **pounds young beets, peeled and cut into matchstick-size julienne**
> 2 **tablespoons sugar**
> ½ **teaspoon dry mustard**
> ½ **teaspoon salt**
> ¼ **teaspoon ground ginger**

Bring pear nectar and 2½ cups water to rapid boil. Meanwhile, melt butter in deep large skillet over medium-high heat. Add remaining ingredients and blend well. Pour boiling pear nectar mixture over beets and return to boil. Cook until beets are tender, stirring frequently, about 40 minutes, adding remaining water as necessary. Turn into dish and serve.

GREEN BEANS WITH HAZELNUTS

8 servings

> 2 **pounds green beans, trimmed and halved crosswise**
>
> 3 **tablespoons butter**
> ½ **cup toasted skinned hazelnuts, coarsely chopped**
> 6 **large green onions (white part only), minced (about ⅓ cup)**
> 2 **teaspoons fresh lemon juice**
> **Salt and freshly ground pepper**

Pour water into steamer to within 1 inch of rack. Place over high heat and bring to boil. Add beans, cover and steam until crisp-tender, about 5 to 7 minutes. Rinse under cold water to stop cooking process.

Melt butter in large skillet over medium-low heat. Add nuts and onions and cook until nuts are aromatic, about 3 minutes. Increase heat to medium high, add beans and stir until heated through. Sprinkle with lemon juice. Season with salt and pepper and serve.

ONION-STEAMED BROCCOLI WITH LEMON DILL BUTTER

6 servings

> 6 **large green onions, chopped**
> 6 **uniform large broccoli stalks**
>
> ¾ **cup (1½ sticks) butter**
> 1 to 2 **tablespoons fresh lemon juice**
> 2 **tablespoons chopped fresh dill**
> **Salt and freshly ground pepper**

Pour water into steamer to within 1 inch of rack. Add onions to water; set rack in place. Bring to rapid boil. Add broccoli, cover and steam until crisp-tender, about 10 minutes.

Melt butter in small saucepan over medium-low heat. Add lemon juice, dill and salt and pepper to taste. Pour butter over broccoli and serve.

Capellini with Fresh Tomato Basil Sauce

Spaghettini Primavera

Clockwise from top: Deep-Dish Sausage, Leek, and Mushroom Pie; Devonshire Lamb Hash with Walnut-Plum Catsup and bread rounds; Lemon Scones with assorted jams

Clockwise from bottom: Pizza Piperade, Tommaso's Calzone, Deep-Dish Seafood Pizza

Clockwise from bottom: Goat Cheese and Green Onion Pithiviers, Asparagus in Brown Butter Mayonnaise, Chicken Livers Normandy, Raspberry Poached Pears

*Clockwise from bottom:
Alsatian Charcuterie Plate, Salmon
Trout Fillets with Red Wine Sauce
on Fresh Parsley Noodles, Kirsch
Ice Cream, Lacy Hazelnut Cookies*

ASPARAGUS IN BROWN BUTTER MAYONNAISE

8 servings

- 4 cups beef stock, preferably homemade (see recipe, page 37)
- 1 medium carrot, thinly sliced
- 1 celery stalk, sliced
- 1 lemon, sliced
- ¼ cup chopped onion
- 4 parsley sprigs
- 1 teaspoon salt (reduce or omit if using canned beef stock)
- 3 pounds fresh medium asparagus, trimmed

  Lettuce leaves
  Brown Butter Mayonnaise (see following recipe)

Combine stock, carrot, celery, lemon, onion, parsley and salt in large skillet and bring to boil. Add asparagus. Cover and simmer until almost tender, about 5 minutes. Let cool (asparagus will continue to cook as it cools). Refrigerate asparagus in broth. (*Can be prepared 1 day ahead.*)

Line serving platter with lettuce leaves. Drain asparagus well. Arrange atop lettuce. Serve with Brown Butter Mayonnaise.

Brown Butter Mayonnaise

Can be prepared 1 day ahead; whisk before serving if necessary.

Makes about 1½ cups

- 1 cup (2 sticks) unsalted butter
- 4 egg yolks, room temperature
- 1 tablespoon Dijon mustard
- 1 tablespoon fresh lemon juice
  Salt and fresh ground pepper

Melt butter in heavy small saucepan over low heat. Continue cooking, swirling pan occasionally, until butter is rich chestnut brown, about 20 minutes. Let butter cool 15 minutes.

Combine yolks, mustard and lemon juice in processor or blender. With machine running, pour in butter in slow, steady stream. Season mayonnaise with salt and pepper. Refrigerate until ready to use.

BRUSSELS SPROUTS WITH GRILLED ALMONDS

(Choux de Bruxelles et Amandes Grillées)

6 servings

- 1½ pounds brussels sprouts
- ¼ cup (½ stick) butter
  Salt and freshly ground pepper
- ⅓ cup toasted slivered almonds

Bring large amount of salted water to rapid boil. Meanwhile, remove and discard outer leaves of brussels sprouts. Cut shallow cross in root end of each sprout for even cooking. Boil until crisp-tender, 10 to 12 minutes. Drain well. Melt butter in large skillet until dark golden brown. Remove from heat. Stir in sprouts with salt and pepper to taste. Sprinkle with nuts and serve.

BRUSSELS SPROUTS WITH MUSTARD SEED

12 servings

- 2½ pounds small brussels sprouts
- ¼ cup (½ stick) butter
- 2 tablespoons white mustard seed *or* 1 tablespoon white and 1 tablespoon brown mustard seed*
- ¼ cup coarse French mustard
- 1 teaspoon salt
  Freshly ground pepper

Bring large amount of salted water to rapid boil. Meanwhile, remove and discard outer leaves of brussels sprouts. Cut shallow cross in root end of each sprout for even cooking.

Boil brussels sprouts until crisp-tender, 10 to 12 minutes. Drain well.

Just before serving, stir butter and mustard seed in heavy large skillet over medium heat until butter browns lightly. Blend in mustard and brussels sprouts. Season with salt and pepper. Stir until hot, 2 to 3 minutes. Serve immediately.

*Available at specialty foods stores.

SPRING CARROTS WITH YELLOW RICE

4 servings

- 1⅓ cups chicken stock, preferably homemade (see recipe, page 38)
- ⅛ teaspoon turmeric
  Pinch of salt
- ⅔ cup uncooked rice
- 3 tablespoons butter
- 1 medium onion, minced
- 1 pound carrots, cut into ¼-inch julienne
- 2 teaspoons fresh marjoram leaves *or* ½ teaspoon dried, crumbled
- ¼ teaspoon dried Italian *or* Greek oregano, crumbled
- 1 tablespoon wine vinegar
- ½ teaspoon sugar
  Pinch of cinnamon
- ½ cup chicken stock *or* water
- 2 teaspoons minced fresh parsley

Combine 1⅓ cups stock with turmeric and salt in heavy 2-quart saucepan and bring to boil over high heat. Add rice, reduce heat to low, cover and cook until liquid is absorbed, about 25 minutes. Remove from heat and fluff with fork. Cover and keep warm.

Melt butter in heavy large skillet over low heat. Add onion, cover and cook until softened, about 10 minutes, stirring occasionally. Blend in carrots, increase heat to medium low and cook uncovered 5 minutes. Add marjoram and oregano and cook 5 minutes, stirring frequently. Stir in vinegar, sugar and cinnamon and cook several minutes to blend flavors. Add remaining stock and simmer gently until carrots are crisp-tender and liquid is evaporated, about 20 minutes. Stir carrots into rice. (*Can be prepared 2 days ahead to this point and refrigerated. To reheat, turn into buttered baking dish, cover with foil and bake in preheated 325°F oven until hot, about 30 minutes.*) Mix in parsley and serve hot.

MINTED PEAS IN BOSTON LETTUCE CUPS

8 servings

- 1   10-ounce package frozen peas
- ½   cup (1 stick) unsalted butter
- 1   medium onion, halved and thinly sliced
- ⅓   cup minced fresh mint leaves
- 1   teaspoon sugar
      Salt and freshly ground pepper
- 8   Boston lettuce leaves, washed and dried

Cook peas in large saucepan of boiling salted water 5 minutes. Drain and plunge into cold water.

Heat butter in heavy large skillet over low heat until it begins to brown, 8 to 10 minutes. Increase heat to medium and sauté onion until tender. Stir in peas, mint, sugar, and salt and pepper to taste. Reduce heat to low and cook until peas are hot. Spoon into lettuce leaves and serve immediately.

PUREE OF CELERY ROOT

4 servings

- 1   celery root (about 1 pound)
- ½   lemon
- ⅔   cup whipping cream
- 2   tablespoons (¼ stick) butter
      Salt and freshly ground white pepper

Peel and quarter celery root, rubbing with lemon to prevent discol-

oration. Fit large saucepan with steamer rack. Add enough water to come just below rack. Bring water to boil. Add celery root, cover and steam until tender, about 30 minutes, adding more water to pan as necessary. Transfer celery root to processor or blender and puree. Add cream and butter and blend until smooth. Just before serving, transfer puree to large saucepan. Place over medium-high heat and stir until heated through. Season to taste with salt and pepper.

LEEK CASSEROLE

4 servings

- ¼   cup olive oil
- 2   large onions, coarsely chopped
- 2   pounds leeks (white part only), cut into 2-inch lengths
- 3   medium carrots, sliced
- 2   tomatoes, peeled and coarsely chopped
- 1   teaspoon garlic salt
- 1   teaspoon freshly ground white pepper

Heat oil in large saucepan over medium heat. Add onions and sauté until edges are golden brown. Add leeks, carrots, tomatoes, garlic salt and pepper. Barely cover vegetables with boiling water. Simmer for 1 hour. Remove vegetables and set aside. Continue simmering liquid until reduced to ½ cup. Add vegetables and cook until heated through. Serve immediately.

STIR-FRY OF FRESH FENNEL AND PEAS

6 servings

- 4   to 5 small to medium fennel bulbs, cored and sliced into thin strips*
- 2   tablespoons fresh lemon juice
- 3   tablespoons olive oil
- 3   large shallots, minced
- 2   ounces boiled ham, diced
- ½   teaspoon fresh tarragon *or* ⅛ teaspoon dried, crumbled

- 1½ cups frozen tiny peas, thawed
- 2   green onions, cut into 1-inch lengths
- 2   tablespoons chopped fennel or celery leaves
      Salt and freshly ground pepper

Combine fennel and lemon juice in medium bowl and let stand 10 minutes. Heat olive oil in wok or large skillet over high heat. Add fennel and shallots and stir-fry, tossing constantly, about 2 minutes. Remove from heat and add ham and tarragon. (*Can be prepared 1 hour ahead to this point.*)

About 5 minutes before serving, return mixture to high heat and toss until very hot. Add remaining ingredients and stir-fry just until heated through. Transfer to platter and serve.

One large bunch celery can be substituted. Separate into stalks. Cut in half crosswise, then slice thinly lengthwise.

ALIGOT WITH TURNIPS

8 servings

- 2½ pounds turnips, peeled and cut into ½-inch dice
- ¾   cup (1½ sticks) unsalted butter, cut into chunks
- 6   large garlic cloves
- 2½ pounds unpeeled boiling potatoes
- 4   ounces Gruyère, shredded (1 cup)
      Freshly grated nutmeg
      Salt and freshly ground white pepper

Bring about 2 quarts water to rapid boil. Add turnips and cook 8 minutes. Drain well. Turn turnips into large skillet. Add butter and garlic. Place over low heat, cover and cook until tender, about 30 minutes, stirring occasionally; *do not brown.* Meanwhile, boil unpeeled potatoes in large amount of salted water until just tender.

Remove turnip mixture from heat and cool slightly. Peel potatoes and dice. Transfer turnip mixture and potatoes to processor or blender (in batches if necessary) and puree until smooth. If not serving immediately, keep puree warm in large metal bowl set over simmering water, stirring occasionally. (*Can be prepared 1 day ahead to this point. Reheat 30 minutes over simmering water.*)

Just before serving, fold cheese into hot aligot until melted and stringy. Season with nutmeg, salt and generous amount of pepper.

SPINACH WITH CARAMELIZED ONIONS

2 to 4 servings

- 3 tablespoons olive oil
- 1 large red onion, thinly sliced
- 1 pound fresh spinach leaves, stemmed
- 1 tablespoon fresh lemon juice
  Freshly ground pepper

Heat oil in heavy large skillet over medium-high heat until hot but not smoking. Add onion and sauté, stirring constantly, until onion is caramelized, about 15 minutes. Continue cooking until some of onion is dark and crisp, about 3 minutes. Add spinach and stir until just wilted but still bright green. Remove from heat. Add lemon juice and pepper. Toss gently and serve.

SAUTEED SPINACH WITH PEAR

4 servings

- 1 teaspoon butter
- 3 tablespoons minced shallot
- 1 pound fresh spinach, cooked until just wilted, squeezed dry and finely chopped
- 1 ripe pear, peeled, cored and finely chopped
  Generous pinch of freshly grated nutmeg
  Salt and freshly ground pepper

Melt butter in large saucepan over medium-high heat. Add shallot and cook until golden. Blend in spinach, pear, nutmeg and salt and pepper. Cook, stirring constantly, until heated through. Serve immediately.

SQUASH AND PECAN SAUTE IN ZUCCHINI SHELLS

4 servings

- 2 large zucchini (1 pound *each*), halved lengthwise
  Salt
- 3 to 4 small zucchini (about 1¾ pounds total)
- 3 to 4 small yellow crookneck squash (about 1¾ pounds total)
- 2½ tablespoons salt

- 1 tablespoon unsalted butter
- ⅔ cup coarsely chopped pecans

- 1 tablespoon unsalted butter, room temperature

- 2 tablespoons (¼ stick) unsalted butter
- 1 to 2 tablespoons fresh lemon juice
- 3 4-inch fresh thyme sprigs (leaves only)
  Salt and freshly ground white pepper

- 4 tablespoons finely chopped pecans
  Pecan halves (garnish)

Scoop pulp from large zucchini leaving ¼-inch shell (if pulp is not too seedy, reserve for another use). Sprinkle inside of zucchini shells generously with salt. Invert on wire rack set in pan. Drain 1 hour. Meanwhile, grate small zucchini and crookneck squash. Alternate layers of grated squash and 2½ tablespoons salt in colander, ending with salt. Cover completely with plate. Weight with heavy object. Let stand in pan or sink about 1 hour to drain.

Melt 1 tablespoon butter in small skillet over medium heat. Stir in coarsely chopped pecans and cook, stirring frequently, until golden, about 3 to 4 minutes. Set aside.

Preheat oven to 350°F. Rinse zucchini shells in cold water to remove salt; pat dry. Spread shells inside and out with 1 tablespoon butter. Invert on baking sheet. Bake zucchini shells just until tender, about 30 minutes.

Rinse grated squash thoroughly in cold water to remove salt; squeeze dry in potato ricer or towel. Melt 2 tablespoons butter in wok or large skillet over high heat. Add grated squash, lemon juice and thyme and stir-fry until all moisture has evaporated, about 2 to 3 minutes. Stir in coarsely chopped pecans. Season with salt and pepper.

Sprinkle inside of each zucchini shell with 1 tablespoon finely chopped pecans. Fill with stir-fried squash. Garnish with pecan halves and serve. (*Can be prepared several hours ahead, covered and kept at room temperature. Reheat in 300°F oven for 10 minutes.*)

BAKED POTATO CHIPS

6 servings

- 3½ pounds red or white boiling potatoes, cut crosswise into ⅛-inch-thick slices
- 6 tablespoons (¾ stick) butter, melted
  Salt and freshly ground pepper

Position racks in upper and lower third of oven and preheat to 500°F. Lightly grease 2 baking sheets. Arrange potato slices in single layer on prepared baking sheets. Brush generously with butter. Bake 7 minutes. Switch pan positions and continue baking until potatoes are crisp and browned around edges, about 7 to 9 minutes. Transfer to heated platter. Sprinkle with salt and pepper. Serve immediately.

SHERRY-SAUTEED MUSHROOMS

Makes about 2 cups

      2 tablespoons (¼ stick) butter
      2 tablespoons olive oil
    12 ounces fresh mushrooms, thickly sliced (5 cups)
    ½ cup chopped onion
      1 cup dry Sherry

          Salt and freshly ground pepper
      1 tablespoon minced fresh parsley

Melt butter with 1 tablespoon olive oil in large skillet over medium-high heat. Add mushrooms and sauté 2 minutes. Remove mushrooms from skillet and set aside. Reduce heat to medium low and add remaining 1 tablespoon olive oil to skillet. Add onion and cook until soft and golden, about 5 minutes. Stir in Sherry, increase heat to high and boil rapidly until reduced by half, about 6 minutes.

Reduce heat to medium low. Return mushrooms to skillet. Season with salt and pepper. Simmer gently 5 minutes. (*Can be prepared ahead to this point and reheated just before serving.*) Stir in minced parsley and serve immediately.

CONFIT OF ONIONS WITH CARAWAY

(Fondue d'Oignons au Carvi)

Can be prepared 2 days ahead and refrigerated. Reheat before serving.

6 servings

      2 tablespoons (¼ stick) butter
      2 pounds small white onions, peeled, shallow cross cut in root ends
          Pinch of sugar
          Salt and freshly ground pepper
      1 teaspoon white wine vinegar
    ½ teaspoon caraway seed, or to taste

Melt butter in heavy large skillet over medium heat. Add onions and sauté until lightly colored, shaking pan frequently, about 10 minutes. Sprinkle with sugar. Season with salt and pepper to taste. Reduce heat to very low, cover and cook until onions are tender and falling apart, about 1¾ hours, stirring occasionally. Stir in vinegar and caraway seed. Cool 10 minutes before serving.

BREAD AND ONION SAUSAGE

(Knepfle au Torchon)

This classic Germanic dish was originally developed at a time when flour was scarce and not a single crumb of bread was to be wasted. Brioche and challah are generally used because of their capacity to absorb the onion-flavored egg mixture. The egg-soaked crumbs are rolled in cheesecloth to form a large sausage, then poached. The cooked egg holds the crumbs together. The sausage is then sliced and sautéed in browned butter to hearty perfection.

6 servings

    ¼ cup (½ stick) unsalted butter
      2 medium onions, finely chopped
      2 medium leeks (white part only), finely chopped
      2 shallots, finely chopped
      2 medium garlic cloves, finely chopped
          Salt and freshly ground pepper
    1¼ cups half and half
      4 eggs
      2 cups ½-inch cubes stale challah with crust, toasted until golden (about ½ loaf)
    1½ tablespoons chopped fresh chives
    ¼ teaspoon freshly grated nutmeg

          Corn oil
      2 beef bouillon cubes
    ¼ cup (½ stick) butter, heated to dark golden and cooled

          Sour cream (garnish)

Melt unsalted butter in heavy large skillet over low heat. Stir in onions, leeks, shallots and garlic. Cover and cook until vegetables are translucent, about 10 minutes. Season to taste with salt and pepper. Remove skillet from heat.

Beat half and half with eggs in medium bowl until well blended. Stir bread cubes, chives and nutmeg into vegetables. Blend in egg mixture. Set mixture aside until bread cubes absorb liquid, about 30 minutes.

Bring large amount of water to rapid boil in stockpot. Meanwhile, cut three 12 × 36-inch rectangles of cheesecloth. Stack cheesecloth to form 3 layers. Brush top layer generously with corn oil. Turn bread mixture onto cheesecloth about 6 inches from 1 short end and several inches from sides. Fold 6-inch border over, then continue to roll mixture up in cheesecloth. Twist ends to enclose bread mixture and tie securely with string. Add bouillon cubes to boiling water and stir to dissolve. Add sausage and return water to boil. Reduce heat and simmer sausage until firm to touch, about 40 minutes.

Remove sausage from water and cool to lukewarm. Remove cheesecloth. Brush sausage with some of browned butter. Set aside and let cool completely.

Cut sausage into ⅔-inch-thick slices. Reheat browned butter in heavy large skillet over medium heat. Add sausage slices (in batches if necessary) and cook until light golden. Serve immediately with sour cream.

POTATO AND CORN GRATIN

4 to 6 servings

      2 pounds baking potatoes (8 medium), peeled and sliced into thin rounds
          Salt and freshly ground white pepper

4 **medium ears corn, grated (about 1 cup)**
5 **tablespoons butter, cut into small pieces**
2 **cups buttermilk**
2 **tablespoons minced fresh chives *or* green onion (optional garnish)**

Preheat oven to 375°F. Generously butter 9 × 12-inch gratin or other baking dish. Arrange half of potato slices in single layer in bottom, overlapping slightly. Season with salt and pepper. Sprinkle with ½ cup corn and dot with 2½ tablespoons butter. Repeat layering. Pour buttermilk over. Bake until milk is absorbed and potatoes are browned and crusty, about 1 to 1¼ hours. Sprinkle with minced chives and serve immediately.

PEARS COOKED IN VERJUICE

Verjuice, acidic juice extracted from large unripened grapes, was used in cooking during the Renaissance. Prepare dish three days ahead to allow syrup to permeate pears. The syrup can be frozen and reused to poach other fresh seasonal fruits.

10 servings

5 **cups tart grapes with seeds (preferably red), stemmed**
4 **cups light-bodied red wine (such as Beaujolais) *or* rosé**
½ **cup red wine vinegar**
3 **cups dry white wine**
1½ **cups sugar**
4 **whole cloves**
2 **3-inch cinnamon sticks, broken into pieces**
1 **teaspoon whole black peppercorns, lightly crushed**
10 **small slightly underripe pears, preferably Seckel**
3 **tablespoons fresh lemon juice**

Crush grapes in processor or blender using several on/off turns. Blend with red wine and vinegar in nonaluminum bowl. Refrigerate overnight.

Strain mixture through fine sieve into 5-quart nonaluminum saucepan. Stir in white wine, sugar, cloves, cinnamon sticks and peppercorns. Cover pan partially and cook over low heat until sugar dissolves, about 10 minutes, swirling pan occasionally.

Meanwhile, peel pears, core through bottom and cut thin slice from bottom so pears stand upright. As pears are peeled, place in large bowl of water to which lemon juice has been added.

Drain pears; add to liquid (it should be barely shaking) and poach until pears are barely resistant when pierced with knife, about 10 minutes. Cool in liquid, turning often. Cover and refrigerate 3 days, turning once a day. Drain thoroughly before serving.

WARM FRUIT COMPOTE

Also excellent as a dessert.

6 servings

2 **medium apples, peeled, cored and sliced**
6 **ounces dried pitted prunes (1 cup)**
6 **dried figs, sliced**
3 **ounces dried apricots (⅔ cup)**
⅓ **cup water**
⅓ **cup apple juice**
   Juice of ½ lemon
2 **to 3 cinnamon sticks**
½ **teaspoon ground cloves**
2 **medium pears, peeled, cored and sliced**
2 **medium oranges, peeled, seeded and sectioned**
1 **cup seedless grapes**
   Plain yogurt

Combine apples, prunes, figs, apricots, water, apple and lemon juices and spices in large saucepan and bring to simmer over medium heat. Let simmer 5 minutes. Add pears and continue cooking just until fruit is tender, about 5 minutes. (*Can be prepared up to 2 days ahead to this point. Let cool, cover and refrigerate until ready to use.*)

Just before serving, return mixture to simmer. Stir in orange sections and grapes and cook 2 minutes. Discard cinnamon. Serve warm with yogurt.

NATIVE AMERICAN CRANBERRY SAUCE

Can be prepared 3 days ahead.

Makes about 4 cups

1½ **cups pure maple syrup**
½ **cup water**
1 **teaspoon ground ginger**
4 **cups fresh cranberries**

Bring syrup, water and ginger to boil in heavy 2½-quart saucepan over medium heat. Stir in cranberries. Simmer until berries begin to pop, about 5 minutes, stirring occasionally. Turn into bowl and let cool. Cover and refrigerate.

APPLE AND SWEET POTATO PUREE

6 servings

1 **pound sweet potatoes (about 2 medium)**
8 **tablespoons (1 stick) butter**
1½ **pounds Pippin or Granny Smith apples, peeled, cored and sliced**
1 **tablespoon fresh lemon juice**
1½ **teaspoons salt**
2 **to 3 pieces preserved ginger**
½ **teaspoon cinnamon**

Preheat oven to 375°F. Bake potatoes until tender, about 50 minutes. Discard skin; reserve pulp.

Melt 1 tablespoon butter in large skillet over medium heat. Add apples, cover and cook until soft and mushy, about 12 minutes, stirring occasionally. Transfer apples to processor. Add sweet potatoes, lemon juice, salt, ginger, cinnamon and remaining 7 tablespoons butter and mix, using on/off turns, until smooth. Serve hot.

Grains and Pasta

CAJUN MAQUE CHOUX

A traditional Louisiana side dish for simply grilled meats or fish.

8 servings

½ cup bacon drippings
1 green bell pepper, finely chopped
1 medium onion, chopped
1 large garlic clove, minced
4 cups corn kernels
2 medium tomatoes, peeled, seeded and chopped
½ teaspoon ground red pepper
  Salt and freshly ground pepper
1 cup chicken stock, preferably homemade (see recipe, page 38)

Melt bacon drippings in heavy large skillet over medium heat. Add green pepper, onion and garlic and sauté 5 minutes. Stir in corn, tomatoes, ground red pepper and salt and pepper and cook, stirring occasionally, 5 minutes. Pour in stock. Reduce heat to medium low, cover partially and cook until liquid is almost totally absorbed, about 45 minutes. Serve immediately.

RISOTTO CASSEROLE WITH PORCINI

6 to 8 servings

Mushroom Compote
1 ounce dried porcini mushrooms
  Hot water

3 tablespoons butter
8 ounces fresh mushrooms, sliced
2 tablespoons minced fresh parsley
2 garlic cloves, pureed
  Salt and freshly ground pepper

Zucchini
  Flour
  Salt and freshly ground pepper
1 medium zucchini, cut into ⅓-inch rounds
  Olive oil

Risotto
¼ cup (½ stick) butter
1 medium onion, finely chopped
2 cups arborio rice*
4 to 6 cups chicken stock *or* veal stock (preferably homemade), heated

5 ounces Taleggio cheese, grated or crumbled
1 cup half and half
2 eggs
½ teaspoon freshly grated nutmeg

For compote: Soak porcini in hot water to cover until soft, about 30 minutes. Rinse well and drain, reserving liquid. Strain liquid through cheesecloth. Discard hard center cores from porcini. Slice porcini into ¼-inch strips.

Melt butter in heavy medium saucepan over high heat. Sauté porcini and mushrooms until all liquid evaporates. Blend in parsley and garlic. Season with salt and pepper to taste.

For zucchini: Season flour with salt and pepper. Coat zucchini rounds with flour, shaking off excess. Heat ¼ inch olive oil in heavy large skillet over medium heat until hot but not smoking. Sauté zucchini until brown, about 10 minutes. Drain on paper towels.

For risotto: Melt butter in heavy large saucepan over medium heat. Add onion, cover and cook until translucent, about 10 minutes. Add rice and stir until opaque, about 1 to 2 minutes. Pour in porcini soaking liquid and enough hot stock to cover rice and bring to boil. Reduce

heat and simmer until almost all liquid is absorbed, stirring constantly. Add another ½ cup stock and cook, stirring until absorbed. Continue adding stock, ½ cup at a time, stirring constantly, until rice is tender but al dente, about 30 minutes (rice should be moist but not soupy). Season with salt and pepper.

Preheat oven to 325°F. Butter 1½- to 2-quart baking dish. Spread half of rice in dish. Arrange zucchini rounds over top. Sprinkle with salt and pepper and cover with all but 3 tablespoons cheese. Top with mushroom mixture. Spread on remaining rice. Blend half and half, eggs and nutmeg in bowl. Pour over rice. Sprinkle with remaining cheese. Bake until top is browned, about 30 minutes. Serve risotto immediately.

*Available at Italian markets.

FRESH PARSLEY NOODLES
(Nouilles au Persil Frais)

6 servings

1 cup packed parsley leaves, blanched 2 minutes and completely dried
3 cups unbleached all purpose flour, or more
3 egg yolks, room temperature
2 to 3 eggs, room temperature
1 teaspoon salt

¾ cup (1½ sticks) butter

Puree parsley leaves in processor; leaf particles will be visible. Mound 3 cups flour on work surface and make well in center. Place egg yolks, 2 eggs, salt and pureed parsley in well and blend with fork. Gradually draw small amount of flour from inner edge of well into egg mixture with fork, stirring constantly until all flour is incorporated. Knead mixture until smooth dough forms, kneading in another egg if dough is dry and sprinkling dough lightly with flour if sticky.

Divide dough into 4 to 6 pieces. Wrap all but 1 piece of dough in plastic or towel to prevent drying; set aside. Flatten remaining piece of dough with heel of hand, then fold in half. Turn pasta machine to widest setting and run dough through. Continue folding and kneading process with pasta machine until dough is smooth and velvety, about 10 more times (number will depend on how vigorously dough was kneaded by hand). Dust dough lightly with more flour as necessary.

Adjust pasta machine to next narrower setting. Run dough through machine *without folding,* dusting lightly with flour if sticky. Repeat, narrowing rollers after each run until machine is on second to narrowest setting; pasta should be less than 1/16 inch thick.

Knead and shape remaining dough into sheets, kneading each piece slightly before running through machine. Set aside until sheets look firm and leathery and edges begin to curl up slightly but are not brittle (this will take 10 to 30 minutes depending on dryness of dough and temperature and humidity of kitchen). *Pasta must be cut at this point or dough will break.*

Cut dough sheets into 1/4-inch-wide noodles. Arrange pasta on kitchen towel set over baking sheet to dry. Set aside until ready to cook. (*Pasta can be prepared several days ahead; store dry noodles airtight at room temperature.*)

Fill pasta cooker or stockpot 3/4 full with salted water, cover and bring to boil over high heat. Add pasta and stir vigorously to prevent sticking. Cook uncovered until al dente, about 5 to 20 seconds for freshly made pasta and up to 3 minutes for thoroughly dried; taste often to prevent overcooking. Drain well.

Melt butter in large skillet over medium-high heat. Add pasta, toss gently and serve.

RYE RICE PILAF

The rye flakes add a toothsome crunch reminiscent of wild rice.

8 servings

½ cup (1 stick) butter
¼ cup vermicelli, broken into ¾-inch pieces (about 1 ounce)
1 cup uncooked rice
1 cup rye flakes*
¼ cup minced onion
4 cups boiling water
1½ teaspoons salt, or more to taste
Freshly ground pepper

Melt butter in heavy 2-quart saucepan over medium-high heat. Add vermicelli and sauté until lightly browned, 2 to 3 minutes. Stir in rice, rye flakes and onion and sauté until rice is *very* hot, vermicelli is browned and onion is soft. Pour in boiling water. Blend in salt and season with pepper. Reduce heat to low. Cover pan with 3 paper towels, then with tight-fitting lid. Cook 20 minutes. Remove lid and paper towels and, if necessary, continue cooking until all moisture evaporates. Fluff pilaf with fork. Turn pilaf into dish and serve immediately.

*Available in natural foods stores.

WILD RICE PANCAKES

Serve these pancakes with whipped butter as a savory side dish, or dress them with melted butter and sugared strawberries, blueberry syrup, honey or butter-sautéed apple slices with cinnamon sugar for breakfast or brunch.

Makes about 36

⅓ cup wild rice, rinsed thoroughly
2 cups milk
2 tablespoons (¼ stick) butter, melted
1 teaspoon salt
4 eggs, separated, room temperature
1 cup blanched toasted almonds, finely chopped (5 ounces)

1 cup all purpose flour
Pinch of cream of tartar

2 tablespoons (or more) clarified butter *or* 1 tablespoon butter and 1 tablespoon oil (or more)

Bring 1 cup salted water to boil in medium saucepan. Add rice, cover and simmer over low heat until tender and all water is absorbed, about 45 minutes to 1 hour (*rice can be cooked ahead and set aside*). Blend in milk, melted butter and salt. Beat yolks until light in color, about 3 minutes. Mix into rice. Stir in chopped nuts and flour. Beat whites with cream of tartar until stiff but not dry; fold into batter.

Preheat oven to 175°F. Melt 2 tablespoons clarified butter on griddle or in heavy large skillet over medium heat. Ladle 2½-inch pancakes onto griddle and cook until bottom is golden brown and pancakes begin to set, about 2 to 3 minutes. Turn and brown second side. Repeat with remaining batter, adding more butter to griddle as necessary. Arrange finished pancakes in single layer on baking sheet and keep warm in oven until all are cooked. Serve immediately.

BUTTERED FRUIT RICE

(*Tupa Menda*)

6 servings

½ cup (1 stick) butter
2 cups rice, rinsed and drained
3½ cups water
¼ teaspoon salt
½ cup raisins
½ cup diced dried apricots

Melt butter in heavy large saucepan over medium heat. Add rice and stir until golden, 2 to 3 minutes. Blend in water and salt and bring to boil. Reduce heat to low, cover and simmer 5 minutes. Stir in raisins and apricots. Cover and continue simmering until rice is dry and soft, about 12 minutes. Turn heat off and let rice stand, covered, 15 minutes before serving.

10 ❖ Salads and Dressings

Main Dish Salads

CRABMEAT SALAD IN SHELLS

6 servings

12 **hard-shell blue crabs***

8 **ounces small pasta shells**

4 **ounces trimmed asparagus, stems peeled**

3 **medium tomatoes, peeled, seeded and chopped (about 1 pound)**

3 **egg yolks, room temperature**

1½ **tablespoons fresh lemon juice**

2½ **teaspoons snipped fresh chives**

1½ **teaspoons Dijon mustard**

1½ **teaspoons grated lemon peel**

1 **tablespoon minced fresh tarragon *or* large pinch dried, crumbled**

1 **cup plus 2 tablespoons olive oil**

6 **tablespoons vegetable oil**

Watercress sprigs (garnish)

Combine crabs in stockpot with enough cold water to cover. Cover and bring to boil over high heat. Let boil 5 minutes. Drain and cool. Remove legs and body from top shells. Scrub top shells; dry shells and refrigerate until ready to use. Remove meat from legs, claws and bodies. Transfer to bowl.

Bring large amount of salted water to rapid boil. Add pasta shells, stir, and cook until al dente, about 7 to 8 minutes. Drain and pat dry with paper towels. Add pasta shells to crabmeat.

Meanwhile, bring large pot of salted water to rapid boil. Add asparagus and cook until crisp-tender, 2 to 3 minutes. Drain and plunge into cold water to stop cooking process. Drain and dry well. Cut asparagus stalks diagonally into ¾-inch pieces. Add asparagus to crabmeat mixture. Blend in tomatoes.

Combine egg yolks, lemon juice, chives, mustard, lemon peel and tarragon in processor or blender. With machine running, gradually add olive and vegetable oils in slow, steady stream and mix until thick and creamy. Pour dressing over crabmeat mixture and toss gently. Cover salad and refrigerate for up to 2 hours.

To serve, divide crab salad among reserved shells. Garnish with watercress sprigs.

*Two cups cooked flaked king crab, Dungeness or stone crab can be substituted.

ROASTED PEPPER SALAD WITH FETA AND SHRIMP

A perfect main course for summer. Serve with country bread, a fruity white wine and an iced fruit soufflé.

4 to 6 servings

1 **cup plain yogurt**

5 **fresh mint leaves *or* ½ teaspoon dried, crumbled**

1 **small garlic clove, chopped**

3 **green bell peppers, rinsed and dried**

3 **sweet red bell peppers, rinsed and dried**

2 **yellow sweet peppers,* rinsed and dried**

1 **tablespoon olive oil**

1 **tablespoon wine vinegar**

8 **inner leaves of romaine lettuce**

1 **pound jumbo shrimp, cooked, shelled and deveined**

8 **ounces feta *or* fresh goat cheese, coarsely crumbled**

½ **cup Greek olives**

3 **small green onions, shredded**

Combine yogurt, mint and garlic in processor or blender and puree.

Preheat broiler. Pierce each pepper near stem with sharp, thin knife. Arrange peppers on broiler pan and roast on all sides until blistered (but not charred). Transfer to plastic or paper bag, close tightly and steam 15 minutes. Slip off skins; discard stems and seeds. Slice peppers into thin strips. Transfer to large bowl. Add olive oil and vinegar and toss gently until blended.

Arrange romaine leaves in fan pattern on serving platter. Mound peppers in center. Drizzle some yogurt dressing over top. Scatter shrimp, cheese, olives and green onion around peppers. Cover and chill slightly before serving with remaining dressing.

*If unavailable, substitute 1 additional green and 1 additional red pepper.

WARM SCALLOP AND AVOCADO SALAD

2 servings

- 2 cups chicken stock, preferably homemade (see recipe, page 38)
- 5 to 6 ounces fresh sea scallops
- ¼ cup olive oil
- 1½ tablespoons Sherry vinegar
- 1 teaspoon Dijon mustard
  Salt and freshly ground pepper
- 8 large spinach leaves, stemmed (about 3 ounces after stemming)
- 1 medium avocado, peeled, pitted and thinly sliced lengthwise
- 6 walnut halves, toasted

Heat stock just to simmer in medium saucepan. Add scallops and poach just until opaque, about 2 to 3 minutes; *do not let broth boil and do not overcook or scallops will be tough.* Chill scallops in stock by setting pan in large bowl of ice water for at least 30 minutes.

Just before serving, slice scallops into thin rounds. Combine oil, vinegar, mustard and salt and pepper in small saucepan and bring to simmer. Stack spinach leaves and roll up lengthwise. Cut crosswise into chiffonade. Divide spinach between 2 heated salad plates. Arrange scallops and avocado decoratively atop spinach. Garnish with walnut halves. Pour warm dressing over salads and serve immediately.

MUSSEL SALAD WITH POTATOES VINAIGRETTE

Light and fresh, with most of the preparation done ahead, this is a perfect change-of-pace dish. Precede with a lightly creamed carrot soup and follow with a hot apple tart.

4 main-course or 6 to 8 first-course servings

- 2½ pounds mussels, scrubbed and debearded (discard any that are opened or broken)
- 1 tablespoon cornmeal
- ½ cup water
- 1½ pounds White Rose, red *or* new potatoes
- ¼ cup cider vinegar
- 1 tablespoon olive oil
- 1 large shallot, minced
  Salt and freshly ground pepper
- ¼ cup olive oil
- 4 to 5 shallots, thinly sliced (about 1 cup)
- 1½ tablespoons chopped fresh basil leaves *or* 1½ teaspoons dried, crumbled
- 1 teaspoon grated orange peel
- 2 large garlic cloves, minced (about 2 teaspoons)
- 1 teaspoon tomato paste
- 7 ounces fresh young spinach, stemmed, rinsed and dried
- 4 large tomatoes, hollowed out and diced *or* 8 canned plum tomatoes, seeded, drained and diced (2 cups diced)
- 3 tablespoons fresh lemon juice
  Freshly ground pepper

Combine mussels in large bowl with enough cold water to cover and sprinkle with cornmeal. Chill 8 to 24 hours.

Drain mussels. Transfer to 4-quart saucepan. Add ½ cup water, cover and place over medium-high heat. Cook until shells open, about 5 minutes. Remove opened mussels from pan using slotted spoon. Cook remaining mussels until opened, about 5 more minutes; discard any that do not open. Set mussels aside to cool; reserve liquid. Remove mussels from shells. Reserve about 6 shells for garnish; discard remaining shells. Refrigerate mussels in cooking liquid until ready to use.

Combine potatoes in saucepan with enough water to cover. Place over medium-high heat and bring to boil. Let boil until potatoes are tender, 15 to 20 minutes; cool *slightly.* Peel potatoes and slice into ⅛- to ¼-inch rounds; keep warm.

Place vinegar in large bowl. Whisk in 1 tablespoon olive oil 1 drop at a time. Add minced shallot with salt and pepper to taste. Add potatoes and toss gently to blend. Refrigerate until 2 hours before serving. (*Can be prepared to this point up to 24 hours ahead.*)

About 30 minutes before serving, heat ¼ cup olive oil in heavy large nonaluminum skillet over medium-high heat. Add sliced shallots and sauté until soft, about 3 minutes. Stir in basil, orange peel and garlic and cook about 2 minutes, watching carefully so garlic does not brown. Blend in tomato paste and reserved mussel liquid and boil until reduced by ⅓. Set sauce aside.

Arrange spinach leaves in overlapping pattern on 12-inch round platter. Spoon potato salad into center. Bring sauce to boil over medium-high heat. Add diced tomato and cook 10 seconds. Reduce heat to medium, add reserved mussels and cook just until heated through; *do not overcook or mussels will toughen.* Stir in lemon juice. Season generously with pepper. Pour sauce over potatoes. Garnish with shells. Serve at room temperature.

SMOKED TROUT SALAD

You will need 2 cups of hickory chips for smoking the trout.

6 servings

- 2 pounds fresh trout (about 4 small), cleaned but not boned
- 1 pound green beans
  Escarole leaves
- 1 bunch radishes, shredded
- 2 large tomatoes, peeled, seeded and chopped
  Chuck's Special Dressing (see following recipe)

Soak 2 cups hickory chips in water 20 minutes. Arrange in bottom of electric smoker.* Place tray half filled with water over chips. Set trout on grill, cover and smoke 1 hour; do not remove lid while cooking. (*Procedure may vary with manufacturer's instructions. Trout can be refrigerated up to 2 weeks after cooking in smoker.*)

Transfer trout to work surface. Remove skin, bone carefully and cut fish into narrow strips. Wrap fish tightly in foil and refrigerate until ready to use.

French cut beans. Blanch in boiling salted water until crisp-tender, about 2 minutes. Plunge into cold water to stop cooking process. Drain beans well; gently pat dry with paper towels.

Cover serving platter with escarole leaves. Place beans down center of platter. Arrange trout in lengthwise strip over beans. Set narrow strip of radishes on each side of beans. Arrange tomatoes at top and bottom of platter. Refrigerate at least 1 hour. (If salad has been chilled more than 3 hours, let stand at room temperature 15 minutes before serving.) Serve immediately with Chuck's Special Dressing.

If commercial smoker is not available, soak 2 cups hickory chips in water 20 minutes. Meanwhile, line very heavy skillet or lidded casserole with heavy-duty aluminum foil, bringing enough foil up above rim so it will completely cover lid and form tight seal. Arrange hickory chips in single layer in bottom of skillet. Sprinkle 1 tablespoon sugar over chips. Set rack about 2 to 3 inches above chips. Generously butter rack. Arrange trout on rack and cover skillet with lid. Bring foil up over lid, folding and pleating to make tight seal. Smoke fish over high heat 20 minutes; do not overcook.

Chuck's Special Dressing

Makes about 1 cup

- ½ cup olive oil
- ¼ cup fresh lemon juice
- 3 tablespoons white wine vinegar (preferably French)*
- 1 egg yolk
- ¼ teaspoon dried thyme, crumbled
  Salt and freshly ground pepper

Mix oil, lemon juice, vinegar, egg yolk and thyme in small bowl. Season with salt and pepper. Cover tightly. Refrigerate until ready to use.

For a milder dressing, use only 1½ tablespoons white wine vinegar.

CURRIED CHICKEN SALAD WITH APPLES ON SPICED FRUIT BREAD

Bread and salad are both delicious on their own but are especially good combined in a sandwich. You will have enough bread for a double recipe of the curried chicken salad.

Makes two 9 × 5-inch loaves and about 5 cups chicken salad.

Spiced Fruit Bread

- 2 cups warm milk (105°F to 115°F)
- 2 tablespoons sugar
- 1 envelope dry yeast
- 2 bananas, mashed (1 cup)
- 1 cup raisins
- ¼ cup (½ stick) butter, melted
  Grated peel of 2 oranges
- 2 tablespoons cinnamon
- 1 tablespoon salt
- 5 to 6 cups bread flour *or* unbleached all purpose flour

- 1 egg
- 1 tablespoon milk

Chicken Salad

- 3 cups chopped cooked chicken
- 1 large red apple, cored and finely diced
- ½ cup plain yogurt
- ⅓ cup mayonnaise
- 2 tablespoons plus 2 teaspoons fresh lemon juice
- 1 tablespoon curry powder, or to taste
- ⅓ cup chopped fresh parsley leaves
- ¼ cup grated onion
  Salt and freshly ground pepper

  Crushed peanuts
  Boston lettuce leaves

For bread: Oil very large bowl and set aside. Pour ½ cup warm milk into another large bowl. Add sugar and yeast and stir until dissolved. Let stand until foamy, 5 to 10 minutes. Blend in 1½ cups warm milk, bananas, raisins, melted butter, orange peel, cinnamon and salt. Using wooden spoon, stir in flour 1 cup at a time until dough can be kneaded. Turn dough out onto floured surface and knead until smooth and elastic, about 10 to 15 minutes, adding remaining flour as necessary. Transfer dough to oiled bowl, turning to coat entire surface. Cover with damp towel. Let stand in warm draft-free area until doubled, about 1½ hours.

Grease two 9 × 5-inch loaf pans. Punch dough down and knead lightly. Divide dough in half. Shape each half into loaf and transfer to prepared pans. Cover with damp towel. Let dough stand in warm draft-free area until doubled, about 35 minutes.

Preheat oven to 375°F. Blend egg and remaining 1 tablespoon milk in cup. Brush tops of loaves with egg mixture to glaze. Bake until loaves sound hollow when tapped, about 50 minutes. Cool completely on racks before slicing.

For salad: Combine chicken and apple in large bowl. Blend yogurt, mayonnaise, lemon juice and curry powder in small bowl. Add to chicken mixture and toss to coat. Stir in parsley, onion and seasoning. Cover and chill until ready to serve.

For sandwiches, spread slice of bread with chicken salad. Sprinkle with peanuts. Top with lettuce and second bread slice.

SMOKED CHICKEN, APPLE AND WALNUT SALAD

Accompany this salad with a crisp Chenin Blanc.

6 servings

- 4 whole smoked chicken breasts (about 2 pounds), skinned and cut into thin strips

3 medium Granny Smith
  apples, cored and diced
6 celery stalks, sliced (1½
  cups)
4 cups chopped watercress
  leaves
1 cup Lemon-Mustard
  Dressing (see following
  recipe)
  Freshly ground pepper

  Boston or romaine lettuce
  leaves
  Watercress sprigs (garnish)
1¼ cups chopped toasted
  walnuts (5 ounces)

Toss chicken strips, apple, celery and watercress in large bowl. Blend in lemon dressing and pepper. Cover and refrigerate up to 4 hours.

To serve, line platter with lettuce. Mound salad in center. Garnish with watercress sprigs. Sprinkle with nuts.

* Smoked turkey breast can be substituted.

Lemon-Mustard Dressing

Makes 1 cup

4 teaspoons fresh lemon juice
4 teaspoons Dijon mustard
1 egg yolk
¼ teaspoon *each* salt and
  freshly ground pepper
1 cup olive oil
1 tablespoon fresh lemon
  juice

Combine 4 teaspoons lemon juice with mustard, yolk and salt and pepper in processor or blender. With machine running, add olive oil through feed tube in slow, steady stream and mix until thickened. Blend in remaining lemon juice.

BEEF SALAD WITH ASPARAGUS AND BROCCOLI

4 servings

1 small flank steak

4 cups fresh asparagus,
  diagonally sliced into 2-inch
  pieces
1 bunch broccoli, cut into
  bite-size florets

Ginger Dressing

⅓ cup light soy sauce
¼ cup vinegar
3 tablespoons sesame oil
1 1½-inch piece fresh ginger,
  peeled and grated
1 teaspoon sugar
  Freshly ground white
  pepper

Broil or pan-fry flank steak to desired doneness. Cool and slice.

Bring large pot of salted water to rapid boil. Add asparagus and blanch 30 seconds. Remove with slotted spoon or strainer and set aside to cool. Add broccoli to same water and blanch 30 seconds. Drain well and let cool.

For dressing: Combine all ingredients and whisk to blend.

When ready to serve, toss beef slices with dressing. Add vegetables and toss again. Serve at room temperature.

DUCK AND ORANGE SALAD WITH PECANS

2 servings

2 duck legs and thighs,
  trimmed
2 teaspoons fresh lemon juice
1 teaspoon minced fresh
  tarragon *or* ¼ teaspoon
  dried, crumbled
1 teaspoon minced fresh
  parsley
  Salt and freshly ground
  pepper

¼ cup minced green onion
  (about 3)
3 tablespoons olive oil
1½ tablespoons fresh lemon
  juice
  Grated peel of 1 orange
  Salt and freshly ground
  pepper

1 tablespoon butter
1 garlic clove, unpeeled
¼ cup coarsely chopped pecans

1 medium orange, peeled,
  thinly sliced and seeded
  Lettuce leaves

Arrange duck in shallow pan. Combine 2 teaspoons lemon juice with tarragon, parsley and salt and pepper in small bowl. Brush over duck. Let stand at room temperature about 1 hour.

Preheat broiler. Place duck in broiling pan and broil until browned and crisp, turning once, about 5 minutes per side. Let duck cool completely before cutting.

Cut meat into strips; discard bones (or use in stock). Combine duck and onion in medium bowl. Whisk olive oil, remaining lemon juice, orange peel and salt and pepper to taste in small bowl. Pour over duck. Refrigerate at least 2 hours, stirring occasionally.

Meanwhile, melt butter in small skillet. Add garlic and cook over low heat 1 to 2 minutes. Discard garlic. Add pecans to skillet and cook until browned and crisp, stirring frequently. Remove from heat and set aside.

When ready to serve, add orange slices to duck and toss well. Taste and adjust seasonings. Arrange lettuce leaves on plates and spoon salad over. Sprinkle with pecans and serve.

MARINATED LAMB SALAD

After marinating, lamb can be frozen up to one month.

12 servings

Marinade

1½ cups olive oil *or* peanut oil
1 cup minced fresh parsley
½ cup dry vermouth
8 green onions, minced
6 tablespoons minced fresh
  mint leaves
4 to 6 tablespoons fresh
  lemon *or* lime juice, or to
  taste
2 to 3 tablespoons minced
  garlic
2 tablespoons Grand Marnier
1 tablespoon dried rosemary,
  crumbled
  Salt and freshly ground
  pepper
1 5- to 6-pound leg of lamb,
  boned, trimmed and cut
  into 1½ × ½-inch cubes

1   tablespoon olive oil *or* peanut oil
4   cups chopped onion
5   to 6 kiwi fruit, thinly sliced (reserve 1 or 2 slices for garnish)
5   tablespoons minced cilantro (coriander) leaves
3   to 6 whole green chilies, seeded, deveined and shredded
3   to 6 tablespoons capers, rinsed and drained
1   cup roasted cashews
1   cup minced fresh parsley
1   6-ounce can water chestnuts, drained and thinly sliced
¼   to ½ cup fresh mint leaves, chopped
¼   to ½ cup watercress leaves
½   cup toasted sesame seed (optional)
4   to 6 tablespoons lemon juice, or to taste
     Salt and freshly ground pepper

Combine first 9 ingredients with salt and pepper in large mixing bowl. Add lamb, tossing to coat. Cover and chill 1 to 2 days; turn once or twice each day.

Heat 1 tablespoon oil in large skillet over medium-high heat. Add onion and cook until browned, being careful not to burn. Remove with slotted spoon.

Drain lamb. Stir-fry in small batches in same skillet over high heat until just pink. *Do not overcook; test by cutting one piece in each batch.* Transfer lamb to large bowl using slotted spoon. Let cool to room temperature.

Add onion, kiwi slices, cilantro, chilies, capers, cashews, parsley, water chestnuts, mint, watercress, sesame seed, lemon juice and salt and pepper to lamb and blend well. Arrange on large platter and garnish with reserved kiwi slices. Serve at room temperature.

❖

HAM AND ASPARAGUS SALAD

A main-dish salad with oriental overtones. Accompany with assorted breads, a chilled white wine and pineapple sorbet for dessert.

4 servings

4   large dried shiitake mushrooms
⅓   cup boiling water

1   pound asparagus, cut diagonally into ¾- to 1-inch lengths (about 2 cups)

Oriental Dressing

1   ounce tofu* (about 2 tablespoons)
1   small garlic clove
¼   cup vegetable oil
1   tablespoon sesame oil
1   tablespoon tamari soy sauce
1½   teaspoons rice vinegar
     Large pinch of ground red pepper
     Pinch of sugar
     Pinch of coarse salt
⅛   teaspoon freshly ground pepper (optional)

6   ounces cooked ham, cut into 2-inch strips (about 1½ cups)
½   cup peeled jícama julienne
¼   cup diagonally sliced green onion
2½   tablespoons toasted sesame seed

White Wine Vinaigrette

2   teaspoons white wine vinegar
½   teaspoon Dijon mustard
½   teaspoon coarse salt
⅛   teaspoon freshly ground black pepper
¼   cup vegetable oil

3   cups romaine lettuce, cut into 1-inch-wide strips
1   cup watercress sprigs
8   cherry tomatoes, halved (garnish)

Combine mushrooms and boiling water in small bowl. Let stand 30 minutes. Remove mushrooms, gently squeezing out excess water. Cut out woody stems and discard.

Slice mushrooms into thin strips; set aside.

Bring large amount of water to rapid boil. Add asparagus and blanch 2 minutes. Drain immediately. Rinse under cold water until cool. Drain and set aside.

For dressing: Puree tofu and garlic in processor or blender, scraping down sides of container. Combine oils, soy and vinegar. With machine running, add oil mixture in slow steady stream, then add red pepper, sugar and salt and blend well. Taste and add freshly ground pepper if desired.

Combine ham, jícama, onion, 1½ tablespoons sesame seed and reserved mushroom strips in large bowl. Toss with all but 2 tablespoons dressing.

For vinaigrette: Blend vinegar, mustard, salt and pepper in another large bowl. Whisk in oil 1 drop at a time.

Toss vinaigrette with lettuce and watercress and spread on large platter. Spoon ham and asparagus salad down center. Spoon remaining 2 tablespoons dressing over top. Garnish with tomatoes. Sprinkle with remaining sesame seed and serve.

* Two tablespoons mayonnaise or ½ egg yolk can be substituted for tofu.

CHARCUTERIE SALAD

A good do-ahead recipe. This buffet or supper dish can be doubled easily. Crusty bread and beer or a light, dry wine are good companions.

4 to 6 servings

1   pound cooked well-marbled pork, trimmed of all fat and cut into thin sticks
¼   cup light olive oil
¼   cup Spanish Sherry vinegar
6   cornichons, cut julienne
2   green onions, minced
1   large shallot, minced

1   pound new potatoes

¼   cup wine vinegar
3   tablespoons light olive oil

3 tablespoons minced sweet red onion
1 heaping teaspoon Dijon mustard
 Salt and freshly ground pepper

1 large head romaine lettuce
1 cup julienne of roasted sweet red peppers
 Salt and freshly ground pepper
2 green onions, cut into very thin 2-inch strips
1 tablespoon capers, rinsed and drained

Combine pork, ¼ cup oil, Sherry vinegar, cornichons, minced green onions and shallot in medium bowl and toss gently. Cover and refrigerate 1 to 2 days.

Boil potatoes in large saucepan in water to cover until tender. Drain well. Return to hot pan and place over heat to dry, shaking pan constantly. Let stand until cool enough to handle, then peel and cut into medium dice.

Combine potatoes, wine vinegar, 3 tablespoons oil, red onion,

mustard and salt and pepper in another bowl and toss lightly. Cover and refrigerate overnight.

To serve, arrange lettuce leaves on large platter, leaving center almost empty. Add peppers to pork mixture and toss well. Taste and season with salt and pepper. Arrange potato salad over lettuce in shallow ring and sprinkle with green onions. Mound pork in center; top with capers. Serve lightly chilled.

Side Dish Salads

CURRIED RICE SALAD

12 servings

Garlic-Mustard Dressing

2 tablespoons fresh lime juice
1 egg, room temperature
½ teaspoon dry mustard
½ teaspoon salt
½ medium garlic clove
1¼ cups vegetable oil
½ cup sour cream
1 tablespoon curry powder, or to taste, mixed with enough water to form paste

2 tablespoons (¼ stick) butter
12 pearl onions
½ cup dried currants
5 tablespoons dark rum
4 cups cooked rice, room temperature
1½ cups ¼-inch-thick banana slices
1 cup fresh pineapple chunks
½ cup slivered almonds
 Cherry tomatoes (garnish)

For dressing: Mix lime juice, egg, mustard, salt and garlic in processor or blender. With machine running, add oil in slow steady stream, mixing until thick. Blend in sour cream and curry.

Melt butter in heavy large skillet over low heat. Add onions, cover and cook 10 minutes. Remove cover, increase heat to medium and cook until brown, 5 to 10 minutes. Combine currants and rum in large bowl and let marinate 10 minutes. Drain currants and return to bowl. Add rice, banana, pineapple and almonds and toss gently. Fold in onions. Blend in dressing. Garnish with tomatoes. Serve at room temperature.

RICE SALAD WITH BRAISED BROCCOLI

16 to 18 servings

Rice

6 cups chicken stock, preferably homemade (see recipe, page 38)
3 cups uncooked converted rice
6 tablespoons vegetable oil
¼ cup white wine vinegar
 Salt and freshly ground pepper

Broccoli

3½ pounds broccoli
6 tablespoons vegetable oil
6 large shallots, coarsely chopped
2 large pinches of sugar
 Salt and freshly ground pepper
2 cups chicken stock
8 large green onions, cut diagonally into ¾-inch pieces

Dressing

¼ cup white wine vinegar
2 large shallots, chopped
2 teaspoons Dijon mustard
¼ teaspoon Hungarian sweet paprika
 Large pinch of ground red pepper
¾ cup vegetable oil
 Salt and freshly ground pepper

8 large Boston lettuce leaves
3 green onion tops, minced

For rice: Bring stock to boil in heavy large saucepan. Stir in rice. Reduce heat to low, cover and cook 20 minutes. Fluff rice with fork. Turn into bowl. Stir in oil and vinegar. Cool. Season rice mixture with salt and pepper. (*Can be prepared 1 day ahead and refrigerated.*)

For broccoli: Peel stems; cut diagonally into pieces ½ inch thick. Divide heads into florets. Heat oil in wok or heavy large skillet over high heat until hot but not smoking. Add broccoli stems and stir-fry until edges begin to brown, about 30 seconds. Add florets and shallots and stir-fry until florets brown slightly, about 1½ minutes. Stir in sugar and salt and pepper.

Pour in stock and bring to boil, stirring often. Continue cooking until broccoli is barely tender. Remove with slotted spoon and arrange on platter to cool. Cook liquid over high heat until reduced to 1 cup. Cool. Transfer broccoli to bowl. Add green onion and reduced liquid and toss gently. (*Can be prepared 1 day ahead and refrigerated.*)

For dressing: Mix vinegar, shallots, mustard, paprika and red pepper in processor or blender until smooth. With machine running, add oil in slow steady stream. Season with salt and pepper. Stir into rice. Refrigerate. (*Can be prepared up to 6 hours ahead and refrigerated.*)

About 4 hours before serving, gently fold broccoli and liquid into rice. Line platter with lettuce leaves. Mound rice mixture atop lettuce. Garnish with green onion. Refrigerate. Let stand at room temperature for 30 minutes before serving.

VIETNAMESE COLD NOODLES WITH SHRIMP

10 buffet servings

- 8 ounces mai fun (rice sticks)*
- 1½ pounds (about) cooked small fresh shrimp
- 2 cups fresh bean sprouts
- 2 cups shredded lettuce
- 2 cups Nuoc Cham Sauce (see following recipe)
- 1 cup snipped chives *or* minced green onion
- 1 cup fresh mint leaves
- 1 cup fresh cilantro (coriander) leaves
- 1 cup roasted unsalted peanuts, coarsely chopped
- ½ cup fresh hot green chilies, seeded and shredded

Cook mai fun according to package directions. Drain and rinse in cold water. Drain again. Transfer to platter. Surround with remaining ingredients in individual serving bowls.

* Available in Vietnamese markets.

Nuoc Cham Sauce

A popular dipping sauce in Vietnam.

Makes about 2 cups

- 1 cup fish sauce (nuoc mam)*
- 1 cup water
- ⅓ cup fresh lime juice
- ¼ cup sugar
- 4 to 5 fresh red *or* green chilies, seeded and quartered
- 4 medium garlic cloves, halved

Puree all ingredients in blender until smooth. Refrigerate mixture in covered container for up to 2 weeks.

* Available in Vietnamese markets.

COUSCOUS-STUFFED TOMATOES

6 servings

- 6 medium-large tomatoes Salt

- 1½ cups water
- 1 tablespoon butter
- ¼ teaspoon salt
- ¾ cup quick-cooking couscous

- 3 tablespoons olive oil
- 1 medium zucchini, coarsely grated
- 1 medium carrot, coarsely grated
- 1 green onion, minced
- 2 tablespoons chopped fresh parsley
- 2 medium mushrooms, chopped

- 1 tablespoon red wine vinegar Salt and freshly ground pepper Snipped fresh chives (garnish)

Carefully hollow out tomatoes, leaving ¼- to ½-inch shell (save pulp for another use). Salt tomatoes lightly and invert on rack to drain.

Combine water, butter and salt in heavy large saucepan and bring to boil over medium-high heat. Add couscous and continue boiling, stirring occasionally, until water is almost completely absorbed, about 2 minutes. Remove from heat, cover tightly and cool 10 to 15 minutes. Fluff with fork.

Heat olive oil in large skillet over medium-high heat. Add zucchini, carrot, onion, parsley and mushrooms and sauté until crisp-tender, about 3 to 5 minutes. Set aside to cool.

Stir vinegar into vegetables. Add vegetables to couscous and mix well. Season with salt and pepper. Spoon filling into tomatoes. Garnish with chives and serve.

BREAD SALAD (Panzanella)

8 servings

- 1 1-pound loaf very stale Italian Country bread (see recipe, page 168) *or* French bread, cut into ½-inch cubes
- 1 cup olive oil
- ⅓ cup white wine vinegar
- 2 tomatoes, cored, seeded and coarsely chopped
- 2 hard-cooked eggs, chopped
- 1 cucumber, peeled, seeded and coarsely chopped
- 1 onion, finely chopped
- 1 carrot, thinly sliced
- 1 celery stalk, thinly sliced
- 3 anchovy fillets, chopped
- 2 tablespoons chopped fresh basil, or more
- 1 generous tablespoon capers Chopped fresh mint leaves Salt and freshly ground pepper

Place bread cubes in large bowl. Add enough cold water to cover. Let stand 30 minutes. Drain bread well; squeeze dry and fluff with fingers.

Transfer to large serving bowl. Add remaining ingredients and toss thoroughly. Adjust seasoning. Chill until serving time.

WARM SALAD OF GREENS WITH PANCETTA

Kale, nasturtium leaves, red leaf lettuce, arugula, radicchio or watercress can also be used for this salad in any combination.

8 servings

- 8 ounces green Swiss chard
- 8 ounces red Swiss chard

- 5 to 6 ounces pancetta *or* slab bacon, sliced ¼-inch thick Olive oil, if needed

- 4 to 5 tablespoons red wine vinegar *or* Sherry vinegar
- 1 teaspoon Dijon mustard
- ⅓ cup olive oil Salt and freshly ground pepper

- 1 red bell pepper, cut lengthwise into strips ½ inch wide
- 2 large shallots, minced
- 8 ounces curly endive, preferably inner leaves
- 8 ounces spinach, stems removed

Cut stems off chard. Trim ends, halve stems lengthwise and cut into 2-inch lengths. Blanch stems in boiling water until crisp-tender, about 4 minutes. Drain, rinse with cold water and drain again.

Trim pancetta or bacon so proportion of fat to lean is 50:50. Cut into ½-inch cubes. Sauté in Dutch oven or heavy very large skillet over medium-high heat until light brown. Remove meat with slotted spoon. Reserve 3½ tablespoons fat for vinaigrette; leave 2 to 3 tablespoons fat in Dutch oven, adding olive oil if necessary.

Mix vinegar and mustard in small bowl. Whisk in ⅓ cup olive oil and 3½ tablespoons pancetta fat, 1 tablespoon at a time. Season with salt and pepper.

Heat Dutch oven with pancetta fat over medium heat. Add bell pepper and shallots and sauté until shallots are translucent. Gradually add chard, chard stems, endive and spinach. Cover and cook until slightly wilted, about 4 minutes. Add vinaigrette and pancetta and toss until salad is just warm. Serve immediately.

ASPARAGUS SALAD WITH SOY-LEMON DRESSING

4 servings

Soy-Lemon Dressing

- 1½ tablespoons vegetable oil
- ¼ teaspoon minced fresh ginger
- 2 green onions, minced
- ½ cup chicken stock, preferably homemade (see recipe, page 38)
- 1 tablespoon cider vinegar
- 1 teaspoon Japanese soy sauce
- ½ teaspoon sugar

- 1 to 1¼ pounds pencil-thin asparagus stalks, cut diagonally into 1½-inch lengths
- 11 green onions

- 1 head romaine lettuce, cut crosswise into ½-inch strips
- ¼ cup chopped salted cashews
- ⅛ teaspoon freshly ground pepper, or more Salt to taste Fresh lemon juice to taste

For dressing: Heat oil in small saucepan over medium-high heat. Add ginger and stir until beginning to color. Blend in green onions and cook 3 to 4 seconds. Mix in stock, 1 tablespoon vinegar, soy sauce and sugar. Set aside. (*Dressing can be prepared 2 hours ahead to this point.*)

Pour water into steamer to within 1 inch of rack; set rack in place. Bring water to rapid boil over high heat. Add asparagus, cover and steam until crisp-tender, about 5 minutes. Rinse under cold water to stop cooking process and set color. Drain and cool. Steam 8 green

onions until just barely tender. Rinse under cold water; drain.

Just before serving, mince remaining 3 onions. Transfer to large bowl. Add whole green onions, lettuce, cashews and asparagus. Bring dressing to boil over medium-high heat. Let boil 30 seconds. Stir in ⅛ teaspoon pepper. Taste and add salt, lemon juice and additional vinegar and pepper to attain tart, peppery flavor. Toss salad with simmering dressing and serve.

ENDIVE, BACON AND PECAN SALAD

The nuts can be toasted ahead of time, but this salad is best put together just before serving.

6 servings

- 1 head butter lettuce, coarsely torn
- ½ head curly endive, sliced or coarsely torn
- ¾ cup minced red onion
- ¾ cup toasted pecan halves (3½ ounces)

- 6 thick bacon slices, cut into ½-inch pieces (8 ounces)
- 1½ teaspoons firmly packed brown sugar
- ¼ cup white *or* red wine vinegar
- ¼ teaspoon salt, or to taste Freshly ground pepper

Combine greens, onion and pecans in large salad bowl and toss lightly.

Cook bacon in large skillet over medium heat until crisp, turning once. Drain on paper towels. Pour off all but ¼ cup fat from skillet. Add brown sugar to skillet, return to medium heat and stir until dissolved. Blend in vinegar and salt and bring to boil. Pour hot dressing over salad. Top with bacon. Season salad with pepper and toss gently. Serve immediately.

❖

CARROT SALAD IN BERRY VINAIGRETTE

Carrot Salad can be prepared up to 4 days ahead.

6 servings

- 1½ pounds carrots, very thinly sliced (5 cups)
- ⅓ cup olive oil
- 3 tablespoons raspberry *or* strawberry vinegar
- ½ cup minced fresh parsley leaves
- ⅓ cup minced green onion
  Salt and freshly ground pepper

Bring 2 quarts salted water to rapid boil over high heat. Add carrots and boil just until crisp-tender. Drain well. Transfer to bowl. While still hot, toss with oil and vinegar. Cool.

Add parsley, onion and salt and pepper to carrots and toss gently. Refrigerate overnight. Bring to room temperature before serving.

SALAD OF ROASTED PEPPER AND ESCAROLE

6 servings

- 1 large red bell pepper
- 1 large head escarole, torn into bite-size pieces
- 3 tablespoons red wine vinegar
- ½ cup plus 1 tablespoon olive oil
  Freshly ground pepper

Preheat broiler. Set red pepper on broiler pan. Roast 6 inches from heat source, turning until blackened on all sides. Transfer to plastic bag and seal tightly. Let steam 10 minutes. Peel pepper; cut in half, discarding veins and seeds. Rinse, if necessary, and pat dry with paper towels. Slice pepper lengthwise into ½-inch strips. Transfer to salad bowl and add

escarole. Place vinegar in small bowl and whisk in oil 1 drop at a time. Season with pepper. Pour vinaigrette over salad and toss gently. Serve immediately.

MOZZARELLA, TOMATO AND FRESH BASIL PESTO SALAD

4 servings

- 4 large ripe beefsteak tomatoes, each cut into 4 to 6 slices
- 8 ounces fresh mozzarella (preferably buffalo milk mozzarella), Italian Fontina *or* bel paese cheese, cut into same number of slices as tomatoes
- ½ cup Fresh Basil Pesto, room temperature (see recipe, page 7)
- ¼ to ½ cup virgin olive oil
  Salt and freshly ground pepper

Divide tomatoes and cheese into 4 equal portions. Arrange 1 slice of cheese over each tomato slice. Spread thin layer of pesto over cheese. Continue layering in same order for each portion, ending with pesto. Arrange in circle on platter, overlapping slightly. Serve at room temperature. Serve olive oil and salt and pepper separately.

MINTED ZUCCHINI AND SWEET CORN SALAD

16 to 18 servings

- 3 tablespoons olive oil, preferably extra virgin
- 4 pounds small zucchini, cut into 2 × ¼-inch julienne
- 2 medium onions, minced
- 2 large garlic cloves, minced
- ⅓ cup wine vinegar, or more
- 1½ teaspoons fresh oregano *or* ½ teaspoon dried, crumbled
- 3 tablespoons well-packed minced fresh mint leaves *or* 1 to 2 tablespoons dried, crumbled

- 1½ cups fresh corn kernels
  Salt and freshly ground pepper
  Mint sprigs (garnish)

Heat 1 tablespoon oil in heavy large skillet over high heat. Add ⅓ of zucchini and toss until lightly browned, 3 to 5 minutes. Transfer to large bowl. Repeat with remaining oil and zucchini. Reduce heat to medium low and add onions to skillet. Cover and cook until soft, about 10 minutes. Add garlic and cook 1 minute. Stir in ⅓ cup vinegar and oregano; simmer 2 minutes. Pour over zucchini. Mix in mint. Let mixture cool completely.

Add corn to boiling water. When water returns to boil, drain corn and rinse with cold water; drain again. Cool.

Add corn to zucchini. Taste and add more vinegar if desired. Season with salt and pepper. Arrange salad on large platter. Garnish with mint and serve immediately.

BACON AND MUENSTER SALAD (*Salade au Lard et au Muenster*)

6 servings

- 1 head escarole
- 1 head curly chicory
- 1 3-ounce slab bacon (rind discarded), cut into ⅓-inch dice
- 1½ tablespoons wine vinegar
- 1½ teaspoons strong Dijon *or* Düsseldorf mustard
- ¼ cup plus 2 tablespoons corn oil *or* sunflower oil
- ½ teaspoon crushed caraway seed
  Salt and freshly ground pepper

- 4 ounces Alsatian Muenster cheese *or* Liederkranz (crust discarded), diced

Remove all dark green leaves from escarole and chicory and reserve for soup. Roll light green and white leaves in towel. Refrigerate until ready to use.

Cook bacon in heavy skillet over low heat until soft and light golden, about 15 minutes, watching carefully so bacon does not crisp.

Remove from skillet using slotted spoon and drain on paper towels. Degrease skillet. Cool skillet slightly to prevent spattering when vinegar is added. Place over medium-high heat and stir in vinegar, scraping up any browned bits. Pour vinegar mixture into large bowl. Blend in mustard. Whisk in oil 1 drop at a time. Add caraway. Season with salt and pepper. Set aside for about 15 minutes to allow flavors to mellow.

Just before serving, tear chilled greens into large bowl. Add half of dressing and toss gently. Sprinkle cheese, bacon and remaining dressing over and toss gently to blend. Serve immediately.

Dressings

ONION SALAD DRESSING

Makes about 1 cup

½ cup finely chopped onion
¼ cup cider vinegar
¼ cup sugar
½ teaspoon salt
½ teaspoon dry mustard
¼ teaspoon celery seed
½ cup oil

Combine all ingredients except oil in processor or blender and mix well, stopping as necessary to scrape down sides of container. With machine running, add oil in slow steady stream, blending until dressing is creamy. Transfer to container with tight-fitting lid and refrigerate before using. Whisk or shake if dressing separates on standing.

MUSTARD-DILL DRESSING

Makes about 3½ cups

½ cup Dijon mustard
½ cup cider vinegar
1½ teaspoons dried tarragon, crumbled

1½ teaspoons dried dillweed
2 cups safflower oil *or* sunflower oil
2 tablespoons grated Parmesan cheese
2 tablespoons half and half

Combine mustard, vinegar, tarragon and dillweed in medium bowl and let stand 10 minutes. Add oil in slow steady stream, whisking constantly until mixture is thickened and smooth. Blend in Parmesan and half and half. Transfer to container with tight-fitting lid and refrigerate until ready to use.

CHEDDAR CHEESE SALAD DRESSING

Makes about 2½ cups

1½ cups mayonnaise
½ cup buttermilk
½ cup finely shredded cheddar cheese
Dash of Worcestershire sauce
Dash of red wine vinegar, or to taste

Pinch *each* of salt, freshly ground pepper and ground red pepper

Combine all ingredients in medium bowl and blend thoroughly. Store dressing in tightly covered container in refrigerator.

MANGO DRESSING

Makes about 1 cup

1 medium-size very ripe mango

2 tablespoons dry vermouth
1 tablespoon chopped fresh summer savory
Salt and freshly ground pepper
¾ cup safflower oil *or* light vegetable oil

Roll unpeeled mango on counter to soften. Cut off one end. Squeeze mango over small bowl to catch as much juice as possible.

Add vermouth, summer savory and salt and pepper. Whisk in oil 1 drop at a time. Adjust seasoning. Let stand at room temperature 1 hour before using.

11 ❖ Sauces and Condiments

Sauces

SPICY RED WINE SAUCE WITH GLAZED APPLES

Makes about 2¼ cups

3 large golden apples
  (preferably
  Golden Delicious)
3 tablespoons unsalted butter
⅛ teaspoon minced garlic
6 tablespoons sugar

1½ cups dry red wine
¾ cup water
2 teaspoons hoisin sauce, or
  to taste
¼ teaspoon cornstarch
  dissolved in 1 tablespoon
  water
1 teaspoon red wine vinegar
½ teaspoon coarse salt
⅛ to ¼ teaspoon freshly
  ground pepper
1 tablespoon unsalted butter

Peel, core and quarter apples. Cut each quarter into 4 slices. Melt 3 tablespoons butter in heavy large skillet over high heat. Add garlic. Stir in apples, spreading in single layer as much as possible. Sprinkle with sugar and turn to coat. Cook until golden brown and almost tender, about 5 minutes, shaking skillet occasionally.

Pour wine and water into skillet and stir, scraping up any browned bits. Remove apples from skillet using slotted spoon. Stir hoisin sauce and mustard into skillet. Reduce sauce to 1¾ cups. Add apples, salt and pepper and simmer until apples are tender, about 10 minutes. Whisk in butter and serve.

LIGHT CURRY SAUCE

French chefs use curry powder with a light hand to obtain delicate sauces like this one. Serve it with eggs, seafood, chicken or pasta; to use cold, omit last 3 tablespoons butter.

Makes ¾ cup

4 tablespoons (½ stick)
  unsalted butter
2 tablespoons minced shallot
3 tablespoons dry white wine
2 tablespoons water
  Salt

¾ cup whipping cream
1 teaspoon curry powder

Melt 1 tablespoon butter in heavy-bottomed medium saucepan over low heat (keep remaining 3 tablespoons butter refrigerated). Add shallot and cook until soft but not brown, about 5 minutes, stirring occasionally. Blend in wine, water and small pinch of salt. Increase heat to medium and boil until mixture is reduced to about 2 tablespoons, about 4 minutes, watching carefully and stirring constantly.

Blend in cream and curry powder. Cook, stirring frequently, until sauce is slightly reduced and thick enough to coat back of spoon, about 7 minutes. (*Can be prepared 2 days ahead to this point and refrigerated.*)

Just before serving, bring sauce to boil, whisking constantly. Reduce heat to low and add remaining 3 tablespoons butter 1 tablespoon at a time, whisking constantly. Immediately remove sauce from the heat. Taste and adjust seasoning.

PUMPERNICKEL MUSTARD SAUCE

This quick sauce, perfect for baked ham, is thickened with a slice of bread and laced with vodka.

Makes about 1 cup

1½ cups chicken stock,
  preferably homemade (see
  recipe, page 38)
2 tablespoons minced onion
¼ teaspoon minced garlic
1 1-ounce slice stale dark
  pumpernickel bread (with
  crust), coarsely torn
½ teaspoon caraway seed
  (optional)
  Freshly ground pepper
1¼ tablespoons coarse mustard
1½ teaspoons Dijon mustard
1½ tablespoons vodka
1 tablespoon snipped fresh
  chives

Combine stock, onion and garlic in medium saucepan. Cover and bring to simmer over high heat. Simmer until onion is cooked through, about 10 minutes. Add bread and cook until saturated, about 30 seconds. Pour mixture into processor or blender and blend until smooth. Return sauce to pan. Stir in caraway seed and pepper. Place over medium-high heat and continue cooking until thickened and reduced to about 1 generous cup, approximately 6 minutes. Blend in mustards, vodka and chives just before serving.

HOT PEANUT SAUCE

A full-flavored sauce inspired by the spicy cuisine of Thailand. Spoon it over satés of pork, beef or chicken.

Makes 1¼ cups

- ½ cup dry vermouth
- ½ cup rice vinegar
- ¼ teaspoon dried red pepper flakes
- ¼ cup whipping cream
- ¼ cup water
- 3 tablespoons diagonally sliced green onion
- 2 tablespoons firmly packed dark brown sugar
- 1 tablespoon fish sauce (nam pla)*
- 1½ teaspoons tamari soy sauce
- 1 to 2 small green chilies, seeded and finely chopped
- ¼ teaspoon finely chopped garlic
  Pinch of freshly ground pepper
- 5 tablespoons chunky peanut butter

Combine vermouth, vinegar and red pepper flakes in medium saucepan and bring to boil over medium-high heat. Continue boiling until reduced to ¼ cup, stirring occasionally. Stir in cream, water, onion, brown sugar, fish sauce, soy sauce, green chilies, garlic and freshly ground pepper and return to boil. Cook, stirring constantly, until sauce is slightly thickened. (*Sauce can be prepared ahead to this point. Rewarm before continuing.*) Reduce heat to very low. Whisk in peanut butter 1 tablespoon at a time, blending until smooth. Serve immediately.

*Available at oriental markets. If unavailable, add 1 tablespoon light soy sauce and ½ teaspoon salt to recipe.

TARRAGON CREAM PESTO

A smoky, faintly anise-flavored pesto made with crushed tarragon leaves and crisp walnuts. Toss it lightly with hot green beans or use on fish.

Makes 2 cups

- 1 cup packed fresh tarragon leaves
- 2 large garlic cloves
- ½ teaspoon salt
- 1 tablespoon green peppercorns, drained
- ½ cup fine fresh white breadcrumbs
- 1 tablespoon fresh lemon juice
- 1 cup walnut halves
- ½ cup olive oil
- ¼ cup (about) warm water

If using mortar and pestle, crush tarragon in mortar to fine paste. Add garlic and salt and work into paste. Add peppercorns and continue to work into paste. Add breadcrumbs and lemon juice and beat until smooth. Gradually add walnut halves and crush to paste. Pour olive oil, then water, into mixture in slow steady stream, stirring constantly, until mixture forms creamy paste. Serve at room temperature.

If using processor, combine tarragon, garlic and salt in work bowl and blend to fine paste, scraping down sides of bowl as necessary. Add peppercorns and breadcrumbs and process until smooth. Add lemon juice and walnut halves and continue mixing until smooth. With machine running, pour oil through feed tube in slow steady stream. Add water in same manner and process until mixture is consistency of thick mayonnaise. Serve at room temperature.

TOMATO CREAM SAUCE

Serve with chicken, veal or pasta.

Makes about 1 cup

- 1 tablespoon butter
- 1 medium onion, chopped
- 2 garlic cloves, minced (optional)
- 1½ pounds ripe tomatoes,* peeled, seeded, juiced and chopped
- 5 parsley stems
- 1 fresh thyme sprig *or* ¼ teaspoon dried, crumbled
- 1 small bay leaf
  Salt and freshly ground pepper
- 1 cup whipping cream
- 1 teaspoon tomato paste (optional)

Melt butter in heavy-bottomed skillet over low heat. Add onion and cook, stirring frequently, until soft but not brown, about 4 minutes. Add garlic and stir 30 seconds. Blend in tomatoes, parsley, thyme and bay leaf with pinches of salt and pepper. Increase heat to medium and cook, stirring frequently, until very thick puree forms and mixture is reduced to about 1¼ cups and beginning to stick to skillet, about 25 minutes. (*Can be prepared 2 days ahead to this point and refrigerated.*)

Just before serving, bring sauce to boil over medium heat, whisking constantly. Add cream and return to boil, whisking frequently. Reduce heat and simmer until slightly thickened, about 4 minutes. Strain sauce through fine sieve set over small saucepan, pressing on vegetables with back of spoon to extract all liquid and scraping puree from underside of sieve with rubber spatula. Reheat sauce. For deeper color, whisk in 1 teaspoon tomato paste. Taste and adjust seasoning.

*One 28-ounce can Italian plum tomatoes can be substituted. Drain well and chop.

MINTED SPINACH SAUCE

Makes about 2 cups

- ½ cup dry white wine
- 1 cup whipping cream
  Pinch of ground red pepper
- 1 tablespoon unsalted butter
- 3 tablespoons chopped green onion
- 3 cups packed spinach leaves (about 6 ounces)
- ¼ cup fresh mint leaves
- 1 teaspoon fresh lemon juice
  Salt

Boil wine in small saucepan over medium-high heat until reduced to 1 tablespoon, about 3 to 5 minutes. Stir in ¼ cup cream and cook until reduced to about 2 tablespoons. Stir in remaining cream. Blend in pepper; set aside.

Cream-based Sauces

Cream is definitely not a new ingredient in the French kitchen—yet cream-based sauces are relatively new and currently in favor in France. Unlike the classic *sauce crème*, a cream-enriched béchamel, these modern versions contain neither flour nor starch. Instead, they are thickened either by reduction or by a vegetable puree.

Although these blends are luxurious enough to serve on the most special occasions, they are simple to prepare and convenient, too, since they can be served hot or cold and can be made ahead and reheated.

The flavor and texture of cream-based sauces are perfect for delicate foods such as chicken, veal and sweetbreads; poached, steamed or sautéed seafood; and poached eggs. They will embellish vegetables elegantly, particularly the more assertive broccoli and cauliflower. Or, with the addition of a few chopped or minced fresh herbs, they can be used to enhance pasta dishes. Cream-based sauces can even be served as dips for vegetables.

The first step consists of preparing the reduction, usually a combination of dry white wine and shallot that is cooked down to a fraction of its original volume. Then cream is added and the sauce is simmered, reducing and thickening the cream and concentrating all of the flavors.

Since it is the cream that characterizes the sauce, it is important to use the freshest and best-tasting variety possible. For this reason, pasteurized whipping cream is preferable to the ultrapasteurized. Crème fraîche can be substituted for whipping cream, but the result will be heavier. It will impart a tangy flavor, however, especially to sauces that are served cold.

Tips

♦ Reheat sauces over hot (not boiling) water to avoid separation.

♦ If serving sauces cold, reduce them slightly less than you would hot sauces, as they will thicken when chilled.

♦ When a sauce is too thick, gradually stir in a few tablespoons whipping cream until it achieves the desired consistency. Adjust seasoning just before serving.

Melt butter in large skillet over medium-high heat. Add onion and sauté 10 seconds. Add spinach and stir until wilted, about 2 minutes. Blend in mint leaves. Drain mixture and squeeze dry. Transfer to processor and chop finely using on/off turns. Bring cream to boil. Pour into spinach mixture and puree finely. Return sauce to pan. Season with lemon juice and salt. Place over medium-high heat and warm through. Serve immediately.

GREEN SAUCE

An easy no-cook sauce that is perfect with slices of cold ham.

Makes about 1 cup

- 1 cup packed fresh spinach leaves
- 1 cup packed fresh parsley leaves
- ½ cup packed fresh cilantro (coriander) leaves
- 2 tablespoons capers, rinsed and drained
- 2 green onions (white part only), each cut crosswise into 3 pieces
- 1 large garlic clove
- ½ cup olive oil
- 1½ tablespoons red wine vinegar
- ⅛ to ¼ teaspoon coarse salt
- ⅛ teaspoon freshly ground black pepper
  Dash of hot pepper sauce

Combine spinach, parsley, cilantro, 1 tablespoon capers, green onions and garlic in processor and mix using on/off turns until coarsely chopped, scraping down sides of bowl several times. With machine running, quickly pour in ⅓ cup oil. Pour mixture into small bowl. Whisk in remaining oil. Blend in vinegar, salt, pepper and hot pepper sauce. Stir in remaining capers. Refrigerate until ready to serve.

APRICOT SCALLION SAUCE

When served warm, this sauce is mellow and buttery. At room temperature it becomes more piquant.

Makes about 1⅔ cups

- 2 cups water
- ⅔ cup dried apricots, cut into strips (4 ounces)
- 2 tablespoons sliced green onion (white part only)
- 1¼ teaspoons grated fresh ginger
- ½ teaspoon minced garlic
- 2 teaspoons sugar
- 1 teaspoon white wine vinegar
- ½ teaspoon coarse salt
- ⅛ teaspoon freshly ground pepper
- 3 tablespoons unsalted butter
- 2 tablespoons diagonally sliced green onion (green part only)

Bring water, apricots, onion, 1 teaspoon ginger and garlic to boil in medium saucepan over high heat. Reduce heat, cover and simmer until apricots are very tender and beginning to break apart, about 15 minutes.

Using fork, stir mixture vigorously to coarse puree. Blend in sugar, vinegar, salt, pepper and remaining ¼ teaspoon ginger. (*Can be prepared ahead to this point and set aside at room temperature.*) Before serving, place sauce over low heat. Whisk in butter 1 tablespoon at a time. Stir in onion.

HONEY SHALLOT SAUCE

This recipe uses ham jelly, the result of chilling the pan drippings from ham after the fat has been skimmed off. Extra ham jelly is also delicious served on the side.

Make about 1 cup

- ¾ cup very thinly sliced shallots
- 2 tablespoons herb honey, such as sage
- 2 cups chicken stock, preferably homemade (see recipe, page 38)
- ⅓ cup dry white wine
- ⅛ teaspoon minced garlic
- 1 tablespoon degreased ham jelly *or* ham cooking liquid
- 2 tablespoons (¼ stick) unsalted butter, room temperature
- 1 tablespoon all purpose flour

- 1½ teaspoons fresh lemon juice
- ¼ teaspoon coarse salt
- ¼ teaspoon freshly ground pepper
- 1 tablespoon snipped fresh chives *or* parsley

Combine shallots and honey in medium saucepan and bring to boil over medium-high heat. Cook 1 minute. Add stock and cook until shallots are very tender. Remove all but about 3 tablespoons shallots from pan using slotted spoon. Add wine and garlic to pan and boil until

reduced to 1½ cups, about 15 minutes. Blend in ham jelly and continue cooking until reduced to slightly more than 1 cup. Meanwhile, mash butter with flour in small bowl to smooth paste.

Reduce heat to medium and gradually whisk butter mixture into sauce. Return sauce to boil. Let boil 2 minutes. Stir in reserved shallots. Season sauce with lemon juice, salt and pepper. Stir in chives and serve immediately.

WARM ANCHOVY BUTTER WITH MELTED ONION AND GARLIC

Drizzle this aromatic butter on Schiacciata (see recipe, page 178) and top with roasted peppers.

16 to 18 servings

- ¾ cup plus 2 tablespoons (1¾ sticks) unsalted butter
- 18 large garlic cloves
- 2 large onions, finely diced
- 7 anchovy fillets, or to taste Freshly ground pepper
- 1 tablespoon minced fresh Italian parsley

Melt butter in heavy small saucepan over low heat. Add garlic and onions. Cover and cook until garlic is very soft and almost purees when pressed, 30 to 40 minutes, stirring occasionally. Stir in anchovies and cook uncovered until melted into sauce, about 15 minutes. Season to taste with pepper. (*Can be prepared 2 days ahead. Remelt just before serving.*) Top with parsley.

ORANGE RUM GLAZE

This glaze requires some cooking to thicken into a syrup. Garnish the platter with Maple-soaked Orange Slices and fresh watercress sprigs.

Glaze (*makes about ½ cup*)

- ½ cup maple syrup
- ½ cup orange juice
- ¼ cup fresh lemon juice

- 2½ tablespoons dark rum
- 2 teaspoons Dijon mustard
- 2 teaspoons grated orange peel

Maple-soaked Orange Slices (*makes 10 slices*)

- ⅓ cup maple syrup
- ⅓ cup water
- 10 uniform ⅛-inch-thick orange slices (1 to 2 oranges)

For glaze: Bring maple syrup, orange and lemon juices, 2 tablespoons rum, mustard and 1 teaspoon orange peel to boil in medium saucepan over medium-high heat. Cook, stirring occasionally, until thickened and reduced to ½ cup, about 8 minutes. Blend in remaining rum and orange peel. Brush ham with glaze every 15 minutes *after* first hour of baking; use all glaze.

For orange slices: Bring syrup and water to boil in large skillet over high heat. Add orange slices to syrup mixture. Reduce heat to medium and cook until peel appears translucent, about 12 minutes, turning slices once or twice. Cool completely.

VEGETABLE JULIENNE CREAM SAUCE

Serve with poached eggs, fish, shellfish, chicken breasts or fresh pasta. If serving sauce cold, stir carrot, leek and celery into hot sauce and then set aside to cool before refrigerating.

Makes about 1 cup

- 1 small or ½ large leek
- 1 carrot
- ½ small celery stalk
- 6 very white large mushroom caps

- ¼ cup dry white wine
- 1 tablespoon white wine vinegar
- 1 tablespoon minced shallot Salt and freshly ground white pepper
- 1 cup whipping cream

Trim and discard root and top of leek, leaving white part and about 2 inches of deep green. Using sharp knife, slit leek lengthwise, starting from center and cutting toward end (leave small section in center uncut to keep leek in 1 piece). Rinse leek in cold water, separating pieces to remove all dirt. Cut leek, carrot and celery into thin julienne about 1½ inches long. Slice mushroom caps crosswise into ovals. Cut ovals into thin strips.

Combine wine, vinegar and shallot in heavy-bottomed medium saucepan and bring to simmer over medium heat. Let simmer until reduced to about 2 tablespoons, about 3 minutes, watching carefully and stirring occasionally to prevent burning. Add mushroom julienne with pinches of salt and pepper. Bring mixture to boil. Stir in cream and simmer until mushrooms are tender and sauce is thick enough to coat back of spoon lightly, about 6 minutes, stirring occasionally. Remove sauce from heat and set aside.

Fill large saucepan with water and bring to boil. Add carrot, leek and celery and boil 3 minutes. Drain well. (*Sauce and vegetable julienne can be prepared several hours ahead. Store in separate containers in refrigerator.*)

Just before serving, reheat sauce to just below boiling point. Stir in carrot, leek and celery and bring almost to boil. Remove from heat. Adjust seasoning.

Condiments

CURRY PICKLES

For best flavor, age pickles for three months before opening. Excellent with cold pork, chicken or roast lamb.

Makes about 7 pints

>   8   **pounds slender small cucumbers, well scrubbed**
>
> 2½   **quarts cider vinegar**
>   ⅓   **cup sugar**
>   ⅓   **cup coarse salt**
>   ⅓   **cup dry mustard**
>   ⅓   **cup curry powder**
>   ⅓   **cup mixed pickling spice**
>   ¼   **cup mustard seed**
> 1½   **teaspoons turmeric**
>   ½   **teaspoon ground red pepper**

Bring large amount of water to boil in stockpot over high heat. Meanwhile, trim all stems and blossoms from cucumbers, discarding any cucumbers that are soft. Add cucumbers to boiling water and blanch 30 seconds. Drain well, pat dry. Pack tightly into clean, hot jars to ½ inch from top.

Combine remaining ingredients in stockpot and bring to rapid boil. Ladle enough hot brine into 1 jar just to cover cucumbers. Run plastic knife or spatula between cucumbers and jar to release any air bubbles. Clean rim and threads of jar with damp cloth. Seal jar with new, scalded, very hot lid. Repeat with remaining jars. Transfer jars to gently simmering (180°F to 190°F) water bath and process for 10 minutes. Let jars cool on rack. Test for seal. Store pickles in cool dry place.

WALNUT-PLUM CATSUP

Makes 2 quarts

>   5   **pounds ripe red *or* purple plums**
>   4   **cups sugar**
>
>   2   **cups cider vinegar**
>   1   **teaspoon cinnamon**
>   ½   **teaspoon freshly grated nutmeg *or* ground mace**
>   ¼   **teaspoon ground cloves**
>
>   1   **cup walnuts, toasted and finely chopped**

Cook plums and sugar in heavy large nonaluminum stockpot over medium heat until mixture just simmers; if plums are not juicy, mash slightly with back of spoon to break skins and release enough juices to mix with sugar. Reduce heat to low, cover and simmer until plums are tender, stirring occasionally, about 30 minutes. Mash plums slightly with back of spoon and cook uncovered 10 minutes.

Strain mixture through fine sieve into very large bowl, pressing to release liquid and most of pulp. Transfer back into original stockpot. Discard skins and pits remaining in sieve.

To flavor vinegar, barely simmer vinegar and spices in nonaluminum medium saucepan 5 minutes. Stir into plum mixture. Cook over medium heat until reduced to about 2 quarts, stirring occasionally, about 30 minutes.

Remove from heat and stir in walnuts. Ladle into clean, tall glass bottles or jars, using funnel as aid if necessary. Cool completely. Cap tightly and refrigerate.

BASIC MAYONNAISE

Makes about 1¾ cups

>   2   **egg yolks, room temperature**
>   1   **tablespoon flavored vinegar *or* fresh lemon juice**
> 1½   **cups oil (olive, peanut, vegetable, safflower *or* a combination)**
>   2   **tablespoons boiling water**
>   ¾   **teaspoon salt**

If preparing by hand, combine yolks and vinegar or lemon juice in medium bowl. Gradually whisk in ½ cup oil a drop at a time, stirring

Mayonnaise

When the French celebrated their 1756 victory over the British at the Mediterranean port of Mahon with a banquet, legend has it that the chef served a sauce created especially for the occasion. He obviously could not have realized that centuries later the battle would long be forgotten, but his culinary triumph, *mahonnaise* or mayonnaise, would grace the shelves of every American supermarket. And if the chef who devised this sauce could step forward in time to sample the bottled version, he would likely be surprised: The commercial variety we have come to know bears little resemblance to the original in taste, color or consistency.

Similar in style to the other emulsion sauces, hollandaise and béarnaise, mayonnaise is a magical marriage of eggs and oil. The magic? Beating the oil slowly into the egg yolks and watching them whip into a luscious creamy cloud. The trick is a bit of kitchen chemistry: Acid such as lemon juice or vinegar binds the eggs and oil together and produces the familiar thick and smooth texture. This simple formula gives rise to limitless, delectable variations you will never find in any store.

More important, though, homemade mayonnaise, unlike its packaged cousin, is virtuous in its lack of preservatives, additives or excessive salt. You choose your own fresh eggs, and since polyunsaturated oils make perfect mayonnaise, saturated oils can be avoided entirely. It therefore contains very little cholesterol per tablespoon.

Whisking mayonnaise by hand takes just a few minutes, but with an electric mixer, food processor or blender, it is absolutely effortless. If you are making mayonnaise by hand, avoid an aching arm by stirring consistently, rather than beating vigorously. The addition of boiling water at the end of some of these recipes lightens the mayonnaise and also gives it a paler color. These mixtures will last up to ten days, covered, in the refrigerator–if you have a lot of self-control.

Tips

- Be sure all ingredients are at room temperature. Cold eggs will not emulsify and the result will tend to be soupy rather than thick.
- To bring cold ingredients to room temperature quickly, place the bottle of oil and the eggs (still in the shell) in a bowl of hot, but not boiling, water for a few minutes.

- Each egg yolk can absorb only ¾ cup oil. Using more will cause the mayonnaise to break down. Add the oil to the egg yolks *slowly* or the mixture will curdle.
- To rescue separated or curdled mayonnaise, beat an extra egg yolk in another bowl, then add the mayonnaise to it by the teaspoonful, stirring well after each addition until thoroughly blended. Continue until all the mayonnaise has been added, then blend in remaining oil slowly.

Variations

- Blend ½ cup Basic Mayonnaise with 4 cups shredded cabbage, 1 cup chopped fresh pineapple (with juice) and ½ cup raisins for a tangy pineapple coleslaw perfect for luncheon.
- Use flavored vinegars in mayonnaise recipes to vary the taste. Or add mustard, garlic and herbs to mayonnaise for use in tuna, chicken or tossed green salads.
- Combine several leaves of fresh spinach and 2 to 3 tablespoons minced fresh herbs with mayonnaise for a quick sauce for either steamed vegetables or poached ocean fish.

---

mixture constantly until absorbed. Stir in remaining oil 1 tablespoon at a time; do not add oil all at once or mayonnaise will not thicken. Mix in boiling water and salt.

If preparing in processor or blender, combine yolks and vinegar or lemon juce and blend well. With machine running, add oil in slow steady stream, mixing until mayonnaise is smooth and thick. Mix in boiling water and salt.

PESTO MAYONNAISE

An excellent dressing for potato, pasta, chicken, fish and beef salads.

Makes about 1¾ cups

- **2 egg yolks, room temperature**
- **2 garlic cloves, halved**
- **1 tablespoon garlic vinegar**
- **1½ cups firmly packed fresh basil leaves**
- **2 fresh spinach leaves, stemmed**
- **1 cup oil**
- **¾ teaspoon salt, or to taste**

Mix yolks, garlic and vinegar in processor or blender. Blend in basil and spinach. With machine running, add oil in slow steady stream, blending until mayonnaise is smooth and thick. Season with salt to taste.

HERBED ROASTED RED AND YELLOW PEPPERS

16 to 18 servings

- 10 large red bell peppers *or* 5 large red and 5 large yellow bell peppers
- 3 tablespoons olive oil (preferably extra virgin)
- 1 tablespoon fresh marjoram *or* ¾ teaspoon dried, crumbled
- ¾ teaspoon fresh thyme *or* large pinch of dried, crumbled
  Salt and freshly ground pepper

Prepare barbecue or preheat boiler. Roast peppers 6 inches from heat source, turning until skins blister and blacken. Place in plastic bag and steam 10 minutes. Peel away skins and remove seeds, rinsing if necessary. Pat dry and cut into small dice. Toss with oil and herbs in serving bowl. Season with salt and pepper. (*Can be prepared 2 days ahead, covered and refrigerated.*) Serve at room temperature.

PEAR AND SHALLOT CONFIT WITH RED GRAPES

A colorful relish for any ham.

Makes about 1½ cups

- 1¼ to 1½ cups whole shallots, preferably small (about 13)
- 3 very firm pears
- 1½ cups water
- 1 garlic clove, flattened
- 1 1-inch diameter ⅛-inch-thick slice fresh ginger
- 1 cup seeded red grapes *or* other dark grapes, halved
- ¼ cup sugar
- 2 teaspoons fresh lemon juice
  Pinch of coarse salt
  Pinch of freshly ground white pepper

Peel outside of shallots until bulbs divide into 2 pieces or shallots are small and remain in 1 piece; shallots should measure about 1 cup. Transfer peelings to large saucepan.

Peel and core pears. Add peel and cores to shallot peelings. Slice pears to approximately same size as shallots; set aside. Add water, garlic and ginger to peelings. Place over high heat and cook 10 minutes, stirring occasionally.

Strain liquid into another large saucepan, pressing on peelings with back of spoon to extract all liquid. Discard peelings; rinse pan. Bring liquid to boil over medium-high heat. Add grapes and blanch 20 seconds. Transfer grapes to medium bowl using slotted spoon. Add shallots to liquid and cook 3 minutes, then add pears and cook 2 minutes. Transfer shallots and pears to previously used pan. Sprinkle with 1 tablespoon cooking liquid. Pour any juice that has exuded from grapes into remaining cooking liquid. Place liquid over medium-high heat and reduce to 1 to 2 tablespoons.

Sprinkle shallots and pears with sugar and 1 teaspoon lemon juice. Place over high heat and cook until deep caramel color, about 15 minutes, stirring frequently (mixture will darken). Reduce heat to low and add reduced cooking liquid, blending well. Stir in salt and pepper with remaining lemon juice. Remove from heat. Turn confit into bowl and cool to room temperature.

Add grapes and toss gently. Serve chilled or at room temperature.

CAPONATA

16 to 18 servings

- 3½ to 4 pounds eggplant, cut into ¼-inch dice
- 2 tablespoons salt
- ⅔ cup olive oil, or more (preferably extra virgin)
- 1¼ cups minced celery
- 2 medium onions, minced
- 2 garlic cloves, minced
- 3 tablespoons minced fresh basil *or* 1 tablespoon dried, crumbled
- 1½ teaspoons fresh oregano leaves *or* ½ teaspoon dried, crumbled
- 2¼ cups veal stock *or* chicken stock, preferably homemade (see recipe, page 38)
- 7 tablespoons tomato paste
- 1½ teaspoons sugar
- 4 to 5 tablespoons cider vinegar
- ⅛ teaspoon freshly ground pepper
- 1 cup California black olives, pitted and chopped
- ½ cup mild Greek olives, pitted and chopped
- 2½ tablespoons drained capers, minced if large

Toss eggplant with salt in large colander. Drain 2 hours. Rinse; place in kitchen towel and squeeze dry.

Heat ⅔ cups oil in heavy large skillet over medium heat. Add celery and onions and cook, stirring often, until softened but not brown, about 5 minutes. Increase heat to medium high, add eggplant and cook, stirring often, until lightly browned, 10 to 15 minutes, adding more oil to skillet as necessary. Stir in garlic and herbs and cook 30 seconds. Reduce heat to medium low. Blend in stock, tomato paste and sugar and simmer until thick, about 10 minutes. Stir in vinegar and pepper and cook 2 to 3 minutes. Cool. Stir in olives and capers. (*Can be prepared 2 days ahead and refrigerated.*) Taste and adjust seasoning. Turn into bowl. Serve at room temperature.

HOT CHILI CHUTNEY
(Seme Mandu)

If a chutney with more texture is desired, simply chop all of the ingredients coarsely and mix well.

Makes 1 cup

- 1 large ripe tomato
- 3 large garlic cloves
- 6 tablespoons fresh cilantro (coriander) leaves and stems
- 2 tablespoons sliced fresh red chilies

Puree all ingredients in processor or blender using on/off turns until smooth paste forms. Sieve through fine strainer into bowl. Serve at room temperature.

Jams and Preserves

PRUNE BUTTER WITH QUETSCH
(Beurre de Pruneaux à la Quetsche)

Makes 1½ cups

- 1 **pound pitted prunes**
- 1 **cup (about) very strong hot Lapsang Souchong tea**
- 1½ **tablespoons quetsch *or* slivovitz (plum brandies) Dash of Quatre-Epices (see recipe, page 5)**

Place prunes in large bowl and add enough tea barely to cover. Set aside until softened, about 2 hours. Puree prune mixture in processor or blender (puree will be thick). Press through strainer to remove skins. Blend in plum brandy and spice mixture. Pack into small crock and serve. (*Can be prepared up to 1 week ahead and refrigerated. Serve at room temperature.*)

PLUM RUM CONSERVE

Makes 4 pints

- 4 **pounds firm red-fleshed plums, pitted and thinly sliced**
- 1 **cup water**
- 3 **cups sugar**
- 1 **cup coarsely chopped walnuts**
- ⅓ **cup dark rum**

Combine plums and water in large saucepan and bring to simmer over medium-high heat. Let simmer 3 minutes. Remove mixture from heat, cover and let stand at room temperature overnight.

Immerse four 1-pint jars in boiling water. Boil 15 minutes; keep immersed until ready to use. Place plum mixture over medium-high heat and bring to gentle boil. Add

Step by Step to Perfect Preserving

1. Select jars and clean thoroughly in hot soapy water; keep hot.
2. Place dome lids and sealing rings in pan of simmering water.
3. Ladle hot prepared mixture into jars, arranging attractively and filling to within one-half inch of top. Pack jars as full as possible.
4. Check for air pockets by running thin plastic knife or spatula, or chopstick, between mixture and jar.
5. Clean rims and threads of jars with damp cloth to ensure a seal. Place dome lids on jars and screw on rings.
6. Transfer jars to canner or heavy Dutch oven with enough very hot water to cover the lids by at least one inch. Simmer gently at 180°F to 190°F for amount of time specified in the recipe; *do not boil*.
7. Transfer jars to towels or wire rack to cool (contact with a cold surface could cause hot jars to crack), spacing well apart so air can circulate. Cool several hours or overnight.
8. Test for seal by pressing center of each lid. If the dome is down or stays down when pressed, there is a good seal. (Occasionally a jar may not seal for 24 hours, so be patient.)

sugar and cook until mixture falls in sheets from spoon and jelly or candy thermometer registers 220°F to 222°F, about 20 minutes, stirring almost constantly. Blend in walnuts and rum. Pour hot conserve into 1 hot jar to ½ inch from top. Run plastic knife or spatula between conserve and jar to release any air bubbles. Clean rim and threads of jar with damp cloth. Seal jar with new, scalded, very hot lid. Repeat with remaining jars. Let jars cool on rack. Test for seal. Store in cool dry place until ready to use.

RED AND BLUE JAM

Makes about 5 pints

- 4 **cups fresh raspberries**
- 2 **cups fresh blueberries**
- 7 **cups sugar**
- ⅓ **cup fresh lemon juice**
- 6 **ounces liquid pectin**

Immerse five 1-pint jars in boiling water. Boil 15 minutes; keep immersed until ready to use. Combine berries in large pot and crush lightly. Add sugar and lemon juice and blend well. Place over high heat and bring to rapid boil, stirring constantly for 1 minute. Remove from heat and stir in pectin, blending well. Skim foam if necessary. Ladle jam into 1 hot jar to ½ inch from top. Run plastic knife or spatula between jam and jar to release any air bubbles. Clean rim and threads of jar with damp cloth. Seal with new, scalded, very hot lid. Repeat with remaining jars. Let jars cool on rack. Test for seal. Store jam in cool dry place.

12 ❖ Baking: Breads

Yeast Breads

ITALIAN COUNTRY BREAD

Makes 2 loaves

Cornmeal
2½ cups warm water (105°F to 115°F)
  4 envelopes dry yeast
  1 tablespoon sugar
  4 to 5 cups unbleached all purpose flour
  2 to 3 cups whole wheat flour
  1 tablespoon salt

Set baking stones* in oven and sprinkle with cornmeal. Oil large bowl and set aside. Combine warm water, yeast and sugar in another large bowl. Let stand until foamy, about 5 minutes. Blend in 4 cups all purpose flour and 2 cups whole wheat flour with salt. Add more of each flour to make workable dough. Turn out onto lightly floured surface and knead until smooth, about 10 minutes. Form dough into ball. Dust with flour. Transfer to prepared bowl, turning to coat entire surface. Cover with towel and let stand in warm draft-free area until dough is doubled in size, about 40 to 45 minutes.

Punch dough down. Turn out onto work surface and divide in half. Shape each half into round or oblong loaf. Transfer to prepared baking stones. Cut 3 to 4 diagonal slashes into top of each loaf using sharp knife or razor blade. Brush loaves with water. Set oven temperature to 350°F and bake until loaves are golden and sound hollow when tapped, about 1 hour. Transfer loaves to racks to cool completely before slicing and storing.

If unavailable, bread can also be prepared on large baking sheets sprinkled with cornmeal. Do not preheat oven.

CLASSIC FRENCH BREAD

For the best French bread, allow the dough to mature slowly. Baked loaves can be wrapped tightly and refrigerated 1 to 2 days. Reheat briefly in 400°F oven before serving.

Makes 2 loaves

2½ cups cool water (about 50°F)
2½ cups unbleached all purpose flour (10 ounces)
2½ teaspoons dry yeast
  3 to 3½ cups unbleached all purpose flour (12 to 14 ounces)
2½ teaspoons salt

Cornmeal

Combine water, 2½ cups flour and yeast in processor and mix 30 seconds (or beat by hand 2 minutes). Transfer to large bowl. Cover with plastic wrap and let stand at room temperature for about 4 to 5 hours.

Lightly grease large bowl. Add 3 cups flour and salt to yeast mixture, blending well. Stir in enough additional flour to make soft, slightly sticky dough. Knead until dough is very elastic, adding more flour as necessary, about 15 minutes. Transfer to prepared bowl, turning to coat entire surface. Cover with plastic wrap and let rise until 2½ times original size, about 3 to 4 hours. Press down on dough using palm of hand. (*Dough can be prepared ahead to this point, covered and refrigerated overnight. Adjust time for second rising for chilled dough.*)

Cover dough and let rise again until 2½ times original size, about 2½ to 3 hours.

Generously sprinkle flat baking sheet or peel with cornmeal. Press dough down using palms of hands. Turn out onto lightly floured surface. Divide dough in half. Pat each into oval. Fold each in half lengthwise, pressing edges together. Flatten slightly and fold lengthwise again. Arrange seam side down on work surface. Using sides of hands, stretch, smooth and shape dough into taut cylinder. Starting at center of each cylinder, gently stretch until each loaf is about 13 inches long. Arrange loaves on prepared baking sheet, spacing about 6 inches apart. Sprinkle lightly with flour. Cover loaves with towel and let rise at room temperature until more than doubled in size, about 2 to 3 hours.

Arrange unglazed quarry tiles on center rack of oven and preheat to 450°F. Place broiler pan on lowest rack. Pour 1 cup water into broiler pan. Generously sprinkle tiles with cornmeal. Cut 4 horizontal slits in top of each loaf using razor or very sharp knife. Slide loaves from baking sheet onto hot tiles. Bake 15 minutes. Remove broiler pan from oven. Continue baking loaves until bottoms sound hollow when tapped, about 20 minutes. Cool on rack at least 1 hour before slicing.

Left to right: Bacon-wrapped Chutney Bananas, Curried Rolled Soufflé, Fresh Mint Chutney, Papaya with Raspberry Lime Sauce, India Cup

*Clockwise from bottom right:
White Cheese Tart, Bischofswein,
Alsatian Smoked Bacon,
Confit of Onions with Caraway,
Kugelhopf accompanied by
Prune Butter*

*Clockwise from top right:
Swiss Chard-Basil Soup,
Timbale Rustica,
Walnut and Corn Bran
Muffins, Port and
Honey Zabaglione*

Clockwise from far right:
Wild Rice Pancakes, Scallop-filled
Salmon Medallions with Lettuce Sauce,
Sherry-sauteed Mushrooms, Orange-
glazed Bananas, Carrot Salad
in Berry Vinaigrette

*Poached Leeks
with Sauce Verte*

A Brief Guide to Breadmaking

Flours

If possible, use stone-ground, preservative-free flours found in natural foods stores and refrigerate them to ensure freshness. The term "hard wheat" indicates a high gluten content, while "soft wheat" indicates lower gluten. These are some of the types of flour:

All purpose unbleached white flour. A combination of hard and soft wheats. Its moderate gluten content develops good texture, and this is an ideal flour for French bread and most other breads made with white flour.

Bread flour. Since this hard wheat flour has a high gluten content, it is the perfect candidate for blending with whole grain or low gluten flours (rye, whole wheat, soy or oatmeal) to encourage higher rising.

Whole wheat flour. This comes in two types: low gluten, best for pastrymaking, and higher gluten, best for breadmaking. Both give a fine, nutty flavor to any loaf, but the high gluten variety gives the best texture to most loaves.

Rye flour. There are three varieties: light, medium and dark, the light being the most highly sifted and the dark containing the most fiber. Use according to personal taste. Rye flours are low in gluten and produce loaves that are dense and moist.

Pumpernickel flour. A flaked rye flour that results in a very coarse, fibrous grain. Adds interesting texture to loaves.

Soy flour. A fine source of vitamins and minerals with no gluten. Add small quantities to breads for a much higher nutritional value.

Liquids

Use an instant-reading thermometer for accuracy in checking temperatures of all liquids. If mixing and kneading dough in food processor, liquid should be very cold; friction of processor can overheat dough and kill yeast if ingredients are warm to begin with.

Water. Produces a slightly chewy texture in loaves. Often used in preparing dough for French- and Italian-style breads.

Milk. Makes a cakelike crumb, and is favored for rich breads such as brioche.

Sour cream. Produces an even richer result than milk and adds a subtle tang.

Beer. Gives a malty, sweet flavor, and usually boosts rising power.

Cider and fruit juices. Add flavor and make a more cakelike bread.

Yeast

When substituting fresh cake yeast for dry granulated yeast, a ⅗-ounce yeast cake equals one tablespoon dry yeast. One envelope dry yeast contains one tablespoon. Use dry, preservative-free yeast and store it in the refrigerator or freezer. Always check the expiration date of yeast.

Salt

Salt tempers the growth of yeast and is hence used not only for flavor but also to control rising. It can be eliminated without any radical changes to the finished loaf of bread.

Sweeteners

Sugar, molasses, maple syrup and fruit syrups will encourage rising as well as add flavor to breads. Sugar doesn't belong in a French- or Italian-style bread.

Techniques

Proofing. To determine whether yeast is alive, dissolve it in water with sugar according to directions and allow it to stand for about 10 to 15 minutes or until bubbly and *proofed.*

Kneading. Bread can be mixed and kneaded by hand or in food processor or heavy-duty electric mixer. Allow at least 10 minutes for hand kneading and follow manufacturer's instructions for both mixer and processor.

Rising. The key to fine bread texture and flavor lies in a long, slow maturation. To achieve this, use cooler liquid (90°F to 105°F) to dissolve yeast and a relatively small amount of yeast and sugar in proportion to flour. Give breads three rises at room temperature rather than the usual two in a "warm place," allowing them to reach between two and three times their size during each rise. If desired, dough can be refrigerated to slow down a rise.

Equipment

Baking tiles. Bread baked on a baking stone or an oven rack lined with ½-inch-thick quarry tiles will have a crisper crust than loaves baked on a baking pan. Preheat stone for 30 minutes before baking bread.

Utensils. To tranfer bread to stone, use a flat baking sheet, wooden baker's peel or thin piece of plywood that has been generously sprinkled with flour or cornmeal before loaf is placed on it.

Proof box. Professional bakers pamper their yeast doughs with a warm, humid mini-environment called a "proof box." To simulate those ideal conditions: Choose a bowl slightly larger than the one in which the bread will rise. Pour two to four cups hot tap water into the bottom of this large bowl. Slip the slightly smaller dough bowl inside the large one. Stretch plastic wrap over the rims of both bowls. As usual, set in a warm place to rise, but keep in mind that rising time may be shorter.

FOCACCIA

Italian peasant loaves made from an olive oil–enhanced yeast dough that is shaped into large flattened rounds. Each variation is distinctively flavored and then decorated with the herbs or other seasonings that will be found inside. Tie a red, green and white striped ribbon around the bread or present it in a rustic napkin-lined basket. Best served warm or at room temperature within several hours of baking.

Makes one 12-inch round loaf

 1 **envelope dry yeast**
 ½ **teaspoon sugar**
 ¼ **cup warm water (105°F to 115°F)**

 ¾ **cup lukewarm water (95°F)**
 1 **tablespoon olive oil**
 1 **teaspoon salt**
 1 **teaspoon sugar**
 3¼ **to 3½ cups all purpose flour**
     Variation (see below)
     Olive oil

 1 **egg beaten with 2 teaspoons water (glaze)**
     Garnishes (herbs or other seasonings corresponding to Variation)

Stir yeast and ½ teaspoon sugar into ¼ cup warm water in large bowl. Cover with towel and let stand until mixture is foamy, about 5 minutes.

Add ¾ cup lukewarm water, olive oil, salt and 1 teaspoon sugar to yeast. Mix in 1 cup flour and Variation (see below). Blend in remaining flour 1 cup at a time until soft, slightly sticky dough forms. Turn dough out onto lightly floured surface and knead until smooth and elastic, about 5 minutes, kneading in additional flour as necessary. Brush large bowl with olive oil. Add dough, turning to coat entire surface. Cover bowl with plastic wrap and towel. Let dough rise in warm draft-free area until doubled in size, about 1 hour.

Line heavy baking sheet with parchment paper. Punch dough down. Turn out onto lightly floured surface and knead until smooth, 2 to 3 minutes; then knead dough into smooth ball. Place dough on prepared pan. Let rest 10 minutes. Roll out gently into round 1¼ inches thick. Cover with towel. Let rise at room temperature until almost doubled, about 25 minutes.

Position rack in lower third of oven and preheat to 375°F. Brush top of loaf with egg glaze. Arrange appropriate garnishes decoratively atop loaf. Brush garnishes with glaze. Bake until loaf is golden brown and sounds hollow when tapped on bottom, about 35 minutes (if top browns too quickly, cover with brown paper). Transfer bread to rack. Cool at least 1 hour before slicing. (*Can be wrapped and stored at room temperature 3 days or frozen up to 1 month. Reheat thawed unwrapped bread in 350°F oven 5 minutes.*)

Variations

For rosemary-raisin: Add 1 tablespoon chopped fresh rosemary and ⅓ cup golden raisins soaked in ¼ cup vermouth or Marsala 30 minutes.

For prosciutto, parsley and pepper: Add ⅓ cup coarsely diced prosciutto, 3 tablespoons minced Italian parsley and 1 teaspoon cracked black peppercorns.

For garlic and red onion: Add 2 minced large garlic cloves and ¾ cup coarsely chopped red onion sautéed in 4 teaspoons olive oil with 1 teaspoon sugar and ½ teaspoon salt until just wilted, then cooled to room temperature.

ITALIAN PEPPER BREAD

This easy-to-make bread has tiny bits of crisp salt pork and the zesty bite of coarsely cracked black pepper. It makes wonderful sandwiches. The baked loaves can be wrapped tightly in foil and frozen.

Makes 2 loaves

 1 **pound salt pork, diced**

 2¼ **cups warm water (105°F to 115°F)**
 1 **tablespoon salt**
 2 **teaspoons coarsely cracked black pepper**
 2 **envelopes dry yeast**

 6½ **to 7 cups unbleached all purpose flour**

 1 **egg, lightly beaten**
     Coarse salt (optional)

Oil large bowl and set aside. Warm salt pork in heavy large skillet over low heat until some fat is rendered. Increase heat to medium high and sauté until crisp. Drain pork on paper towels. Reserve ¼ cup fat from skillet.

Combine 1½ cups warm water, reserved pork fat, salt and pepper in large bowl. Dissolve yeast in remaining ¾ cup warm water. Let stand until foamy, about 10 minutes. Add to pepper mixture. Add salt pork and 3 cups flour, stirring vigorously until mixture forms smooth batter. Blend in remaining flour 1 cup at a time to form stiff dough. Turn out onto lightly floured surface and knead until smooth and elastic, about 10 minutes. Transfer to prepared bowl, turning to coat entire surface. Cover and let stand in warm draft-free area until doubled in size, about 1 hour.

Punch dough down. Turn out onto lightly floured surface and cut in half. Divide each half into thirds. Roll each piece into 12-inch-long rope. Place 3 ropes on ungreased baking sheet and braid together, pinching ends to seal. Repeat with remaining dough. Cover lightly and let stand in warm, draft-free area until doubled, 45 minutes.

Preheat oven to 375°F. Brush loaves with beaten egg. Sprinkle with coarse salt. Bake until crust is golden brown and bread sounds hollow when tapped, 40 to 45 minutes. Cool on racks.

SCHIACCIATA

16 to 18 servings (2 loaves)

Sponge

 4 **cups unbleached all purpose flour**
 3 **cups lukewarm water (about 100°F)**
 1 **envelope dry yeast**

Dough

 5 **to 6 cups unbleached all purpose flour**

1 tablespoon salt

4 tablespoons olive oil, or more

For sponge: Mix sponge ingredients with heavy-duty mixer fitted with flat beater on medium speed 1 minute. (Dough can also be made in processor or by hand.) Gradually increase speed to high and beat 5 minutes. Turn into large bowl. Cover with plastic wrap. Let stand at room temperature 24 hours.

For dough: Fit mixer with dough hook. Knead flour and salt into sponge on low speed. Increase speed to medium and knead until dough is smooth and elastic, about 10 minutes. Turn dough out onto lightly floured surface and knead by hand until satiny, 5 to 6 times. (Or knead bread dough completely by hand for 15 minutes.)

Oil large bowl with some of olive oil. Place dough in bowl, turning to coat entire surface. Cover with plastic wrap. Let rise at room temperature until almost 2½ times original size.

Lightly coat two 10 × 15 × 1-inch baking pans with olive oil. Punch dough down. Divide in half. Roll out half of dough on lightly floured surface into rectangle same size as pan, ¼ inch thick. Fit into pan, patting dough to ensure even thickness. Cover with towel. Repeat with other half of dough. Let rise at room temperature until doubled.

Preheat oven to 375°F. Sprinkle each loaf with 1 tablespoon olive oil. Bake 1 pan on middle shelf and 1 pan on bottom shelf until loaves are golden brown and sound hollow when tapped, about 45 minutes; halfway through baking, switch places so loaves bake evenly. Invert onto rack to cool. (*Can be prepared up to 1 month ahead, wrapped tightly and frozen. Thaw overnight, still wrapped, in refrigerator.*)

Before serving, preheat oven to 375°F. Rewarm bread until crisp, about 5 minutes. Slice bread in half horizontally then, with top half on, cut each loaf into 24 squares.

Breakfast and Tea Breads

❖ ❖ ❖ ❖ ❖ ❖ ❖ ❖ ❖ ❖ ❖ ❖ ❖ ❖

ORANGE-SCENTED CRANBERRY BREAD

Serve with Whipped Honey Butter and a cinnamon and rosehips tea.

Makes one 9 × 5-inch loaf

2 cups whole wheat pastry flour

2 teaspoons baking powder (without aluminum salts)

1 teaspoon baking soda

½ teaspoon cinnamon

¼ teaspoon freshly grated nutmeg

1 cup honey

⅓ cup almond oil *or* vegetable oil

2 eggs, beaten

1 cup whole fresh cranberries

1 cup chopped pecans *or* walnuts

⅔ cup raisins

2 tablespoons grated orange peel mixed with 1 tablespoon grated lemon peel

2 tablespoons plain yogurt

Preheat oven to 350°F. Grease 9 × 5-inch loaf pan. Combine flour, baking powder, soda, cinnamon and nutmeg in medium bowl. Combine honey and oil in small saucepan and warm over low heat. Transfer honey mixture to another medium bowl. Add eggs and mix well. Add to dry ingredients and stir just until moistened; *do not overmix*. Fold in cranberries, nuts, raisins, peel and yogurt. Pour into prepared pan. Bake until tester inserted in center comes out clean, about 65 minutes. Turn loaf out onto wire rack and let cool slightly. Serve warm. (*Bread can be frozen. Cover tightly with plastic wrap and aluminum foil. Rewarm slices in 350°F oven for 10 to 15 minutes; rewarm whole loaf in 350°F oven for 25 minutes.*)

PEAR-PECAN BREAD

Makes one 9 × 5-inch loaf

1 cup sugar

½ cup vegetable oil

2 eggs

¼ cup sour cream

1 teaspoon vanilla

2 cups sifted all purpose flour

1 teaspoon baking soda

½ teaspoon salt

¼ teaspoon cinnamon

¼ teaspoon freshly grated nutmeg

1½ cups coarsely chopped peeled pears (about 2 to 3)

⅔ cup coarsely chopped pecans

½ teaspoon grated lemon peel

Preheat oven to 350°F. Grease 9 × 5-inch loaf pan. Combine sugar and oil in large bowl of electric mixer and beat well. Add eggs one at a time, beating well after each addition. Mix in sour cream and vanilla. Sift flour, soda, salt, cinnamon and nutmeg. Beat into sour cream mixture. Stir in pears, pecans and lemon peel. Spoon batter into prepared pan. Bake until tester inserted in center comes out clean, about 1 hour. Cool in pan 10 to 15 minutes. Turn loaf out onto rack and cool completely before slicing.

BASIC DANISH PASTRY DOUGH

Makes 1 recipe

> 2 eggs, room temperature
>   Warm water (105°F to 115°F)
> 2 envelopes dry yeast
> 3¾ cups unbleached all purpose flour
> ½ cup milk, warmed to 115°F
> ¼ cup sugar
> 1 teaspoon vanilla
>
> 2 teaspoons salt
> 2 cups (4 sticks) chilled unsalted butter, cut into ½-inch pieces

Combine eggs in 1-cup measure with enough warm water to equal ¾ cup total. Transfer to medium bowl. Stir in yeast. Let stand until mixture bubbles, about 5 minutes. Whisk in ¾ cup flour with milk, sugar and vanilla and stir until smooth. Cover bowl with plastic wrap. Let stand in warm area (about 75°F) 1½ to 2 hours to mature (an oven preheated to lowest setting 1 minute and then turned off works well). About halfway through rising process, batter will bubble up, then sink down; if preparation is to be interrupted at this point, stir bubbles out of batter and refrigerate up to 24 hours (maturing process will continue).

Combine remaining 3 cups flour with salt in large bowl. Add well-chilled butter and mix, flattening butter pieces slightly between fingertips and working quickly so butter remains firm. (To ensure flaky layers, butter should remain in pieces the size of lima beans and should not be totally incorporated into dough.) Refrigerate mixture if yeast batter is not ready to use. Pour yeast batter into flour mixture and carefully fold in using large rubber spatula, just moistening flour mixture without breaking up any of butter pieces; dough will be crumbly.

Turn dough out onto lightly floured surface. Pat dough down and roll into 12 × 18-inch rectangle; if dough is sticky, sprinkle top lightly with flour, brushing off excess. Using metal spatula, fold right ⅓ of dough toward center, then fold left ⅓ over to cover (as for business letter); dough will still be slightly rough. Lift folded dough from work surface, scrape surface clean and sprinkle lightly with flour. Repeat patting, rolling and folding dough 3 more times. (*If butter starts to soften and run, immediately wrap dough in plastic and freeze 10 to 15 minutes; butter pieces must remain layered throughout dough to ensure flaky pastry.*) Cover dough with plastic wrap and refrigerate for at least 45 minutes (or up to 24 hours).

BEARCLAWS WITH NUT STREUSEL AND APPLE BUTTER FILLING

Makes about 16

Nut Streusel

> ¾ cup all purpose flour
> ½ cup firmly packed brown sugar
> ¼ cup (½ stick) chilled butter, cut into ½-inch pieces
> ½ cup chopped toasted almonds
> 2 egg yolks
>   Pinch of salt
>
> 1 recipe Basic Danish Pastry Dough (see preceding recipe)
>   Apple butter (homemade or commercial)
> 1 egg beaten with 1 tablespoon milk (glaze)
>
>   Grated unsweetened coconut (garnish)

For streusel: Combine flour and brown sugar in small bowl. Using pastry blender, cut in butter until mixture resembles coarse meal. Stir in almonds, egg yolks and salt.

Line 2 rimmed baking sheets with parchment paper. Divide dough into 4 pieces. Return 3 pieces to refrigerator. Divide remaining piece into 4 equal portions. Roll 1 portion out on lightly floured surface into 4½ × 9-inch rectangle. Spread 2 tablespoons apple butter over top, leaving ½-inch border on all sides. Sprinkle about 2 rounded tablespoons streusel over apple butter. Fold rectangle into thirds (as for business letter), sealing edges. Using very sharp knife, make several perpendicular slashes along 1 folded side. Transfer pastry to prepared baking sheet. Repeat with remaining 3 portions. Brush pastries with egg glaze. Repeat process with remaining 3 pieces of dough. Let rest at room temperature 30 minutes (dough will rise only slightly).

Position rack in center of oven and preheat to 450°F. Reglaze pastries with egg mixture. Sprinkle coconut evenly over tops. Transfer pastries to oven and immediately reduce temperature to 400°F. Bake until golden brown, about 20 minutes. Cool on wire racks. Serve warm or at room temperature.

ALMOND COMBS

Makes 3 dozen

Nut Filling

> 1 cup ground toasted almonds*
> ¼ cup (½ stick) butter, room temperature
> 3 tablespoons sugar
> 1½ tablespoons dark rum (optional)
> 1 egg, beaten
> ¼ teaspoon almond extract
> ¼ teaspoon vanilla extract
>
> 1 recipe Basic Danish Pastry Dough (see recipe, this page)
> 1 egg beaten with 1 tablespoon milk (glaze)
>
> ¼ cup apricot preserves
>   Sliced toasted almonds (garnish)

For filling: Combine ground almonds, butter, sugar, rum, egg and extracts in medium bowl.

Line 2 rimmed baking sheets with parchment paper. Divide dough into 4 pieces. Return 3 pieces to refrigerator. Roll remaining piece out on lightly floured surface to form square slightly larger than 12 × 12 inches. Using ruler and pastry wheel, trim dough to square exactly 12 × 12 inches. Divide into nine 4-inch squares. Spread 2 teaspoons filling in ¾-inch-thick strip in center of right half of each square. Brush egg mixture around filling. Fold left side over filling, pressing to seal edges. Using very sharp knife, make eight to ten 1-inch-long perpendicular slashes along folded side of pastry. Spread pastry slightly at slashes. Transfer to prepared baking sheet. Repeat with remaining dough. Brush pastries with egg glaze. Let rest at room temperature 30 minutes (dough will rise only slightly). Reglaze with egg mixture.

Position rack in center of oven and preheat to 450°F. Transfer pastries to oven and immediately reduce temperature to 400°F. Bake until golden brown, about 12 to 15 minutes.

Meanwhile, press apricot preserves through fine strainer into small saucepan and bring to boil over medium heat. Remove from heat. Remove pastries from oven and transfer to wire rack. Immediately brush with apricot glaze. Press almonds into tops. Serve warm or at room temperature.

*Hazelnuts can be substituted for almonds.

WALNUT CORN BRAN MUFFINS

Makes about 1 dozen muffins

- 1 cup milk
- ½ cup bran flakes

  Walnut oil
- ¼ cup (½ stick) unsalted butter
- 3 tablespoons firmly packed dark brown sugar
- 1 egg, room temperature
- 1 teaspoon walnut oil (optional)
- 1 cup all purpose flour
- ½ cup cornmeal
- ½ cup walnuts, toasted and coarsely chopped

- 2 teaspoons baking powder
- ½ teaspoon salt

Combine milk and bran flakes in medium bowl. Let stand at room temperature for at least 8 hours or overnight.

Preheat oven to 400°F. Generously coat twelve 2½-inch muffin cups with walnut oil. Cream ¼ cup butter with sugar in large mixing bowl. Stir in egg and walnut oil, blending well. Fold in flour, cornmeal, walnuts, baking powder, salt and bran mixture until dry ingredients are just moistened. Divide batter evenly among muffin cups. Bake until muffins are brown and tester inserted in centers comes out clean, about 20 to 25 minutes. Cool in pan 7 minutes before serving.

BROWN BUTTERMILK BRAN MUFFINS

Serve these warm with butter.

Makes about 24 muffins

- ½ cup (1 stick) butter
- 1¼ cups sugar
- 2 cups buttermilk
- 2 eggs
- 3 cups whole bran cereal

- 3 cups all purpose flour
- 2 teaspoons baking soda
- 1 teaspoon salt
- ½ cup raisins, chopped nuts *or* coconut (optional)

Preheat oven to 350°F. Generously grease muffin tins or paper baking cups. Cream butter with sugar in large bowl. Stir in buttermilk and eggs. Add cereal and mix well. Let stand about 5 minutes.

Sift flour, baking soda and salt. Add to cereal mixture, blending well. Stir in raisins, nuts or coconut. Divide batter evenly among prepared tins. Bake until tester inserted in centers comes out clean, about 30 minutes. Serve warm.

LEMON SCONES

Light, crumbly and fragrant with lemon peel, these scones are brushed with cream just before baking for a rich sheen. Serve hot with sweet butter, jams and marmalades.

Makes 16 to 20

- 4 cups all purpose flour sifted 3 times with 2 tablespoons baking powder
- ¼ cup sugar
- ¼ teaspoon salt
- 3 tablespoons grated lemon peel
- ½ cup (1 stick) unsalted butter, cut into ½-inch pieces
- 2 eggs, room temperature, beaten to blend
- ⅔ cup milk *or* buttermilk

  Whipping cream

Preheat oven to 450°F. Grease and flour baking sheets. Sift flour, sugar and salt into deep bowl. Stir in peel. Cut in butter until mixture resembles coarse meal. Blend in eggs and just enough milk or buttermilk to form soft but not sticky dough.

Turn dough out onto lightly floured surface. Gently roll or pat dough to about ½-inch thickness, lightly flouring as necesary to prevent sticking. Cut out rounds using 2-inch floured biscuit cutter. Set ½ inch apart on prepared baking sheets. Brush with cream. Bake until scones are golden brown, 12 to 15 minutes. Serve immediately.

❖

13 ❖ Baking: Cakes, Tarts and Cookies

Cakes

❖ ❖ ❖ ❖ ❖ ❖ ❖ ❖ ❖ ❖ ❖ ❖ ❖ ❖ ❖

KUGELHOPF

There are thousands of Kugelhopf recipes in Alsace, since each family has its own formula.

8 to 10 servings

⅓ cup golden raisins
2 tablespoons kirsch

½ cup warm milk (105°F to 115°F)
3 tablespoons sugar
1 envelope dry yeast
3 cups sifted all purpose flour
2 tablespoons cornstarch
1 teaspoon coarse salt
4 eggs, room temperature
¾ cup (1½ sticks) butter, softened until almost oily

2 tablespoons clarified butter (see recipe, page 62)
Grated peel of ½ lemon
½ cup blanched whole almonds (or halve lengthwise)

Powdered sugar
Unsalted butter
Prune Butter with Quetsch (see recipe, page 165)

Combine raisins and kirsch in small bowl and set aside for several hours.

Combine milk, sugar and yeast in small bowl and let stand until mixture bubbles, about 10 minutes. Resift flour with cornstarch and salt onto work surface.* Shape mixture into mound and make well in center. Break eggs into well and beat with fork, gradually adding bubbling yeast mixture. Gather into loose mass. Arrange butter in 4 evenly spaced mounds around dough. Gradually cream butter into flour

mixture using fingertips and moving counterclockwise. Knead dough with fingertips several times. Transfer to large bowl; dough will be very sticky. Cover bowl with towel. Let dough rise at room temperature until doubled in size, about 2 hours.

Brush 2½-quart tube pan or kugelhopf mold with clarified butter. Punch dough down, simultaneously mixing in lemon peel and undrained raisins. Arrange almonds on bottom of prepared pan. Spoon dough over almonds. Cover pan with towel. (*Cake can be prepared 1 day ahead to this point and refrigerated.*) Let dough rise to rim of pan, about 1 hour (longer, if refrigerated).

Preheat oven to 375°F. Bake until cake sounds hollow when tapped, about 45 minutes to 1 hour. Remove from oven and loosen cake from edge of pan with tip of knife. Unmold cake onto rack. Cool. Dust lightly with powdered sugar. Serve with butter and prune butter.

*Cake can also be prepared in electric mixer. Sift flour mixture into large bowl of electric mixer. Make well in center. Pour bubbling yeast mixture into well. Add eggs and beat at low speed until blended.

BURNT SUGAR CROWN CAKE
(*Couronne au Sucre Brûlé*)

An Alsatian specialty, traditionally decorated with fresh red currants. More easily obtainable glacéed fruit can also be used.

12 servings

Cake

1½ tablespoons unsalted butter
1¼ cups sugar
½ cup hot water

6 eggs, room temperature
Pinch of salt
1½ cups sifted all purpose flour
½ cup (1 stick) butter, melted and cooled
2 tablespoons dark rum

Rum Buttercream

1 cup sugar
12 tablespoons (¾ cup) water
¼ cup dark rum

9 egg yolks
1½ cups (3 sticks) unsalted butter, almost room temperature

¼ cup water
¼ cup dark rum
1 tablespoon sugar
1½ cups chopped toasted almonds

6 glacéed cherries, halved
12 small triangular pieces green glacéed fruit

For cake: Coat inside of 3-quart bundt pan with 1½ tablespoons unsalted butter. Combine sugar with ¼ cup hot water in heavy-bottomed large saucepan over low heat and swirl pan gently until sugar is dissolved. Increase heat to high and cook until mixture caramelizes and is deep mahogany color. Remove from heat and cool slightly. Blend in remaining ¼ cup water.

Preheat oven to 350°F. Beat eggs with salt in large bowl of electric mixer at high speed until foamy. Gradually add caramel in thin steady stream, beating constantly until mixture forms a ribbon when beaters are lifted, 8 to 10 minutes. Resift flour over egg mixture in 3 batches, folding gently after each addition. Gently fold in melted butter and rum. Turn batter into prepared pan. Bake until tester inserted near center comes out clean, 30 to 35 minutes. Cool on rack.

For buttercream: Combine 1 cup sugar with 6 tablespoons water in heavy-bottomed large saucepan until sugar is dissolved. Increase heat to high and cook until mixture caramelizes and is deep mahogany color. Remove from heat and cool slightly. Add ¼ cup rum with remaining 6 tablespoons water to caramel (be careful; mixture may spatter) and blend thoroughly.

Beat yolks in large bowl of electric mixer at high speed until mixture forms a ribbon when beaters are lifted; continue beating, adding caramel in thin steady stream, until mixture is cold. Add butter 1 tablespoon at a time, beating until mixture is smooth and creamy.

To assemble, cut cake horizontally into 4 equal layers. Combine ¼ cup water, ¼ cup rum and 1 tablespoon sugar in small bowl and stir until sugar is dissolved. Moisten bottom layer of cake with 2 tablespoons rum mixture. Spread ¼-inch-thick layer of buttercream over top. Repeat with next two layers. Brush remaining 2 tablespoons rum mixture over bottom of last layer, then invert layer onto cake. Spread ⅛-inch-thick layer of buttercream over cake. Sprinkle with toasted almonds.

Spoon remaining buttercream into pastry bag fitted with small star tip. Pipe 6 rosettes around top rim of cake. Top each rosette with glacéed cherry half and piece of green glacéed fruit. Pipe 6 more rosettes around base of cake. Top each rosette with glacéed cherry half and piece of green glacéed fruit. Refrigerate. Let stand at room temperature 15 minutes before serving.

❖

ALMOND CAKE WITH RASPBERRY SAUCE

12 servings

Almond Cake

    8 ounces almond paste
    ¾ cup sugar
    ½ cup (1 stick) unsalted butter, room temperature
    3 eggs
    1 tablespoon kirsch *or* Triple Sec
    ¼ teaspoon almond extract
    ¼ cup all purpose flour
    ⅓ teaspoon baking powder
       Powdered sugar

Raspberry Sauce

    1 pint (2 cups) fresh raspberries *or* one 12-ounce package frozen, thawed
    2 tablespoons sugar, or to taste (omit if using frozen raspberries)

For cake: Preheat oven to 350°F. Generously butter and flour 8-inch round cake pan. Combine almond paste, sugar and butter in medium mixing bowl and blend well. Beat in eggs, liqueur and almond extract. Add flour and baking powder, beating until just mixed through; *do not overbeat.* Turn batter into prepared pan. Bake until tester inserted in center of cake comes out clean, about 40 to 50 minutes. Let cool. Invert onto serving platter and dust lightly with powdered sugar.

For sauce: Combine raspberries with sugar in processor or blender and puree. Gently press sauce through fine sieve to remove seeds. Serve sauce as an accompaniment to Almond Cake.

TRIPLE MOCHA SQUARE

With coffee in the cake, filling and buttercream frosting, this dessert is sure to be popular with mocha lovers.

16 servings

Mocha Cake

    ¼ cup boiling water
    2 tablespoons instant espresso powder

    1 cup all purpose flour
    1 teaspoon baking powder
    3 eggs, room temperature, separated
    1 cup sugar
    ¼ teaspoon cream of tartar

Chocolate Mocha Filling

    3½ ounces semisweet chocolate, broken into small pieces
    2 tablespoons coffee liqueur
    5 tablespoons unsalted butter, cut into pieces

Mocha Buttercream

    2 tablespoons instant espresso powder
    2 teaspoons boiling water
    1 cup (2 sticks) unsalted butter, cut into ¼-inch slices

    2 eggs
    6 tablespoons sugar

       Chocolate coffee beans (garnish)

For cake: Preheat oven to 300°F. Butter and flour 9 × 12-inch cake pan. Combine water and espresso powder in small bowl and set aside. Sift flour with baking powder and set aside.

Beat egg yolks in large bowl until thick and pale yellow. Gradually add sugar, beating constantly. Stir in flour mixture. Blend in espresso. Beat egg whites in another bowl with cream of tartar until stiff and glossy. Carefully fold egg whites into yolk mixture.

Pour batter into prepared pan, spreading evenly. Bake until edges of cake shrink slightly from pan and tester inserted in center comes out clean, about 25 to 30 minutes. Remove cake from pan and let cool on wire rack.

For filling: Combine chocolate and coffee liqueur in top of double boiler and melt over hot (not boiling) water, stirring occasionally until smooth. Remove from heat. Add butter one piece at a time and beat with wooden spoon until mixture is consistency of mayonnaise. If not thick enough, set in bowl of ice water and beat to proper consistency, about 1 to 2 minutes.

For buttercream: Combine espresso powder and boiling water in small bowl and stir until dissolved. Set aside. Cream butter in another bowl until soft and fluffy.

Beat eggs in top of double boiler. Add sugar and beat until thick and pale yellow. Place over simmering water and cook, beating constantly with electric mixer at medium-high speed until thick and creamy, about 4 minutes. Transfer to bowl. Blend in espresso. Gradually add butter, beating constantly. Continue beating until mixture is cool, thick, glossy and slightly lightened in color, 3 to 5 minutes.

Slice cake crosswise into 2 sections using serrated knife. Carefully split each section horizontally, making 4 layers. Reserve top layer. Spread filling thinly and evenly over remaining 3 layers. Stack layers on serving platter filling side up, topping with reserved unfilled layer cut side down.

Spread half of buttercream over top and sides of cake. Spoon remainder into pastry bag with decorative tip. Pipe rosettes around rim and several over top. Place chocolate coffee beans in centers of rosettes. Refrigerate until 1 hour before serving. To serve, cut crosswise into strips and cut each strip in half through center.

CAKE ROLL WITH WHOLE EGGS

Depending on eggs for its leavening, this cake requires only two techniques to guarantee its success: beating the eggs to maximum volume and folding in dry ingredients without deflating the batter. An electric heavy-duty mixer makes these tasks a snap. If one is not available, facilitate beating by first whisking eggs in a mixing bowl over simmering water until warm to the touch or soaking unbroken eggs in a bowl of very hot water for one hour before beating. If using a portable electric mixer, move it around the bowl in concentric circles to incorporate as much air into the eggs as possible.

10 to 12 servings

  6 **eggs, room temperature**
  1 **cup (16 tablespoons) sugar**
  2 **teaspoons vanilla *or* 1 tablespoon fresh lemon juice *or* 3 tablespoons liqueur**
     Finely grated peel of 1 orange *or* lemon (optional)
1¼ **cups cake flour *or* 1 cup plus 1½ tablespoons all purpose flour, sifted**
⅛ **teaspoon salt**

     Powdered sugar

Preheat oven to 350°F. Line 10 × 15-inch jelly roll pan with parchment or waxed paper, allowing 3-inch overhang on short sides. Generously grease paper and sides of pan. Dust lightly with flour, shaking off excess. Place eggs in large bowl of electric mixer. Beat in sugar on medium-high speed 1 tablespoon at a time. Continue beating until eggs have thickened and tripled in volume, about 10 minutes. Beat in flavoring and peel. Combine flour and salt and sift into batter about ¼ cup at a time, folding carefully to prevent deflating.

Turn batter into prepared pan, pushing it into corners and smoothing top with metal spatula. Tap pan lightly on counter. Bake until cake is golden brown, springy to the touch and a tester inserted in center comes out clean, about 12 minutes. Immediately loosen edges of cake using tip of knife. Sprinkle clean kitchen towel with powdered sugar. Set over cake sugared side down, folding ends under pan. Pulling ends of towel tautly to secure cake, invert pan onto counter. Remove pan and peel off paper lining. Fold end of towel down on top of cake and roll cake lengthwise in towel. Let cool completely on rack. If not filling immediately, unroll cake and remove towel to prevent sticking. Reroll cake in waxed paper or aluminum foil. Store in refrigerator overnight or in freezer several weeks (thaw completely in refrigerator before filling).

To fill, unroll cake and trim off any crusty edges on long sides. Spread filling evenly over top, covering to ends. Roll cake up length-wise, using towel as aid. Trim off ends of cake and discard. Cover cake with topping or glaze if desired. Arrange seam side down on serving platter using 2 spatulas. (*Can be prepared 1 day ahead and refrigerated overnight. Let stand at room temperature 30 minutes before serving.*) Slice cake using serrated knife in rocking motion to prevent mashing filling.

CAKE ROLL WITH SEPARATED EGGS

This batter contains less flour and sugar than the Cake Roll with Whole Eggs.

8 to 10 servings

  6 **eggs (room temperature), separated**
½ **cup (8 tablespoons) sugar**
  2 **teaspoons vanilla *or* 1 tablespoon fresh lemon juice *or* 3 tablespoons liqueur**
     Finely grated peel of 1 orange *or* lemon (optional)
⅔ **cup cake flour *or* ⅔ cup all purpose flour minus 4 teaspoons, sifted**

¼ **teaspoon cream of tartar**
⅛ **teaspoon salt**
  2 **tablespoons sugar**

Preheat oven to 350°F. Line 10 × 15-inch jelly roll pan with parchment or waxed paper, allowing 3-inch overhang on short sides. Generously grease paper and sides of pan. Dust lightly with flour, shaking off excess. Place yolks in large bowl of electric mixer. Beat in ½ cup sugar on medium-high speed 1 tablespoon at a time. Continue beating until mixture thickens and forms ribbon when beaters are lifted, about 5 minutes. Beat in flavoring and peel. Gradually fold flour into egg yolks, being careful not to deflate batter.

Beat egg whites with cream of tartar and salt in another bowl until soft peaks form. Beat in remaining sugar 1 tablespoon at a time. Continue beating until whites are stiff

Rolled Cakes: Plain or Fancy

The versatile rolled cake is a delectable dessert for any occasion. Its presentation ranges from the simple jelly roll that grandmother loved to bake to Bûche de Noël, the classic Yule log cake from France. The airy sponge batter is baked in a shallow rectangular pan and then rolled into its characteristic shape while still warm. When cool, it can be lavished with fillings and frostings.

Here are two versions of the basic batter: one made with beaten whole eggs and the other in which the whites are beaten separately and folded into the batter. The cake roll with whole eggs will be higher, the one with separated eggs lighter and more delicate. Both are delicious.

Fillings

Cakes can be filled with 1½ to 2 cups jam, buttercream or frosting or 2 to 4 cups mousse, custard, lemon curd, fruit puree, chestnut spread or whipped cream and fresh fruit. For an ice cream roll, fill cake with 1½ to 2 pints of softened ice cream, then roll up and freeze until firm, about 4 hours.

Toppings and Glazes

Rolled cakes can be frosted with the same buttercream or icing with which they are filled, glazed with melted jelly or topped with meringue or almond paste. When the focus is on the filling, finish the cake simply by sifting powdered sugar or a mixture of 1 tablespoon cocoa to 3 tablespoons powdered sugar over top. To decorate, arrange a stencil or strips of waxed paper on cake before sprinkling with sugar. Caramelize the sugar, if desired, by placing under broiler for 1 to 2 minutes. Garnish with ground nuts, praline (see recipe, page 191), coconut or chocolate curls.

Variations

Chocolate Sponge Cake: Substitute ½ cup dark Dutch process cocoa for ½ cup flour in either recipe. Sift cocoa with flour before folding into cake batter.

Nut Sponge Cake: Substitute ½ cup ground toasted nuts for ¼ cup flour in Cake Roll with Whole Eggs, or use ⅓ cup ground toasted nuts for ⅓ cup flour in Cake Roll with Separated Eggs.

Great Hints

♦ To moisten cake before filling, brush with syrup or fruit poaching liquid, or sprinkle lightly with orange juice, fresh coffee or a good fruit-based liqueur.

♦ Batter for both types of cake can be baked in two round 8-inch pans.

♦ Sponge sheet can be sliced lengthwise in half or thirds and stacked instead of rolled. Fill as desired.

♦ Jam or other fillings that will not be affected by heat can be added when cake is first rolled immediately after baking.

♦ Add subtle flavoring to cake by brushing lined jelly roll pan with either almond oil or melted browned butter.

♦ Crusts trimmed from cake can be mixed with custard or buttercream and used for pudding or cake filling.

♦ For a springy texture, substitute cornstarch for half of the flour in Cake Roll with Separated Eggs.

---

and glossy. Gently fold ¼ of whites into batter to loosen; fold in remaining whites.

To bake, roll and fill, follow directions for Cake Roll with Whole Eggs (see preceding recipe).

APRICOT AND WALNUT DACQUOISE CAKE

10 servings

Apricot Filling

1¾ cups water
8 ounces dried apricots
2 tablespoons fresh lemon juice
4 ½-inch-wide (about) strips of orange peel
½ cup sugar
3 to 4 tablespoons orange liqueur *or* dark rum

Walnut Dacquoise

¾ cup sugar
⅓ cup cornstarch
¼ cup walnut pieces, lightly toasted
3 egg whites, room temperature
½ teaspoon vanilla
⅛ teaspoon cream of tartar
Pinch of salt

Cake

⅔ cup sugar
4 eggs, separated, room temperature
1 teaspoon vanilla
½ teaspoon orange extract
½ cup all purpose flour
⅓ cup cornstarch
Salt
2 tablespoons (¼ stick) unsalted butter, melted

1 cup whipping cream, well chilled
2 tablespoons powdered sugar
1 tablespoon orange liqueur *or* dark rum
¼ cup walnut pieces, lightly toasted

For filling: Combine water, apricots, lemon juice and orange peel in large saucepan over medium-low heat. Cover partially and cook until apricots are soft and water is reduced by half, about 15 minutes (depending on dryness of the apricots).

Stir in sugar and continue cooking, uncovered, until syrup is thickened and reduced by half again, about 12 minutes. Cool 10 minutes. Transfer to processor and coarsely puree. Add enough liqueur to make puree spreadable. (*Filling can be prepared 1 day ahead and refrigerated. Bring to room temperature before continuing with recipe.*)

For dacquoise: Combine ¼ cup sugar, ⅓ cup cornstarch and ¼ cup toasted walnuts in processor and mix until finely ground. Beat egg whites with vanilla, cream of tartar and salt in large bowl of electric mixer until soft peaks form. Add remaining ½ cup sugar 1 tablespoon at a time, beating until whites are stiff but not dry. Gently fold in ground walnut mixture. Spoon into pastry bag fitted with No. 7 or No. 8 tip. Set aside while preparing cake.

For cake: Set rack at lowest position of oven and preheat to 350°F. Butter two 8-inch round cake pans. Line bottoms with waxed paper; butter paper. Lightly dust pans with flour.

Combine ⅓ cup sugar, yolks, vanilla and orange extract in large bowl of electric mixer and beat until mixture is pale yellow and forms a ribbon when beaters are lifted. Sift flour 3 times with cornstarch and pinch of salt. Combine whites with pinch of salt in another large bowl and beat until soft peaks form. Add remaining ⅓ cup sugar 1 tablespoon at a time, beating until stiff but not dry. Gently fold whites into yolks alternately with flour. Gently fold in butter.

Divide batter evenly between prepared pans. Starting in center, pipe dacquoise in spiral pattern over tops to edges. Bake until dacquoise is lightly browned and tester inserted in center of cake comes out clean, about 35 minutes. Run knife around edge of cake and carefully invert onto rack. Remove waxed paper. Lay another rack over cake and quickly invert dacquoise side up. Cool completely. (*Cake can be made 1 day ahead to this point. Cover with plastic wrap and set aside at room temperature.*)

To assemble, arrange 1 layer on serving platter dacquoise side up. Spread with half of apricot filling. Repeat with remaining layer and filling. (*Cake can be prepared several hours ahead to this point.*) Whip cream to soft peaks. Add powdered sugar and orange liqueur and whip until slightly stiffer. Spoon cream into pastry bag fitted with star tip. Pipe 8 rosettes around top rim of cake and 1 in center. Garnish rosettes with remaining walnuts. Pipe diagonal stripes of cream decoratively around sides of cake. Serve immediately. Use serrated knife to slice.

APPLE LADYFINGER LAYER CAKE WITH CIDER BUTTERCREAM

Best prepared one day before serving.

8 servings

Apple Ladyfinger Layers

  4 eggs, separated, room temperature
½ cup (8 tablespoons) sugar
⅔ cup all purpose flour, sifted
½ cup peeled grated apple
¼ cup husked hazelnuts, toasted and ground

⅛ teaspoon salt
⅛ teaspoon cream of tartar

Poached Apple Filling

  3 large apples, peeled, halved and cored
½ cup cider
½ cup sugar
  3 strips lemon peel
  1 teaspoon vanilla

Cider Buttercream

  4 egg yolks, room temperature

  1 cup (2 sticks) unsalted butter, cut into 16 pieces, room temperature
  1 tablespoon Calvados

¼ cup apricot preserves, melted
½ cup hazelnuts, toasted and chopped

For ladyfinger layers: Preheat oven to 300°F. Line 2 baking sheets with parchment paper. Butter and flour paper, shaking off excess. Draw 9-inch circle on each. Beat egg yolks with 6 tablespoons sugar until mixture is lemon colored and forms a ribbon when beaters are lifted. Mix in flour, grated apple and hazelnuts.

Beat egg whites until foamy. Add salt and cream of tartar and continue beating until soft peaks form. Add remaining 2 tablespoons sugar 1 tablespoon at a time and continue beating until whites are stiff but not dry. Gently stir ¼ of whites into yolk mixture, then fold yolk mixture back into remaining whites. Spoon into pastry bag fitted with ½-inch plain tip and pipe out in concentric circles on each baking sheet so no paper shows through (or divide batter between 2 baking trays and spread with metal spatula). Bake until layers are just firm to the touch and lightly browned on top, about 20 minutes. Slide off onto rack and let cool.

For filling: Chop apples coarsely. Combine cider, sugar and lemon peel in 2-quart saucepan and cook over low heat until sugar dissolves. Add apples, cover and poach, stirring occasionally, until tender when pierced with fork. Remove from heat and stir in vanilla. Let apples cool completely in liquid.

For buttercream: Drain apples (reserve liquid) and pat dry with paper towels; set aside. Simmer liquid in small saucepan until reduced to about ½ cup.

Begin beating yolks in medium mixing bowl. Gradually pour in reduced liquid and continue beating until mixture is lemon colored and forms a ribbon when beaters are lifted. Add butter 1 piece at a time and continue beating until smooth. Stir in Calvados.

Place 1 ladyfinger layer on rack set over baking sheet. Brush with preserves. Mix poached apples with ¼ of Cider Buttercream and spread over ladyfinger layer. Top with second ladyfinger layer bottom side up. Frost top and sides of cake with remaining buttercream. Press nuts around sides of cake. Transfer to serving platter and refrigerate overnight. Let stand at room temperature 30 minutes before serving.

INDIVIDUAL BAKED ALASKAS

Recipe can be halved if you wish.

Makes 14

Chocolate Ice Cream with Brandied Currants

3½ cups whipping cream
6 ounces semisweet chocolate, coarsely chopped
1 ounce unsweetened chocolate, coarsely chopped
½ cup sugar
¼ cup water

3 egg yolks, room temperature
Pinch of salt
1 teaspoon vanilla

½ cup dried currants
¼ cup brandy

Chocolate Brownie Cake

1 cup (2 sticks) unsalted butter
4 ounces unsweetened chocolate, coarsely chopped
2 cups sugar
3 eggs, room temperature
1 teaspoon vanilla
½ teaspoon salt
1 cup cake flour
¼ cup ground walnuts (preferably black walnuts)

8 egg whites, room temperature
1 teaspoon cream of tartar
¾ cup sugar
2 teaspoons vanilla

For ice cream: Combine 1 cup cream and both chocolates in heavy medium saucepan over low heat and whisk until melted and smooth.

Heat sugar and ¼ cup water in another heavy saucepan over low heat, swirling pan occasionally, until sugar dissolves. Increase heat to medium high and boil until mixture registers 230°F (thread stage) on candy thermometer.

Meanwhile, slowly beat yolks and salt in large bowl of electric mixer 1 minute. Increase speed to high and beat in hot syrup in thin stream. Blend in chocolate mixture until well combined. Add remaining 2½ cups cream and vanilla. Cover and refrigerate until well chilled, at least 2 hours. (*Can be prepared 1 day ahead to this point.*)

Meanwhile, marinate currants in brandy at least 1 hour, stirring occasionally; drain thoroughly.

Transfer chocolate mixture to ice cream maker and freeze according to manufacturer's instructions. Fold drained currants into ice cream. Divide mixture among fourteen 3-inch-diameter ramekins, packing tightly. Cover and freeze until firm, at least 3 hours. (*Can be prepared 1 day ahead to this point.*)

For cake: Preheat oven to 350°F. Butter 10½ × 16½-inch jelly roll pan. Line pan with parchment, extending paper 1 inch beyond ends. Butter and flour paper. Melt ½ cup butter and chocolate in top of double boiler, stirring until smooth. Remove from over water. Cream remaining ½ cup butter and 2 cups sugar in large bowl until fluffy. Beat in eggs 1 at a time. Blend in chocolate mixture, 1 teaspoon vanilla and salt. Fold in flour and walnuts. Spread batter evenly in prepared pan. Bake until firm to the touch, about 20 minutes. Cool in pan 15 minutes. Invert onto rack and cool completely. Trim off crisp ends and cut cake into 3-inch rounds, using cookie cutter or glass. (*Can be prepared 1 day ahead. Wrap cakes tightly and refrigerate.*)

Arrange cake rounds on baking sheets, spacing 2 inches apart. One at a time, dip ice cream molds into tepid water 3 seconds. Run knife around edge and unmold each atop cake round. Freeze desserts until ready to serve.

Just before serving, preheat oven to 450°F. Beat whites and cream of tartar in large bowl of electric mixer until soft peaks form. Add sugar 1 tablespoon at a time, beating until meringue is stiff and shiny. Blend in 2 teaspoons vanilla. Spoon meringue into pastry bag and pipe decoratively over each ice cream cake round, covering completely. Bake until meringue is light brown, about 3 minutes, watching carefully. Serve immediately.

STRAWBERRY-GLAZED CREAM CHEESE CAKE

10 to 12 servings

Crust

¾ cup coarsely ground walnuts (3 ounces)
¾ cup finely crushed graham crackers
3 tablespoons unsalted butter, melted

Filling

4 8-ounce packages cream cheese, room temperature
4 eggs
1¼ cups sugar
1 tablespoon fresh lemon juice
2 teaspoons vanilla

Topping

2 cups sour cream
¼ cup sugar
1 teaspoon vanilla

Strawberry Glaze

4 cups medium strawberries
1 12-ounce jar red raspberry jelly
1 tablespoon cornstarch
¼ cup orange liqueur
¼ cup water

Position rack in center of oven and preheat to 350°F. Lightly butter 9- or 10-inch springform pan.

For crust: Combine walnuts, graham cracker crumbs and butter. Press firmly onto bottom of pan.

For filling: Beat cream cheese in large bowl of electric mixer until smooth. Add eggs, sugar, lemon juice and vanilla and beat thoroughly. Spoon over crust.

Set pan on baking sheet to catch any butter that may drip out. Bake 10-inch cake 40 to 45 minutes or 9-inch cake 50 to 55 minutes. (Cake may rise slightly and crack in several areas; it will settle again, cracks will minimize and topping will cover them up.) Remove from oven and let stand at room temperature for 15 minutes. Retain oven temperature at 350°F.

For topping: Combine sour cream, sugar and vanilla and blend well. Cover and refrigerate. When cake has finished baking, spoon topping over, starting at center and extending to within ½ inch of edge. Return to oven and bake 5 minutes longer. Let cool, then refrigerate cheesecake for at least 24 hours or, preferably, 2 to 3 days.

For glaze: Several hours before serving, wash and hull berries and let dry completely on paper towels. Combine a little jelly with cornstarch in saucepan and mix well. Add remaining jelly, liqueur and water and cook over medium heat, stir-ring frequently, until thickened and clear, about 5 minutes. Cool to lukewarm, stirring occasionally.

Using knife, loosen cake from pan; remove springform. Arrange berries pointed end up over top of cake. Spoon glaze over berries, allowing some to drip down sides of cake. Return to refrigerator until glaze is set.

CHEESECAKE CAPPUCCINO

10 to 12 servings

½ cup graham cracker crumbs

9 egg yolks
1 cup sugar
1 teaspoon fresh lemon juice
½ teaspoon vanilla
   Pinch of salt
   Finely grated peel of ¼ lemon

2½ pounds cream cheese, room temperature
¾ cup (1½ sticks) butter, room temperature
¾ cup sugar
½ cup sour cream
½ cup all purpose flour

6 ounces semisweet chocolate, melted
½ cup chopped toasted almonds

Preheat oven to 325° F. Butter and flour 10-inch springform pan, shaking out excess flour. Sprinkle bottom with crumbs.

Combine yolks, 1 cup sugar, lemon juice, vanilla, salt and lemon peel in medium bowl and whisk until light and fluffy. Set aside.

Combine cream cheese, butter, ¾ cup sugar, sour cream and flour in large bowl and beat until smooth and creamy. Stir in chocolate and almonds. Gradually add egg mixture, stirring constantly until just blended; *do not overmix.* Pour batter into prepared pan to within ¾ inch of rim. Set pan in baking dish. Add enough warm water to come halfway up sides of pan. Bake until set, about 1½ hours. Remove cake from water bath and let cool completely (cake may fall slightly). Remove springform. Refrigerate cake 24 hours. Let stand at room temperature 30 minutes before serving.

Tarts and Pastries

COOKIE CRUST TART WITH BOYSENBERRY PUREE

8 servings

Cookie Crust

½ cup sliced blanched almonds
5 tablespoons sugar
1¼ cups (2½ sticks) unsalted butter
2 tablespoons plus 1½ teaspoons almond paste
1 jumbo egg yolk

1½ cups plus 2 tablespoons all purpose flour

Boysenberry Puree

4 cups boysenberries
¾ cup sugar, or more to taste
1 teaspoon fresh lemon juice

   Powdered sugar (garnish)

For crust: Grind almonds with half of sugar in processor. Beat ground almonds, remaining sugar, butter, almond paste and egg yolk in large bowl of electric mixer until light and fluffy. Blend in flour just until mix-ture forms ball; do not overmix. Flatten into disc. Wrap dough in plastic or waxed paper and refrigerate while making puree.

For puree: Puree berries in processor or blender. Transfer to heavy medium saucepan. Add sugar and lemon juice and stir over medium heat until thick, about 12 minutes. Strain puree through very fine sieve.

Place 9-inch flan ring or tart pan with removable bottom on baking sheet. Spoon dough into pastry bag fitted with No. 6 tip and pipe (if too sticky to pipe, add a bit more flour) in concentric circles to cover bottom of pan, then pipe around side. Refrigerate for about 30 minutes.

Preheat oven to 375°F. Spoon puree into crust. Pipe lattice design over top with remaining dough. Bake until crisp and golden, 45 minutes. Before serving, dust with powdered sugar.

LEMON PRALINE TART

All components can be prepared one to two days in advance, and the tart can be assembled several hours ahead.

6 to 8 servings

Pastry

- 1 cup all purpose flour
- ¼ cup cake flour
- 2 tablespoons sugar
- ½ teaspoon grated lemon peel
  Pinch of salt
- 6 tablespoons (¾ stick) chilled unsalted butter, cut into ½-inch pieces
- 1 to 1½ tablespoons cold water
- 1 egg yolk
- ½ teaspoon vanilla

Lemon Filling

- 7 tablespoons unsalted butter
- 1 cup sugar
  Grated peel of 2 large lemons
  Juice of 3 large lemons
  Juice of 1 lime
- 3 eggs, room temperature
- 3 egg yolks, room temperature
  Pinch of salt
- ½ teaspoon almond extract

Praline

- ½ cup sugar
- 2 tablespoons water
- 1 teaspoon fresh lemon juice
- ½ cup sliced toasted almonds

For pastry: Mix flours, sugar, lemon peel and salt in processor. Add butter and mix using on/off turns until mixture resembles coarse meal. Beat together 1 tablespoon water, yolk

and vanilla to blend. Drizzle yolk mixture over flour. Mix using on/off turns until dough just begins to mass together. If dough appears dry, sprinkle with additional ½ tablespoon water and mix until just blended. Pat dough into disc, wrap in plastic and refrigerate at least 1 hour. (*Dough can be prepared several days ahead and refrigerated.*)

Grease 9-inch tart pan with removable bottom. Roll dough out between sheets of plastic wrap to thickness of less than ⅛ inch. Fit dough into prepared pan; trim edge or crimp decoratively. Refrigerate at least 1 hour.

Preheat oven to 425°F. Line chilled pastry shell with buttered parchment or aluminum foil. Fill with dried beans or pie weights. Bake until set, about 10 minutes. Remove beans and foil, prick bottom of crust with fork and continue baking until golden brown, about 10 minutes. Cool on rack.

For filling: Melt butter in top of double boiler set over gently simmering water. Remove from heat. Stir in sugar, lemon peel and juice and lime juice. Beat in eggs, yolks and salt. Replace over simmering water and whisk constantly until mixture is thick and thermometer registers 160°F. Remove from heat. Stir in almond extract. Let cool. Refrigerate until well chilled. (*Can be prepared 2 days ahead.*)

For praline: Oil heavy baking sheet or pan. Combine sugar, water and lemon juice in heavy small saucepan over medium-low heat and swirl pan gently until sugar dissolves, brushing down any crystals from side of pan with wet pastry brush; *do not stir or syrup will crystallize.* Increase heat to medium-high and boil until syrup just caramelizes. Set aside 2 tablespoons almonds. Stir remaining almonds into caramel and immediately pour mixture onto prepared baking sheet. Cool until hardened. Break into chunks. Mix in processor or blender until reduced to powder. (*Praline can be prepared several months ahead and stored in airtight container at room temperature.*)

To assemble, pour filling into pastry and smooth top. Sprinkle with 3 to 4 tablespoons praline, then with reserved almonds. Refrigerate for 4 to 5 hours before serving.

LEMON RASPBERRY TART

8 to 10 servings

Pastry

- 2 cups all purpose flour
- 2 tablespoons sugar
- 1 teaspoon grated lemon peel
  Pinch of salt
- ½ cup (1 stick) chilled unsalted butter, cut into ½-inch pieces
- 3 tablespoons chilled solid vegetable shortening
- 1 tablespoon Cognac
- 2 to 4 tablespoons ice water

Lemon Filling

- 1½ cups sugar
- ½ cup (1 stick) unsalted butter, melted and cooled
- 7 tablespoons fresh lemon juice
- 3 extra-large eggs, room temperature, beaten to blend
- 2 egg yolks, room temperature, beaten to blend
- 1 to 2 tablespoons minced lemon peel

- 4 cups fresh raspberries

For pastry: Combine flour, sugar, peel and salt in large bowl. Cut in butter and shortening until mixture resembles coarse meal. Add Cognac, then gradually blend in water until mixture can be gathered into ball. Flatten dough into disc. Wrap in plastic and refrigerate 1 hour. (*Can be made up to 3 days ahead and refrigerated.*)

Butter 10- to 11-inch quiche pan. Roll dough out on lightly floured surface into 12- to 13-inch circle ⅛ inch thick. Fit into pan; form edges. Freeze pastry until firm. (*Can be made up to 1 month ahead and frozen.*)

Preheat oven to 450°F. Prick pastry shell with fork. Line with buttered parchment paper, then fill with dried beans or pie weights. Bake 5 minutes. Reduce oven temperature to 350°F and bake 10 minutes. Remove paper and weights. Continue baking until well browned, about 20 minutes.

For filling: Combine all ingredients in heavy medium saucepan and stir constantly over low heat until thick, 15 to 20 minutes; *do not boil.* Let cool. (*Can be prepared 2 days ahead. Place plastic wrap directly on surface of filling after cooling. Refrigerate until ready to use.*)

Spoon filling into crust. Arrange raspberries decoratively over top and serve.

FRUIT EMPANADAS

Fresh flour tortillas, enveloping a tropical fruit filling, are deep fried, then sprinkled with powdered sugar.

Makes 10 pastries

- 10 ounces guava *or* quince paste, fresh *or* canned mango *or* fresh papaya, cut into ¼ × 1-inch strips
- 2 8-ounce packages cream cheese, cut into ¼ × 1-inch strips
- 10 ¼-inch-thick, 5½-inch-diameter uncooked flour tortillas (see recipe, page 11)
   Peanut oil (for deep frying)
   Powdered sugar (garnish)

Divide guava paste and cream cheese evenly among tortillas. Fold tortillas in half, allowing rounded edge of bottom half to extend about ¼ inch beyond top half. Fold bottom edge up and over top about ½ inch; crimp edges decoratively to seal. Pour oil into medium saucepan or deep fat fryer to depth of 2 to 3 inches and heat to 375°F. Add empanadas 1 at a time and fry until golden brown on both sides, 1 to 2 minutes, spooning oil over top to encourage puffing. Remove from pan using slotted spoon and drain on paper towels. Dust generously with powdered sugar and serve.

CREME BRULEE TART JIMMY

8 to 10 servings

Pâte Sucrée

- 1 cup all purpose flour
- 2½ tablespoons sugar
   Pinch of salt
- 7 tablespoons chilled unsalted butter, cut into ½-inch pieces
- 1 egg yolk

Crème

- 6 egg yolks, room temperature
- 6 tablespoons sugar
- 2 cups whipping cream
- 1 cup sour cream
- 1 teaspoon vanilla
- ¼ cup (½ stick) unsalted butter, cut into pieces, room temperature
- 3 ounces semisweet chocolate, melted
- 2 cups blackberries
   Brown sugar

For pâte: Combine flour, sugar and salt in large bowl. Cut in butter until mixture resembles coarse meal. Add yolk and mix until dough just holds together. Flatten into disc. Wrap in plastic. Refrigerate 1 hour. (*Can be made up to 3 days ahead and refrigerated.*)

Butter 8- or 9-inch cake pan. Roll dough out on lightly floured surface into circle ⅛ inch thick. Fit into pan; trim and form edges. Prick shell and freeze until firm. (*Can be prepared 1 month ahead and frozen.*)

Preheat oven to 400°F. Line shell with buttered parchment paper and fill with dried beans or pie weights. Bake 15 minutes. Reduce oven temperature to 350°F and bake 10 minutes. Remove paper and weights. Continue baking until brown, about 8 minutes.

For crème: Whisk yolks and sugar in bowl set over pan of gently simmering water (water should not touch bottom of bowl). Add cream, sour cream and vanilla and continue cooking, whisking occasionally, until very thick, 30 to 35 minutes; *do not boil or crème will curdle.* Remove bowl

from over water and whisk in butter. Cool 20 minutes.

Preheat broiler. Spread melted chocolate over crust. Cover with berries. Top with crème, smoothing surface with spatula. Sift brown sugar over entire top. Broil until sugar caramelizes, watching carefully to prevent burning. Let cool; refrigerate. Serve tart well chilled.

MARZIPAN TART

Best served on the day it is prepared.

8 to 10 servings

Pâte Sucrée

- 1½ cups all purpose flour
- ¼ cup sugar
   Pinch of salt
- 10 tablespoons (1¼ sticks) chilled unsalted butter, cut into ½-inch pieces
- 1 egg

Marzipan Filling

- ½ cup (1 stick) unsalted butter, room temperature
- 8 ounces almond paste, room temperature
- 2 eggs, room temperature
- 3 tablespoons Cognac
- 2 teaspoons all purpose flour
- 5 cups fresh boysenberries
- 1 12-ounce jar boysenberry jam, melted, strained and heated with dash of Cognac

For pâte: Combine flour, sugar and salt in large bowl. Cut in butter until mixture resembles coarse meal. Add egg and mix until dough just holds together. Flatten into disc. Wrap tightly in plastic and refrigerate for at least 1 hour. (*Can be made up to 3 days ahead and refrigerated.*)

Butter 11-inch tart pan. Roll dough out on lightly floured surface into 13-inch circle ⅛ inch thick. Fit into pan; trim and form edges. Prick with fork. Freeze until firm. (*Can be made up to 1 month ahead and frozen.*)

Preheat oven to 425°F. Line pastry shell with buttered parchment paper, then fill with dried beans or pie weights. Bake 5 minutes. Reduce oven temperature to 350°F and continue baking 15 minutes. Remove paper and weights. Bake until pastry browns, about 10 minutes. Cool while preparing filling. Retain oven at 350°F.

For filling: Cream butter and almond paste in medium bowl. Beat in eggs one at a time. Blend in Cognac and flour. Pour into crust. Bake until filling is dry and light brown, about 30 minutes. Cool completely. (*Can be prepared early on day of serving to this point and stored at room temperature.*)

To serve, arrange berries atop filling. Brush with melted jam, thinning glaze with additional Cognac if necessary.

PLUM FINGER PASTRIES

These pastries, inspired by tiny Italian tortas, can be made several days ahead and refrigerated.

Makes 5 to 6 dozen

Filling

½ 750-ml bottle full-bodied dry red wine
1½ teaspoons cider vinegar
1 bay leaf
½ star anise*
1 cup sugar
2 pounds purple plums *or* red plums, halved and pitted
Dash of salt

Pastry

¾ cup (1½ sticks) chilled unsalted butter
6 tablespoons lard
1 cup sugar
6 egg yolks
3 to 4 tablespoons Marsala
2 teaspoons grated lemon peel
3 cups unbleached all purpose flour
1½ cups cake flour

1 egg, beaten to blend

For filling: Boil wine, vinegar, bay leaf and anise in heavy nonaluminum large saucepan until reduced by ¾. Stir in sugar and boil until dissolved. Remove bay leaf and anise. Add plums and salt to pan. Reduce heat and simmer, uncovered, until very thick, about 1½ to 2 hours, stirring occasionally at first and constantly during last 20 minutes. (*Can be prepared up to 1 month ahead and refrigerated.*)

For pastry: Beat butter and lard at medium speed in bowl of electric mixer until light and fluffy. Gradually add sugar and beat 2 minutes. Beat in yolks one at a time. Blend in 3 tablespoons Marsala and lemon peel. Reduce speed to low and gradually beat in flours until just combined (overbeating will make dough tough). If dough appears dry, add remaining Marsala. Wrap in plastic and refrigerate overnight. (*Can be prepared up to 4 days ahead.*)

Let dough stand at room temperature 30 minutes. Divide dough in half. Roll each half out on lightly floured surface into circle ⅛ inch thick. Using 3-inch cutter, cut dough into rounds. Gather scraps and refrigerate 30 minutes. Reroll and cut additional circles.

Place 1 teaspoon filling on half of each circle leaving small margin. Brush margin with egg. Fold dough in half over filling, pinching edges together with fingertips to seal. Crimp edges with fork tines.

Preheat oven to 350°F. Grease baking sheet. Arrange pastries on prepared baking sheet and brush with egg. Bake until edges are brown, about 15 minutes. Let cool on wire rack.*

*Available in oriental markets.

BAKED ALMOND APPLES IN PASTRY

The pastry can be prepared up to 5 days ahead. Apples can be baked, wrapped in almond paste and pastry and chilled up to 2 days. Sauce can be prepared 1 day ahead.

4 servings

Pastry

1 cup all purpose flour
½ teaspoon sugar
½ teaspoon finely grated lemon peel
Pinch of salt
½ cup (1 stick) chilled unsalted butter, cut into ½-inch pieces
2 tablespoons cold water
All purpose flour

Apples

½ cup whipping cream
½ cup cider
2 tablespoons vanilla
Pinch of cinnamon
4 small baking apples
½ lemon
2 teaspoons unsalted butter

Sauce

Whipping cream

3 egg yolks, room temperature
⅓ cup sugar
1 tablespoon unsalted butter
Freshly grated nutmeg

7 ounces almond paste
1 egg white
Sifted powdered sugar

½ cup apricot preserves, melted, strained and cooled

1 egg, lightly beaten with 1 tablespoon water
½ cup apricot preserves, melted, strained and cooled (optional)

For pastry: Combine 1 cup flour, sugar, lemon peel and salt in medium bowl. Mix in butter using fingertips until mixture is consistency of fine meal. Add water and gather ingredients into a ball. Turn out onto counter and do a *fraisage* (push dough out along counter with heel of hand). Reform ball; repeat fraisage. Sprinkle dough with flour, wrap tightly in plastic and chill at least 1 hour.

For apples: Preheat oven to 350°F. Mix cream, cider, vanilla and cinnamon in baking pan. Peel and core apples; rub with cut lemon to prevent discoloration. Place apples upright in pan; top each with ½ teaspoon butter. Cover with foil and bake until apples are half cooked, about 15 minutes. Transfer to plate to cool; reserved baking liquid.

For sauce: Measure baking liquid and add enough cream to make 1¼ cups. Transfer to saucepan and heat through.

Place egg yolks in medium bowl. Gradually beat in sugar until yolks are lemon colored and mixture forms a ribbon when beaters are lifted. Beating constantly, add warm baking liquid and cream.

Return mixture to saucepan. Place over medium-low heat and stir with wooden spoon until mixture is thick enough to leave path when finger is drawn across spoon. Remove from heat and stir in butter and nutmeg. Place plastic wrap on surface of sauce to prevent skin from forming. Let cool, then chill thoroughly in refrigerator.

Crumble almond paste onto work surface. Moisten with egg white and knead until smooth enough to roll, adding sifted powdered sugar as necessary. Divide into 4 parts. Roll each between 2 pieces of plastic wrap into 7-inch circle.

One at a time, dry apples with paper towels. Paint inside and outside with preserves. Discard top piece of plastic wrap from almond paste circle and set apple in center. Bring almond paste up around apple and pinch edges together on top. Peel off bottom piece of plastic wrap. Set apples on small platter without sides touching and refrigerate.

Grease baking sheet. Divide pastry into 4 parts, reserving small piece to form 4 pastry leaves and stems. One at a time, roll each between 2 pieces of plastic wrap into 7-inch circle. Discard top piece of plastic wrap. Using metal spatula to lift apple from platter, place an apple in center of pastry. Bring pastry up around apple and pinch edges together on top. Peel off bottom piece of plastic and set apple seam side down on baking sheet. Form leaves and stems from reserved pastry and set on apples. Chill at least 1 hour before baking.

One hour before serving, preheat oven to 425°F. Paint apples with beaten egg and bake until well browned, about 30 minutes. Let cool 15 minutes. Transfer apples to individual plates. Pipe thin ribbon of melted preserves around base of each apple if desired and surround with band of chilled sauce.

Cookies

GINGER COIN COOKIES

Minced crystallized ginger gives these refrigerator cookies their unusual flavor. The dough can be made well ahead and frozen. Let thaw slightly before slicing into cookie rounds. The cookies can also be baked ahead, wrapped tightly in foil and frozen.

Makes about 5 dozen

  1 **cup (2 sticks) unsalted butter, room temperature**
  1 **cup powdered sugar, sifted**
2½ **cups sifted all purpose flour**
  3 **tablespoons minced crystallized ginger**
  1 **teaspoon ground ginger**
  ¼ **teaspoon salt**

Cream butter with powdered sugar in large bowl. Add all remaining ingredients and blend well. Form dough into cylinder about 1¾ inches in diameter. Wrap in plastic and refrigerate until firm enough to slice, at least 2 hours, or freeze about 45 minutes.

Preheat oven to 400°F. Cut dough into ¼-inch-thick slices. Arrange slices on ungreased baking sheets. Bake until lightly browned, about 8 minutes. Transfer cookies to wire racks to cool. Store in airtight container.

LACY HAZELNUT COOKIES

(Palets aux Noisettes)

These can be prepared 1 week ahead and stored in an airtight container at room temperature.

Makes about 6 dozen

1¼ **cups chopped hazelnuts (about 5 to 6 ounces)**
  ⅔ **cup sugar**
  3 **tablespoons all purpose flour**
  1 **tablespoon cornstarch Pinch of salt**
  3 **tablespoons butter, melted and cooled**
  1 **teaspoon vanilla**
  1 **teaspoon cinnamon**
  3 **egg whites**

Mix hazelnuts, sugar, flour, cornstarch and salt in large bowl. Blend butter, vanilla and cinnamon in small bowl. Add butter mixture to hazelnut mixture and blend well. Add whites and mix until smooth. Chill 30 minutes.

Preheat oven to 400°F. Line baking sheet with foil. Drop batter onto prepared baking sheet by half teaspoons, spacing 2 inches apart. Dip small metal spatula into cold water. Spread cookies to width of 1¼ inches, moistening spatula for each cookie. Bake until cookies are deep golden and 2 inches wide, about 7 to 8 minutes. Transfer to rack using spatula and cool.

GLACEED ORANGE PEEL

Honey adds flavor and keeps peel soft. Any citrus peel can be glacéed.

Makes about 1 pound

  4 **large oranges, washed**
 12 **cups water**

1¾ **cups water**
1½ **cups sugar**
  ½ **cup honey**

Score oranges into quarters; remove peel with any white pith that clings to it. (Reserve oranges for another use.) Cut peel into ⅜-inch-wide strips. Boil with 6 cups water in heavy large saucepan 10 minutes. Drain. Repeat with 6 cups fresh water. Drain well.

Combine 1¾ cups water, sugar and honey in same saucepan. Heat over low heat, swirling pan occasionally, until sugar dissolves. Increase heat and bring to boil. Mix in peel. Boil gently until peel is tender and syrup is reduced to ¾ cup, stirring frequently, about 40 minutes. Cool in colander, stirring occasionally. Store in airtight container. *(Glacéed Orange Peel can be refrigerated up to 2 months.)*

FRUIT-AND CHOCOLATE-FILLED COOKIE ROLLS (*Cucidati*)

A traditional Sicilian treat.

Makes about 3 dozen

Filling

> 2 ounces semisweet chocolate
> 2 ounces dried figs, stemmed and halved
> 2 ounces (scant ½ cup) raisins
> 2 ounces dried apricots, peaches, pears, apples or combination
> 1½ ounces Glacéed Orange Peel (see preceding recipe), coarsely chopped
> ¼ cup honey
> ⅛ teaspoon ground allspice
> ⅛ teaspoon cinnamon

Pastry

> ¼ cup (½ stick) butter, room temperature
> ¼ cup sugar
> 1 egg
> 1 teaspoon grated lemon peel
> 1¼ cups all purpose flour
> 1 teaspoon baking powder

For filling: Coarsely chop chocolate in processor or food grinder. Add all dried fruit and orange peel and chop finely. Blend in honey and spices. Refrigerate in airtight container 2 hours. *(Filling can be stored up to 2 weeks.)*

For pastry: Cream butter and sugar with electric mixer. Beat in egg and lemon peel. Mix in flour and baking powder until smooth dough forms. Wrap with plastic. Cover and refrigerate dough at least 1 hour or overnight.

Preheat oven to 375°F. Divide pastry and filling into thirds. Roll one portion of pastry out on lightly floured surface to 3 × 13-inch strip. Trim edges. Form one portion of filling into 13-inch rope. Arrange atop pastry 1 inch from one long edge. Fold far edge of pastry over filling. Brush with water and fold up near edge to enclose filling. Pinch edges to seal. Cut pastry diagonally into 1-inch pieces. Arrange seam side down on ungreased baking sheets, spacing 1 inch apart. Repeat with remaining dough. Bake until cookies are golden, about 14 minutes. Cool completely on racks. Store cookies in airtight container.

SARDINIAN RAISIN AND NUT COOKIES (*Papassinos*)

Shortbread-type cookies loaded with fruit, almonds and walnuts and delicately flavored with Marsala.

Makes about 3½ dozen

> ½ cup (1 stick) unsalted butter, room temperature
> ¾ cup sugar
> 2 teaspoons grated orange peel
> 2 eggs
> 2 tablespoons Marsala, Sherry or fresh orange juice
> 1½ cups all purpose flour
> ¼ teaspoon salt
> ⅔ cup raisins
> ⅔ cup coarsely chopped toasted almonds
> ⅔ cup coarsely chopped walnuts

> ⅓ cup powdered sugar, sifted
> 1 scant tablespoon fresh orange juice

Cream butter, ¾ cup sugar and orange peel using electric mixer. Beat in eggs 1 at a time. Blend in Marsala. Stir in flour and salt, then raisins and nuts. Wrap dough in plas-

tic. Refrigerate at least 4 hours or overnight.

Preheat oven to 350°F. Roll dough out on well-floured surface to thickness of ⅜ inch. Cut into 1½-inch diamonds or squares using floured knife. Arrange on ungreased baking sheets, spacing 1 inch apart. Bake until light golden, about 23 minutes. Transfer to racks. Mix powdered sugar with orange juice. Brush glaze over warm cookies. Cool to room temperature. Store in airtight container.

LITTLE YELLOW DIAMONDS (*Gialletti*)

These sturdy golden cookies feature cornmeal, a northern Italian staple. For finest texture, grind cornmeal in processor four to five minutes.

Makes about 4 dozen

> ½ cup golden raisins
> ½ cup dark rum

> ½ cup sugar
> 2 egg yolks
> ⅔ cup butter, melted
> 2 teaspoons grated lemon peel
> 1 teaspoon vanilla
> Pinch of salt
> 1⅓ cups all purpose flour
> 1 cup fine yellow cornmeal
> ⅓ cup pine nuts
> Powdered sugar

Combine raisins and rum in small bowl. Cover and let stand overnight.

Preheat oven to 375°F. Drain raisins well (discarding rum); chop coarsely. Beat sugar and yolks with electric mixer at low speed until blended. Increase speed to high and beat until pale yellow and slowly dissolving ribbon forms when beaters are lifted, about 7 minutes. Beat in butter in thin stream. Blend in lemon peel, vanilla and salt. Using wooden spoon, stir in raisins, flour, cornmeal and pine nuts. Let dough rest about 10 minutes.

Roll dough out on wooden surface to thickness of ½ inch. Cut into diamonds with 1-inch sides. Arrange on ungreased baking sheet, spacing 1 inch apart. Reroll scraps and cut additional cookies. Bake until golden, about 15 minutes. Transfer to racks. Cool completely. Dust cookies with powdered sugar just before serving.

MUSTACHES
(Mostaccioli)

A Neapolitan specialty, made almost entirely of ground nuts. Mostaccioli are best the day after baking.

Makes about 2½ dozen

  1 **cup hazelnuts (about 4 ounces)**
  1 **cup walnuts (4 ounces)**
  ⅓ **cup honey**
  1 **egg white**
  1 **tablespoon unsweetened cocoa powder**
  ½ **teaspoon cinnamon**
  ⅛ **teaspoon ground cloves**
     Pinch of salt
  ⅓ **cup all purpose flour**

     Powdered sugar

Icing

  ½ **cup powdered sugar, sifted**
  1 **tablespoon egg white, beaten to blend**
  1 **to 2 teaspoons orange liqueur**

Preheat oven to 275°F. Grease baking sheet. Finely grind nuts in processor. Add honey, egg white, cocoa, spices and salt and blend to paste. Add flour and mix using on/off turns until just incorporated (dough will be sticky).

Place dough on work surface heavily dusted with sifted powdered sugar. Sift more sugar over dough. Gently roll dough out to thickness of ⅜ inch. Cut into 1 × 1½-inch bars using knife dusted with powdered sugar. Arrange on prepared sheet, spacing 1 inch apart. Bake cookies until firm and tops appear dry, 25 to 30 minutes. Cool cookies completely on racks.

For icing: Blend ½ cup powdered sugar and egg white. Mix in enough liqueur to make thick but pourable icing.

Set racks on waxed paper; arrange cooled cookies on racks with edges touching. Drizzle icing over cookies in irregular lines. Separate cookies. Let stand until icing is dry. Store in airtight container.

SWEET BEANS
(Fave Dolci)

Chewy cookies from southern Italy that are served on All Souls' Day. The custom stems from the ancient tradition of offering beans to Pluto and Proserpina, god and goddess of the underworld in Roman mythology.

Makes about 5 dozen

  1 **cup unblanched almonds**
  1 **cup sugar**
  ⅓ **cup unsalted butter, cut into ½-inch pieces**
  1 **egg**
  2 **teaspoons grated lemon peel**
  1 **teaspoon orange flower water**
  ½ **teaspoon cinnamon**
  ½ **cup plus 2 tablespoons all purpose flour**

Grind almonds finely in processor using on/off turns. Add sugar and blend until powdery. Add butter, egg, lemon peel, orange flower water and cinnamon and process to paste. Mix in flour until just incorporated, using several on/off turns (dough will be sticky). Transfer to medium bowl. Cover with plastic. Refrigerate dough overnight.

Preheat oven to 350°F. Grease and flour baking sheets. Roll rounded teaspoons of dough into short thick cylinders. Arrange on prepared sheets, spacing 2 inches apart. Using finger or handle of wooden spoon, press indentation in side of each to form into lima bean shape. Flatten slightly with hands. Bake until cookies are just beginning to color, about 16 minutes. Cool on baking sheets 5 minutes; transfer to racks and cool completely. Store in airtight container.

HAZELNUT COOKIES
(Biscottini Di Nocciole)

This dough is ready in seconds.

Makes about 2½ dozen

  ¾ **cup hazelnuts (4 ounces)**
  ⅔ **cup sugar**
  2 **egg yolks**
  1 **teaspoon vanilla**

  ½ **teaspoon grated lemon peel**
     Pinch of salt

     Sugar

Halve 15 hazelnuts, using sharp knife; set aside. Finely grind remaining nuts in processor. Blend in sugar thoroughly. With machine running, add yolks, vanilla, lemon peel and salt through feed tube and process until mixture forms ball, adding drops of water if necessary to make workable dough. Wrap dough in plastic or foil. Refrigerate 2 hours. *(Can be prepared 1 day ahead to this point.)*

Preheat oven to 350°F. Grease baking sheets. Form dough into ¾-inch balls. Arrange on prepared sheets, spacing 3 inches apart. Flatten to ⅛-inch thickness using bottom of glass dipped in sugar, twisting glass to prevent sticking. Firmly press hazelnut half, cut side down, into each cookie. Bake until cookies are dry and slightly golden, about 10 minutes. Immediately transfer cookies to racks. Cool completely. Store in airtight container.

ORANGE WAFERS
(Gallettine All'Arancia)

Lacy rounds that are a cross between a cookie and a candy. They tend to soften at room temperature, but stay crisp if stored in the freezer.

Makes about 3 dozen

  ¾ **cup unblanched almonds (4 ounces)**
  ½ **cup coarsely chopped Glacéed Orange Peel (see recipe, page 194)**
  3 **tablespoons unsalted butter**
  ⅓ **cup sugar**
  ¼ **cup whipping cream**
  1 **tablespoon orange liqueur**
     Pinch of salt
  2 **tablespoons all purpose flour**

Preheat oven to 375°F. Line baking sheets with parchment. Finely chop almonds and orange peel in processor. Melt butter with sugar and cream in heavy small saucepan over low heat, stirring frequently. Increase heat to medium-high and bring to boil. Remove from heat and stir in almond mixture, liqueur and salt. Stir in flour until batter is just blended.

Drop mixture by teaspoons onto prepared sheets, spacing 2 inches apart. Spread evenly to ⅛-inch-thick rounds using knife. Bake cookies until golden brown, 10 to 12 minutes. Transfer parchment with cookies to rack. Let stand until almost cool, then peel cookies from parchment. Cool completely on racks. Store in freezer in airtight container. Serve cold.

BUTTERBALLS
(Pallottole Al Burro)

Makes about 3 dozen

- ½ cup (1 stick) butter, room temperature
- ¼ cup sugar
- 2 tablespoons honey
- 1 cup plus 2 tablespoons all purpose flour
- ¼ teaspoon (scant) baking soda
- 2 tablespoons dark rum
- 1¼ cups coarsely ground walnuts *or* Brazil nuts

  Powdered sugar

Cream butter, sugar and honey with electric mixer until smooth. Stir in flour and baking soda. Blend in rum, then nuts. Wrap dough in plastic and refrigerate until firm enough to handle, at least 1 hour, or overnight.

Preheat oven to 325°F. Lightly grease and flour baking sheets. Roll dough into 1-inch balls. Arrange on prepared sheets, spacing 1½ inches apart. Bake until firm and just beginning to color, 15 to 20 minutes. Cool slightly on racks. Roll in powdered sugar while still warm. Cool completely on racks. Store in airtight container.

QUEEN'S COOKIES
(Biscotti Di Regina)

A very crisp cookie distinguished by the flavor of sesame seed.

Makes about 4½ dozen

- 1½ cups all purpose flour
- ⅔ cup sugar
- ¾ teaspoon baking powder
- 6 tablespoons (¾ stick) butter, melted
- 1 egg, beaten to blend
- 1½ teaspoons vanilla
- ¾ cup sesame seed

Preheat oven to 350°F. Combine flour, sugar and baking powder in medium bowl. Blend in butter, egg and vanilla with wooden spoon. Press dough together with hands.

Roll about ½ cup dough into ¾-inch-thick rope. Cut into 1½-inch lengths. Roll in sesame seed to coat completely. Arrange cookies on ungreased baking sheets, spacing ½ inch apart. Repeat with remaining dough. Bake until cookies are light golden, about 18 minutes. Cool completely on racks. Store cookies in airtight container.

Variation: Add 2 teaspoons grated orange peel or ¾ teaspoon aniseed to dough.

SWEET RAVIOLI
(Ravioli Dolci)

A specialty of Liguria, the area around Genoa on Italy's northwest coast. Potato flour produces a very crisp cookie with a delicate crumb.

Makes about 3 dozen

- ½ cup (1 stick) unsalted butter, room temperature
- ½ cup sugar
- 1 egg
- 2 tablespoons brandy
- 1 teaspoon grated lemon peel
- 1 teaspoon vanilla
- 1¼ cups all purpose flour
- 1 cup potato flour*
- ⅛ teaspoon salt

  Thick apricot or cherry jam
  Powdered sugar

Cream butter and ½ cup sugar with electric mixer. Beat in egg, brandy, lemon peel and vanilla. Blend in both flours and salt. Refrigerate dough at least 2 hours or overnight.

Preheat oven to 350°F. Butter baking sheets. Roll half of dough out on generously floured surface into ⅛-inch-thick rectangle (keep remaining dough refrigerated).

Using fluted pastry wheel guided with ruler, cut dough into 2-inch squares. Arrange on prepared sheets. Top each with ½ teaspoon jam, leaving ¼-inch border. Roll and cut remaining dough as above. Brush borders of jam-covered squares with water. Top each with second dough square, pressing edges to seal. Bake until cookies are beginning to brown, about 18 minutes. Cool completely on racks. Store in airtight container. Sift powdered sugar lightly over cookies before serving.

*Also called potato starch. Available at European markets and in kosher products section of most markets. Do not use the coarser flour sold at natural foods stores.

UGLY BUT GOOD
(Brutti Ma Buoni)

From Florence, a combination of fruit and nuts that is really not ugly, just somewhat irregularly shaped.

Makes about 3 dozen

- 1⅓ cups blanched almonds (8 ounces)
- 1⅓ cups powdered sugar
- ¼ teaspoon vanilla
- ¼ teaspoon almond extract
  Pinch of salt
- 1 egg white
- ⅓ cup coarsely chopped walnuts
- 3 tablespoons minced moist dried apricots

Preheat oven to 350°F. Grease and flour baking sheet. Grind almonds in processor until finely powdered and beginning to hold together, stopping occasionally to scrape down sides of work bowl, about 3 minutes. Blend in sugar, vanilla, almond extract and salt. With machine running, pour egg white through feed tube and blend until mixture forms ball. Transfer to medium bowl. Knead in walnuts and apricots. Form dough into 1-inch balls. Pinch into irregular shapes. Arrange on prepared sheet, spacing 1 inch apart. Bake until just beginning to brown, 13 to 15 minutes. Cool on racks. Store in airtight container.

14 ✦ Desserts

199

Ice Creams

❖ ❖ ❖ ❖ ❖ ❖ ❖ ❖ ❖ ❖ ❖ ❖ ❖ ❖

KIRSCH ICE CREAM (*Creme Glacée au Kirsch*)

Makes about 1 quart

- 8 **egg yolks, room temperature**
- ½ **cup sugar**
- ⅔ **cup cold milk**
- 1 **tablespoon vanilla**
- ½ **teaspoon ground cardamom**
  Pinch of salt
- 1 **cup whipping cream**
- ¼ **cup Kirschwasser (cherry brandy)**
- 3 **tablespoons chopped toasted skinned hazelnuts**

Combine yolks and sugar in heavy 2-quart saucepan and whisk until slowly dissolving ribbon forms when whisk is lifted, about 5 to 7 minutes. Whisk in half of cold milk. Place pan over medium heat and cook until thickened, about 12 minutes, whisking constantly and gradually adding remaining milk as custard thickens (custard will resemble sabayon because of incorporation of air when whisked). Cool 1 hour. Blend in vanilla, cardamom and salt.

Whip cream to soft peaks. Blend in Kirschwasser. Gently fold cream into cooled custard. Refrigerate mixture thoroughly, at least 1 hour (or overnight).

Transfer mixture to ice cream maker and process according to manufacturer's instructions.* Turn mixture into container with tight-fitting lid and freeze for up to 2 days.

To serve, spoon 2 small scoops of ice cream into individual Champagne glasses. Sprinkle with nuts.

*If ice cream maker is unavailable, freeze mixture in shallow metal trays. Mix in blender or processor until smooth. Refreeze.

FLORENTINE FROZEN CREAM WITH FRUIT

10 to 12 servings

- 4 **egg yolks**
- 1 **cup sugar**
- ¼ **cup water**
- 3 **cups ground toasted almonds**
- 3 **to 4 tablespoons Galliano liqueur**
- 1½ **cups whipping cream**
- ½ **cup Galliano liqueur**

  Fresh strawberries, sliced papaya, golden raisins, figs *or* prunes, and sliced almonds (garnish)

Beat yolks with electric mixer until thick and pale, about 5 minutes.

Meanwhile, combine sugar and water in 1-quart saucepan over low heat and stir until dissolved. Increase heat and cook until syrup registers 235°F (softball stage) on candy thermometer. Gradually beat syrup into yolks and continue beating until thick and fluffy, about 15 minutes. Cool in refrigerator.

Moisten almonds with enough liqueur to bind. Press evenly onto bottom and sides of 8- or 9-inch springform pan.

Whip cream until soft peaks form. Fold into yolk mixture with ½ cup liqueur. Pour into springform pan. Freeze until firm, about 6 hours or overnight.

Let dessert stand at room temperature for 15 minutes before serving. Carefully remove springform. Cut frozen cream into wedges. Garnish each serving with fruits and almonds.

WHITE CHOCOLATE ICE CREAM

This dense and creamy mixture does not require an ice cream maker.

Makes about 1 quart

- 1 **cup water**
- ¾ **cup sugar**
- 6 **egg yolks**
- 1 **tablespoons vanilla**
- 10 **ounces white chocolate (preferably Swiss or French), melted**
- 2 **cups whipping cream**

Blend water and sugar in heavy medium saucepan. Cook over low heat until sugar dissolves, swirling pan occasionally. Bring to boil. Let boil 5 minutes. Meanwhile, combine yolks and vanilla in large bowl of electric mixer and beat at high speed until light and fluffy, about 7 minutes. Slowly add hot syrup to yolk mixture, beating constantly until thickened and completely cool, about 10 minutes. Gradually add white chocolate and continue beating until cool, about 7 minutes. Stir in cream. Cover and freeze until set, at least 5 hours, or overnight.

TARTUFI

Tartufi can be prepared up to one month ahead.

10 servings

- 1 cup superfine sugar
- ⅔ cup Dutch process cocoa
- 2 teaspoons instant espresso powder
- ⅓ cup water
- 4 egg yolks
- 10 maraschino cherries, stemmed, pitted, rinsed, drained and soaked in 2 tablespoons rum
- 1 cup whipping cream
- ⅔ cup coarsely chopped semisweet chocolate
- ⅓ cup chopped toasted almonds

  Chopped or shaved chocolate (garnish)

Sift sugar, cocoa and espresso powder into heavy medium saucepan. Whisk in water. Place over medium heat and bring to boil. Cook, stirring constantly, until all sugar is dissolved and mixture is smooth, about 10 minutes.

Beat egg yolks in large bowl of electric mixer at high speed until light and fluffy. Reduce speed to medium, add hot chocolate mixture in slow steady stream and continue beating until cool, stopping once to scrape down sides and bottom of bowl. Chill 1 hour.

Remove maraschino cherries from rum using slotted spoon and set aside to drain. Mix rum into cooled chocolate.

Whip cream in medium mixing bowl until stiff peaks form. Stir

---

Ice Cream: Tips and Techniques

- ◆ Ice cream will be even better if basic mixtures are allowed to chill in refrigerator overnight before processing in the ice cream freezer.
- ◆ Use the freshest and purest flavoring. These ice creams will be only as good as the ingredients that go into them.
- ◆ Do not use metal bowls for any ingredients that are the slightest bit acidic, including most fruits. Mixtures can discolor and flavor will be altered.
- ◆ Because alcohol slows down freezing, it is better to add it toward the end of processing. Keep the measured amount in the freezer (it will not freeze) until ready to use.
- ◆ Almond extract will also slow down the freezing process and should be added sparingly at the end.
- ◆ Do not oversweeten any basic mixture or it will become too sticky.
- ◆ Fresh fruit should be finely chopped before adding because it will harden firmly with freezing.
- ◆ Create new combinations by processing batches of two different flavors and layering them, ¼ at a time, in the plastic container before final freezing. To serve, be sure the scoop dips both flavors simultaneously for a rippled effect.

---

1 large spoonful of whipped cream into chocolate mixture to loosen, blending well. Gently fold in remaining cream, ⅔ cup coarsely chopped semisweet chocolate and chopped toasted almonds; *be careful not to deflate whipped cream.*

Arrange 10 decorative foil-lined paper cups in muffin pan. (Mixture can also be spooned into individual cups.) Fill each cup ⅓ full with chocolate mixture. Arrange cherry in center and fill to ⅔ full. Sprinkle lightly with chopped or shaved chocolate and freeze at least 4 hours. (If freezing longer, cover with plastic and foil.) Serve directly from freezer.

LA MYSTERE

This dessert may be found in one guise or another on the menus of many Parisian bistros.

6 servings

- 2 8¾-ounce cans chestnut spread (crème de marrons)*
- 2 ounces unsweetened chocolate, coarsely chopped
- ¼ cup (½ stick) unsalted butter, chopped
- 4 to 6 tablespoons whipping cream
- 1 quart rich vanilla ice cream
- ¾ cup whipping cream, whipped with ¼ teaspoon vanilla
- ½ cup sliced toasted almonds
- 6 glacéed chestnuts*

Stir chestnut spread, chocolate and butter in top of double boiler set over hot (not boiling) water until mixture is smooth. Stir in enough cream to make thick sauce. (*Can be prepared up to 3 days ahead, covered and refrigerated.*)

Before serving, remelt sauce over low heat, stirring frequently. Place 2 scoops ice cream into dessert dishes. Spoon about ¼ cup sauce over each. Top with whipped cream, almonds and a glacéed chestnut.

*Available at specialty foods stores and in some supermarkets.

Puddings and Custards

❖ ❖ ❖ ❖ ❖ ❖ ❖ ❖ ❖ ❖ ❖ ❖ ❖ ❖

PORT AND HONEY ZABAGLIONE WITH FIGS

4 servings

12 to 16 fresh figs, peeled
½ cup Port, or more

6 egg yolks
3 tablespoons honey
1½ teaspoons vanilla
¾ teaspoon fresh lemon juice

Make a slit in each fig with sharp knife. Combine figs and ½ cup Port in large bowl and let stand at room temperature several hours or overnight, turning occasionally.

Drain Port into measuring cup and add more Port as necessary so liquid measures ½ cup. Arrange figs in individual goblets and set aside.

Combine Port, egg yolks, honey, vanilla and lemon juice in top of double boiler set over simmering water and whisk until mixture thickens and triples in volume (scraping down sides and bottom of pan as you beat), about 5 to 7 minutes; *do not let water boil or yolks will curdle.* Spoon zabaglione over figs. Serve hot or chilled.

RANCH PUDDING WITH WHISKEY WHIPPED CREAM

6 to 8 servings

1 cup firmly packed dark brown sugar
¾ cup light corn syrup
4 eggs
¼ cup whiskey, rum *or* brandy
¼ cup (½ stick) butter, melted
1 teaspoon vanilla
½ teaspoon salt
1 cup chopped toasted pecans *or* walnuts (4 ounces)
1 cup raisins
½ cup toasted pecan *or* walnut halves (2 ounces)

Whiskey Whipped Cream (see following recipe)

Position rack in center of oven and preheat to 400°F. Butter 9-inch square or round baking dish. Beat brown sugar, corn syrup, eggs, whiskey, melted butter, vanilla and salt in medium bowl until well blended. Sprinkle chopped nuts and raisins evenly into prepared dish. Pour egg mixture over. Arrange nut halves decoratively over top. Bake 10 minutes, then reduce oven temperature to 325°F and continue baking until set, about 20 to 25 minutes. Serve warm with Whiskey Whipped Cream.

Whiskey Whipped Cream

Makes about 2 cups

1 cup whipping cream
2 tablespoons whiskey, rum *or* brandy
1 tablespoon sugar

Combine all ingredients in large bowl and whip until soft peaks form.

BREAD PUDDING (Capirotada)

8 servings

Filling

⅔ cup walnuts, pecans or sliced almonds, chopped
1 large apple, peeled, cored and coarsely chopped
¼ cup golden seedless raisins

Syrup

1 cup firmly packed brown sugar
¾ cup water
2 tablespoons Sherry (optional)
1 teaspoon aniseed
2 whole cloves
1 3-inch cinnamon stick

9 ½-inch-thick slices stale French bread, crusts trimmed
¾ cup (1½ sticks) butter
4 ounces queso fresco *or* cream cheese, chilled and crumbled

Topping

2 egg whites, room temperature
⅓ cup walnuts, pecans or sliced almonds, chopped
3 tablespoons firmly packed brown sugar
1 teaspoon cinnamon
Whipped cream (garnish)

For filling: Combine nuts, apple and raisins in small bowl; set aside.

For syrup: Combine sugar, water, Sherry, aniseed, cloves and cinnamon stick in medium saucepan and bring to boil over medium-high heat. Let boil 30 seconds. Strain and set aside.

Preheat oven to 350°F. Butter 1½-quart casserole (at least 3 inches deep) or soufflé dish. Melt about 5 tablespoons butter in large skillet over medium-high heat. Add bread slices in batches and sauté on both sides until just beginning to color, about 2 minutes total, adding more butter if necessary. Remove from skillet. Melt remaining butter.

Arrange 3 bread slices in bottom of prepared dish. Cover with ⅓ of filling. Sprinkle with ⅓ of cheese, then drizzle with ⅓ of syrup. Repeat layering twice, alternating bread slices to cover empty spaces. Pour remaining melted butter over top. Press down gently on bread slices to soak well.

For topping: Beat egg whites in large bowl until stiff but not dry. Combine nuts, sugar and cinnamon. Gently fold sugar mixture into whites. Spread topping over pudding. Bake 35 minutes. Turn oven off and let pudding stand in oven 15 minutes before serving. Pass whipped cream separately.

Mousses, Charlottes and Soufflés

FROZEN MOKA MOUSSE

4 to 6 servings

- ⅓ cup water
- 3 tablespoons instant espresso powder
- 1¼ teaspoons unflavored gelatin

- ⅔ cup sugar
- 2 eggs, separated, room temperature
- ½ teaspoon vanilla

- 1 cup whipping cream
  Pinch of cream of tartar
  Pinch of salt

  Chocolate coffee beans (garnish)
  Jamaican Chocolate Sauce (see following recipe)

Lightly oil 1-quart charlotte mold. Bring water to boil in small saucepan. Add espresso powder and stir until dissolved. Cool. Sprinkle gelatin over top. Set aside to soften.

Beat sugar and egg yolks in nonaluminum large bowl using portable electric mixer. Set bowl over barely simmering water and continue beating until mixture is pale yellow and just warmed through; *do not boil or yolks will curdle.* Stir espresso mixture over medium heat to dissolve gelatin. Beat espresso mixture into yolks. Cool to room temperature. Stir in vanilla.

Whip cream in large bowl to soft peaks. Beat whites in another large bowl until foamy. Add cream of tartar and salt and continue beating to soft peaks. Quickly fold cream into yolk mixture, then gently fold in whites. Turn into prepared mold and smooth top. Cover and freeze at least 12 hours. (*Can be prepared several days ahead.*)

To serve, dip mold briefly in hot water and invert onto rimmed plate; melted exterior of mousse will form pool around base. Refrigerate about 1 hour to soften before serv-ing. Garnish with coffee beans. Pass sauce separately.

Jamaican Chocolate Sauce

An easy and delicious topping for the frozen mousse or ice cream.

Makes about 1½ cups

- ¾ cup Italian *or* French roast coffee beans
- ⅓ cup powdered sugar
- 1½ tablespoons butter
- 2 tablespoons dark rum
- 1 cup half and half, room temperature
- 1 teaspoon vanilla

- 2 ounces semisweet chocolate, coarsely chopped
- 1 ounce unsweetened chocolate, coarsely chopped

Place coffee beans in processor or blender and lightly crush using 1 or 2 on/off turns; do not grind. Transfer to medium skillet. Add sugar and butter. Place over low heat and cook until sugar is melted, about 3 minutes, stirring frequently. Stir in rum and simmer gently until mixture begins to caramelize, adjusting heat as necessary to avoid burning, about 7 minutes. Add half and half and stir until hot but not boiling. Remove from heat. Blend in vanilla. Cover; let stand 30 minutes.

Melt chocolates in nonaluminum medium bowl set over hot water. Strain coffee bean mixture through fine sieve into chocolate (still over hot water) and stir until completely blended. Let cool. Cover and refrigerate. (*Sauce can be prepared 2 days ahead.*) To serve, set sauce over gently simmering water and stir until warmed through.

COCO-AMARETTO MOUSSE

6 servings

Coconut-Chocolate Crust

- 2 cups flaked sweetened coconut

- 6 ounces semisweet chocolate chips
- 2 tablespoons (¼ stick) unsalted butter
- 1 tablespoon light corn syrup

Chocolate Cigars (garnish)

- 6 ounces semisweet chocolate chips

Almond Mousse Filling

- ¼ cup amaretto
- 2 teaspoons unflavored gelatin
- ½ cup sour cream, room temperature
- 1½ cups whipping cream
- 1 cup powdered sugar
- ¾ cup lightly toasted finely ground almonds
  Chopped toasted almonds (optional garnish)

For crust: Lightly grease 9- to 10-inch pie plate or deep square serving dish. Place coconut in medium bowl and warm in 150°F oven.

Combine chocolate chips, butter and corn syrup in top of double boiler over hot (not simmering) water. Stir until melted and smooth. Pour chocolate over warmed coconut and mix with 2 forks until thoroughly blended. Press coconut mixture evenly into bottom and sides of pie plate or dish. Chill.

For chocolate cigars: Melt chocolate in top of double boiler over hot water, stirring until smooth. Spread chocolate over back of baking sheet into 4 × 6-inch rectangle. Cool to room temperature (65°F to 70°F) (or refrigerate to firm, but chocolate must be room temperature to shape). Using cheese-shaver server (wire cheese cutter will not work), start an inch from short end of chocolate and pull server toward you in slightly upward motion so that chocolate will curl up and around. Use fingers to aid curling. Wrap cigars in plastic and refrigerate.

For filling: Combine ¼ cup liqueur with gelatin in small heat-proof cup and mix until softened. Place cup in simmering water and heat until gelatin is liquefied, about 2 to 3 minutes. Transfer gelatin to large bowl. Add sour cream, blending well. Stir in cream and powdered sugar. Whip until stiff. Fold in almonds and spoon into shell. Decorate with chocolate cigars and chopped toasted almonds if desired. Refrigerate until set, at least 2 hours.

ALMOND CHARLOTTE

10 servings

Raspberry-Grand Marnier Sauce

- 2   10-ounce packages frozen raspberries, thawed
- 2   to 4 tablespoons sugar
- 1   tablespoon Grand Marnier

Almond Filling

- 2½ cups (about 1 pound) almond meal (finely ground blanched almonds)
- 2½ cups powdered sugar
- 1¾ cups (3½ sticks) unsalted butter, room temperature
- 2   tablespoons kirsch
- ½   teaspoon almond extract
- 1¾ cups whipping cream

     Powdered sugar
- 18 to 20 4-inch ladyfingers

- ½   cup whipping cream
- 2   tablespoons powdered sugar
- 1   teaspoon kirsch
     Fresh raspberries (garnish)

For sauce: Sieve raspberries over medium bowl to remove seeds. Whisk in sugar and Grand Marnier. Refrigerate sauce until ready to serve.

For filling: Combine almond meal and 2½ cups powdered sugar in processor or blender and mix just until well blended; do not form

---

❖   ❖

Charlottes: Tips and Techniques

- ◆ Before substituting another mold, determine how much it holds by measuring its capacity with water.
- ◆ Use tin-washed or ceramic charlotte molds for charlottes that are baked. Aluminum charlotte molds are good only for chilled types.
- ◆ For easy unmolding of chilled charlottes, first line the mold with waxed or parchment paper, especially if it is deep and the filling is delicate.
- ◆ To turn out a charlotte from an unlined pan, dip the mold in warm water to the depth of its contents. Place a serving plate over the top and, holding tightly, invert the plate and mold. Shake them gently and remove the mold carefully. Repeat the process if necessary. Or, place the platter over the mold and, holding tightly, invert. Soak a kitchen towel in hot water, wring dry and press all around the pan. Shake mold gently and remove. If the charlotte does not slide out easily, reapply the hot, damp towel until it does.

❖   ❖

---

paste. Sift almond mixture, discarding any remaining granules. Beat butter in large bowl until light and smooth. Add almond mixture and continue beating rapidly until light and fluffy. Blend in kirsch and almond extract. Beat 1¾ cups cream in another large bowl just until soft peaks form. Gently fold cream into almond-butter mixture.

Lightly butter 8-cup (No. 18) charlotte mold. Dust mold with powdered sugar, shaking out excess. Line bottom with waxed paper. Trim 1 rounded end of each ladyfinger to square off. Line sides of mold with ladyfingers, trimmed end down and rounded side out. Spoon filling into large pastry bag fitted with ⅝-inch tube tip. Pipe filling into mold. Tap mold lightly on work surface to remove air pockets and distribute filling evenly. Refrigerate charlotte until set, several hours or overnight.

To serve, dip mold in hot water several seconds to loosen charlotte. Invert charlotte onto rimmed large platter. Spoon raspberry sauce around charlotte. Whip ½ cup cream with 2 tablespoons powdered sugar and 1 teaspoon kirsch until mixture holds stiff peaks. Spoon cream into small pastry bag fitted with small star tip. Pipe rosettes of cream around rim of charlotte. Garnish rosettes and top with raspberries.

SOUFFLE GLACE PRALINE

The remaining praline can be stored in an airtight container. Use as a topping for ice cream, cake or sliced fresh fruit.

8 to 10 servings

Praline

     Vegetable oil
- ½   cup sugar
- ¼   cup water
- ½   cup hazelnuts, toasted and husked
- ½   cup blanched toasted almonds

Soufflé

- 4⅓ cups whipping cream, well chilled
- 1¼ cups sugar
- ⅓   cup water

- 6   eggs, separated, room temperature
- ¼   teaspoon cream of tartar
- 6   tablespoons praline liqueur

- ½   cup coarsely chopped toasted almonds
- 12 chocolate leaves (garnish)

For praline: Brush large baking sheet with oil. Heat sugar and ¼ cup water in heavy small saucepan over low heat until sugar dissolves, swirling pan occasionally. Increase heat and boil until mixture turns a dark caramel color. Stir in nuts, then pour onto prepared baking sheet. Cool completely. Break praline into small pieces. Coarsely crumb in processor or blender, using on/off turns. Measure ¾ cup praline to use in soufflé and set aside.

For soufflé: Wrap strip of foil around 8-cup soufflé dish, extending 3 inches above edge. Tie string around dish to secure collar. Whip cream in very large bowl to soft peaks. Cover and refrigerate. Heat sugar and ⅓ cup water in heavy medium saucepan over low heat until sugar dissolves, swirling pan occasionally. Increase heat to medium and cook until mixture registers 235°F (soft-ball stage) on thermometer.

Meanwhile, working quickly, beat yolks in large bowl of electric mixer until a ribbon forms when beaters are lifted. Pour half of hot syrup into yolks in thin stream and beat until cool. Beat whites and cream of tartar in another large bowl to soft peaks. Add remaining hot syrup in thin stream and beat until stiff and cool, about 5 minutes. Fold ¾ cup praline and liqueur into yolks. Gently fold ¼ of whites into yolks to lighten, then fold in remaining whites. Fold in whipped cream. Spoon mixture into prepared dish. Freeze for at least 10 hours, or overnight.

Just before serving, gently remove collar from soufflé dish. Press almonds into exposed edge. Top with leaves.

HOT BROWNIE SOUFFLE WITH VANILLA ICE CREAM SAUCE

Tastes like a rich, moist brownie.

6 servings

  Sugar (for dish)
½ **cup (1 stick) butter, cut into small pieces**

4 **ounces unsweetened chocolate, coarsely chopped**
1 **cup sugar**
4 **egg yolks, room temperature**
1 **tablespoon instant coffee powder dissolved in 1 tablespoon rum *or* orange liqueur**
1 **teaspoon vanilla**
¼ **cup all purpose flour**

5 **egg whites, room temperature**
  Vanilla Ice Cream Sauce (see following recipe)

Position rack in center of oven and preheat to 450°F. Butter 1-quart soufflé dish and sprinkle with sugar. Melt ½ cup butter with chocolate in heavy large saucepan over very low heat, stirring until smooth. Blend in ½ cup sugar, yolks, coffee mixture and vanilla. Stir in flour. (*Can be prepared several hours ahead and set aside at cool room temperature. Reheat before continuing.*)

Beat whites in large bowl until soft peaks form. Gradually add remaining ½ cup sugar, beating constantly until whites are stiff but not dry. Fold ¼ of whites into chocolate, then fold chocolate back into remaining whites (be careful not to deflate mixture; a few streaks of white may remain). Turn batter into prepared dish. Sprinkle lightly with sugar. Bake 5 minutes. Reduce oven temperature to 400°F and continue baking until soufflé is puffed, about 20 minutes (center will be moist). Serve immediately with sauce.

Vanilla Ice Cream Sauce

Makes 2 cups

1 **pint rich vanilla ice cream**
2 **tablespoons rum *or* orange liqueur**

Place ice cream in medium bowl. Let soften at room temperature 10 minutes (or in refrigerator 30 minutes). Add rum and beat until smooth. Turn into small bowl and serve immediately.

COLD AMARETTO SOUFFLE

6 servings

2 **dozen (about) whole *or* 1 dozen split ladyfingers**

½ **cup cold water**
1 **envelope unflavored gelatin**
¾ **cup amaretto**

6 **eggs, separated, room temperature**
¾ **cup sugar**
1 **tablespoon fresh lemon juice**
1 **cup whipping cream**
  Toasted slivered almonds (garnish)

Cut strip of waxed paper 8 inches wide and 2 inches longer than circumference of 7-inch-diameter soufflé dish. Fold in half lengthwise. Generously butter 1 side. Wrap around top of dish buttered side in, allowing at least 2½ inches of collar to rise above rim. Staple or pin overlap. Tie string around dish to secure collar. Stand ladyfingers upright around dish (trimming 1 end flat if necessary) with sides touching.

Pour cold water into small heatproof bowl. Sprinkle gelatin over top. Let stand 5 minutes. Set bowl in pan of simmering water and stir until gelatin is dissolved. Remove from heat. Blend liqueur into gelatin. Let cool. Refrigerate until slightly thickened, about 30 minutes, stirring occasionally.

Beat yolks in large bowl until frothy. Gradually add ¼ cup sugar, beating until mixture is thick and lemon colored. Add gelatin mixture and beat until light. Beat whites in large bowl until soft peaks form. Gradually beat in remaining ½ cup sugar. Add lemon juice and beat until whites are stiff but not dry. Whip cream in another bowl until soft peaks form. Fold whites into yolk mixture, then fold in cream. Carefully spoon mixture into prepared soufflé dish, smoothing top. Chill until firm, about 3 hours or up to 2 days. Sprinkle nuts over top before serving.

Fruit Desserts

AUTUMN APPLE MERINGUE

6 servings

¼ cup raisins
¼ cup rum

Caramel

⅔ cup sugar
⅓ cup water
⅛ teaspoon cream of tartar

Apple Meringue

5 tart medium cooking apples, preferably Pippin *or* Greening (about 1¼ pounds)
½ lemon
2 tablespoons (¼ stick) unsalted butter
½ cup water

1 cup egg whites (about 8), room temperature
⅛ teaspoon salt
⅛ teaspoon cream of tartar
1 cup (16 tablespoons) sugar
⅓ cup chopped toasted walnuts

Apple Rum Cream Sauce

3 egg yolks, room temperature
⅓ cup sugar
1 cup whipping cream
1 teaspoon vanilla

Combine raisins and rum; set aside.

For caramel: Lightly grease wire rack and baking sheet. Combine sugar, water and cream of tartar in 2-quart charlotte or other mold. (If using porcelain mold that cannot be placed over direct heat, combine ingredients in saucepan.) Place over low heat and swirl mold occasionally until sugar is dissolved. Increase heat and continue cooking until sugar caramelizes, washing down any crystals clinging to sides of pan using brush dipped in cold water, about 10 minutes. Remove from heat and quickly tilt mold until caramel covers bottom and sides. Invert on rack set over baking sheet and let stand 5 minutes.

For apple meringue: Preheat oven to 350°F. Butter baking pan. Peel apples and rub with cut lemon. Quarter and core apples; chop coarsely into ⅓-inch pieces. Spread in baking pan and dot with 2 tablespoons butter. Cover and bake, stirring occasionally, until apples are tender when pierced with knife, about 15 minutes. Drain through sieve set over bowl. Return ¾ cup of apples with drained juice to pan (let remaining apples cool completely). Add water to pan, cover and bake until apples are soft enough to mash. Set aside for sauce.

Drain raisins (reserving rum) and pat dry with paper towels. Beat egg whites until foamy. Add salt and cream of tartar and continue beating until soft peaks form. Add sugar 1 tablespoon at a time and continue beating until meringue is stiff and glossy. Fold in raisins, walnuts and apple pieces. Turn into caramelized mold, smoothing top. Top mold on counter and set in deep baking pan. Fill pan with enough simmering water to come ¾ up sides of mold. Bake until meringue is browned and has begun to shrink from sides of mold, 40 to 45 minutes. Let cool to room temperature, then refrigerate at least 3 hours.

For sauce: Beat egg yolks with sugar in medium bowl until lemon colored and mixture forms a ribbon when beaters are lifted. Combine apples for sauce and reserved rum in processor or blender and mix until smooth. Transfer to heavy large saucepan and add cream. Bring to simmering point, then gradually stir into beaten yolk mixture. Return to saucepan over low heat and stir with wooden spoon until mixture thickens and finger leaves a path when drawn across spoon; *do not boil or egg yolks will curdle.* Remove from heat and stir in vanilla. Place piece of plastic wrap on surface of sauce. Let cool, then chill thoroughly.

To serve, unmold meringue onto serving platter and surround with sauce.

PAPAYA WITH RASPBERRY-LIME SAUCE

Raspberry-Lime Sauce can be prepared up to 2 days ahead and refrigerated. Bring to room temperature before serving.

6 servings

2 10-ounce packages frozen sweetened raspberries, thawed
2 tablespoons fresh lime juice
2 tablespoons sugar
3 papayas, halved and seeded

Combine raspberries, lime juice and sugar in processor or blender and puree until sugar is dissolved and mixture is smooth. Strain to remove seeds. Place papaya halves on individual plates. Spoon raspberry sauce into cavities and serve immediately.

ORANGE-GLAZED BANANAS

6 servings

6 bananas, halved lengthwise
¾ cup fresh orange juice
¼ cup Grand Marnier
3 tablespoons unsalted butter
⅓ cup chopped walnuts
⅓ cup firmly packed brown sugar
  Vanilla ice cream *or* sour cream

Preheat oven to 450°F. Arrange bananas in shallow baking dish. Combine orange juice and liqueur and pour over bananas. Dot with butter. Bake 10 minutes, basting occasionally. Sprinkle with nuts and brown sugar and continue baking until sugar is melted and nuts are glazed and toasted, about 5 minutes. Serve warm with ice cream or sour cream.

APPLE CREPES WITH CIDER BEURRE BLANC

6 servings

Crepes

Makes 24 6½-inch crepes

1 cup all purpose flour
1½ cups milk, room temperature
¼ cup water
¼ cup Calvados
3 eggs, room temperature
2 egg yolks, room temperature
2 tablespoons sugar
⅛ teaspoon freshly ground cardamom
⅛ teaspoon freshly grated nutmeg
⅛ teaspoon cinnamon

4 tablespoons (½ stick) unsalted butter

Caramel Apple Filling

12 medium cooking apples, preferably Pippin *or* Greening (about 3 pounds)
1 to 2 tablespoons fresh lemon juice

2 cups sugar
1 cup water
6 walnut halves, toasted
¼ cup (½ stick) unsalted butter, cut into small pieces
¼ cup sugar, or to taste

2 tablespoons (¼ stick) unsalted butter, melted
  Cider Beurre Blanc (see following recipe)

For crepes: Place flour in medium bowl. Whisk in about ⅔ cup milk a little at a time to make smooth paste. Gradually whisk in remaining milk with water, Calvados, eggs and egg yolks. Stir in sugar, cardamom, nutmeg and cinnamon. Strain batter if any lumps remain. Cover and let stand at room temperature for 1 hour.

Melt butter in crepe pan or 6- to 7-inch skillet. Let cool, then mix 2 tablespoons into batter. Pour remaining butter into small cup and spoon off foam. Heat crepe pan over medium-high heat. Brush with some of melted butter and heat until almost smoking. Remove pan from heat. Ladle about 3 to 4 tablespoons batter into corner of pan, then tilt pan until bottom is covered with thin layer of batter; pour out any excess. Return pan to medium-high heat, loosen edges of crepe with knife tip and cook until bottom of crepe is browned, about 1 minute, shaking pan in circle so crepe doesn't stick. Turn crepe and cook another minute until second side is browned. Slide crepe out onto plate. Repeat with remaining batter, stacking crepes on top of each other. Let cool completely. Cover with plastic wrap and refrigerate. (*Freeze crepes if they are going to be kept more than 4 days.*)

For filling: Peel, quarter and core apples. Cut into slices ¼ inch thick and transfer to bowl. Toss with lemon juice.

Preheat oven to 400° F; grease small plate. Combine sugar and water in small saucepan and cook over low heat, swirling pan occasionally, until sugar is dissolved. Increase heat and cook until syrup is light brown,

washing down any crystals clinging to sides of pan using brush dipped in cold water. Remove from heat. Using trussing needle, quickly dip walnuts one at a time into caramel, then push off onto greased plate. Return caramel to very low heat just long enough to remelt, then pour into 9 × 12-inch gratin pan, tilting pan so caramel covers bottom evenly.

Sprinkle apples over caramel. Dot with pieces of butter. Cover with buttered parchment paper buttered side down. Bake, stirring occasionally with wooden spoon, until apples are tender when pierced with knife, about 25 minutes. Taste and add sugar if needed. Let apples cool completely, stirring occasionally.

Butter large shallow baking pans. Spread crepes with apples and baking juices. Fold into triangles and arrange in single layer in pans. Cover with foil until serving time. (*Crepes can be filled up to 1 day ahead and refrigerated. Bring to room temperature before baking.*)

Preheat oven to 400°F. Drizzle melted butter over crepes. Re-cover with foil and bake until heated through, about 5 minutes. Spoon Cider Beurre Blanc into center of 6 heated dinner plates. Arrange 4 crepes with tips toward center on each. Place caramelized walnut in middle and serve immediately.

Cider Beurre Blanc

Makes about 1 cup

1 cup cider (preferably hard)
¼ cup cider vinegar
1 teaspoon vanilla
  Pinch of cinnamon
2 tablespoons sugar

1 cup (2 sticks) chilled unsalted butter, cut into 16 pieces

Combine cider, vinegar, vanilla and cinnamon in heavy small saucepan and bring to boil. Let boil until reduced to about 2 tablespoons, about 20 minutes. Reduce heat to low, add sugar and cook, swirling pan occasionally, until sugar is dissolved. Remove from heat and whisk in 2 pieces of butter. Return to low heat and whisk in remaining butter 2 pieces at a time. (*Mixture should be creamy; if at any time butter looks as though it is melting rather than thickening sauce, remove from heat before adding more butter.*) Serve sauce warm.

FRESH ORANGES WITH ORANGE ZABAGLIONE

6 servings

 4 to 6 oranges, peeled (white pith discarded) and cut crosswise into ½-inch-thick slices

Orange Zabaglione

 6 egg yolks
 1 tablespoon sugar
 ¾ cup fresh orange juice
 ¼ cup orange liqueur
  Sliced toasted almonds *or* hazelnuts (garnish)

Arrange orange slices in 6 dessert dishes and chill while preparing Orange Zabaglione.

For zabaglione: Combine yolks and sugar in top of double boiler and beat with whisk or electric mixer until thick and lemon colored. Set pan over simmering water. Gradually add orange juice and liqueur, beating constantly until thick. Spoon over orange slices. Sprinkle with toasted nuts and serve.

RASPBERRY POACHED PEARS

8 servings

 2 10-ounce packages frozen raspberries, thawed (do not drain)
 ½ cup crème de cassis
 8 firm ripe pears
 ¼ cup finely chopped raw pistachio nuts

Puree raspberries until smooth in processor or blender. Strain through fine sieve to remove seeds. Add crème de cassis to puree. (*Can be prepared ahead.*)

Peel pears. Core from bottom, leaving stem intact. Cut thin slice from bottom so pears stand upright. Arrange pears upright in large saucepan. Pour raspberry mixture over. Bring to simmer, then cover and simmer gently until tender, about 8 to 10 minutes. Remove pears from pan. Cool, then chill.

Transfer cooking liquid to smaller saucepan and boil until reduced to thick syrup, about 10 to 12 minutes. Let cool. (*Can be prepared ahead.*)

To serve, spoon some of syrup onto individual dessert plates. Top with pear. Drizzle additional syrup over. Sprinkle pears with chopped pistachio nuts.

PEAR-CRANBERRY CRISP

Vanilla ice cream is the natural partner for this old-fashioned dessert.

6 to 8 servings

 4 firm ripe pears, peeled, cored and sliced (2½ pounds)
 12 ounces cranberries
 ⅓ cup sugar
 ½ teaspoon cinnamon
 ¾ cup rolled oats
 ⅔ cup firmly packed brown sugar
 ½ cup (1 stick) butter, cut into ½-inch pieces
 ½ cup all purpose flour
  Pinch of salt

Position rack in center of oven and preheat to 375°F. Toss pears, cranberries, sugar and ¼ teaspoon cinnamon in 10-inch round baking dish until blended. Combine oats, brown sugar, butter, flour, salt and remaining ¼ teaspoon cinnamon in large bowl and blend with fingertips until mixture resembles coarse meal. Sprinkle over fruit mixture and pat down lightly. Bake until pears are tender and topping is golden, about 45 minutes. Cool about 1 hour. Serve warm.

PEAR BRANDY GRATIN

(Gratin de Poire Williams)

8 to 10 servings

 6 egg yolks
 ⅓ cup sugar
 1¼ cups half and half
 2½ tablespoons Poire Williams (pear brandy)*
 ¼ teaspoon ground ginger
  Pinch of salt

 1 tablespoon butter
 6 almost ripe large Bosc pears, peeled, halved and cored
 ½ cup water
 ⅓ cup sugar

Mix yolks with ⅓ cup sugar in large saucepan. Scald half and half in small saucepan. Gradually add hot half and half to yolk mixture in slow steady stream, whisking constantly. Place over medium heat and cook until thickened, about 7 minutes. Remove from heat and whisk to cool rapidly to lukewarm. Blend in brandy, ginger and salt. (*Custard can be prepared 1 day ahead and refrigerated. Let stand at room temperature 30 minutes before using.*)

Preheat oven to 350°F. Coat 10-inch round ceramic tart or quiche dish with 1 tablespoon butter. Cut pear halves crosswise into slices ¼ inch thick. Gently open slices to fan shape. Arrange pears in prepared dish in flower petal pattern. (*Pears can be prepared 1 day ahead to this point. Cover dish with plastic wrap and refrigerate.*) Add water to dish. Sprinkle sugar over pears. Bake pear mixture until tender and caramelized, checking frequently.

Preheat broiler. Pour custard over hot pears. Broil until top of gratin is golden, about 2 minutes. Serve lukewarm.

An additional ¾ teaspoon ground ginger can be substituted for pear brandy.

❖

*Coco-Amaretto Mousse (top),
individual Tartufi*

*Counter clockwise from top left: Cookie Crust Tart
with Boysenberry Puree, Lemon Raspberry Tart,
Marzipan Tart with boysenberries, Chocolate Confection
with Raspberries, Crème Brûlée Tart Jimmy*

Clockwise from left: Baked Almond Apples in Pastry, Apple Crepes with Cider Beurre Blanc, Apple Ladyfinger Cake with Cider Buttercream, Autumn Apple Meringue in Rum Cream

*Top to bottom: Fruit-and-Chocolate-filled
Cookie Rolls, Sardinian Raisin and
Nut Cookies, Orange Wafers, Little Yellow
Diamonds, Mustaches, Butterballs,
Sweet Beans, Queen's Cookies,
Hazelnut Cookies, Sweet Ravioli,
Ugly but Good Cookies, Butterballs*

*Clockwise from right:
Creamy Caramels,
English Butter Toffee,
Rocky Road*

Confections

CREAMY CARAMELS

Nothing like the kind you buy.

Makes about 7 dozen 1-inch squares

1½ cups half and half
1½ cups whipping cream
 2 cups sugar
 ¼ teaspoon salt
1⅓ cups light corn syrup

 2 teaspoons vanilla
 1 cup chopped toasted
   walnuts (optional)

Butter 9-inch square pan. Combine half and half and cream in 4-cup measure. Mix sugar, salt, corn syrup and 1 cup of the combined creams in heavy 3- or 4-quart saucepan. Cook over medium-high heat, stirring constantly, until syrup reaches 235°F on candy thermometer (softball stage).

   Add 1 more cup of cream and stir until mixture again reaches 235°F. Add remaining cream and stir until mixture reaches 250°F (hardball stage); *this may take up to 1 hour.* Remove from heat and stir in vanilla and nuts. Pour into pan and refrigerate until just firm but not hard. Cut in pieces about 1-inch square and wrap in cellophane, plastic wrap or waxed paper.

ROCKY ROAD

Makes 3 dozen 1½-inch squares

 8 ounces milk chocolate
 8 ounces semisweet chocolate
 1 tablespoon unsalted butter
   Pinch of salt
 1 teaspoon vanilla
20 marshmallows, snipped into
   quarters
 ¾ cup coarsely chopped
   toasted walnuts

Butter 8-inch square pan. Melt chocolate with butter and salt in top of double boiler over very hot, not boiling, water. Add vanilla, marshmallows and nuts and stir thor-

oughly. Spread in pan and chill until firm. Cut into squares. (*If candy is difficult to cut, let stand at room temperature about 10 minutes.*)

CHOCOLATE CONFECTION WITH RASPBERRIES

A terrific hostess gift. Roasted or caramelized whole almonds can be substituted for raspberries.

10 to 12 servings

13 ounces semisweet chocolate
 4 lemon or other waxy leaves
   with stems, washed and
   dried
 4 cups fresh raspberries

   Tiny strawberry leaves with
   buds (optional garnish)

Melt chocolate in top of double boiler set over gently simmering water, stirring until smooth. Spread some of chocolate on underside of leaves with small spatula (do not let chocolate drip onto top of leaves). Freeze until chocolate is firm, about 10 minutes. Dip hands in ice water and dry. Remove leaf from chocolate by pulling gently from stem. Make 4 perfect leaves and return them to freezer.

   Line baking sheet with waxed paper. Set 14-inch rectangular flan mold on top. Remelt chocolate if necessary. Reserve 1 teaspoon melted chocolate. Spread remainder evenly inside bottom of mold (do not spread sides). Arrange berries decoratively atop chocolate; do not press down or chocolate may crack. Refrigerate only until chocolate begins to set, about 12 minutes.

   Run thin-bladed knife around bottom inside edge of mold and remove. Refrigerate chocolate until completely firm. Carefully tip chocolate and remove paper. Set chocolate on serving platter. Using reserved 1 teaspoon melted choco-

late (remelted if necessary), attach chocolate leaves decoratively. Refrigerate. Let stand at room temperature 30 minutes before serving. Garnish confection with tiny strawberry leaves if desired.

ENGLISH BUTTER TOFFEE

Makes 1 pound 6 ounces

 1 cup sugar
 1 cup (2 sticks) unsalted
   butter
 ¼ cup water
 ½ teaspoon salt
 1 teaspoon vanilla

 4 ounces milk chocolate
 4 ounces sweet cooking
   chocolate
 ¼ cup finely chopped toasted
   pecans *or* walnuts

Butter 10 × 15-inch baking sheet. Combine sugar, butter, water and salt in heavy saucepan. Place over medium-high heat and bring to boil, stirring until sugar is dissolved. Continue boiling, shaking pan occasionally, until candy thermometer registers 305°F (hard-crack stage). Remove from heat and stir in vanilla. Pour onto baking sheet in 10 × 10-inch square. Let stand until cool and hardened.

   Melt 2 ounces of each chocolate* in small pan over very low heat. Spread chocolate evenly with spatula on top side of toffee. Immediately sprinkle with half of nuts. Refrigerate for 30 minutes.

   Using spatula, carefully turn toffee over. Repeat layering procedure with remaining chocolate and nuts. Return to refrigerator and chill for at least 30 minutes.

   When firm enough to handle, break toffee into pieces. Store in airtight container in cool, dry place.

*Instead of combining chocolates, toffee can be coated with 8 ounces of either type.

Index

Credits and Acknowledgments

Project editor: Jan Stuebing

The following people contributed the recipes included in this book:

Aubergine, Munich, Germany, Eckart Witzigmann, chef-owner
Margot Bachman
Nancy Baggett
James Beard
Bernard's, Los Angeles, California, Bernard Jacoupy, owner; Roland Gilbert, executive chef
Odette Bery
Blue Boar, San Francisco, California
Boca Raton Hotel & Club, Boca Raton, Florida
Anita Borghese
Michelle Braden
Jean Brady
Jennifer Brennan
Cabell's, Charleston, South Carolina
Cafe Cappuccino, Pittsburgh, Pennsylvania
Biba Caggiano
George Caloyannidis and Christine Tittel
Hugh Carpenter
Christmas Farm Inn, Jackson, New Hampshire
Maria Rondinelli Ciferri
Elyn and Phil Clarkson
Peter and Susan Coe
Shirley Collins
Charlotte Combe
Patricia Connell
Dinah Corley
Diane Darrow and Tom Maresca
Narsai David
Deirdre Davis and Linda Marino

Déjà-Vu, Philadelphia, Pennsylvania, Salomon Montezinos, chef-owner
Veronica di Rosa
Myra Dorros
El Torito, California
Olivia Erschen and Charlotte Walker
Rodney Eubanks
Joe Famularo
Helen Feingold
Chuck Flannery-Jones
Lawrence Forgione
Garnet Hill Lodge, North River, New York
Peggy Glass
Rhoda Gordon
Freddi Greenberg
Bess Greenstone
Anne Greer
The Harvest, Cambridge, Massachusetts
Jacki Horwitz
Bill Hughes
John Hurst
Izaak Walton Inn, Glacier National Park, Montana
John Clancy's, New York, New York
Ruth Hartley Johnson
Jane Helsel Joseph
Peggy Jurjevich
Madeleine Kamman
Kapalua Bay Resort, Maui, Hawaii
Shari Karney
Barbara Karoff
Lynne Kasper
Sophie Kay
Lori Kuhn

La Cheminée, King's Beach, California, Jean-Pierre Doignon and Tommy Cortopassi, owners
La Côte Basque, New York, New York
Le Cirque, New York, New York, Joseph Jensen, chef
Faye Levy
Abby Mandel
Amy C. Marchaud
Copeland Marks
Perla Meyers
Henry Miller
Jinx and Jefferson Morgan
Doris Muscatine
Louise Natenshon
Helen Cassidy Page
Marsha Palanci
Elise Pascoe
Richard Perry Restaurant, St. Louis, Missouri
Vicki Pierson
Paul Prudhomme
Rabbit Hill Inn, Lower Waterford, Vermont
Neil Romanoff
Julie Sahni
Edena Sheldon
Sitmar Cruises
Sky Garden, St. Moritz on the Park, New York, New York
Shirley Slater
Susan Snyder
Leon Soniat
Terry Thompson
May Wong Trent
Valentino, Santa Monica, California, Abbye Silverman, pastry chef
Maggie Waldron

Jan Weimer
Gina Wilson
Woerne's European Pastry Shop and Restaurant, Seattle, Washington

Additional text was supplied by:

Biba Caggiano, *Pasta*
Olivia Erschen and Charlotte Walker, *Charlottes: Tips and Techniques*
Lynne Kasper, *A Brief Guide to Breadmaking*
Loni Kuhn, *Step by Step to Perfect Preserving*
Faye Levy, *Cream-based Sauces, Cream Soups & Veloutés*
Helen Cassidy Page, *Mayonnaise*
Elise Pascoe, *Ice Cream: Tips and Techniques*
Jan Weimer, *Rusks, Toasts, Croutons and Croûtes, Rolled Cakes: Plain or Fancy, Pizza Primer*

Photographers

Jerry Friedman: 94–95
Irwin Horowitz: 25, 26–27, 32, 49, 89, 96, 135, 136, 169, 170–171, 174–175, 209, 210–211, 212–213
Alan Krosnick: 134
Brian Leatart: 28–29, 30, 92–93, 129, 214–215, 216
Rudy Legname: 130–131, 176
Victor Scocozza: 31, 50–51, 52–53, 56, 90–91, 132–133, 172–173
Dan Wolfe: cover, 54–55
Food and prop stylist for cover: Edena Sheldon

Accessories information

for cover photo: dinnerware, candlesticks and candles, decorative plates, flower jug, table linens, cheese tray courtesy Williams-Sonoma, P.O. Box 7456, San Francisco, California, 94120
Handpainted fruit bowl, Armatale service plates, flatware, stemware courtesy The Brass Tree, 9044 Burton Way, Beverly Hills, California, 90211

Special thanks to:

Marilou Vaughan, *Editor, Bon Appétit*

Bernard Rotondo, *Art Director, Bon Appétit*
William J. Garry, *Managing Editor, Bon Appétit*
Barbara Varnum, *Articles Editor, Bon Appétit*
Jane Matyas, *Associate Food Editor, Bon Appétit*
Brenda Koplin, *Copy Editor, Bon Appétit*
Judith Strausberg, *Copy Editor, Bon Appétit*
Robin G. Richardson, *Research Coordinator, Bon Appétit*
Leslie A. Dame, *Assistant Editor, Bon Appétit*
Donna Clipperton, *Manager, Rights and Permissions, Knapp Communications Corporation*
Karen Legier, *Rights and Permissions Coordinator, Knapp Communications Corporation*
Patricia Connell
Rose Grant
Tyra Mead
Edena Sheldon

The Knapp Press
is a wholly owned subsidiary of
KNAPP COMMUNICATIONS
 CORPORATION
*Chairman and Chief Executive
 Officer:* Cleon T. Knapp
President: H. Stephen Cranston
Senior Vice-Presidents:
 Rosalie Bruno *(New Venture
 Development)*
 Betsy Wood Knapp *(Adminis-
 trative Services/Electronics)*
 Harry Myers *(Magazine Group
 Publisher)*
 William J. N. Porter *(Corporate
 Product Sales)*
 Paige Rense *(Editorial)*
 L. James Wade, Jr. *(Finance)*

THE KNAPP PRESS
 President: Alice Bandy; *Admin-
 istrative Assistant:* Beth Bell;
 Editor: Norman Kolpas; *Man-
 aging Editor:* Pamela Mosher;
 Associate Editors: Colleen Dunn
 Bates, Jan Koot, Diane Rossen
 Worthington; *Assistant Editor:*
 Nancy D. Roberts; *Editorial
 Assistant:* Teresa Roupe; *Art
 Director:* Paula Schlosser;
 Designer: Robin Murawski;
 Marketing Designer: Barbara
 Kosoff; *Book Production Man-
 ager:* Larry Cooke; *Book Produc-
 tion Coordinators:* Veronica
 Losorelli, Joan Valentine; *Direc-
 tor, Rosebud Books:* Robert
Groag; *Creative Director, Rose-
bud Books:* Jeff Book; *Financial
Manager:* Joseph Goodman;
Financial Assistant: Julie
Mason; *Fulfillment Services
Manager:* Virginia Parry; *Direc-
tor of Public Relations:* Jan B.
Fox; *Marketing Assistants:*
Dolores Briqueleur, Randy
Levin; *Promotions Managers:*
Joanne Denison, Nina Gerwin;
Special Sales Manager: Lynn
Blocker; *Special Sales Coordina-
tor:* Amy Hershman

This book is set in Galliard.
Composition was on the Mergenthaler Linotron 202 by Graphic Typesetting Service.
Book design by Robin Murawski. Page layout by Tanya Maiboroda.
Text stock: Knapp Cookbook Opaque Basis 65.
Color plate stock: Mead Northcote Basis 80.
Furnished by WWF Paper Corporation West.
Color separations by NEC Incorporated.
Printing and binding by R. R. Donnelley and Sons.